discover
ALASKA

CATHERINE BODRY
GREG BENCHWICK, JIM DUFRESNE

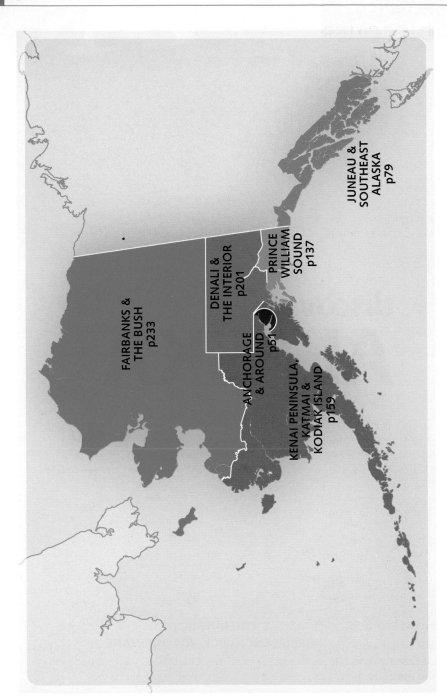

FAIRBANKS & THE BUSH p233

DENALI & THE INTERIOR p201

JUNEAU & SOUTHEAST ALASKA p79

PRINCE WILLIAM SOUND p137

ANCHORAGE & AROUND p51

KENAI PENINSULA, KATMAI & KODIAK ISLAND p159

DISCOVER ALASKA

Anchorage & Around (p51) Boutiques and bistros meld with urban moose and hiking trails in the state's largest city.

Juneau & Southeast Alaska (p79) A foggy emerald maze of fishing towns and ferry routes, plus the state's capital.

Prince William Sound (p137) A kayaker's delight, the Sound abounds with islands, glaciers and hidden coves.

Kenai Peninsula, Katmai & Kodiak Island (p159) Enjoy an accessible wilderness playground on the Kenai Peninsula or watch bears in Katmai National Park.

Denali & the Interior (p201) It's not just the tallest mountain in North America, but also the backcountry surrounding it.

Fairbanks & the Bush (p233) Chug along the Chena River, soak in hot springs, or spot your first polar bear.

↘CONTENTS

FAIRBANKS &
THE BUSH
p233

DENALI &
THE INTERIOR
p201

ANCHORAGE
& AROUND
p51

PRINCE
WILLIAM
SOUND
p137

KENAI PENINSULA,
KATMAI &
KODIAK ISLAND
p159

JUNEAU &
SOUTHEAST
ALASKA
p79

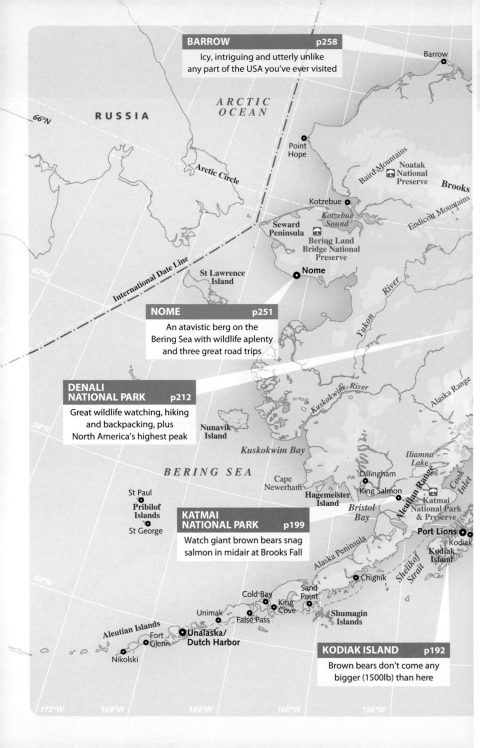

BARROW p258

Icy, intriguing and utterly unlike any part of the USA you've ever visited

ARCTIC OCEAN

Barrow

RUSSIA

66°N

Point Hope

Arctic Circle

Baird Mountains

Noatak National Preserve

Brooks

Kotzebue

Kotzebue Sound

Endicott Mountains

Seward Peninsula

Bering Land Bridge National Preserve

62°N

International Date Line

St Lawrence Island

Nome

Yukon River

NOME p251

An atavistic berg on the Bering Sea with wildlife aplenty and three great road trips

Kuskokwim River

Alaska Range

DENALI NATIONAL PARK p212

Great wildlife watching, hiking and backpacking, plus North America's highest peak

58°N

Nunavik Island

Kuskokwim Bay

Iliamna Lake

BERING SEA

Cape Newerham

Dillingham

King Salmon

Cook Inlet

Aleutian Range

Katmai National Park & Preserve

St Paul

Pribilof Islands

St George

KATMAI NATIONAL PARK p199

Watch giant brown bears snag salmon in midair at Brooks Fall

Hagemeister Island

Bristol Bay

Port Lions

Kodiak

Shelikof Strait

Kodiak Island

Chignik

54°N

Sand Point

Cold Bay

King Cove

Alaska Peninsula

Shumagin Islands

Unimak

False Pass

Aleutian Islands

Fort Glenn

Unalaska/ Dutch Harbor

KODIAK ISLAND p192

Brown bears don't come any bigger (1500lb) than here

Nikolski

172°W   168°W   164°W   160°W   156°W

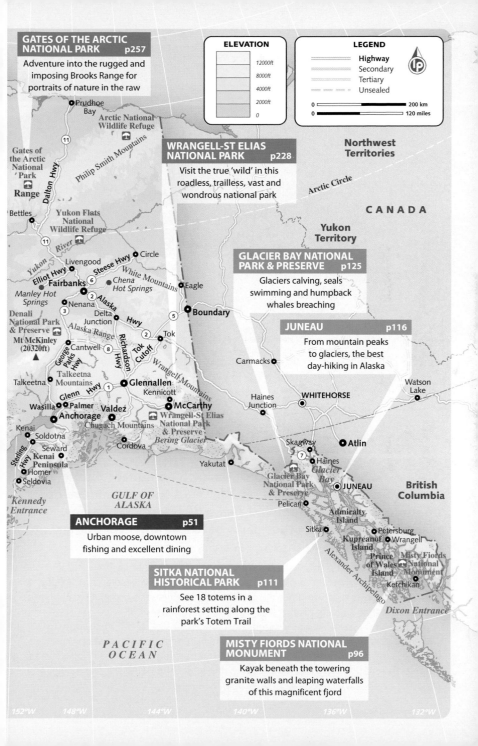

ELEVATION

12000ft
8000ft
4000ft
2000ft
0

LEGEND

Highway
Secondary
Tertiary
Unsealed

0 ————— 200 km
0 ————— 120 miles

GATES OF THE ARCTIC NATIONAL PARK p257

Adventure into the rugged and imposing Brooks Range for portraits of nature in the raw

WRANGELL-ST ELIAS NATIONAL PARK p228

Visit the true 'wild' in this roadless, trailless, vast and wondrous national park

GLACIER BAY NATIONAL PARK & PRESERVE p125

Glaciers calving, seals swimming and humpback whales breaching

JUNEAU p116

From mountain peaks to glaciers, the best day-hiking in Alaska

ANCHORAGE p51

Urban moose, downtown fishing and excellent dining

SITKA NATIONAL HISTORICAL PARK p111

See 18 totems in a rainforest setting along the park's Totem Trail

MISTY FIORDS NATIONAL MONUMENT p96

Kayak beneath the towering granite walls and leaping waterfalls of this magnificent fjord

Prudhoe Bay

Arctic National Wildlife Refuge

Northwest Territories

Gates of the Arctic National Park

Range

Philip Smith Mountains

Arctic Circle

CANADA

Bettles

Yukon Flats National Wildlife Refuge

Yukon Territory

Yukon River

Livengood

Steese Hwy

Circle

Elliot Hwy

Fairbanks

White Mountains

Eagle

Manley Hot Springs

Chena Hot Springs

Alaska

Boundary

Nenana

Delta Junction

Hwy

Carmacks

Denali National Park & Preserve

Alaska Range

Tok

Mt McKinley (20320ft)

Cantwell

Richardson Hwy

Tok Cutoff

George Parks Hwy

Talkeetna Mountains

Glennallen

WHITEHORSE

Watson Lake

Talkeetna

Glenn Hwy

Kennicott

Wrangell Mountains

Haines Junction

Wasilla

Palmer

Valdez

McCarthy

Anchorage

Chugach Mountains

Wrangell-St Elias National Park & Preserve

Skagway

Atlin

Kenai

Soldotna

Cordova

Bering Glacier

Haines

Glacier Bay

Seward

Kenai Peninsula

Yakutat

JUNEAU

British Columbia

Sterling Hwy

Homer

Seldovia

Glacier Bay National Park & Preserve

Kennedy Entrance

GULF OF ALASKA

Pelican

Sitka

Admiralty Island

Petersburg

Kupreanof Island

Wrangell

Prince of Wales Island

Misty Fiords National Monument

Ketchikan

PACIFIC OCEAN

Alexander Archipelago

Dixon Entrance

152°W   148°W   144°W   140°W   136°W   132°W

↘ THIS IS ALASKA

Alaska is where human beings stand on an equal footing with nature. Nowhere else in the USA is there such an undeveloped, unpopulated and untrampled place. There are mountains, glaciers and rivers in other parts of North America, but few are on the same scale as those in Alaska.

This state has 17 of the country's 20 highest peaks, and 5000 glaciers, including one larger than Switzerland. In Alaska, there are king crabs that measure 3ft from claw to claw, brown bears that stand more than 12ft tall, farmers who grow 125lb cabbages and glaciers that discharge icebergs the size of small houses.

Because of its size – Alaska is more than twice the size of the next-largest state, Texas – it's better to pick one or two regions to visit on a shorter vacation than try to fly around the entire state in two weeks. In the Interior, you'll find massive glacial rivers and North America's highest mountain, while in Southeast Alaska things feel a bit

more snug. Here, the US's largest national forest, the Tongass, cradles fishing towns and stretches across islands and fjords, with the Alaska Marine Highway weaving through it all. Anchorage provides museums, excellent restaurants and good local hiking, while the Kenai Peninsula and Prince William Sound offer kayaking and opportunities to spot both marine and land animals. In the Bush and the Southwest you'll learn what 'wide open spaces' really means, as the mostly roadless regions are impossibly remote and wild.

'Alaska offers more outdoor activities than most people do in a lifetime'

Alaska offers more outdoor activities than most people can do in a lifetime, from climbing mountains to rafting rivers. And if spotting a grizzly bear, catching a wild salmon, kayaking a fjord, walking on a glacier, or simply spinning down a scenic highway is your thing, you've chosen the right destination.

↘ ALASKA'S TOP 25 EXPERIENCES

1

↘ SEE THE GREAT ONE

Prepare to have your mind blown by the sheer size of Mt McKinley (p213) if you catch it on a clear day. North America's tallest mountain, also called Denali, is truly humbling, and you won't want to do anything but stare at her as long as she's on show.

↘ JUNEAU

The only US capital inaccessible by road, Juneau (p116), is a stunner. With green mountains, shrouded in fog, rising straight out of downtown, and with ships gliding down the channel, the city has an almost ethereal quality to it. The state's largest brewery and most oft-visited glacier are also here.

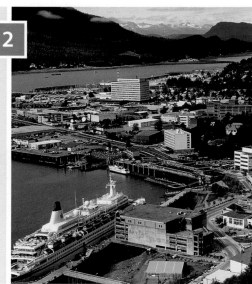

↘ ALASKA MARINE HIGHWAY

Alaska's water highway stretches from Southeast Alaska to the long wisp of the Aleutian Chain and stops at many ports along the way. Riding the Alaska Marine Highway Ferry is a fun way to witness travel the way locals do it in a mostly roadless state.

1 LEE FOSTER; 2 JAMES MARSHALL; 3 JOHN HYDE / ALASKASTOCK.COM

1 Mt McKinley (p213); 2 Juneau (p116); 3 Humpback whale and ferry, Alaska Marine Highway

↘ SEE THE MIDNIGHT SUN

4

There are places in Alaska, such as **Barrow** (p258), where the sun won't set for three months. But you don't have to fly that far north to bask in midnight rays: **Fairbanks** (p242) enjoys nearly 24 hours of daylight in the summer months, and even hosts late-night baseball games to celebrate it.

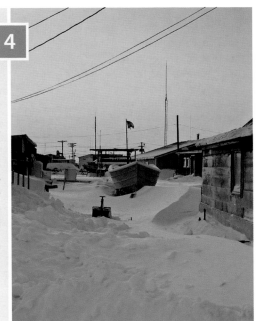

5

↘ TAKE THE TRAIN

The Alaska Railroad offers a relaxing and scenic alternative to driving or flying. The coolest ride is from Talkeetna to Hurricane Gulch on the **Hurricane Turn** (p72), America's last flag-stop train. This is a locals' route, filled with hikers and fishers out to spend a couple of days in the backcountry.

↘ KATMAI NATIONAL PARK & PRESERVE

It's just like in the photos: giant grizzly bears standing on top of a small waterfall, catching flying salmon as they try to jump upstream. It's remote and wild, but Katmai National Park (p199) is the place to witness one of Alaska's archetypal scenes and well worth the trip.

6

4 ROBERT DESTEFANO / ALAMY; 5 LEE FOSTER; 6 SHANNON NACE

4 Barrow (p258); 5 Passengers alight from Alaska Railroad (p72); 6 Grizzly bear atop waterfall

↘ WATCH FOR WHALES

With so much coastline, you have a great shot at spotting whales on your trip to Alaska. Take a whale-watching tour or search from the deck of a ferry. A few of the best places include **Prince William Sound** (p137), **Kenai Fjords National Park** (p180) and **Glacier Bay National Park** (p125).

7

8

↘ TREK ON A GLACIER

You'll have no problem finding a glacier to walk on or someone to take you up to do it. Exit Glacier (p180) is a favorite, as is the Matanuska Glacier (p228). In Talkeetna (p223), you can take a helicopter tour that actually lands on one of Denali's glaciers.

↘ CATCH THE NORTHERN LIGHTS

9

Seeing the shimmering curtain of lights for the first time borders on a spiritual experience. You're not going to see them in summer, but if you take a winter trip head up to Chena Hot Springs Resort (p249), which specializes in Northern Lights tours. What's better than watching the light spectacle while soaking in hot mineral water?

7 MARK NEWMAN ; 8 MICHAEL JONES / ALASKASTOCK.COM; 9 MARK NEWMAN

7 Humpback whale; 8 Exit Glacier (p180); 9 Northern Lights

ALASKA'S TOP 25 EXPERIENCES

10

⬎ PAN FOR GOLD

You might not strike it rich, but you'll certainly come across plenty of folks who are still hoping they might. In Hope (p171), folks still exercise mining claims. Over in Nome (p251) you'll find sluices along a sandy beach in town, or you can just enjoy the gold-rush history in Skagway (p130) or Fairbanks (p242).

⬎ NORTHERN HOT SPRINGS

11

Several hot springs near Fairbanks beckon to the weary traveler: the most accessible is Chena Hot Springs (p249), with a geothermal resort on-site, but the most delight-ful is Manley Hot Springs (p251). Here you'll find a few pools lounging in a tropical garden. You'll also find Pilgrim Hot Springs (p255) outside of Nome.

COPPER RIVER HIGHWAY

12

Spin across 50 miles of gorgeous gravel road along one of the Pacific Coast's largest wetlands. The highway (p155) crosses through the Copper River Delta, an area rich with glaciers, rivers and trails. At the end is the Million Dollar Bridge and grumbling Childs Glacier.

13

WRANGELL-ST ELIAS NATIONAL PARK

The US's largest national park is the size of six Yellowstones and has nine of the country's highest 16 peaks. Set yourself up at end-of-the-road, McCarthy (p229), and take your time exploring the seemingly endless supply of glaciers and rivers.

10 EMILY RIDDELL; 11 RANDY BRANDON / ALASKASTOCK.COM; 12 © NIEBRUGGE IMAGES / ALAMY; 13 JIM WEST / IMAGEBROKER

10 Gold panners; 11 Chena Hot Springs (p249); 12 Million Dollar Bridge, Copper River Hwy (p155); 13 Ice climber, Wrangell-St Elias National Park (p228)

14

↘ EAT YOUR VEGGIES

Summer may be short in Alaska, but the days are not. Evidence of the non-stop sunshine can be found in the Matanuska Valley (p76), Alaska's only farming community. Here you can find veggies such as kale and record-breaking cabbage – the world record was set here in 2009 at 125.6lb!

⬏ COMBAT FISH FOR SALMON

In Alaska rivers are so choked with salmon that hundreds of anglers will line up, shoulder to shoulder, snagging fish. It's an odd and uniquely Alaskan sight. The **Kenai** and **Russian Rivers** (p182) are a good place to photograph this phenomenon, as is Anchorage's **Ship Creek Viewing Platform** (p58).

15

14 PATRICK ENDRES / ALASKASTOCK.COM; 15 GRANT KLOTZ / ALASKASTOCK.COM

14 Farm building, Matanuska Valley (p76); 15 Combat fishing, Kenai Peninsula

ALASKA'S TOP 25 EXPERIENCES

↘ CLIMB A MOUNTAIN

Anchorage's **Flattop Mountain** (p61) is a great place to warm up your climbing muscles. A short but steep climb to the summit offers sweeping city-and-beyond views and a feeling of satisfaction at scaling your first mountain. The hike is kid-friendly and is the first peak most Anchorage residents climb as youngsters.

16

17

⬎ PHOTOGRAPH URBAN WILDLIFE

It's unique but not rare: a bald eagle perched on a telephone pole, a moose mowing down someone's garden, a black bear darting across a city trail. Even Alaska's biggest city, **Anchorage** (p58), is perched on the edge of the wilderness, and is a good place to spot some wild animals.

⬎ CELEBRATE FOURTH OF JULY

18

In a state that knows how to party, the Fourth of July celebration in **Seward** (p173) is legendary. The highlight event is the Mt Marathon race, where runners climb straight up and then fly back down the namesake mountain, often finishing bruised and muddy.

16 JOHN R. DELAPP / ALASKASTOCK.COM; 17 GRAEME CORNWALLIS; 18 JOCHEN TACK / IMAGEBROKER

16 Summit of Flattop Mountain (p61); 17 Bald eagles; 18 Children celebrate the Fourth of July

⬊ WANDER THE ARCTIC

The spine of the Brooks Range runs through the massive swatch of land that is **Gates of the Arctic National Park** (p257), where you can lose yourself for weeks. Raft the rivers, hike across the tundra or simply fly in to a remote site. Time is the only limiting factor.

19

ALASKA'S TOP 25 EXPERIENCES

20

⬐ HEAD WEST

Southwest Alaska (p159) is a veritable no man's land, full of treeless islands and active volcanoes. But there's also rich salmon fishing, excellent crabbing (remember *The Deadliest Catch*?), and little-known WWII history. Bear watching is also at its best in the region, thanks to the abundance of salmon.

19 CHRIS BELL; 20 SUNE WENDELBOE

19 Gates of the Arctic National Park & Preserve (p257); 20 Fishermen work the nets on a salmon boat

21

↘ FLY THROUGH MISTY FIORDS

A flightseeing tour of Misty Fiords National Monument (p96) is a great way to get a bird's-eye view of this stunning landscape. Floatplane tours will even land on the water. Vertical cliffs with tumbling waterfalls rise out of deep fjords and are covered in fog and deep green trees.

↘ GO ACROSS THE BAY

22

Kachemak Bay, that is. A muse for Homer's artist, Kachemak Bay State Park (p191) is a boat or short plane ride away. Overnight in pretty little Seldovia and kayak the coastline or hike up to Grewingk Glacier.

⬊ ICE FIELDS

Fly up to the **Juneau Ice Field** (p121) or take a long hike up to Kenai Fjords National Park's **Harding Ice Field** (p180). Remnants of the ice age exist here in the form of massive sheets of ice, from which scenic glaciers form. It's surreal – you'll feel like you're standing on sky.

⬊ SPOT A POLAR BEAR

Head on up towards the top of the world and you'll find **Barrow** (p258). There are definitely polar bears up here, but you should sign up for a tour to show you. While scoping for the big mammals, you might also catch sight of a walrus. But remember, there aren't any penguins up here...

21 CHIP PORTER / ALASKASTOCK.COM; 22 BERND ZOLLER / IMAGEBROKER; 23 JOHN HYDE / ALASKASTOCK.COM; 24 ERNEST MANEWAL

21 Misty Fiords National Monument (p96); 22 Kachemak Bay State Park (p191); 23 Juneau Ice Field (p121); 24 Traveling polar bears

↘ EXPLORE NATIVE CULTURE

Alaska's first residents, spread across the state, have their own cultures and languages. You can see totem poles in Sitka (p109), or hear Yupik spoken on the western coast. A good introduction is at the Alaska Native Heritage Center (p61) in Anchorage.

25

25 BRENT WINEBRENNER

25 Totem pole, Sitka National Historical Park (p111)

↘ ALASKA'S TOP ITINERARIES

FAMILY RAILROAD ADVENTURE

FIVE DAYS FAIRBANKS TO SEWARD

This land-based itinerary takes advantage of the scenic Alaska Railroad corridor. It's possible to drive the same route, but on a train it's easier to entertain the kids; they can walk around, eat in the dining car, or watch for wildlife out the windows.

❶ FAIRBANKS

Start in the north with some family fun at Pioneer Park (p242) or drive out to Chena Hot Springs (p249), where you'll find pools of varying warmth to splash around in. After a day in Fairbanks, hop onto the Alaska Railroad and head south.

❷ DENALI NATIONAL PARK

Put aside a day to ride the shuttle bus (p212) into the park for a chance to spot wildlife. Stop off at Savage River (p213) for a mellow walk, or when you're back to the park walk the Horseshoe Lake Trail (p217), where moose are often spotted. After a pizza dinner at Lynx Creek Pizza & Pub (p221), rest up and get back on the train the next day.

❸ ANCHORAGE

Your next stop is Alaska's biggest city, Anchorage (p58), which, not surprisingly, has plenty to entertain the whole family for at least a couple of days. If you missed wildlife in Denali, spend a few hours at

Alaska Railroad

LEE FOSTER

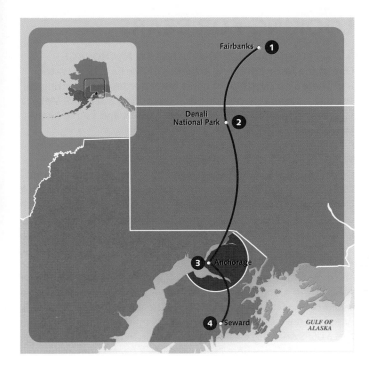

the Alaska Zoo (p62), where you'll be able to see a polar bear. At the Anchorage Museum (p58) kids will have fun in the new Imaginarium (p63). Everyone will get a feeling of satisfaction after summiting Flattop Mountain (p61).

❹ SEWARD

You'll take the train one last time, to its terminus in Seward. This is the place to appreciate Alaska's marine world. First stop: the awesome Alaska SeaLife Center (p176). Indulge in a behind-the-scenes tour or a Puffin Experience; kids will love getting up close to the animals. Later, head out to Exit Glacier (p180), where you can take an easy walk to the ice. The next day, board one of the tour boats for a trip into Kenai Fjords National Park (p180). You're sure to see sea lions and if you're lucky, whales.

LOOKING FOR BEARS

10 DAYS KATMAI NATIONAL PARK TO ANCHORAGE

One of the fastest growing activities in Alaska is bear watching. There's no shortage of bears here, nor tourists wanting to see one – preferably catching and devouring a salmon. Make it to at least one of the following destinations and you're likely to spot one.

❶ KATMAI NATIONAL PARK & PRESERVE

One of the most famous bear-viewing sites is Brooks Falls in **Katmai National Park** (p199). Fly into King Salmon, Katmai's hub, or book a cot at **Hallo Bay Bear Camp** (p199), located on a remote stretch of coast along the Alaska Peninsula, and watch big brownies snap jumping salmon from the waterfall.

❷ JUNEAU & SOUTHEAST ALASKA

The most affordable bear watching is found in **Juneau & Southeast Alaska** (p79). It's supereasy to catch brown and black bears feasting on salmon at Juneau's **Steep Creek** (p125), near the Mendenhall Glacier. At **Anan Creek Wildlife Observatory** (p100) near Wrangell you can rent a USFS Anan Bay Cabin that comes with four bear-watching permits to the stream where brown and black bears come in July and August.

❸ DENALI NATIONAL PARK

A bit more accessible than Katmai, **Denali National Park** (p212) sits on the road system. Jump on to a park **shuttle bus** (p212) and press

MARK NEWMAN

Brown bear cubs

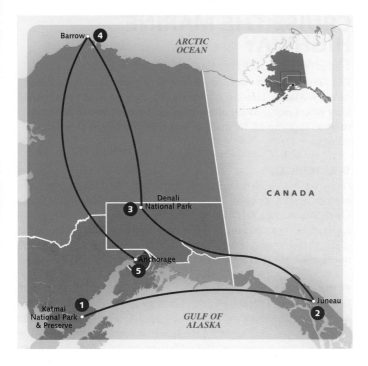

your face against the glass as you scour the sweeping landscape for both brown and black bears. Though you're likely to spot one of these legendary beasts, you'll probably also catch sight of caribou and moose.

❹ BARROW

We saved the best for almost-last. To see a polar bear head to **Barrow** (p258) at the top of the world. A guided tour to **Point Barrow** (p258) will take you just out of town, where you might also spy a walrus or two. Don't walk around on your own.

❺ ANCHORAGE

Finally, if you haven't had the luck to be in the right spot at the right time, you can always head to the **Alaska Zoo** (p62). Here you can see, all in the same hour, a black bear, a grizzly, and the magnificent polar bear. It's not quite as cool as seeing a bear in its natural setting, but you can get much closer to them, and it's a lot safer.

CRUISE THE MARINE HIGHWAY
TWO WEEKS KETCHIKAN TO KODIAK ISLAND

The Alaska Marine Highway is one of the greatest parts about travel in Alaska. Linking communities with no road access, the ferry offers not only an alternative to a cruise, but also opportunities to jump off in small towns that the cruise ships can't access.

❶ KETCHIKAN

Begin in the 'canned salmon capital of Alaska,' **Ketchikan** (p90), and explore highlights such as the **Totem Heritage Center** (p92) and **Creek Street** (p90). Additionally, consider a floatplane tour (or multi-day paddle) into absurdly pretty **Misty Fiords National Monument** (p96). After returning to Ketchikan you'll sail north, threading through the Inside Passage's foggy green islands.

❷ WRANGELL

The small town of **Wrangell** (p98) offers an antidote to bustling tourist towns; cruise ships only visit once a week. Since the ferry docks downtown, you can hop off for quick visit while in port or use the town as a base for exploring the wilds surrounding it. No matter what, be sure to visit **Petroglyph Beach** (p99), with its close to 50 primitive rock carvings on its sandy shores.

SUNE WENDELBOE

Columbia Glacier (p150), Prince William Sound

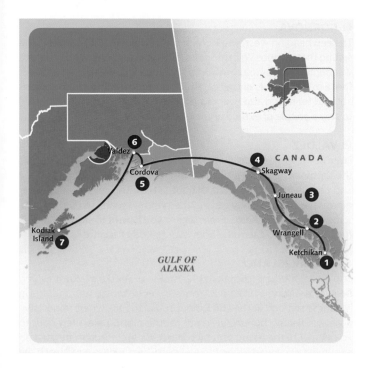

ALASKA'S TOP ITINERARIES

CRUISE THE MARINE HIGHWAY

❸ JUNEAU

The ferry will arrive in the state's mountainous **capital** (p116) at Auke Bay. Enjoy the city's natural wonders with a ride up the **Mt Roberts Tramway** (p118), or head out to the **Mendenhall Glacier** (p124). Dramatic mountains rise straight out of downtown, and you head straight into the middle of them on the **Perseverance Trail** (p119). Finally, relax with a beer at the **Alaskan Brewery Company** (p124).

❹ SKAGWAY

You have many options for detours at this point; head up to **Skagway** (p130), where the Marine Highway meets the 'real' road. Like Juneau, Skagway has numerous hiking trails that run straight out of downtown. You can practically tumble off of the ferry onto the **Dewey Lakes Trail System** (p132). But by far the highlight in Skagway is a trip up the **White Pass & Yukon Route Railroad** (p134). Ride in parlor cars up the narrow-gauge line that was laid during the Klondike Gold Rush of 1898. Prep for your trip up the pass with a visit to the **Klondike Gold Rush National Historical Park Visitor Center** (p131).

❺ CORDOVA

To keep heading west, you'll cruise to **Cordova** (p152), a jewel in the setting that is Prince William Sound. Give yourself at least a day here to wander the **small-boat harbor** (p152) and explore the **Copper River Delta** (p155) with its glaciers, trails, fishing and birding. Opportunities abound for hiking and river rafting, and it's easy to convince yourself to stay a couple of extra days.

❻ VALDEZ

From Cordova, float north up to **Valdez** (p148), where you'll cruise past the terminus of the oil pipeline. Switch to a smaller boat – a kayak – and paddle up to **Columbia Glacier** (p150). This massive tidewater glacier has been actively calving the past few years, so the bay is littered with giant icebergs. From Valdez you'll need to sail to **Whittier** (p156) in order to catch the boat over to Kodiak Island.

❼ KODIAK ISLAND

Sup on seafood on **Kodiak** (p192), home of Alaska's largest fishing fleet. After taking a hike up **Barometer Mountain** (p195), indulge in Japanese seafood at the **Old Powerhouse** (p198), where you'll have a view of fishing boats cruising in for the night. Take a few days to **kayak** (p196) the island's many protected coves. From here you can continue sailing west along the Aleutian Chain, where you'll reach the end of the ferry's line but not the end of your adventure.

EMILY RIDDELL

Kayaks & fishing boats, Valdez (p148)

PLANNING YOUR TRIP

ALASKA'S BEST...

ALASKA'S BEST...

⬆ HIKING

- **Juneau** (p116) Trails commence right in the city.
- **Denali National Park** (p212) Choose from ranger-led hikes or multiday backcountry jaunts.
- **Seward** (p173) Surrounded by mountains and Resurrection Bay, it's a hikers' paradise.
- **Kachemak Bay State Park** (p191) Head across the bay from Homer for idyllic hiking.

⬆ PADDLING

- **Prince William Sound** (p137) A massive green cirque full of coves and islands.
- **Kenai Fjords National Park** (p180) An accessible wilderness outside Seward.
- **Glacier Bay National Park** (p125) Eleven tidewater glaciers are your backdrop.

- **Misty Fiords National Monument** (p96) This ethereal landscape is breathtaking.

⬆ GLACIER VIEWING

- **Mendenhall** (p124) Great glacier viewing and scenic trails in the state's capital.
- **Exit** (p180) A small glacier in Kenai Fjords National Park.
- **Childs** (p155) The rumble of calving ice alerts you to the glacier's presence before you even see it.
- **Matanuska** (p228) Stop to gawk from the Glenn Hwy.

⬆ DINING

- **Anchorage** (p67) Bistros and salmon bakes, breakfast joints and steakhouses.
- **Girdwood** (p75) More good restaurants than we can list.

BRENT WINEBRENNER

Cruise ship passengers, Sitka Sound

- **Palmer** (p76) Enjoy the fruits of the Matanuska Valley's harvest.

ROAD TRIPPING

- **Seward Hwy** (p170) More than 120 miles of scenic byway in the Chugach National Forest.
- **Copper River Hwy** (p155) Spin across one of the US's largest continuous wetlands.
- **Alaska Marine Highway** (p268) The only All-American Road that floats.
- **Nome–Council Rd** (p255) Drive along this gravel road out of Nome.

FISHING

- **Russian & Kenai Rivers** (p182) Get cozy with other anglers when the salmon are running.
- **Ship Creek** (p58) Watch massive salmon run right through downtown Anchorage.
- **Homer** (p182) Take a halibut charter and bring home hundreds of pounds – of one fish.
- **Kodiak** (p192) Alaska's largest fishing fleet resides here.

WILDLIFE WATCHING

- **Katmai National Park & Preserve** (p199) The place to see grizzlies.
- **Point Barrow** (p258) You might spot a polar bear here.
- **Denali National Park** (p212) Besides bears, there are moose, caribou and all sorts of smaller critters.
- **Glacier Bay National Park** (p125) A dramatic setting to spot marine life.

RIVER RUNNING

- **Gates of the Arctic National Park** (p257) Multiday float trips are possible in this remote wilderness.
- **Denali National Park** (p212) The Nenana River is the most oft-rafted river in Alaska.
- **Sheridan River** (p152) Take a float trip outside Cordova.
- **Talkeetna River** (p223) A placid, scenic float for mellower folks.

THINGS YOU NEED TO KNOW

AT A GLANCE

- **Currency** USD
- **ATMs** Found almost anywhere.
- **Credit cards** You can expect most places to accept credit and debit.
- **Tipping** In restaurants, 18% to 20% and a few bucks to any kind of guide or tour operator.
- **Language** Though you might hear a bit of Yupik or Iñupiat, English is spoken everywhere.
- **Visas** Apply for one through the US Consulate, and if you're coming from the Lower 48 through Canada, make sure you have more than a single entry visa.
- **Cell phones** Coverage is surprisingly good, even in remote corners.

ACCOMMODATIONS

- **Wilderness lodges** (p300) Often luxurious affairs in gorgeous locations, sometimes remote.

- **Roadhouses** Like a roadside motel, but usually with a restaurant and gas station on site.
- **B&Bs** (p300) Run the gamut from suburban home to historic inn.
- **Cabins** May or may not have running water and electricity; USFS maintains wilderness cabins while others are privately owned and as comfy as home.
- **Camping** Free in national forests and fairly inexpensive on private land. Your best budget option.

ADVANCE PLANNING

- **Three months ahead** Book flights into the state, plan your itinerary, and research accommodation and tours.
- **Two months ahead** Book your accommodation, multiday tours, and rental car.

BRENT WINEBRENNER

Tourists contemplate Sitka Sound

- **Two weeks ahead** Break in your hiking boots, purchase binoculars and exercise your fishing (or drinking) arm.

BE FOREWARNED

- **Wildlife** Be sure to read up on bear and moose safety; remember to make noise when you hike and store food away from your tent.
- **Weather** Prepare for the worst, even in summer. The weather can change within minutes.
- **Wilderness hiking** Make sure you're prepared with a compass and map, and know how to cross a river safely.

COSTS

- **Budget** Expect to pay $60 to $70 per day if you camp, cook two meals a day, and participate in low-cost activities such as hiking.
- **Midrange** Anywhere from $100 (for a solo traveler) to $300 (for a family of four) for lodging, rental car and tours.
- **Top end** If you're flying into remote lodges or taking multiday tours, the sky's the limit.

EMERGENCY NUMBERS

- **Police, Fire, Ambulance** ☎ 911 Throughout the state, this is the number to call.

GETTING AROUND

- **Air** Often the only way to reach remote sights and villages.
- **Ferry** An easy way to get around Alaska's coastal communities.
- **Car** National car-rental companies are widespread.
- **Public transport** Can be limited in small towns, though most will have a taxi service.

GETTING THERE & AWAY

- **Air** Major carriers fly into the bigger cities.
- **Boat** The Alaska Ferry sails from Bellingham, WA, and cruise ships run from Vancouver, BC.
- **Car** The Alaska Hwy runs through Canada and is a long, scenic drive.

◥ TECH STUFF

- **Internet** Widely available; wi-fi is becoming common.

◥ TRAVEL SEASONS

- **Best months** June through August
- **Beat the crowds** May and September

◥ WHAT TO BRING

- **Warm clothes** The weather can change rapidly; be prepared with synthetic or wool underclothes, hats and mittens.
- **Waterproof outerwear** A rain jacket that packs into a daypack is useful, as is an umbrella for city walking.
- **Sturdy shoes** Hiking boots are best for tundra and rough trail, while running shoes will suffice for everything else. Make sure your boots are broken in before your trip.

- **Other handy items** Outside bigger cities and towns, things get scarce and prices go up. Consider bringing extra camera batteries, sunscreen and insect repellent.

◥ WHEN TO GO

- **June through August** The most popular time, with the best weather. Book accommodations in advance.
- **May & September** You might get snowy peaks and a bit more rain, but prices and demand are lower.
- **Winter** Traveling outside major cities requires special planning since many places close.

BRENT WINEBRENNER

Pig hurdling fence, Alaska State Fair (p49)

GET INSPIRED

BOOKS

- **Coming into the Country** John McPhee follows Alaska's emergence into statehood in a timeless classic.
- **Ordinary Wolves** Seth Kantner draws on personal experience to weave a tale about a boy growing up white in Bush Alaska and his struggle to be accepted by the village Iñupiat.
- **Into the Wild** Jon Krakauer recounts why a young man from a well-to-do family abandons civilization and walks alone into the Denali wilderness.
- **Arctic Dreams** Is a compelling look at the Far North and author Barry Lopez' personal journey.
- **The Last New Stand: Stories of Alaska Past and Present** An anthology of writings on the Far North, from Tlingit myths to Robert Service's poetry.

FILMS

- **Grizzly Man** A Werner Herzog documentary following grizzly activist Timothy Treadwell's life (and death) among the bears.
- **Alone in the Wilderness** Dick Proenneke films himself building a cabin by hand in the 1960s.
- **Into the Wild** Sean Penn's film adaptation of Jon Krakauer's novel.
- **North to Alaska** John Wayne plays the lead in this gold rush comedy (filmed mostly in California).
- **Insomnia** Al Pacino stars as a man who can't get any sleep under the midnight sun.

MUSIC

- **Pamyua** This Inuit band describes their music as 'tribal funk' and incorporates traditional music and new-world groove.
- **Anchorage** A song by Michelle Shocked about being 'anchored down in Anchorage.'
- **Hobo Jim** Alaska's own balladeer's most famous song is 'Iditarod Trail,' with the catchy lyrics 'I did I did I did the Iditarod Trail.'
- **North to Alaska** A oldie hit by Johnny Horton.

WEBSITES

- **Alaska Public Lands Information Centers** (www.nps.gov/aplic/center) Before you hit the trails, head here.
- **Alaska Travel Industry Association** (www.travelalaska.com) The official tourism marketing arm for the state.
- **Explore North** (www.explorenorth.com) A site dedicated to Alaska and the circumpolar north.
- **Lonely Planet** (www.lonelyplanet.com) Travel news and summaries, the Thorn Tree bulletin board and links to more web resources.

PLANNING YOUR TRIP

GET INSPIRED

CALENDAR

| JAN | FEB | MAR | APR |

CLARK JAMES MISHLER / ALASKASTOCK.COM

Alaska Native performers, Alaska State Fair (p49)

↘ JANUARY

**POLAR BEAR JUMPOFF
FESTIVAL   MID-JAN**
A favorite of costumed masochists who plunge into frigid **Resurrection Bay** with a smile, all to raise money for cancer.

↘ FEBRUARY & MARCH

ICEWORM FESTIVAL   FEB
Cordova's famous home-grown and tongue-in-cheek event is held at the beginning of February, and was first started in 1961 as an antidote to the long dark days of winter. The festival draws mainly locals and their friends and families, who honor the minuscule glacier-dweller *Mesenchytraeus solifugus* by parading a 150ft-long puppet of him through the streets.

**ANCHORAGE FUR
RENDEZVOUS   FEB-MAR**
The place to get fresh-trapped furs is still the 'Rondy,' but most folks prefer to sculpt ice, ride the Ferris wheel in freezing temperatures in February or March, or watch the 'Running of the Reindeer.'

↘ APRIL & MAY

ALASKA FOLK FESTIVAL   MID-APR
Musicians from across Alaska and the Yukon head to Juneau for a week of music and dancing. Who cares if it rains every day? See www.akfolkfest.org.

**COPPER RIVER DELTA
SHOREBIRD FESTIVAL   EARLY MAY**
Birders invade Cordova for some of the greatest migrations in Alaska; see www.cordovachamber.com.

| MAY | JUN | JUL | AUG | SEP | OCT | NOV | DEC |

KACHEMAK BAY SHOREBIRD FESTIVAL   EARLY MAY

If the birders aren't gathering in Cordova then they're nesting in Homer, enjoying workshops, field trips and birding presentations; see www.homeralaska.org.

JUNEAU JAZZ & CLASSICS   MID-MAY

Jazz and blues fills the air for 10 days in Alaska's beautiful capital city; see www.jazzandclassics.org.

KODIAK CRAB FESTIVAL   LATE MAY

Cheer on the survival-suit racers then grab a plate and dig into all the king crab you can eat; see www.kodiak.org.

⬇ JUNE

SUMMER MUSIC FESTIVAL

Chamber music, concerts and lots of cultural events held throughout June by the sea in beautiful Sitka. Book tickets in advance; see www.sitka musicfestival.org.

COLONY DAYS   MID-JUN

A parade and other activities, including a bed race down Main St, in honor of the first farmers arriving in Palmer; see www.palmerchamber.org.

MIDNIGHT SUN FESTIVAL   JUN 21

Celebrate solstice in Fairbanks with music from 40 banks on three stages, the Yukon 800 Power Boat Races and a baseball game that starts at midnight but doesn't need any lights; see www. explorefairbanks.com.

BRENT WINEBRENNER

Competitors, Mt Marathon Race (p48)

PLANNING YOUR TRIP

CALENDAR

CALENDAR

JAN   FEB   MAR   APR

Nalukataq (Whaling Festival)

PATRICK ENDRES / ALASKASTOCK.COM

JULY

INDEPENDENCE DAY PARADE   JUL 4
Soapy Smith, Alaska's most lovable scoundrel, rode at the head of Skagway's first parade in 1898, and this small town has been staging a great one ever since; see www.skagway.com.

MT MARATHON RACE   JUL 4
An exhausting 3.1-mile run up a 3022ft-high peak. The record is around 43 minutes.

GOLDEN DAYS   MID-JUL
A midsummer festival when Fairbanks cheers on the hairiest legs and the biggest moustaches in town; see www.explorefairbanks.com.

MOOSE DROPPING FESTIVAL   MID-JUL
Talkeetna is invaded by Mountain Mothers to the delight of men everywhere and everybody takes a turn tossing a moose nugget; see www.talkeetnachamber.org.

AUGUST

TALKEETNA BLUEGRASS & MUSIC FESTIVAL   EARLY AUG
The best campout music festival in Alaska, when more than 30 bluegrass bands jam for 20 hours; see www.talkeetnabluegrass.com.

MAYOR'S MIDNIGHT SUN MARATHON   JUN 21
On the longest day of the year there's more than enough time to join 3500 other runners for a 26.2-mile race in and around Anchorage; see www.mayorsmarathon.com.

NALUKATAQ (WHALING FESTIVAL)   LATE JUN
Join Barrow residents to celebrate another successful whaling season with dancing, blanket tosses and a taste of *muktuk* (whale blubber); see www.cityofbarrow.org.

GOLD RUSH DAYS   LATE JUN
A family affair with logging events, mining competition and a whole lot of food vendors; see www.traveljuneau.com.

MAY	JUN	JUL	AUG	SEP	OCT	NOV	DEC

TANANA VALLEY FAIR   EARLY AUG
Nine days of big veggies, midway rides and a truck mud bog competition in Fairbanks; see www.tananavalley fair.org.

FIRE TIRE FESTIVAL   EARLY AUG
Grab your mountain bike and ride the road to McCarthy. Lots of families ride the scenic, 60-mile route; see www. arcticbike.org.

GOLD RUSH DAYS   EARLY AUG
Five days of bed races, dances and fish feeds in Valdez. Oh, and a little gold-rush history, too; see www.val dezalaska.org.

ALASKA STATE FAIR   LATE AUG
Palmer's showcase for 100lb cabbages and the best Spam recipes in the state; see www.alaskastatefair.org.

≫ SEPTEMBER & OCTOBER

**KODIAK STATE FAIR
& RODEO   LABOR DAY**
Breakin' broncos and wrestling steers in Kodiak. For the noncowboys there are pie-eating and halibut-cleaning contests; see www.kodiak.org.

**SEWARD MUSIC & ARTS
FESTIVAL   LATE SEP**
Artists and more than 20 musical acts and theatrical companies gather on the shores of Resurrection Bay in Seward; see www.sewardak.org.

BLUEBERRY BASH   LATE SEP
Alaska's largest wild blueberries are found in Unalaska, which is why this bake-off and festival sends everybody home with blue teeth and purple tongues; see www.unalaska.info.

**GREAT ALASKA
BEER TRAIN   EARLY OCT**
All aboard! The *Microbrew Express* is a special run of the Alaska Railroad from Anchorage to Portage, loaded with happy passengers sipping the best beer made in Alaska; see www. alaskarailroad.com.

**ALASKA DAY
CELEBRATION   MID-OCT**
Sitka dresses the part in celebrating the actual transfer ceremony when the United States purchased Alaska from Russia in 1867; see www.sitka.org.

≫ NOVEMBER

WHALEFEST!   EARLY NOV
Whales galore in Sitka, so many you don't even need a boat to view them; see www.sitkawhalefest.org.

↘ ANCHORAGE & AROUND

Seward Highway (p72)

CLARK JAMES MISHLER / ALASKASTOCK.COM

ANCHORAGE AREA

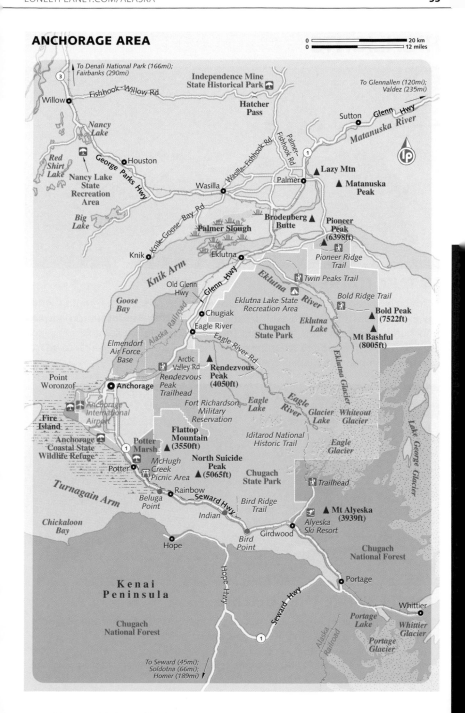

0 ___ 20 km
0 ___ 12 miles

To Denali National Park (166mi);
Fairbanks (290mi)

Independence Mine
State Historical Park

To Glennallen (120mi);
Valdez (235mi)

Hatcher
Pass

Willow

Fishhook–Willow Rd

Sutton

Glenn Hwy

Matanuska River

Nancy
Lake

Red
Shirt
Lake

George Parks Hwy

Houston

Nancy Lake
State
Recreation
Area

Wasilla

Wasilla–Fishhook Rd

Palmer–Fishhook Rd

Palmer

Lazy Mtn

Matanuska
Peak

Big
Lake

Palmer Slough

Brodenberg
Butte

Pioneer
Peak
(6398ft)

Knik

Knik-Goose-Bay-Rd

Eklutna

Glenn Hwy

Pioneer Ridge
Trail

Knik Arm

Old Glenn
Hwy

Eklutna River

Twin Peaks Trail

Bold Ridge Trail

Goose
Bay

Chugiak

Eklutna Lake State
Recreation Area

Eklutna
Lake

Bold Peak
(7522ft)

Alaska Railroad

Eagle River

Chugach
State Park

Mt Bashful
(8005ft)

Elmendorf
Air Force
Base

Eagle River Rd

Eklutna Glacier

Lake George Glacier

Point
Woronzof

Arctic
Valley Rd

Anchorage

Rendezvous
Peak
Trailhead

Rendezvous
Peak
(4050ft)

Eagle
Lake

Eagle River

Glacier
Lake

Whiteout
Glacier

Fire
Island

Anchorage
International
Airport

Fort Richardson
Military
Reservation

Flattop
Mountain
(3550ft)

Iditarod National
Historic Trail

Eagle
Glacier

Anchorage
Coastal State
Wildlife Refuge

Potter
Marsh

McHugh
Creek
Picnic Area

North Suicide
Peak
(5065ft)

Chugach
State Park

Trailhead

Potter

Turnagain Arm

Beluga
Point

Rainbow

Seward Hwy

Indian

Bird Ridge
Trail

Mt Alyeska
(3939ft)

Alyeska
Ski Resort

Chickaloon
Bay

Hope

Bird
Point

Girdwood

Chugach
National Forest

Kenai
Peninsula

Hope Hwy

Seward Hwy

Portage

Portage
Lake

Whittier

Whittier
Glacier

Chugach
National Forest

Alaska Railroad

Portage
Glacier

To Seward (45mi);
Soldotna (66mi);
Homer (189mi)

HIGHLIGHTS

↘ TAKE TO THE HILLS

Chugach State Park's peaks line the eastern edge of town, beckoning with awesome trails that lead to even better views. **Flattop Mountain** (p61) is an Anchorage must-do: the 3-mile round trip hike to the 3550ft summit is easy to follow (but be prepared to scramble a bit), and you'll return home able to boast that you climbed a mountain in Alaska.

↘ EXPERIENCE THE CULTURE

Museums abound in Anchorage, but two stand out: the **Anchorage Museum** (p58) and the **Alaska Native Heritage Center** (p61). The former boasts a new world-class expansion that focuses on experiential learning, while the latter transports you to a Native Alaska village. Both highlight art and ways of life unique to Alaska.

3

↘ FEAST ON THE FRUITS

Freshly caught seafood abounds in Alaska, and this is especially true in Anchorage. But the **Matanuska Valley** (p76) is also Alaska's only true farmland, producing super-sized veggies that set records. Head north out of Anchorage to shop at farmers markets and dine in restaurants that make the most of the valley's offerings.

4

↘ SPOT THE WILDLIFE

Urban moose. Suburban bears. City salmon. Anchorage is a city at the edge of the wilderness, and every now and then humans and wildlife cross paths. Bring your binoculars and have your camera ready; you never know when a munching moose might stroll across your path. A good place to look for moose is **Far North Bicentennial Park** (p59).

5

↘ CRUISE DOWN THE HIGHWAY

Dall sheep and beluga whales; bore tides and mountain vistas: the Anchorage–Girdwood leg of the **Seward Highway** (p72) is a stunner. Plenty of pullouts allow you to stretch this 45-mile journey to half a day; bring your hiking boots and follow one of the many hiking trails for sky-high views.

1 TOM BOL / ALASKASTOCK.COM; 2 BRENT WINEBRENNER; 3 BRENT WINEBRENNER; 4 MATT HAGE / ALASKASTOCK.COM; 5 RICHARD CUMMINS

1 Hiker, Chugach State Park; 2 Totem pole carving, Alaska Native Heritage Center (p61); 3 Vendors, Anchorage Market & Festival (p71); 4 Cyclist, Far North Bicentennial Park (p59); 5 Turnagain Arm, Seward Highway (p72)

BEST...

◥ BIKE TRAILS

- **Tony Knowles Coastal Trail** (p59) Cruise from downtown to Kincaid Park.
- **Campbell Creek Trail** (p66) Spot salmon as you spin from the Seward Hwy north.
- **Indian-Girdwood Trail** (p74) Look for Dall sheep and beluga whales.
- **Ship Creek Bike Trail** (p66) Catch a glimpse of 'urban combat' fishing.

◥ MUSEUMS

- **Anchorage Museum** (p58) A must-see world-class facility.
- **Alaska Native Heritage Center** (p61) A preserver of culture covering 26 acres.
- **Alaska State Trooper Museum** (p62) Check out the state-issued sealskin police booties.
- **Imaginarium Discovery Center** (p63) A hands-on kid-friendly destination.

◥ CUISINE

- **Marx Bros Café** (p67) Innovative cooking and a 500-bottle wine list.
- **Seven Glaciers Restaurant** (p76) Spectacular glacier views while you dine.
- **Red Beet** (p78) Daily menu showcasing Matanuska Valley produce.
- **Humpy's Great Alaskan Alehouse** (p67) Halibut, salmon and a whole lotta beer.

◥ HIKING TRAILS

- **Flattop Mountain Trail** (p61) A basic climb on every local's bucket list.
- **McHugh Lake Trail** (p62) Picnic friendly with waterfall views.
- **Winner Creek Trail** (p73) With a self-propelled river crossing.
- **Bird Ridge Trail** (p72) The first snow-free trail in spring is a steep climb.

LEFT: GRAEME CORNWALLIS; RIGHT: © PAUL ANDREW LAWRENCE / ALAMY

Left: Imaginarium Discovery Center, Anchorage Museum (p63); Marx Bros Café (p67)

THINGS YOU NEED TO KNOW

⬊ VITAL STATISTICS

- **Population** 283,950 (Anchorage city)
- **Best time to visit** April through September

⬊ LOCALITIES IN A NUTSHELL

- **Anchorage** (p58) Alaska's biggest city.
- **Matanuska Valley** (p76) A Depression-era farming settlement with 100lb produce and equally giant peaks.
- **Girdwood** (p73) Ski town in a picturesque valley with great summertime hiking and amazing restaurants.

⬊ ADVANCE PLANNING

- **Two months ahead** Book your accommodations in advance if you're traveling in June, July or August.
- **One month ahead** Book your rental car.
- **Two weeks ahead** Break in your hiking boots.

⬊ RESOURCES

- **Alaska Public Lands Information Center** (Map p64; ☎ 644-3661; www.nps.gov/aplic; 605 W 4th Ave; ☺ 9am-5pm) Bring photo ID.
- **Log Cabin Visitor Center** (Map p64; ☎ 257-2342; www.anchorage.net; 524 W 4th Ave; ☺ 7:30am-7pm Jun-Aug, 8am-6pm May & Sep) Pamphlets, maps, city guides and bus schedules.

- **USFS Glacier Ranger Station** (☎ 783-3242; Ranger Station Rd, Girdwood) Has topo maps and info on area hikes.
- **Chugach State Park Headquarters** (☎ 345-5014; Mile 115 Seward Hwy; ☺ 10am-4:30pm Mon-Fri) Housed in the Potter Section House; has a free museum with a snowplow train and other artifacts of the era.

⬊ GETTING AROUND

- **Bus** People Mover (p72) serves all of Anchorage.
- **Train** Limited passenger services.
- **Taxi** Plentiful, but you'll need to call rather than flag one down. Try **Anchorage Yellow Cab** (☎ 272-2422) or **Anchorage Checker Cab** (☎ 276-1234).

⬊ BE FOREWARNED

- **Smoking** Banned in indoor bars and restaurants.
- **Crime** There's generally a low rate of crime, but women should take caution when going out in the wee hours.
- **Wildlife** Plenty around – read up on bear and moose safety.

DISCOVER ANCHORAGE & AROUND

Anchorage isn't simply a big city on the edge of the wilderness but a big city *in* the wilderness. The town manages to mingle hiking trails and traffic jams, small art galleries and Big Oil, like no other city. At first, the minimalls and busy streets can be off-putting, but look behind its seemingly soulless sprawl and you'll find independent businesses thriving. Between streets, more than 100 miles of city trails meander in hidden greenbelts. Anchorage may be the only major city where you can watch urban moose munch on neighborhood shrubs and fisherman pull salmon from a downtown creek.

And Anchorage is not just the city – the municipality stretches across 1955 sq miles, all the way past the mountain-ringed ski community of Girdwood to the residential suburbs of Eagle River. Traveling from one end to the other is a day's road trip, but it's one where you might spot beluga whales, Dall sheep, or even a black bear or two.

ANCHORAGE

pop 283,950

SIGHTS

DOWNTOWN ANCHORAGE

ANCHORAGE MUSEUM

This **museum** (Map p64; ☎ 929-9200; www.anchoragemuseum.org; 625 C St; adult/child $10/7; ☺ 9am-6pm) recently emerged from a $75 million renovation that doubled its size. The Anchorage Museum is the best cultural jewel in this rough-and-tumble state. Included is the Art of the North Gallery, with entire rooms of Alaskan masters Eustace Ziegler and Sydney Laurence. The 15,000 sq ft Alaska Gallery is the best place to learn your Alaskan history; it's filled with life-size dioramas that trace 10,000 years of human settlement from early subsistence villages to modern oil dependency.

SHIP CREEK VIEWING PLATFORM

From mid- to late summer, king, coho and pink salmon spawn up Ship Creek, the historic site of Tanaina Indian fish camps. The **overlook** (Map p64) is where you can cheer on those love-starved fish humping their way toward destiny.

OSCAR ANDERSON HOUSE

Housed in the city's oldest wooden-framed home, this little **museum** (Map p64; ☎ 274-2336; www.anchoragehistoric.org; 420 M St; adult/child $3/1; ☺ 1-5pm Mon-Fri) overlooks the delightful Elderberry Park and is open from June through mid-September. Anderson was the 18th person to set foot in Anchorage and built his house in 1915.

4TH AVENUE MARKET PLACE/VILLAGE OF SHIP CREEK CENTER

This **shopping mall** (Map p64; ☎ 278-3263; 333 W 4th Ave; admission free; ☺ 10am-7pm Mon-Sat, 11am-6pm Sun) contains the usual gift shops, but also houses a lot of history. Painted on the walls outside is a historic timeline of Anchorage, while inside are displays devoted to the 1964 Good Friday earthquake. An Alaska Native dance show is staged at 1pm daily.

GREATER ANCHORAGE
ALASKA NATIVE MEDICAL CENTER
This **hospital** (Map p60; ☎ 800-478-1636; 4315 Diplomacy Dr; admission free) has a fantastic collection of Alaska Native art and artifacts: take the elevator to the top floor and wind down the staircase past dolls, basketry and tools from all across the state.

EARTHQUAKE PARK
For decades after the 1964 earthquake, this **park** (off Map p63) remained a barren moonscape, revealing the tectonic power that destroyed nearby Turnagain Heights. Today Earthquake Park, at the west end of Northern Lights Blvd on the Knik Arm, is being reclaimed by nature; you'll have to poke around the bushes to see evidence of tectonic upheaval.

FAR NORTH BICENTENNIAL PARK
Comprising 4000 acres of forest and muskeg in east central Anchorage, this **park** (Map p60) features 20 miles of trails. In the center of the park is Bureau of Land Management's (BLM's) **Campbell Tract**, a 700-acre wildlife preserve where it's possible to see moose and bears in the spring and brilliant fall colors in mid-September. There is an active grizzly population, and it's wise to steer clear of salmon streams during the twilight hours.

ACTIVITIES
CYCLING
Anchorage has 122 miles of paved paths that parallel major roads or wind through the greenbelts, making a bicycle the easiest and cheapest way to explore the city. If you run out of steam before the end of the ride, all People Mover (p72) buses are equipped with bike racks.

Downtown Bicycle Rental (Map p64; ☎ 279-5293; www.alaska-bike-rentals.com; 333 W 4th Ave; per 3/24hr $16/32; ⏲ 8am-8pm) has road, hybrid and mountain bikes as well as tandems, trailers and even clip-in pedals and shoes.

Anchorage's favorite cycling trail is the **Tony Knowles Coastal Trail** (Map p64),

SCULPTURE: 'CRYSTAL LATTICE,' ROBERT PFITZENMEIER / PHOTO: RICHARD CUMMINS

Anchorage Museum

GREATER ANCHORAGE

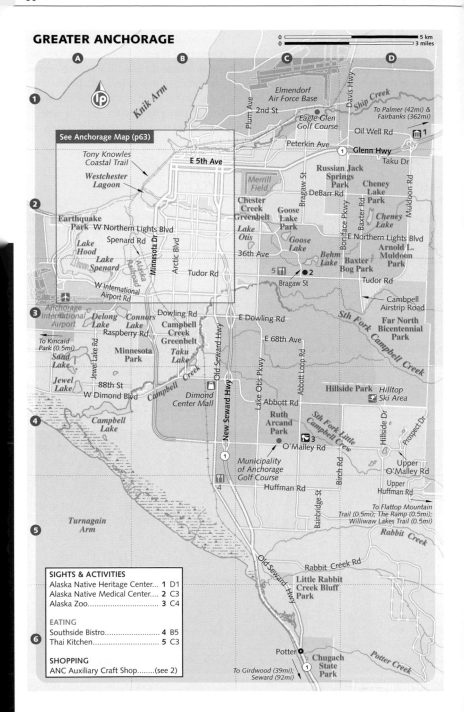

0 — 5 km
0 — 3 miles

A · **B** · **C** · **D**

Knik Arm

Elmendorf
Air Force Base

Plum Ave
2nd St

Davis Hwy

Ship Creek

Eagle Glen
Golf Course

Oil Well Rd

To Palmer (42mi) &
Fairbanks (362mi)

Peterkin Ave

Glenn Hwy

Taku Dr

See Anchorage Map (p63)

Tony Knowles
Coastal Trail

E 5th Ave

Russian Jack
Springs
Park

Cheney
Lake
Park

Muldoon Rd

Westchester
Lagoon

Merrill
Field

Bragaw St

DeBarr Rd

Cheney
Lake

Earthquake
Park   W Northern Lights Blvd

Chester
Creek
Greenbelt

Goose
Lake
Park

E Northern Lights Blvd

Boniface Pkwy

Baxter Rd

Spenard Rd

Lake
Hood

Lake
Spenard

Alaska
Railroad

Minnesota Dr

Arctic Blvd

Tudor Rd

Lake
Otis

36th Ave

Goose
Lake

Behm
Lake

Arnold L.
Muldoon
Park

Baxter
Bog Park

W International
Airport Rd

5 ⚑   ● 2

Bragaw St

Tudor Rd

Campbell
Airstrip Road

Anchorage
International
Airport

Dowling Rd

Connors
Lake

Campbell
Creek
Greenbelt

E Dowling Rd

Sth Fork Campbell Creek

Far North
Bicentennial
Park

Delong
Lake

Raspberry Rd

E 68th Ave

To Kincaid
Park (0.5mi)

Sand
Lake

Jewel Lake Rd

Minnesota
Park

Taku
Lake

Old Seward Hwy

Lake Otis Pkwy

Abbott Loop Rd

Jewel
Lake

88th St

W Dimond Blvd

Campbell Creek

Dimond
Center Mall

New Seward Hwy

Abbott Rd

Sth Fork Little
Campbell Creek

Hillside Park   Hilltop
🎿 Ski Area

Hillside Dr

Prospect Dr

Campbell
Lake

Ruth
Arcand
Park

🏛 3

O'Malley Rd

Birch Rd

Upper
O'Malley Rd

Turnagain
Arm

Municipality
of Anchorage
Golf Course

Huffman Rd

Bainbridge St

Upper
Huffman Rd

To Flattop Mountain
Trail (0.5mi); The Ramp (0.5mi);
Williwaw Lakes Trail (0.5mi)

Rabbit Creek

Rabbit Creek Rd

Little Rabbit
Creek Bluff
Park

Old Seward Hwy

Potter ●

Chugach
State
Park

Potter Creek

To Girdwood (39mi);
Seward (92mi)

SIGHTS & ACTIVITIES
Alaska Native Heritage Center... **1** D1
Alaska Native Medical Center.... **2** C3
Alaska Zoo.............................. **3** C4

EATING
Southside Bistro......................... **4** B5
Thai Kitchen.............................. **5** C3

SHOPPING
ANC Auxiliary Craft Shop........(see 2)

Alaska Native dancer, Alaska Native Heritage Center

BRENT WINEBRENNER

⬃ ALASKA NATIVE HERITAGE CENTER

Experiencing Alaska Native culture firsthand in the Bush is logistically complicated and expensive. Instead, come to the 26-acre **Alaska Native Heritage
Center** and see how humans survived – and thrived – before central heating.

The main building houses meandering exhibits on traditional arts and sci-
ences – including kayaks and rain gear that rival outdoors department store REI's
best offerings. It also features various performances, among them the staccato
Alaghanak song, lost for 50 years: the center collected bits and pieces of the traditional song from different tribal elders and reconstructed it. Outside, examples
of typical structures from the Aleut, Yupik, Tlingit and other tribes are arranged
around a picturesque lake. Docents explain the ancient architects' cunning tech-
nology: check out wooden panels that shrink in the dry summers (allowing light
and air inside) but expand to seal out the cold during the wet winter.

This is much more than just a museum; it represents a knowledge bank of
language, art and culture that will survive no matter how many sitcoms are
crackling through the Alaskan stratosphere. It's a labor of love, and of incal-
culable value.

Things you need to know: Map p60; ☎ 330-8000, 800-315-6608; www.alaskanative.net;
8800 Heritage Center Dr; adult/child $23.50/16; ⏰ 9am-5pm

11 scenic miles that begin at the west
end of 2nd Ave downtown and reach
Elderberry Park a mile away. From there,
the trail winds through Earthquake Park,
around Point Woronzof (Map p53) and
finally to Point Campbell in Kincaid Park.

HIKING
FLATTOP MOUNTAIN TRAIL
The very popular 3-mile round-trip hike to
the 3550ft peak is easy to follow, though
you'll be scrambling a bit toward the summit. Allow three to five hours. From the

OFFBEAT ANCHORAGE

The wildest salmon in Anchorage are nowhere near Ship Creek. They're found spawning along downtown streets as part of the **Wild Salmon on Parade**, an annual event in which local artists turn fiberglass fish into anything but fish. The art competition has resulted in an 'Alaska Sarah Salmon'; a fish with boxing gloves titled 'Socked Eye Salmon'; and 'Marilyn MonROE.' To see them all, pick up a fish tour map at the Log Cabin Visitors Center (Map p64).

A massive sun sits at the corner of 5th Ave and G St, marking the start of the **Anchorage Lightspeed Planet Walk**. This built-to-scale model of the solar system extends from the sun all the way out to Kincaid Park. The scale is set so that walking pace mimics the speed of light, but it'll take you all day to reach marble-sized Pluto at that pace. Travel faster than the speed of light by renting a bike.

Most of us would rather avoid the police. But who can resist the **Alaska State Trooper Museum** (Map p64; ☎ 279-5050; www.alaskatroopermuseum.com; 245 W 5th Ave; admission free; ⏰ 10am-4pm Mon-Fri, from noon Sun)? Dedicated to displaying law enforcement starting from when Alaska was a territory, the storefront museum has a 1952 Hudson Hornet cop car and state-issued sealskin cop boots.

same parking area, you can also access the 2-mile **Blueberry Loop** (perfect for kids) and 11-mile **Powerline Trail**, popular with cyclists.

WILLIWAW LAKES TRAIL

This easy 13-mile **hike** (off Map p60) also begins close to the Flattop Mountain trailhead, leading to the handful of alpine lakes at the base of Mt Williwaw. The trail makes a pleasant overnight hike and many consider it the most scenic outing in the Hillside area of Chugach State Park.

RENDEZVOUS PEAK ROUTE

The 4-mile trek to this 4050ft peak is an easy three- to five-hour trip, rewarding hikers with incredible views of Mt McKinley, Cook Inlet, Turnagain and Knik Arms, and the city far below. From the parking lot, a short trail leads along the right-hand side of the stream up the valley to the northwest. It ends at a pass where a short ascent to Rendezvous Peak is easily seen and climbed.

MCHUGH LAKE TRAIL

This 13-mile trail originates at McHugh Creek Picnic Area, 15 miles south of Anchorage at Mile 111.8 of the Seward Hwy. The route follows the McHugh Creek valley, and in 7 miles reaches Rabbit and McHugh Lakes, two beautiful alpine pools reflecting the 5000ft Suicide Peaks.

ANCHORAGE FOR KIDS
ALASKA ZOO

The unique wildlife of the Arctic is on display at this **zoo** (Map p60; ☎ 346-3242; 4731 O'Malley Rd; adult/child $9/5; ⏰ 9am-6pm Wed, Thu & Sat-Mon, to 9pm Tue & Fri), the only one in North America that specializes in northern animals, including snow leopards, Amur tigers and Tibetan yaks. Alaska native species, from wolverines and moose to caribou and Dall sheep, are abundant.

What kids will love watching, however, are the bears. The zoo has all four Alaskan species (brown, black, glacier and polar) but Ahpun, the polar bear, is clearly the star attraction.

IMAGINARIUM DISCOVERY CENTER

At the **Imaginarium** (Map p64; ☎ 929-9200; 625 C St; adult/child $10/7; ◔ 9am-6pm) kids can hug a life-sized *Tyrannosaurus rex,* stand inside a giant bubble, pick up a sea star from a touch tank or become a human gyroscope.

TOURS
CITY TOURS

Anchorage City Trolley Tours (Map p64; ☎ 775-5603; 612 W 4th Ave; rides $15; ◔ 9am-5pm) One-hour rides in a bright red trolley pass Lake Hood, Earthquake Park and Cook Inlet, among other sights. Tours depart on the hour.

Anchorage Historical Tours (Map p64; ☎ 274-3600; 524 W 4th Ave; adult/child $5/1) Starting at the Old City Hall, the hour-long downtown walking tour run by Anchorage Historical Tours begins at 1pm Monday to Friday.

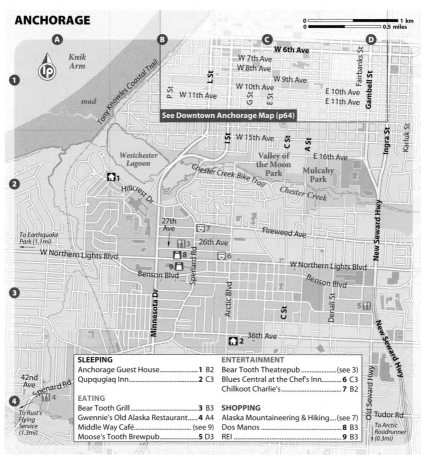

ANCHORAGE

See Downtown Anchorage Map (p64)

To Earthquake Park (1.1mi)

To Rust's Flying Service (1.3mi)

To Arctic Roadrunner (0.3mi)

SLEEPING		ENTERTAINMENT	
Anchorage Guest House	1 B2	Bear Tooth Theatrepub	(see 3)
Qupqugiaq Inn	2 C3	Blues Central at the Chef's Inn	6 C3
		Chilkoot Charlie's	7 B2
EATING			
Bear Tooth Grill	3 B3	SHOPPING	
Gwennie's Old Alaska Restaurant	4 A4	Alaska Mountaineering & Hiking	(see 7)
Middle Way Café	(see 9)	Dos Manos	8 B3
Moose's Tooth Brewpub	5 D3	REI	9 B3

Side tab: ANCHORAGE & AROUND

Side tab: ANCHORAGE

DOWNTOWN ANCHORAGE

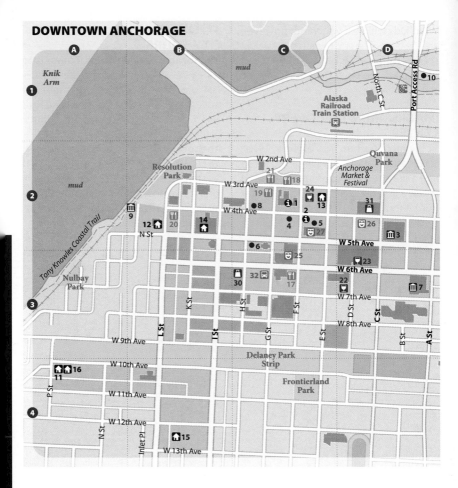

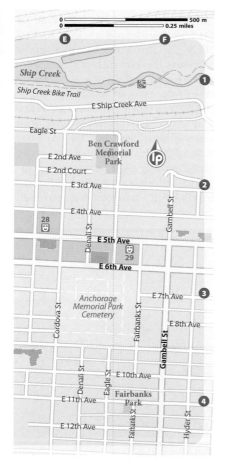

Gray Line (Map p64; ☎ 277-5581, 800-544-2206; www.graylineofalaska.com; 745 W 4th Ave) A three-hour bus tour covers downtown plus the Alaska Native Heritage Center (adult/child $51/26).

FLIGHTSEEING TOURS

Rust's Flying Service (off Map p63; ☎ 243-1595, 800-544-2299; www.flyrusts.com) Rust's offers a three-hour Mt McKinley flight that includes flying the length of Ruth Glacier ($345). It also offers visitors a three-hour Columbia Glacier tour ($340).

DAY TOURS

Alaska Railroad (Map p64; ☎ 265-2494, 800-544-0552; www.akrr.com; 411 W 1st Ave) Has a number of one-day tours from Anchorage that begin with a train ride. The nine-hour Spencer Glacier Float Tour (per person $185) includes a ride to Spencer Lake and a gentle raft trip among the glacier's icebergs.

SLEEPING
BUDGET

ourpick **Qupqugiaq Inn** (Map p63; ☎ 563-5633; www.qupq.com; 640 W 36th Ave; dm $25, s/d with bath $87/104, without bath $69/90; ☒ ☐) This colorful establishment has curved hallways, tiled floors, granite windowsills and a continental breakfast that includes French-pressed coffee and roll-your-own oats. The large dorms sleep eight, and the private rooms are bright and clean. Bus 36 stops right outside.

Anchorage Guest House (Map p63; ☎ 907-274-0408; www.akhouse.com; 2001 Hillcrest Dr; dm $35, r from $80; ☒ ☐) This spacious suburban home feels more like a B&B than a hostel, which is why it costs a bit more. Owner and singer/songwriter Andy Baker offers laundry ($2), bag storage ($1 per day), and bike rentals ($5 per hour) for the nearby coastal trail.

MIDRANGE

City Garden B&B (Map p64; ☎ 276-8686; www.citygarden.biz; 1352 W 10th Ave; r $100-150; ☒ ☐) One of several B&Bs located on a two-block stretch of 10th Ave, this is an open, sunny, gay- and lesbian-friendly place with more cutting-edge art than antiques. The nicest of the three rooms has a private bath.

Oscar Gill House (Map p64; ☎ 279-1344; www.oscargill.com; 1344 W 10th Ave; r $115-135; ☒) This historic clapboard home was built in 1913 in Knik and later moved to its Midtown location. The B&B offers three guest rooms (two that share a bathroom), a fantastic breakfast and free bikes.

TOP END

Copper Whale Inn (Map p64; ☎ 258-7999; www.copperwhale.com; W 5th Ave & L St; r $185-210; ✕ ▣) Recently remodeled rooms make this city-center B&B both elegant and bright. There's a relaxing waterfall pond, and breakfast is served with a view in the living room. It's also gay and lesbian friendly.

Inlet Tower (Map p64; ☎ 276-0110, 800-544-0786; www.inlettower.com; 1200 L St; r $229-269; ✕ ▣) This hotel has 15 floors of spacious suites with kitchenettes, gourmet coffee for the coffeemaker and large TVs with in-room movies. Amazing views.

ourpick Historic Anchorage Hotel (Map p64; ☎ 272-4533, 800-544-0988; www.anchoragehistorichotel.com; 330 E St r from $249; ✕ ▣) This boutique hotel was established only a year after the city was, in 1916, though the current building is from 1936. It's luxurious, and you're sure to receive lots of personal attention.

BRENT WINEBRENNER

Tony Knowles Coastal Trail (p59)

↘ IF YOU LIKE...

If you like cycling the **Tony Knowles Coastal Trail** (p59), we think you'll like Anchorage's other fabulous cycling paths:

- **Ship Creek Bike Trail** This trail runs 2.6 miles from the Alaska Railroad depot along the namesake creek and into the Mountain View neighborhood. Here you can watch aggressive anglers combat fish for salmon as you wind through woods and industry.
- **Chester Creek Trail** This scenic 6-mile path through the Chester Creek Greenbelt connects with the Coastal Trail at Westchester Lagoon and follows a mountain-fed stream to Goose Lake Park.
- **Campbell Creek Trail** Featuring some of the newest paved path in Anchorage, this trail stretches 8 miles from Far North Bicentennial Park to the Seward Hwy, with most of the ride in the Campbell Creek Greenbelt.

COMBAT FISHING

In a place that's mostly natural and wild, there are few sights more unnatural than what happens each summer wherever Alaska's best salmon rivers meet a busy road. When the fish are running, the banks become a human frenzy – a ceaseless string of men, women and children hip-to-hip, hundreds of fishing rods whipping to and fro, the air filled with curses and cries of joy, the waters rippling with dozens of fish dancing on taut and sometimes tangled lines. The banks are a jumble of coolers and tackle boxes and catches-of-the-day. Rub your eyes all you want: the scene is for real. This is combat fishing.

As with any form of combat, there are subtle rules that guide the chaos. Among them: don't wade out in front of other anglers, or snap up their spot on the bank if they briefly step away. (On the other hand, don't let the glares of the earlier arrivals dissuade you from taking your proper place in the fray.) Try to give your neighbor space – and whatever you do, don't foul your line with theirs. Most importantly, if you get a bite, shout 'fish on!' so others can reel in their lines and give you room to wrestle your catch. And while you may be tempted to milk the moment for all it's worth, try to get your trophy to shore quickly. In combat fishing, you don't 'play' a fish; you land it fast, so others can rejoin the fight.

If going into battle doesn't appeal to you, take heart – the combat zone is usually limited to within a few hundred yards of the closest road. Hike half a mile upriver, and you'll likely have all the fish to yourself.

Hotel Captain Cook (Map p64; ☎ 276-6000, 800-843-1950; www.captaincook.com; cnr 4th Ave & K St; r from $250; ⊠ 🖳 🕏) The grand dame of Anchorage accommodations still has the air of an Alaskan aristocrat right down to the doormen with top hats. There are plenty of plush services and upscale shops: Jacuzzis, fitness clubs, beauty salon, jewelry store, and four restaurants including the famed Crow's Nest Bar on the top floor.

EATING
DOWNTOWN
RESTAURANTS

Sack's Café (Map p64; ☎ 274-4022; 328 G St; lunch $9-12, dinner $18-35; 🕑 11am-2:30pm & 5-9:30pm Mon-Thu, 11am-2:30pm & 5-10pm Fri & Sat, 10:30am-2:30pm & 5-9:30pm Sun) A bright, colorful restaurant serving elegant fare that is consistently creative. It is always bustling (reservations recommended) and has the best weekend brunch in town.

Humpy's Great Alaskan Alehouse (Map p64; ☎ 276-2337; 610 W 6th Ave; dinner $12-30; 🕑 11am-2am) Anchorage's most beloved beer place, with 44 draughts on tap. There's also ale-battered halibut, gourmet pizzas, outdoor tables and live music most nights.

Snow Goose Restaurant (Map p64; ☎ 277-7727; 717 W 3rd Ave; medium pizza $13-14; 🕑 11:30am-11:30pm) The outdoor deck on the 2nd floor is positioned to look onto Cook Inlet, Mt Susitna and the sunsets whenever they occur. There are few things nicer than enjoying an Urban Wilderness Pale Ale here on a sunny evening.

ourpick Marx Bros Café (Map p64; ☎ 278-2133; 627 W 3rd Ave; dinner $34-50;

⏰ 5:30-10pm Tue-Sat) Some of Anchorage's most innovative cooking and a 500-bottle wine list are the real reasons this 14-table restaurant is so popular. The menu changes nightly, but the beloved halibut macadamia always stays put. In the summer it's best to book your table a week in advance.

CAFES

our pick **Snow City Café** (Map p64; ☎ 272-2489; 1034 W 4th Ave; breakfast $7-12, lunch $7-9; ⏰ 7am-4pm) Consistently voted best breakfast by *Anchorage Press* readers, this busy cafe serves healthy grub to a mix of clientele that ranges from the tattooed to the up-and-coming.

MIDTOWN
RESTAURANTS

Thai Kitchen (Map p60; ☎ 907-561-0082; 3405 Tudor Rd; dinner $8-12; ⏰ 11am-3pm & 5pm-9pm; ✖) This kid-friendly place comes highly recommended, with more than 100 items on the menu, dozens of which are vegetarian.

our pick **Bear Tooth Grill** (Map p63; ☎ 276-4200; 1230 W 27th St; burgers $8-12, dinner $10-20; ⏰ 4-11pm; ✖) A popular hangout with an adjacent theater (see opposite), it serves excellent burgers and seafood as well as Mexican and Asian fusion dishes. The microbrews are fresh and the cocktails are the best in town – if you're up for a splurge, lash out on the *el Cielo* (the sky) margarita.

Moose's Tooth Brewpub (Map p63; ☎ 258-2537; 3300 Old Seward Hwy; medium pizza $12-21; ⏰ 11am-11pm Mon-Thu, to midnight Fri & Sat, noon-11pm Sun) An Anchorage institution serving 18 custom-brewed beers, including monthly specials. There are also 50 gourmet pizzas on the menu, and it's *the* place refuel after a long day in the Chugach.

CAFES

Middle Way Café (Map p63; ☎ 272-6433; 1200 W Northern Lights Blvd; breakfast $4-9, lunch $6-11; ⏰ 8am-5:30pm Mon-Fri, 10:30am-4:30pm Sat & Sun) This veggie-friendly cafe serves healthy breakfasts (try the huevos rancheros) and organic salads, soups and sandwiches.

BRENT WINEBRENNER

Gwennie's Old Alaska Restaurant

Gwennie's Old Alaska Restaurant (Map p63; ☎ 243-2090; 4333 Spenard Rd; breakfast $6-11, dinner $15-25; ⏰ 6am-10pm Mon-Sat, from 8am Sun) Alaska at its best; lots to look at – totems, stuffed bears and a gurgling stream – and big portions. Non-Alaskans can probably share a reindeer sausage omelet and not be hungry for two days.

SOUTH ANCHORAGE
Arctic Roadrunner (off Map p63; ☎ 561-1245; 5300 Old Seward Hwy; burgers $4-5; ⏰ 10:30am-9pm Mon-Sat; ✗) Since 1964 this place has been turning out beefy burgers and great onion pieces and rings. If your timing is right you can eat outdoors while watching salmon spawn up Campbell Creek.

Southside Bistro (Map p60; ☎ 348-0088; 1320 Huffman Park Dr; dinner $11-36; ⏰ 11:30am-10pm Tue-Thu, to 11pm Fri & Sat) Upscale dining on the south side of town, this bistro is well worth the splurge. We can't get enough of the chevre salad.

DRINKING
With its young and lively population, Anchorage has a lot to do after the midnight sun finally sets. The free *Anchorage Press* and Friday *Anchorage Daily News* both have events listings.

Bernie's Bungalow Lounge (Map p64; 626 D St) Pretty people, pretty drinks: this is the place to see and be seen. On Thursdays bands play on the tiki torch-lit patio, on the weekends it's DJs.

Crush (Map p64; 343 W 6th Ave) This swanky wine bar serves 'bistro bites,' a menu of appetizers and salads. It's great for a nibble and a glass (or bottle) of reasonably priced wine.

F Street Station (Map p64; 325 F St) This is the place where everybody knows your name. The only thing missing in this friendly, music-free drinking hole is Norm sitting at the end of the bar.

There's upscale dining at the **Crow's Nest** (Map p64; 5th Ave & K St), at the top of the Hotel Captain Cook, but most come for a drink and a million-dollar view of Cook Inlet.

ENTERTAINMENT
CLUBS
our pick Chilkoot Charlie's (Map p63; ☎ 272-1010; www.koots.com; 2435 Spenard Rd) More than just Anchorage's favorite meat market, 'Koots,' as the locals call it, is a landmark. The sprawling, wooden edifice has 22 beers on tap, 10 bars, four dancefloors and a couple of stages where basically every band touring Alaska ends up.

GAY & LESBIAN VENUES
Several straight bars are regarded as gay and lesbian friendly: try Bernie's Bungalow Lounge (left) and the Moose's Tooth Brewpub (opposite).

Mad Myrna's (Map p64; 530 E 5th Ave; cover Sat & Sun $5-10) A fun, cruisy bar with line dancing on Thursday, Drag Divas shows on Friday and dance music most nights after 9pm.

Kodiak Bar & Grill (Map p64; 225 E 5th Ave) Charges a $3 cover until 2am, serves alcohol until 3am, and after that this club is open to minglers 18 years and up.

LIVE MUSIC
There's plenty of jazz and blues to be found in Anchorage: **Blues Central at the Chef's Inn** (Map p63; ☎ 272-1341; 825 W Northern Lights Blvd) is an intimate venue with live blues and jazz nightly. Anchorage Museum (p58) offers Jazz After Hours at 7pm on Thursday, free with the cost of museum admission.

CINEMAS
Bear Tooth Theatrepub (Map p63; ☎ 276-4200; www.beartooththeatre.net; 1230 W 27th Ave)

Cruise into this very cool venue (check out the mural on the lobby ceiling) where you can enjoy great microbrews, wine or even dinner while watching first-run movies ($3) – Monday night is 'art house' night, and features foreign and independent films.

Alaska Experience Center (Map p64; ☎ 272-9076; 333 W 4th Ave; adult/child movie $10/6, earthquake exhibit $7/6, combined ticket $13/10; ☺ 10am-9pm) More a tourist trap than movie house, with IMAX nature films and a theatrical simulation of the 1964 Good Friday earthquake.

THEATER & PERFORMING ARTS
Anchorage had an orchestra before it had paved roads, which says a lot about priorities around here.

Alaska Center for the Performing Arts (Map p64; ☎ 263-2900, tickets 263-2787; www.alaskapac.org; 621 W 6th Ave) Impresses tourists with the film *Aurora: Alaska's Great Northern Lights* (adult/child $8.75/$6.75; ☺ on the hour 9am to 9pm) during summer in its Sydney Laurence Theatre. The Alaska Center is also home to the **Anchorage Opera** (☎ 279-2557; www.anchorageopera.org), **Anchorage Symphony Orchestra** (☎ 274-8668; www.anchoragesymphony.org), **Anchorage Concert Association** (☎ 272-1471; www.anchorageconcerts.org) and **Alaska Dance Theatre** (☎ 277-9501; www.alaskadancetheatre.org).

Egan Civic Center (Map p64; ☎ 263-2800; www.egancenter.com; 555 W 5th Ave) Try this place for top-drawer musical groups and other big events.

Eccentric Theatre Company (Map p64; ☎ 274-2599; 413 D St; tickets $12-15) This may well be the best live theater in town, known for staging everything from Shakespeare's *Hamlet* to *Archy and Mehitabel* (comic characters of a cockroach and a cat), Mel Brooks' jazz musical based on the poetry of Don Marquis. Only in Anchorage…

OTHER ENTERTAINMENT
Anchorage Bucs (☎ 561-2827; www.anchoragebucs.com) and **Anchorage Glacier**

Alaska Native Primary Care Center, Alaska Native Medical Center (p59)

Pilots (☎ 274-3627; www.glacierpilots.com) play semipro baseball at Mulcahy Ball Park, where living legend Mark McGuire slammed a few homers. General admission is around $5.

SHOPPING
OUTDOOR GEAR

REI (Map p63; ☎ 272-4565; 1200 Northern Lights Blvd; ⏰ 10am-9pm Mon-Fri, to 8pm Sat, 11am-7pm Sun) Anchorage's largest outdoor store has everything you might ever need, from wool socks to backpacks to kayaks to camp chairs. Besides being able to repair your camp stove or bike tire, it will also rent canoes, bear containers, tents, and bikes.

Alaska Mountaineering & Hiking (Map p63; ☎ 272-1181; www.alaskamountaineering. com; 2633 Spenard Rd; ⏰ 9am-7pm Mon-Fri, to 6pm Sat, noon-5pm Sun) Staffed by experts and stocked with high-end gear, AMH is the place for serious adventurers.

SOUVENIRS

Anchorage Market & Festival (Map p64; ☎ 272-5634; www.anchoragemarkets.com; W 3rd Ave & E St; ⏰ 10am-6pm Sat & Sun) This was called the 'Saturday Market' until it became so popular they opened it on Sundays. A fantastic open market with live music and almost 100 booths stocked with cheap food, Mat-Su Valley veggies and souvenirs from birch steins to birch syrup.

Dos Manos (Map p63; ☎ 569-6800; 1317 W Northern Lights Blvd; ⏰ 11am-6pm Mon-Sat) Across from Title Wave Books, it sells locally crafted art and jewelry, and very cool Alaska-themed T-shirts.

ALASKA NATIVE ARTS & CRAFTS

Alaska Native Arts Foundation Gallery (☎ 258-2623; www.alaskanativearts.org; 500 W 6th Ave; ⏰ 10am-6pm Mon, Wed & Fri, to 7pm Tue & Thu, 11am-5pm Sat) The gallery showcases Native art in a bright, open space.

ANC Auxiliary Craft Shop (Map p60; ☎ 729-1122; 4315 Diplomacy Dr; ⏰ 10am-2pm Mon-Fri, from 11am 1st & 3rd Sat of month) Located on the 1st floor of the Alaska Native Medical Center, it has some of the finest Alaska Native arts and crafts available to the public. It does not accept credit cards.

Oomingmak Musk Ox Producers Co-op (Map p64; ☎ 272-9225; www.qiviut.com; 604 H St; ⏰ 9am-9pm Mon-Fri, to 6pm Sat & Sun) Handles a variety of very soft, very warm and very expensive garments made of Arctic musk-ox wool, hand-knitted in isolated Inupiaq villages.

GETTING THERE & AWAY
AIR

Alaska Airlines (☎ 800-252-7522; www.alaskaair.com) Provides the most intrastate routes to travelers, generally through its contract carrier, ERA Aviation, which operates services to Valdez, Homer, Cordova, Kenai, Iliamna and Kodiak. You can book tickets either online or at the airport.

BUS

Homer Stage Line (☎ 868-3914; www.homerstageline.com) Runs daily in the summer between Anchorage and Cooper Landing ($45), Soldotna ($55), Homer ($65) and Seward ($50).

Seward Bus Line (☎ 563-0800; www.sewardbuslines.net) Runs between Anchorage and Seward ($50) twice daily in summer.

Alaska Yukon Trails (☎ 800-770-7275; www.alaskashuttle.com) Runs a bus up the George Parks Hwy to Talkeetna ($59), Denali National Park ($65) and Fairbanks ($91).

Alaska Park Connection (☎ 800-266-8625; www.alaskacoach.com) Offers daily bus services from Anchorage through to Denali National Park ($79) and Seward ($56), as well as services between Seward and Denali ($135).

RIDING THE ALASKA RAILROAD

In a remote corner of the Alaskan wilderness, you stand along a railroad track when suddenly a small train appears. You wave a white flag in the air – actually yesterday's dirty T-shirt – and the engineer acknowledges you with a sound of his whistle and then stops. You hop onboard to join others fresh from the Bush; fly fishers, backpackers, a hunter with his dead moose, locals whose homestead cabin can be reached only after a ride on the *Hurricane Turn*, one of America's last flag-stop trains.

This unusual service between Talkeetna and Hurricane Gulch along the Susitna River is only one aspect that makes the Alaska Railroad so unique. At the other end of the rainbow of luxury is the railroad's Gold Star Service, two lavishly appointed cars that in 2005 joined the *Denali Star* train as part of the Anchorage–Fairbanks run. The 89ft double-decked dome cars include a glass observation area on the 2nd level with 360-degree views and a bartender in the back serving your favorite libations.

TRAIN

From its downtown depot, the **Alaska Railroad** (Map p64; ☎ 265-2494, 800-544-0552; www.akrr.com; 411 W 1st Ave) sends its *Denali Star* north daily to Talkeetna (adult/child $80/40), Denali National Park ($129/65) and Fairbanks ($179/90). The *Coastal Classic* stops in Girdwood ($49/25) and Seward ($59/30) while the *Glacial Discovery* connects to Whittier ($52/26). You can save 20% to 30% traveling in May and September.

GETTING AROUND
TO/FROM THE AIRPORT

People Mover bus 7 offers hourly service between downtown and the airport.

You can call **Alaska Shuttle Service** (☎ 338-8888, 694-8888; www.alaskashuttle.net) for door-to-door service to downtown and South Anchorage ($30) or Eagle River ($45). These fares are for one to three passengers, so it's cheaper if you can share.

BUS

Anchorage's excellent bus system, **People Mover** (☎ 343-6543; www.people mover.org; Downtown Transit Center, 700 W 6th Ave; ☯ 8am-5pm Mon-Fri), runs services from 6am to midnight Monday to Friday, 8am to 9pm Saturday and 9:30am to 7pm Sunday.

SOUTH OF ANCHORAGE
SEWARD HIGHWAY

Once it leaves Anchorage proper, the highway winds along massive peaks dropping straight into Turnagain Arm. Expect lots of traffic, a frightening percentage of which involves folks who have (1) never seen a Dall sheep before and (2) never driven an RV before; it's a frustrating and sometimes deadly combination. Mile markers measure the distance from Seward.

If you're lucky (or a planner), you'll catch the bore tide (see boxed text, p74), which rushes along Turnagain Arm in varying sizes daily.

Bird Ridge Trail (Mile 102) starts with a wheelchair-accessible loop, then continues with a steep, popular and well-marked path that reaches a 3500ft overlook at Mile 2; this is a traditional turnaround point for folks in a hurry.

GIRDWOOD
pop 1790

Encircled by mighty peaks brimming with glaciers, Girdwood is a laid-back antidote to the bustle of Anchorage.

SIGHTS

The town of Girdwood was named for James Girdwood, who staked the first claim on Crow Creek in 1896. Two years later the **Crow Creek Mine** (☎ 229-3105; www.crowcreekmine.com; Mile 3.5 Crow Creek Rd; adult/child $5/free; ☉ 9am-6pm) was built and today you can still see some original buildings and sluices at this working mine. You can even learn how to pan for gold and then give it a try yourself (adult/child $15/5).

The **Alyeska Ski Resort Tram** (☎ 754-1111; admission $18; ☉ 9:30am-9:30pm) offers the easiest route to the alpine area during the summer. At the top you can dine at Seven Glaciers Restaurant (p76) or just wander above the tree line, soaking up the incredible views.

ACTIVITIES
HIKING

Winner Creek Trail is an easy and pleasant hike that winds 5.5 miles through lush forest, ending in the gorge itself, where Winner Creek becomes a series of pretty cascades. The first half of the trail is a boardwalk superhighway, but toward the end it can get quite muddy. From the gorge you can connect to the **National Historic Iditarod Trail** for a 7.7-mile loop. Either way, you'll cross the gorge on an ultrafun hand-tram. The most popular trailhead is near Arlberg Rd: walk along the bike path past the Alyeska Prince Hotel, toward the bottom of the tram.

The highly recommended **Crow Pass Trail** is a short but beautiful alpine hike that has gold-mining relics, an alpine lake, and often there are Dall sheep on the slopes above. It's 4 miles to Raven

JEFF SCHULTZ / ALASKASTOCK.COM

Log church, Girdwood

ANCHORAGE & AROUND

SOUTH OF ANCHORAGE

CATCHING THE BORE TIDE

One attraction along the Turnagain Arm stretch of Seward Hwy is unique among sights already original: the bore tide. The bore tide is a neat trick of geography that requires a combination of narrow, shallow waters and rapidly rising tides. Swooping as a wave sometimes 6ft in height (and satisfyingly loud), the tide fills the Arm in one go. It travels at speeds of up to 15mph, and every now and then you'll catch a brave surfer or kayaker riding it into the Arm.

So, how to catch this dramatic rush?

First, consult a tide table, or grab a schedule, available at any Anchorage visitors center. The most extreme bore tides occur during days with minus tides between -2.0ft and -5.5ft, but if your timing doesn't hit a huge minus, aim for a new or full moon period. Once you've determined your day, pick your spot. The most popular is Beluga Point (Mile 110), and a wise choice. If you miss the tide, you can always drive further up the Arm and catch it at Bird Point (Mile 96).

Glacier, the traditional turnaround point of the trail, and 3 miles to a **USFS cabin** (☎ 877-444-6777, 518-885-3639; www.recreation. gov; cabins $35).

CYCLING

The most scenic bike ride in this area is the **Indian-Girdwood Trail** – dubbed the Bird-to-Gird – a paved path that leads out of the valley and along the Seward Hwy above Turnagain Arm. The fabulously scenic route extends all the way to Mile 103 of the highway, linking Alyeska Resort with Indian Creek 17 miles away. **Girdwood Ski & Cyclery** (☎ 783-2453; www.girdwoodskicyclery.com; bikes per 3hr/ day $15/30; ☽ 10am-7pm) will rent you the bikes to enjoy it.

The **Alyeska Resort** (☎ 754-1111; www. alyeska.com; mountain bike rentals per day $55) has been working on extensive mountain bike trails suitable for beginners as well as adrenaline addicts. The excellent elevated tread single-tracks are accessible on Chair 7 ($29) or on ascending trails from the main lodge (free). The resort has plans underway to create a number of further cycling trails.

TOURS

Alpine Air (☎ 783-2360; www.alpineairalaska. com; Girdwood airport) Has a one-hour glacier tour that includes a helicopter landing on the ice ($299).

Ascending Path (☎ 783-0505; www.the ascendingpath.com) A climbing-guide service that has a three-hour glacier hike on Alyeska Glacier ($139), including a midnight-sun glacier trek from mid-June to mid-July that begins at 8pm. The company also offers a three-hour rock-climbing outing designed for beginners ($129).

Spencer Whistle Stop Train (☎ 265-2494, 800-544-0552; www.akrr.com) You can now ride the Alaska Railroad to Spencer Glacier viewing area, where you'll find interpretive trails and a group campsite.

SLEEPING

B&Bs make up the bulk of Girdwood's lodging and are the only midrange options. The **Alyeska/Girdwood Accommodations Association** (☎ 222-3226; www.agaa.biz) can find last-minute rooms.

Carriage House B&B (☎ 783-9464, 888-961-9464; www.thecarriagehousebandb. com; Mile 0.3 Crow Creek Rd; r $125-150; ⊠ 🖳) A stunning cedar house within walking distance to the town center. Breakfast is made with eggs from the chickens clucking around outside and is served in a vaulted-ceiling common room that overlooks the mountains.

Hotel Alyeska (☎ 754-2111, www.alyeskaresort.com; 1000 Arlberg Ave; d $199-239, ste $440-2200; ⊠ 🖳 🕿) This place earned four stars from AAA because it deserved them – from the whirlpool with a view to bathrobes and slippers in every room, this place is swanky. For something less swanky you can park your RV in the day lodge for $10 a night and then ride the resort shuttle to use the pool or take a shower.

EATING

For such a tiny place, Girdwood has an amazing selection of restaurants that often pull their patrons in from Anchorage.

Bake Shop (☎ 783-2831; Olympic Circle; mains $3.50-10; ⏱ 7am-7pm Sun-Fri, to 8pm Sat) Always busy, this bright place serves wholesome omelets with fresh-baked breads, all of which you can enjoy at one of the large wooden tables. One of the giant cinnamon rolls is big enough to share with a friend – or not.

our pick Maxine's Glacier City Bistro (☎ 783-1234; Crow Creek Rd; dinner $12-22; ⏱ 5pm-midnight Wed-Mon) Maxine's is a Mediterranean bistro with a Girdwood feel (friendly dogs congregate outside while their owners eat). Share the *meze* or lamb *shwarma* – they're huge – but keep the wonton tacos for yourself. Live music livens up the already colorful place on Friday and Saturday nights.

Chair 5 Restaurant (☎ 283-2500; 5 Lindblad Ave; medium pizza $13-17, dinner $15-26; ⏱ 11am-2am, food served to 10pm) The kind of bar and restaurant skiers love after a long day on the slopes. It features more than 60 beers, including a dozen on tap, gourmet pizzas, big burgers and a lot of blackened halibut.

JAMES MARSHALL

Mural, Seward Highway

Double Musky Inn (☎ 783-2822; Crow Creek Rd; dinner $20-44; ☯ 5-10pm Tue-Thu, 4:30-10pm Fri-Sun) Folks drive down from Anchorage for the New York strip encrusted in cracked peppercorn, the reason you have to wait (reservations are not accepted) two hours on weekends. The cuisine is Cajun accented, hence the masks and mardi-gras beads hanging from the ceiling. The desserts are divine.

Seven Glaciers Restaurant (☎ 754-2237; dinner $28-52; ☯ 5-9:30pm) Sitting on top of Mt Alyeska, 2300ft above sea level, is the best of Alyeska Resort's six restaurants and bars. The hotel tram will take you to an evening of gourmet dining and absolutely stunning views that include Turnagain Arm and, yes, seven glaciers.

GETTING THERE & AWAY

The **Girdwood Shuttle** (☎ 783-1900; www.girdwoodshuttle.com) will take you from several spots in Girdwood to Ted Stevens International Airport, downtown Anchorage, or south to Whittier ($40). **Seward Bus Lines** (☎ 563-0800; www. sewardbuslines.net) can arrange transport to Seward and Anchorage, while **Homer Stage Line** (☎ 868-3914; www.homerstageline. com) can arrange transportation throughout the Kenai Peninsula.

NORTH OF ANCHORAGE

In Anchorage, 5th Ave becomes Glenn Hwy, running 189 miles through Palmer, where it makes a junction with the George Parks Hwy, to Glennallen and the Richardson Hwy. Milepost distances are measured from Anchorage.

PALMER & MATANUSKA VALLEY
pop 5500

Filled with old farming-related buildings, Palmer at times feels more like the Midwest than Alaska, except that it's ringed by mountains. Many downtown venues exude 1930s ambience, with antique furniture and wood floors. Sure, Palmer is subjected to the same suburban

Musk ox

MARK NEWMAN

sprawl as anywhere else, but its charm lies in its unique history and living agricultural community.

SIGHTS & ACTIVITIES

Outside the visitors center is **Matanuska Valley Agricultural Showcase** (☼ 8am-7pm Jun-Aug), a garden featuring flowers and the area's famous oversized vegetables. But you have to be passing through in August if you want to see a cabbage bigger than a basketball.

The friendly **Colony House Museum** (☎ 745-1935; 316 E Elmwood Ave; adult/child $2/1; ☼ 10am-4pm Tue-Sun) is run by Colony children, and their enthusiasm for Palmer's history is evident. Take the time for a guided tour, and you'll leave with an appreciation of the enormity of the colonizing project. The museum itself was a 'Colony Farm House' built during the original settlement of Palmer, and its eight rooms are still furnished with artifacts and stories from that era.

FARMS

South of Palmer, **Pyrah's Pioneer Peak Farm** (☎ 745-4511; Mile 2.8 Bodenberg Loop Rd; ☼ 9am-5pm Mon, to 9pm Tue-Sat) is the largest pick-your-own-vegetables place in the Mat-Su Valley, with would-be farmers in the fields from July to early October picking everything from peas and potatoes to carrots and cabbages.

The **Reindeer Farm** (☎ 745-4000; www.reindeerfarm.com; Mile 11.5 Old Glenn Hwy; adult/child $7/5; ☼ 10am-6pm) is one of the original Colony farms and a great place to bring the kids. Here they will be able to pet and feed the reindeer, and are encouraged to think the reindeer are connected to Santa. There's also elk, moose and bison to take photos of. Rubber boots are provided.

The **Musk Ox Farm** (☎ 745-4151; www.muskoxfarm.org; Mile 50 Glenn Hwy; adult/child $8/6; ☼ 9am-6pm) is the only domestic herd of these big, shaggy beasts in the world. These ice-age critters are intelligent enough to have evolved a complex social structure that allows survival under incredibly harsh conditions. Yes, you'll probably get to pet them, too. Qiviut (pronounced 'kiv-ee-oot'), the incredibly warm, soft and pricey ($40 per ounce) material made from the musk ox's soft undercoat, is harvested here; fine sweaters and hats are for sale in the gift shop. Tours are given every half-hour.

HIKING

The best hike near Palmer is the berry-lined climb to the top of 3720ft **Lazy Mountain**. The 2.5-mile trail is steep at times, but makes for a pleasant trek that ends in an alpine setting with good views of Matanuska Valley farms. Take Old Glenn Hwy across the Matanuska River, turn left onto Clark-Wolverine Rd and then right onto Huntly Rd; follow it to the Equestrian Center parking lot and trailhead, marked 'Foot Trail.' Plan on three to five hours for the round-trip.

SLEEPING

River Crest Manor (☎ 746-6214; www.rivercrestmanor.com; 2655 Old Glenn Hwy; d $90-100; ✕ 🖳) A beautiful, expansive home that provides three guest rooms across the road from the Matanuska River. It's located about 1.5 miles from downtown Palmer.

our pick **Colony Inn** (☎ 745-3330; 325 E Elmwood; r $108; ✕ 🖳) What was constructed in 1935 as the Matanuska Colony Teacher's Dorm is now Palmer's nicest lodge. The 12 rooms are spacious, especially the corner rooms, well-kept and equipped with TVs, pedestal sinks, and whirlpool tubs. There's an inviting parlor for reading, furnished with antiques.

↘ DETOUR: WASILLA

Just 7 miles north of the Glenn Hwy/George Parks Hwy junction, Wasilla was a sleepy little town in the 1970s that served local farmers. Today it's best known to outsiders as the hometown of 2008 Republican vice presidential candidate Sarah Palin, who served as its mayor from 1996 to 2002. Though the major news networks have disappeared from Wasilla's street, Palin still lives there when she's not traveling on the national political circuit.

There's not much to see here besides urban sprawl, but if you need services – banks, auto mechanics etc – you'll find them here and should take advantage of them. Things get sketchier and more expensive between here and Fairbanks.

EATING

Inn Café (☎ 746-6118; 325 E Elmwood; sandwiches $6-10, brunch $15; ☺ 11am-2pm Mon-Fri, 9am-2pm Sun) This former teacher's dorm now houses a pleasant restaurant with the kind of creaky wood-floored ambience expected in Palmer. Sandwiches and salads are served on weekdays, and brunch is on Sunday.

Turkey Red (☎ 746-5544; 550 S Alaska St; lunch $7-11, dinner $11-27; ☺ 8am-9pm Mon-Sat, to 10pm Sat) Palmer's classiest – and its most expensive – joint is an upscale cafe serving fresh dishes made from scratch, homemade dessert, and beer and wine. Vegetarians won't be disappointed, and much of the produce is organic and locally grown.

our pick **Red Beet** (☎ 745-4050; 320 E Dahlia; lunch $11; ☺ 11:30am-late afternoon) Housed in the renovated Palmer Trading Post, this excellent restaurant serves a daily three-course set menu with a dessert option. The food is organic and/or locally grown, and the coffee French-pressed. It's worth it alone just to sit in the wide, wood building, which smells like baking bread and has a view into the open kitchen.

GETTING THERE & AROUND

The Mat-Su Community Transit system, **Mascot** (☎ 376-5000; www.matsutransit.com; single ride/day pass $2.50/6), makes six trips daily between Wasilla and Palmer and three commuter runs from the Valley to the Transit Center in Anchorage.

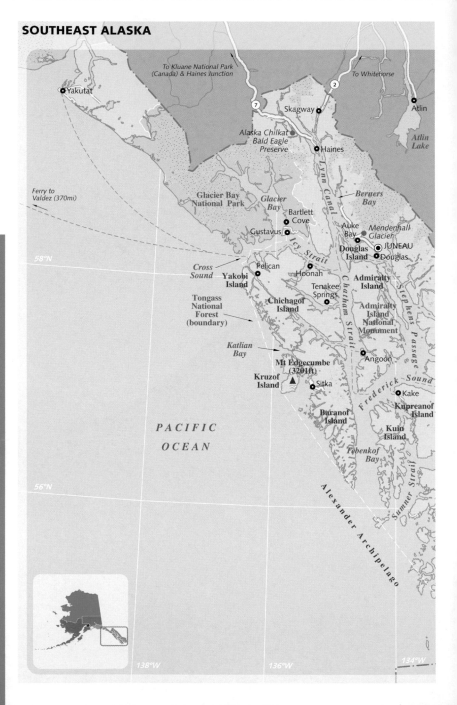

SOUTHEAST ALASKA

To Kluane National Park
(Canada) & Haines Junction

To Whitehorse

2

Yakutat

7

Skagway

Atlin

Atlin
Lake

Alaska Chilkat
Bald Eagle
Preserve

Haines

Ferry to
Valdez (370mi)

Glacier Bay
National Park

Glacier
Bay

Berners
Bay

Bartlett
Cove

Auke
Bay

Mendenhall
Glacier

Gustavus

JUNEAU

Douglas
Island

Douglas

58°N

Cross
Sound

Pelican

Icy Strait

Hoonah

Admiralty
Island

Yakobi
Island

Tenakee
Springs

Chatham Strait

Stephens Passage

Tongass
National
Forest
(boundary)

Chichagof
Island

Admiralty
Island
National
Monument

Katlian
Bay

Mt Edgecumbe
(3201ft)

Angoon

Kruzof
Island

Sitka

Frederick Sound

Kake

Baranof
Island

Kupreanof
Island

Kuin
Island

PACIFIC

OCEAN

Tebenkof
Bay

56°N

Sumner Strait

Alexander Archipelago

138°W

136°W

134°W

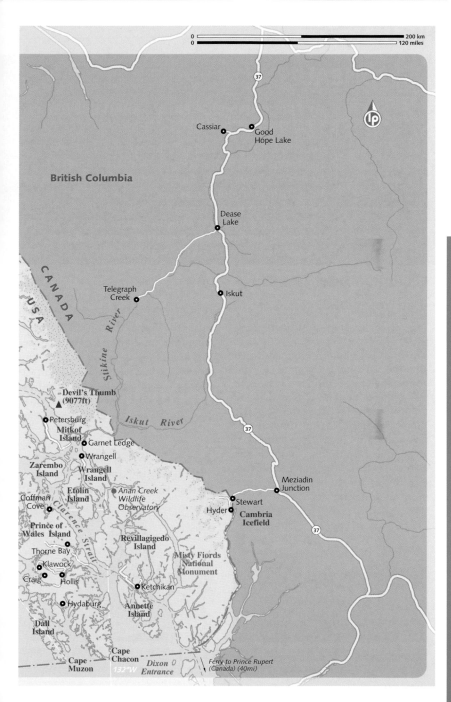

HIGHLIGHTS

1 JUNEAU

BY ERICK HEIMBIGNER, ALASKAN BREWER & LIFELONG JUNEAUITE

Juneau is located within a massive temperate rainforest called the Tongass National Forest, beneath a mountain range and next to the water. Its natural surroundings remind me of a cross between the Ewok forest in *Return of the Jedi* and *The Lord of the Rings'* Middle Earth. I was born and raised in Juneau and no matter how hard I try to leave, there's just no other place like it.

⬊ ERICK'S DON'T MISS LIST

❶ MT ROBERTS TRAMWAY

Though it's located right downtown, the Mt Roberts Tramway (p118) has a great view of Juneau, Douglas Island and the Gastineau Channel. My favorite way to get the same view is to hike up from the Mt Roberts trailhead on 6th St, grab an Alaskan IPA at the Timberline Bar & Grill at the top and take the tram down the mountain. If you're going up to the visitors center, walk the extra half mile up to the cross just shy of the summit for an even more breathtaking view.

❷ MENDENHALL GLACIER

This is the easiest glacier (p124) stemming from the Juneau Ice Field to view and access via the road system. You can walk out, hike or drive up to take photos – it all just depends on how much time you have and how close you want to get. Be sure to watch for bears.

❸ WHALE-WATCHING TOUR

Getting out on the water (p120) is a great way to get a wider view of

Clockwise from top right: Auke Bay (p120); Humpback whale; Mendenhall Glacier (p124)

Southeast Alaska. During the summer months, humpback whales return from the warmer southern waters where some of them give birth. Orcas, sea lions and porpoises are abundant during those months as well.

❹ JUNEAU ICE FIELD HELICOPTER TOUR

If you've got the time, the dime and a nice day, this is an unreal experience. Touring the 1500sq mile Juneau Ice Field (p121) by helicopter provides breathtaking views of countless glaciers, such as Taku, Hole-in-the-Wall and many others.

❺ AUKE BAY

If you are renting a car, take a drive 'out the road' to Auke Bay (p120) and the Shrine of St Therese (p125). The walk along the water at either the Auke Bay Recreation Area or the Shrine of St Therese provides expansive views of the water, the Chilkat Mountains and you can also see local marine life.

⬎ THINGS YOU NEED TO KNOW

Top tip You'll need transport to get out to Mendenhall Glacier or Auke Bay **Clothing advice** It doesn't just rain in Juneau, it dumps! Be prepared with a rain jacket, umbrella and positive outlook. It wouldn't be this green without the rain **For full details on Juneau, see p116**

HIGHLIGHTS

⤷ GAPE AT THE GLACIERS

Eleven tidewater glaciers that spew icebergs of all shapes and sizes make for dramatic cruising in Glacier Bay National Park & Preserve (p125). This world-renowned wilderness is also home to whales, harbor seals, porpoises and sea otters – and that's just the marine life. On shore you might spot brown and black bears, moose, wolves or mountain goats – if you can take your eyes off the glaciers, that is.

⤷ CRUISE THE MARINE HIGHWAY

Spanning 3500 nautical miles, the Alaska Marine Highway is the only All-American Road that floats. As the main thoroughfare throughout Southeast Alaska, the highway hits each soggy fishing town from Ketchikan to Skagway. You can drive on (and off) the ferry, making it an excellent addition to an Alaskan road trip. Rent a cabin and it becomes a cheap alternative to cruising.

4 ⬊ ZIPLINE DOWN A MOUNTAIN

Confront your fear of heights by flying over the Tongass. Ranking high on the list of visitor highlights is to strap onto a cable and zoom over the rainforest. Ziplining has become so popular that companies are sprouting up throughout Southeast Alaska, but the best line is in Ketchikan (p92).

5 ⬊ EXPLORE RUSSIAN HERITAGE

Russians landed in Sitka (p109) as early as 1741 and stayed for more than a century. The town's Russian history is well-preserved and the main attraction for tourists; check out St Michael's Cathedral, Castle Hill and the Russian Bishop's house. All sights are within walking distance of downtown.

6 ⬊ PADDLE THE FJORDS

Tracy Arm (p121), a steep-sided fjord studded with icebergs, and Misty Fiords National Monument (p96), a foggy green wonderland, offer scenic detours from Juneau and Ketchikan. Take a water taxi out to either area, and you'll be rewarded with solace and spectacular scenery.

2 LeConte Glacier (p106), Glacier Bay National Park & Preserve; 3 Cruise ship, Glacier Bay National Park & Preserve (p125); 4 Ziplining (p92), Ketchikan; 5 St Michael's Cathedral (p109), Sitka; 6 Sea kayaker, Tracy Arm (p121)

BEST...

◣ PADDLING

- **Tracy Arm** (p121) You're bound to spot seals and possibly whales at this fjord outside Juneau.
- **Misty Fiords National Monument** (p96) Escape into a foggy wonderland near Ketchikan.
- **Glacier Bay National Park** (p125) Surround yourself with glaciers in the Northern Panhandle.
- **LeConte Glacier** (p106) Thread through icebergs deposited by this massive tidewater glacier.

◣ PLACES TO REST UP

- **Alaska's Capital Inn** (p122) Right across from – you guessed it – the state capital.
- **New York Hotel** (p94) Its creekside location means you can perch on the 2nd floor and watch salmon spawn below.
- **Shee Atiká Totem Square Inn** (p114) Rooms at this central inn overlook Sitka's historic square and harbor.

◣ URBAN HIKING TRAILS

- **Dewey Lakes Trail System** (p132) Walk off a cruise ship and into the mountains of Skagway.
- **Perseverance Trail** (p119) Walk from the capital into Juneau's mining history.
- **Deer Mountain Trail** (p92) A 3-mile hike that begins near Ketchikan's downtown.
- **Indian River Trail** (p112) Follow a salmon stream to Indian River Falls in Sitka.

◣ WATERING HOLES

- **Alaskan Brewing Company** (p124) The state's most well-known beer; visit the brewery and sample all the varieties.
- **Red Dog Saloon** (p122) Also in Juneau, this tourist fave has a sawdust floor and is a replica of the original.
- **Skagway Brewing Co** (p135) Enjoy a Chilkoot IPA after a hard day's hike.

LEFT: KEN HOWARD; RIGHT: RALPH HOPKINS

From left: Skagway Brewing Co (p135); LeConte Bay (p106)

THINGS YOU NEED TO KNOW

➤ VITAL STATISTICS

- **Best time to visit** April through September

➤ LOCALITIES IN A NUTSHELL

- **Juneau** (p116) The only US state capital not accessible by road.
- **Ketchikan** (p90) The first stop on the Alaska Marine Highway.
- **Skagway** (p130) A gold-rush era town at the tip of the Lynn Canal.
- **Sitka** (p109) Well-preserved Russian heritage adds to this already-scenic town.

➤ ADVANCE PLANNING

- **Two months ahead** Book your accommodations and flights.
- **One month ahead** Reserve your ferry tickets.
- **One day ahead** Throw in an extra memory card for your digital camera.

➤ RESOURCES

- **Juneau Visitor Center** (Map p117; ☎ 586-2201, 888-581-2201; www.juneau.com; 101 Egan Dr; ⊗ 9am-5pm)
- **Ketchikan Visitor Information & Tour Center** (Map p91; ☎ 225-6166, 800-770-3300; www.visit-ketchikan.com; City Dock at 131 Front St; ⊗ 7am-5pm)

- **Klondike Gold Rush National Historical Park Visitor Center** (Map p131; ☎ 983-9223; www.nps.gov/klgo; Broadway St at 2nd Ave; ⊗ 8am-6pm)
- **USFS website** (www.fs.fed.us/r10/tongass) Most ranger districts have a Forest Service office; check the website for specific information.
- **Wrangell USFS Office** (☎ 874-2323; 525 Bennett St; ⊗ 8am-4:30pm Mon-Fri)

➤ GETTING AROUND

- **Air** Major carriers service Juneau, Ketchikan and Sitka.
- **Ferry** The Alaska Marine Highway Ferry is your best bet – and it's atmospheric.
- **Car** Roads are limited in Southeast Alaska, but you might want a car to explore bigger areas such as Ketchikan or Juneau.

➤ BE FOREWARNED

- **Rain** Southeast Alaska is soggy, so don't forget your rain jacket!
- **Fog** Southeast Alaska is also foggy, so prepare for low visibility and be flexible with sightseeing plans.

JUNEAU & SOUTHEAST ALASKA ITINERARIES

JUNEAU Three Days

Three days is plenty of time to catch all of the fabulous highlights of **(1) Juneau** (p116). Crane your neck at peaks rising straight from downtown, and then get to the top of at least one of them with a ride up the **(2) Mt Roberts tramway** (p118). Spend the afternoon catching the dreamy Inside Passage view, and then head downtown to check out the state capital and have a rowdy night at the **(3) Red Dog Saloon** (p122).

The next day head out of town to **(4) Mendenhall Glacier** (p124), where you can spend the day photographing icebergs, waterfalls and spawning salmon. Take advantage of the well-maintained trails in the area and have a little hike.

On your third day, either book a sightseeing cruise or paddling trip out to stunning **(5) Glacier Bay National Park** (p125). Spend the day watching tidewater glaciers calve and trying to spot marine and terrestrial wildlife.

HISTORY TOUR Five Days

Even though it's difficult to divert your attention from the natural wonders, get in a little culture with the mix of Russian, Gold Rush and ancient history to be found in Southeast. Start by catching gold fever in **(1) Skagway** (p130), where the Klondike Gold Rush started. A trip up the **(2) White Pass & Yukon Route Railroad** (p134) is a must-do; this narrow-gauge line was laid in 1898 and you can still see mining remnants along the absurdly scenic climb.

After playing in Skagway for a day or two, check out **(3) Sitka's** (p109) photogenic Russian heritage. Several museums showcase this past, including the replicated St Michael's Cathedral. Mingling with these buildings are intricate Tlingit totem poles; be sure to take the 1-mile-long walk past 18 totem poles in Sitka National Historic Park.

As you move south, make a stop in Wrangell to visit **(4) Petroglyph Beach** (p99), where 1000-year-old carvings peer up from beach stones.

Your next stop is **(5) Ketchikan** (p90). The city's colorful history is best illustrated on Creek St, where you can make a visit to Dolly's House. Namesake Dolly was a lady of 'ill reputation'; but from the looks of her digs she knew how to have a good time.

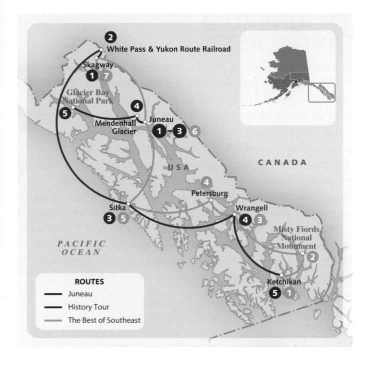

THE BEST OF SOUTHEAST One Week

Ride the Alaska Marine Highway Ferry through the emerald maze of the Inside Passage, hitting the major ports along the way. Your options for detours are only limited by your time; consider some of the smaller fishing ports if you're spending your entire vacation in Southeast. Start in (1) Ketchikan (p90), a full 36-hour ride from the next southern US port, Bellingham, WA. Give yourself time to make a detour to otherworldly (2) Misty Fiords National Monument (p96), whether by kayak or 90-minute flight tour.

Hop back on the ferry to visit (3) Wrangell (p98) and (4) Petersburg (p103), small fishing towns connected by the 'Pinball Alley,' a sight in itself. You can almost reach out and touch the hillsides as you float through these steep green narrows.

From here you'll cruise over to (5) Sitka (p109), a kayaking and hiking destination in its own right.

Your next port of call is (6) Juneau (p116). Enjoy the capital's blend of official and natural while wandering the steep streets past the Governor's mansion and back into the mountains on the Perseverance Trail.

Finally, arrive in (7) Skagway (p130) where you can explore the peaks and valleys and then hit the open highway.

DISCOVER JUNEAU & SOUTHEAST ALASKA

This lush, green and wet region of Alaska, clinging by a thread to the rest of the state, stretches 540 miles from Icy Bay south to Portland Canal but is only 140 miles across at its widest point.

On public ferries or cruise ships you sail past rugged snowcapped mountains that rise steeply from the water to form sheersided fjords embellished by cascading waterfalls. Ice-blue glaciers descend from the peaks and fan out into valleys of green Sitka spruce before melting into waters filled with whales, sea lions, harbor seals and salmon.

The Southeast was once Alaska's heart and soul, and Juneau was not only the capital but the state's largest city. Today the Southeast is characterized by big trees and small towns. You can feel the gold fever in Skagway, see almost a dozen glaciers near Juneau or go to the harbor in Haines and find a fishing boat selling live Dungeness crabs. Each town is unique and offers ample rewards for visitors.

SOUTHERN PANHANDLE

Residents like to call this region of Alaska 'rainforest islands'; lush, green, watery, remote and roadless to the outside world. This is the heart of Southeast Alaska's fishing industry, and the region's best wilderness fishing lodges are scattered in the small coves of these islands.

KETCHIKAN

pop 13,166

Once known as the 'Canned Salmon Capital of the World,' today Ketchikan settles for 'First City,' the initial port for Alaska Marine ferries and cruise ships coming from the south.

If you stay in Ketchikan longer than an hour, chances are good that it will rain at least once. The average annual rainfall is 162in, but in some years it has been known to be more than 200in.

When the skies finally clear, the beauty of Ketchikan's setting becomes apparent. The town is backed by for-

ested hills and faces a waterway humming with floatplanes, fishing boats, ferries and barges hauling freight to other Southeast ports.

SIGHTS

SOUTHEAST ALASKA DISCOVERY CENTER

Three large totems greet you in the lobby of the **center** (☎ 228-6220; 50 Main St; adult/child $5/free; ☀ 8am-5pm) while a school of silver salmon, suspended from the ceiling, leads you toward a slice of nicely re-created rainforest. Upstairs, the exhibit hall features sections on Southeast Alaska's ecosystems and Alaska Native traditions. There's a spotting scope trained on Deer Mountain for mountain goats while underwater cameras in Ketchikan Creek let you watch thousands of salmon struggling upstream to spawn.

CREEK STREET & DOLLY'S HOUSE

Departing from Stedman St is Creek St, a boardwalk built over Ketchikan Creek on

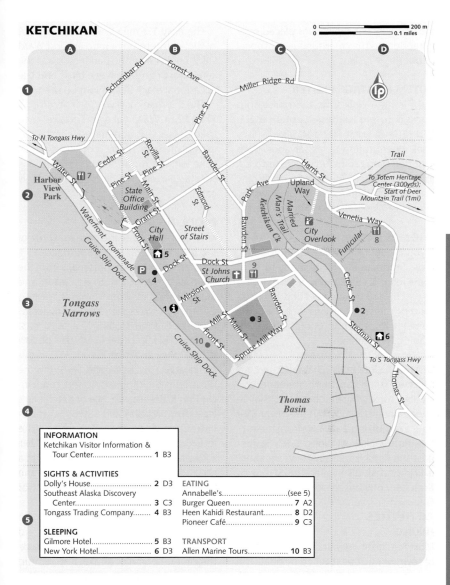

KETCHIKAN

INFORMATION
Ketchikan Visitor Information &
   Tour Center............................ **1** B3

SIGHTS & ACTIVITIES
Dolly's House............................ **2** D3
Southeast Alaska Discovery
   Center................................... **3** C3
Tongass Trading Company........ **4** B3

SLEEPING
Gilmore Hotel............................ **5** B3
New York Hotel......................... **6** D3

EATING
Annabelle's..............................(see 5)
Burger Queen............................ **7** A2
Heen Kahidi Restaurant............. **8** D2
Pioneer Café.............................. **9** C3

TRANSPORT
Allen Marine Tours................. **10** B3

pilings – a photographer's delight. This was Ketchikan's famed red-light district until prostitution became illegal in 1954. During Creek St's heyday, it supported up to 30 brothels and became known as the only place in Alaska where 'the fishermen and the fish went upstream to spawn.' The house with bright red trim is **Dolly's House** (☎ 225-6329; 24 Creek St; adult/child $5/ free; ☉ 8am-5pm or when cruise ships are in), the parlor of the city's most famous madam, Dolly Arthur. You can see the brothel, including its bar, which was placed over a trapdoor to the creek for quick disposal of bootleg whiskey.

TOTEM HERITAGE CENTER

A 15-minute walk from the cruise-ship docks is **Totem Heritage Center** (☎ 225-5900; 601 Deermount St; adult/child $5/free; ☺ 8am-5pm), where totem poles salvaged from deserted Tlingit communities are restored. Inside the center 17 totems are on display in an almost spiritual setting that shows the reverence Alaska Natives attach to them.

THOMAS BASIN

If you thought Creek St was photogenic, cross Stedman St and be ready to burn some megapixels. **Thomas Basin** is home to Ketchikan's fishing fleet and the city's most picturesque harbor. When the boats come in you can photograph them unloading their catch.

STAIRWAYS & BOARDWALKS

All over Ketchikan there are stairways leading somewhere higher. Sure, they're knee-bending climbs, but the reward for your exertion is great views from the top. Heading back west along Dock St, just past the Ketchikan Daily News Building, is Edmond St, also called the **Street of Stairs**, for obvious reasons.

ACTIVITIES
HIKING

Most Ketchikan-area trails are either out of town or must be reached by boat. The major exception is **Deer Mountain Trail**, a well-maintained 2.5-mile trail that begins near downtown. The trailhead is near the southeast end of Fair St and the route climbs to the 3000ft summit of Deer Mountain. Overlooks along the way provide panoramic views – the first is about a mile up the trail.

The easy 1.3-mile **Ward Lake Nature Walk**, an interpretive loop around Ward Lake, begins near the parking area at the lake's north end. Beavers, birds and the occasional black bear might be seen.

The 2.3-mile (one way) **Perseverance Trail** from Ward Lake to Perseverance Lake passes through mature coastal forest and muskeg. The view of Perseverance Lake with its mountainous backdrop is spectacular, and the hiking is moderately easy.

PADDLING

Ketchikan serves as the base for some of the best kayaking in the Southeast. Pick up charts and topographic maps from the Southeast Alaska Discovery Center and outdoor supplies from **Tongass Trading Company** (☎ 225-5101; 201 Dock St), across from the Gilmore Hotel.

Southeast Sea Kayaks (☎ 225-1258, 800-287-1607; www.kayakketchikan.com; 1621 Tongass Ave; kayaks per day single/double $49/59), in the Westflight Building, also offers tours including a 2½-hour paddle of Ketchikan's waterfront (adult/child $89/69). A much better paddling experience, however, is its Orcas Cove trip (adult/child $159/129), a four-hour adventure that begins with a boat ride across the Tongass Narrows and then paddling among protected islands looking for sea lions, orcas and seals.

ZIPLINING

Ketchikan has everything needed to be the zipline capital of Alaska: lush rainforests and elevation. There are two zipline operations now, more are bound to come. The best is **Alaska Canopy Adventures** (☎ 225-5503; www.alaskacanopy.com; 116 Wood Rd; per person $160), which uses eight lines, three suspension bridges and 4WD vehicles to transport you up a mountain so you can zip 4600ft to the bottom.

JUNEAU & SOUTHEAST ALASKA

SOUTHERN PANHANDLE

STEFAN WACKERHAGEN / IMAGEBROKER

Sea kayaking

↘ IF YOU LIKE...

If you like kayaking around **Ketchikan** (p90), check out these off-the-beaten-fjord locations:

- **Betton Island** Due west of Settler's Cove State Park at the north end (Mile 18.2) of N Tongass Hwy is this island and several smaller islands nearby, making it an excellent day paddle if you're staying at the campground.
- **Naha Bay** Also from Settler's Cove State Park, it's an 8-mile paddle to Naha Bay, the destination of an excellent three- or four-day adventure.
- **George & Carroll Inlets** Southeast of Ketchikan, some 7.5 miles down the S Tongass Hwy, you can start an easy one- to four-day paddle north into George or Carroll Inlets, or both. Each inlet is protected from the area's prevailing southwesterlies, so the water is usually calm.

TOURS

Alaska Undersea Tours (☎ 247-8899, 877-461-8687; www.alaskaunderseatours.com; adult/child $49/29) From top of the water to below it, this 1½-hour tour puts you in a semisubmersible vessel with underwater viewing windows so you can see the marine life and seascapes in the Ketchikan harbors.

ourpick **Bering Sea Crab Fishermen's Tour** (☎ 888-239-3816; www.56degreesnorth. com; adult/child $149/99) Ketchikan is a long way from the Bering Sea and they don't catch many king crabs here, but you can experience both on the *Aleutian*

Ballad. The crab boat, once featured on the TV show *Deadliest Catch*, has been modified with a 100-seat amphitheater for a 3½-hour, on-the-water tour of commercial fishing. Right in front of you Bering Sea crabbers pull up huge pots full of tanner, Dungeness and even giant king crabs, as well as bait lines, to catch rockfish and shark.

SLEEPING

Gilmore Hotel (☎ 225-9423, 800-275-9423; www.gilmorehotel.com; 326 Front St; r $115-155; ✕ ☐) Built in 1927 as a hotel and renovated several times since, the Gilmore has

38 rooms that still retain a historical flavor. The rooms are 'historically proportioned' (ie small) but comfortable, with cable TV, coffeemakers and hair dryers. The entire 2nd floor is nonsmoking.

our pick **New York Hotel** (☎ 225-0246, 866-225-0246; www.thenewyorkhotel.com; 207 Stedman St; r $129-144, ste $189-209; ⊠ 💻) A historic, boutique hotel in a great location between Creek St and Thomas Basin. Its 2nd-floor perch means you can watch the salmon spawn in the creek below and the seals that follow them on high tides.

our pick **Black Bear Inn** (☎ 225-4343; www.stayinalaska.com; 5528 N Tongass Hwy; r $160-230; ⊠ 💻) This incredible B&B offers a range of waterfront accommodations 2.5 miles north of the downtown madness. There are four bedrooms in the home and a small apartment on the 2nd floor. Outside is a logger's bunkhouse that was floated to Ketchikan and renovated into a charming cabin. Every room in the house has been beautifully put together by the proprietor who doubles as an artist.

EATING

our pick **Burger Queen** (☎ 225-6060; 518 Tongass Ave; burgers $5-8; 🕑 11am-3pm Mon, 11am-7pm Tue-Sat) Ketchikan's favorite burger joint. Order a burger and fries and it'll be delivered to the Arctic Bar across the street where you can be sipping a beer.

Annabelle's (☎ 225-6009; 326 Front St; chowders $6-9, dinner $18-30; 🕑 10am-9:30pm) At the Gilmore Hotel, this keg and chowder house has a seafood-heavy menu, a wonderful bar and 1920s decor.

Pioneer Café (☎ 225-3337; 619 Mission St; breakfast $8-13, lunch $8-12, dinner $10-17; 🕑 6am-10pm Sun-Thu, 24hr Fri & Sat) One of the few downtown restaurants that was around when the lumber mills were. It serves reindeer sausage at breakfast and some of the best clam chowder in the city.

Heen Kahidi Restaurant (☎ 225-8001; 800 Venetia Way; breakfast $8-12, lunch $10-18, dinner $18-40; 🕑 7am-9pm Mon-Thu, to 9:30pm Fri & Sat, to 8:30pm Sun; ⊠) Generally regarded as Ketchikan's best dining experience, the West Coast Cape Fox Lodge restaurant offers hilltop dining with floor-to-ceiling

ERNEST MANEWAL

Dolly's House (p90)

windows providing a view of the world below. The dinner menu is split between seafood and steaks.

GETTING THERE & AWAY
AIR
Flights to Ketchikan from Seattle, Anchorage and major Southeast communities are all possible with **Alaska Airlines** (☎ 1-800-252-7522; www.alaskaair.com).

Ketchikan has many bush-plane operators, including **Taquan Air** (☎ 225-8800, 800-770-8800; www.taquanair.com; 4085 Tongass Ave) and **Promech Air** (☎ 225-3845, 800-860-3845; www.promechair.com; 1515 Tongass Ave).

BOAT
Northbound Alaska Marine Highway ferries leave almost daily in summer, heading north for Wrangell ($37, six hours), Petersburg ($60, nine hours), Sitka ($83, 20 hours), Juneau ($107, 29 hours) and Haines ($134, 33½ hours). For sailing times call the **ferry terminal** (☎ 225-6181; 3501 Tongass Ave).

The **Inter-Island Ferry Authority** (☎ 225-4838, 866-308-4848; www.interisland ferry.com) operates the MV *Stikine,* which departs Ketchikan at 3:30pm daily and arrives at Hollis on Prince of Wales Island at 6:30pm (one way adult/child $37/18).

GETTING AROUND
TO/FROM THE AIRPORT
The Ketchikan airport is on one side of Tongass Narrows, the city is on the other. A small car-and-passenger ferry ($5 for walk-on passengers) runs between the airport and a landing off Tongass Ave, just northwest of the main ferry terminal. The **Airporter** (☎ 225-9800) bus meets all arriving Alaska Airlines flights at the terminal and will take you to/from downtown for $25, ferry fare included. There isn't a better way to arrive at the First City than

Tongass Water Taxi (☎ 225-8294). Richard Schuerger meets all flights at the baggage-claim area and then gives you a lift on his boat to the dock nearest to your destination.

BUS
Ketchikan's excellent public bus system is called the **Bus** (☎ 225-8726; fare $1), but don't worry, there's more than one of them. The green and red buses run daily, the blues only on weekdays.

PRINCE OF WALES ISLAND
pop 3536

For some tourists, the Alaska they come looking for is only a three-hour ferry ride away from the crowds of cruise-ship tourists they encounter in Ketchikan. At 140 miles long and covering more than 2230 sq miles, Prince of Wales Island (POW) is the USA's third-largest island, after Alaska's Kodiak and Hawaii's Big Island.

This vast, rugged island is a destination for the adventurous at heart, loaded with hiking trails and canoe routes, Forest Service cabins and fishing opportunities. The 990-mile coastline of POW meanders around numerous bays, coves, saltwater straits and protective islands, making it a kayaker's delight. And for someone carrying a mountain bike through Alaska, a week on the island is worth all the trouble of bringing the two-wheeler north.

There are no cruise ships on POW but there are clear-cuts and you must be prepared for them. Blanketing the island is a patchwork quilt of lush spruce-hemlock forest and fields of stumps where a forest used to be. They are a sign that you have reached real Alaska, a resource-based state where people make a living from fishing, mining and cutting down trees.

RALPH HOPKINS

Misty Fiords National Monument

⬎ MISTY FIORDS NATIONAL MONUMENT

This spectacular, 3570-sq-mile national monument, just 22 miles east of Ketchikan, is a natural mosaic of sea cliffs, steep fjords and rock walls jutting 3000ft straight out of the ocean. Brown and black bears, mountain goats, Sitka deer, bald eagles and a multitude of marine mammals inhabit this drizzly realm. The monument receives 150in of rainfall annually, but many people think Misty Fiords is at its most beautiful when the granite walls and tumbling waterfalls are veiled in fog and mist.

Kayaking is *the* best way to experience the preserve. Ketchikan's **Southeast Sea Kayaks** (☎ 225-1258, 800-287-1607; www.kayakketchikan.com; 1621 Tongass Ave) offers a one-day guided paddle in which small groups and their kayaks are transported by boat to the fjords and back (adult/child $399/369).

Flightseeing may be the only option if you're in a hurry, and most tours include landing on a lake and a short walk in the rainforest. But keep in mind that this is a big seller on the cruise ships and when the weather is nice it is an endless stream of floatplanes flying to the same area: Rudyerd Bay and Walker Cove. Throw in the tour boats and one local likened such days to 'the Allie invasion of Omaha Beach.'

Things you need to know: Family Air Tours (☎ 247-1305, 800-380-1305; www.familyairtours.com); Southeast Aviation (☎ 225-2900, 888-359-6478; www. southeastaviation.com); Allen Marine Tours (☎ 225-8100, 877-686-8100; www. allenmarinetours.com; 50 Front St, Ketchikan)

SIGHTS & ACTIVITIES

Of the three totem parks on POW, the **Klawock Totem Park** (Bayview Blvd) is by far the most impressive and obviously a great source of community pride.

Situated on a hill overlooking the town's cannery and harbor, Klawock's 21 totems are the largest collection in Alaska and make for a scenic, almost dramatic setting. The totems are either originals from the former village of Tukekan or replicas.

The **Prince of Wales Hatchery** (☎ 755-2231; Mile 9 Hollis-Klawock Hwy; ☯ 8am-noon & 1-4pm) was established in 1897 and today is the second-oldest one in Alaska. The present facility was built in 1976 and raises coho, king and sockeye salmon, with many released into the adjacent Klawock River.

On the island's southern half, you can watch salmon attempt to negotiate a couple of **fish ladders** during the summer spawning season. Both **Cable Creek Fish Pass** and **Dog Salmon Fish Pass** have viewing platforms, from which you might also see hungry black bears.

The USFS maintains more than 20 hiking trails on POW, with the majority of them being short walks to rental cabins, rivers or lakes. In the south, a good hike can be made to **One Duck Shelter** from a trailhead on the road to Hydaburg, 2 miles south of Hollis junction. The trail is steep, climbing 1400ft in 1.2 miles, but it ends at a three-sided free-use shelter that sleeps four. To spend the night in the open alpine area with panoramic views of the Klawock Mountains is worth the knee-bending climb. To the north the **Balls Lake Trail** begins in the Balls Lake Picnic Area just east of Eagle's Nest Campground and winds 2.2 miles around the lake.

Mountain bikers have even more opportunities than hikers. Bikes can be rented in Coffman Cove from **A5 Outdoor Recreation** (☎ 329-2399; www.a5outdoorrec.com; 103A Sea Otter Dr; per day $25) and then taken on any road to explore the island. One of the most scenic roads to bike is South Beach Rd (also known as Forest Rd 30) from Coffman Cove to Thorne Bay. It's a 37-mile ride along the narrow, winding dirt road that is often skirting Clarence Strait. Along the way is **Sandy Beach Picnic Area** (Mile 6 Sandy Beach Rd), an excellent place to see humpback whales, orcas and harbor seals offshore or examine intriguing tidal pools at low tides.

Opportunities for paddlers are almost as limitless as they are for mountain bikers. At the north end of POW, off Forest Rd 20, is the **Sarkar Lakes Canoe Route**, a 15-mile loop of five major lakes and

Accommodations, Prince of Wales Island

portages along with a USFS cabin and excellent fishing. For a day of kayaking depart from Klawock and paddle into **Big Salt Lake**, where the water is calm and the birding is excellent. A5 Outdoor Recreation also rents kayaks (single/double $50/60 per day) as well as canoes ($55 per day) and will provide transportation for an additional fee.

SLEEPING

Coffman Cove Cabin Rentals (☎ 329-2251; per person $40) A pair of self-contained cabins with fully equipped kitchens and within walking distance of the ferry terminal.

Inn of the Blue Heron (☎ 826-3608; www.littleblueheroninn.com; 406 9th St; s $79-99, d $99-115; ☒ ▢) A delightful B&B overlooking a boat harbor in Craig with three upstairs rooms featuring TVs, small refrigerators and microwaves.

Dreamcatcher B&B (☎ 826-2238; www.dreamcatcherbedandbreakfast.com; 1405 Hamilton Dr; r $105; ☒ ▢) Three guestrooms in a beautiful seaside home in Craig. Big picture windows and a wraparound deck give way to a wonderful view of water, islands, mountains and, of course, clear-cuts.

EATING

Dave's Diner (☎ 755-2986; 6648 Big Salt Rd; breakfast $5-9, lunch $6-11, dinner $11-20; ☽ 11am-7pm Mon-Thu, to 8pm Fri, 8am-8pm Sat, to 7pm Sun) A rambling diner in Klawock with a sloping floor and an attached bus that serves as the kitchen. The burgers are good and the onion rings are great; don't let them roll off the table.

Dockside Restaurant (☎ 826-5544; Front St, Craig; breakfast $6-13, lunch $9-12; ☽ 5:30am-3pm) New owners took over this wonderful breakfast place but its legendary pies ($3.75 per slice) are just as good as before.

Ruth Ann's Restaurant (☎ 826-3377; 300 Front St, Craig; dinner $16-49; ☽ 7am-9pm; ☒) This would be a favorite no matter what Alaskan city it was located in, but in Craig it becomes one of those unexpected joys. The small restaurant with an even smaller bar offers quaint waterfront dining with views of the bay, weathered wharfs and fishing boats returning with their catch that often ends up on your plate: salmon, oysters, steamer clams and giant prawns stuffed with crab.

GETTING THERE & AWAY

The **Inter-Island Ferry Authority** (☎ 866-308-4848, Coffman Cove 329-2345, Hollis 530-4848, Ketchikan 225-4838; www.interislandferry.com) operates a pair of vessels, with the MV *Stikine* departing daily from Hollis at 8am and from Ketchikan at 3:30pm (one way adult/child $37/18). The MV *Prince of Wales* departs Coffman Cove at 7am Friday, Saturday and Monday for Wrangell ($37/18) and then the south end of Mitkof Island ($49/27), where there is road access to Petersburg.

GETTING AROUND

For lengthy stays it's best to rent a car in Ketchikan and take it over on the ferry. Rates for the ferry are based on vehicle length; a subcompact one way is $50. You can also rent a Ford Escort (pavement only) or a 4WD Kia Sportage in Craig through **Wilderness Rent-A-Car** (☎ 800-949-2205; www.wildernesscarrental.com) for $70 per day with unlimited mileage.

WRANGELL & AROUND

pop 2020

Strategically located near the mouth of the Stikine River, Wrangell is one of the oldest towns in Alaska and the only one to have existed under three flags and ruled by four nations – Tlingit, Russia, Britain and America.

The island offers great mountain-biking and bike-camping opportunities; kayakers can explore the Stikine River or myriad islands and waterways around the river's mouth; and local guides lead boat trips to Anan Creek bear observatory and other places of interest.

SIGHTS
WRANGELL MUSEUM
This impressive **museum** (☎ 874-3770; 296 Outer Dr; adult/child/family $5/3/12; ⏲ 10am-5pm Mon-Sat), located in the Nolan Center, is what the colorful history and characters of Wrangell deserve. As you stroll through the museum's many rooms, an audio narration automatically comes on and explains each particular chapter of Wrangell's history, from Tlingit culture and the gold-rush era to the time Hollywood arrived in 1972 to film the movie *Timber Tramps*.

CHIEF SHAKES ISLAND
This **island** (Shakes St) is the most enchanting spot in Wrangell. The small grassy islet is in the middle of the boat harbor and reached by a pedestrian bridge. The tiny island, with its totems, tall pines and the half-dozen eagles usually perched in the branches, is a quiet oasis compared to the hum of the fishing fleet that surrounds it. In the middle is **Shakes Community House**, an excellent example of a high-caste tribal house that contains tools, blankets and other cultural items. It's open only to accommodate cruise ships (call the Wrangell Museum for times). Just as impressive are the six totems surrounding the tribal house, all duplicates of originals carved in the late 1930s.

PETROGLYPH BEACH
Located on the town's north side is a state historic park where you can see primitive rock carvings believed to be at least 1000 years old. The best set is located three-quarters of a mile from the ferry terminal and can be reached by heading north on

ERNEST MANEWAL

Petroglyph Beach

Evergreen Ave where a sign marks the boardwalk that leads to a viewing deck with interpretive displays and petroglyph replicas. Follow the stairway to the beach and then turn right and walk north about 50yd. Before you reach the wrecked fishing vessel (photographers will love it), look for the carvings on the large rocks, many of them resembling spirals and faces. There are almost 50 in the area and you need to hunt around to find most of them. The majority are submerged at high tide so check a tide book before you leave and bring a bottle of water. The carvings are easier to see when wet.

TOTEMS

For its size, Wrangell has an impressive collection of totems, more than a dozen scattered through town. Pick-up the free *Wrangell Guide* at the visitor center and spend an afternoon locating them all. Make sure you stop at **Chief Shakes Grave** to see the killer-whale totems.

ACTIVITIES
BEAR WATCHING

Thirty miles southeast of Wrangell on the mainland, Anan Creek is the site of one of the largest pink salmon runs in Southeast Alaska. From the platforms at **Anan Creek Wildlife Observatory** (Map p80) you can watch eagles, harbor seals, black bears and a few brown bears chowing down gluttonously on the spawning humpies. This is one of the few places in Alaska where black and brown bears coexist – or at least put up with each other – at the same run. Permits ($10) are required from early July through August, or basically when the bears are there, and are reserved online (www.fs.fed.us) or by calling the **USFS Office** (☎ 874-2323; 525 Bennett St; ⏰ 8am-4:30pm Mon-Fri) in Wrangell. Almost half of the daily 60 permits go to local tour opera-

tors. Another 18 are available from March 1 for that particular year and 12 permits are issued three days in advance.

Anan Creek is a 20-minute floatplane flight or an hour boat ride, and almost every tour operator in town offers a trip there. **Alaska Charters & Adventures** (☎ 874-4157, 888-993-2750; www.alaskaupclose.com; 7 Front St) offers an eight-hour trip to the observatory ($198) and **Alaska Waters Inc** (☎ 874-2378, 800-347-4462; www.alaskawaters.com), at the Stikine Inn, has a six-hour boat tour ($245). **Sunrise Aviation** (☎ 874-2319; www.sunriseflights.com; Wrangell Airport) will provide permits and fly you in and out for $375 each way for up to four passengers.

The best way to see the bears, if you can plan ahead, is to reserve the USFS **Anan Bay Cabin** (☎ 877-444-6777; www.recreation.gov; $35), which comes with four permits and is a mile hike from the observation area. This cabin can be reserved six months in advance and during the bear-watching season it pretty much has to be.

HIKING

Other than the climb up Mt Dewey and walking the Volunteer Park Trail, all of Wrangell's trails are off the road and often include muskeg. You'll need a car for the roads and a pair of rubber boots for the trails.

Mt Dewey Trail is a half-mile climb up a hill to a small clearing in the trees, overlooking Wrangell and the surrounding waterways. From Mission St, walk a block and turn left at 3rd St. Follow the street past the houses to the posted stairway on the right. The hike to the top takes 15 minutes or so, but the trail is often muddy. John Muir fanatics will appreciate the fact that the great naturalist climbed the mountain in 1879 and built a bonfire on top, alarming the Tlingit people living in the village below. Ironically, the only signs on top now say 'No Campfires.' The other hike in town is the half-mile **Volunteer Park Trail**, a pleasant forested walk that begins near the park's ball field off 2nd Ave.

Signposted 4.7 miles south of the ferry terminal on the Zimovia Hwy is the **Rainbow Falls Trail**. The trail begins directly across from Shoemaker Bay Recreation Area. It's less than a mile to the waterfalls and then another 2.7 miles along **Institute Creek Trail** to the Shoemaker Bay Overlook Shelter. The lower section of the trail can be soggy at times, the upper section steep. The views are worth the hike, and a pleasant evening can be spent on the ridge.

A 1.4-mile path to the lake, **Thoms Lake Trail** is reached by following Zimovia Hwy to its paved end and then turning east on Forest Rd 6267. About halfway across the island, just before crossing Upper Salamander Creek, turn right on Forest Rd 6290 and follow it 4 miles to the trailhead. The first half-mile of the trail is planked, but the rest cuts through muskeg and can get extremely muddy during wet weather.

PADDLING

One look at a nautical chart of Wrangell will have kayakers drooling and dreaming. Islands and protected waterways abound, though many are across the vast Stikine River flats, where experience is a prerequisite due to strong tides and currents. Novices can enjoy paddling around the harbor, over to Petroglyph Beach or to Dead Man's Island.

Alaska Vistas (☎ 874-2997, 866-874-3006; www.alaskavistas.com; 106 Front St; ☼ 7am-6pm), inside the Java Junkies espresso shed, a wi-fi hot spot at City Dock, rents kayaks (single/double $55/65 per day). The company also runs guided kayak tours including a full-day East West Cove paddle ($210) on the well-protected east side of Wrangell Island.

Rainwalker Expeditions (☎ 874-2549; www.rainwalkerexpeditions.com) also rents kayaks (single/double $40/60 per day) and offers a kayaker drop-off service to the easy-to-explore back side of the island. The company also has Hike-Bike-Kayak tour ($99) that includes paddling to

Totem pole, Ketchikan (p90)

Shoemaker Bay, hiking the Rainbow Falls Trail and biking back to town.

STIKINE RIVER

A narrow, rugged shoreline and surrounding mountains and glaciers characterize the beautiful, wild Stikine River, which begins in the high peaks of interior British Columbia and ends some 400 miles later in a delta called the Stikine Flats, just north of Wrangell. The Stikine is North America's fastest navigable river, and its most spectacular sight is the Grand Canyon of the Stikine, a steep-walled gorge where violently churning white water makes river travel impossible. John Muir called this stretch of the Stikine 'a Yosemite 100 miles long.'

Trips from below the canyon are common among rafters and kayakers. They begin with a charter flight to Telegraph Creek in British Columbia and end with a 160-mile float back to Wrangell.

Travelers arriving in Wrangell with a kayak but insufficient funds to charter a bush plane can paddle from the town's harbor across the Stikine Flats (where there are several USFS cabins) and up one of the Stikine River's three arms.

Wrangell's USFS office can provide information on the Stikine River, including two helpful publications: *Stikine River Canoe/Kayak Routes* ($5) and *Lower Stikine River Map* ($5), the latter covering the river up to Telegraph Creek.

Several Wrangell guide services run trips on the Stikine or offer drop-off services for kayakers. **Stikeen Wilderness Adventures** (☎ 800-874-2085; www.akgetaway. com) provides a water-taxi service for kayakers and rafters, charging $225 per hour for up to six passengers or $205 if you rent kayaks from Alaska Vistas. Also providing tours or transport up the Stikine River is **Alaska Charters & Adventures** (☎ 874-4157, 888-993-2750; www.alaskaupclose.com).

SLEEPING

Alaskan Sourdough Lodge (☎ 874-3613, 800-874-3613; www.akgetaway.com; 1104 Peninsula St; s/d $104/114; ☒ ▣) This family-owned lodge was hosting visitors when there were still lumber mills in Wrangell. It offers 16 rooms, a sauna, steam bath, free transportation to/from the ferry or airport and a front deck full of wicker furniture with a view of the harbor.

Rooney's Roost (☎ 874-2026; www. rooneysroost.com; 206 McKinnon St; r $110-130; ☒ ▣) Within easy walking distance from the ferry, just a short way up 2nd St, is this antique-filled B&B. There are four guestrooms with queen-size beds, TV and private baths. In the morning you enjoy a full breakfast, and in the afternoon you can relax on the deck with views of Wrangell.

Grand View B&B (☎ 874-3225; www. grandviewbnb.com; Mile 1.9 Zimovia Hwy; r $115-135; ☒ ▣) Just beyond City Park is this seaside B&B with its entire ground devoted to guests. That includes three spacious rooms, a large kitchen and outdoor covered patio. The best part is the living room that features four comfy recliners positioned in front of a row of picture windows looking out at Zimovia Strait.

Stikine Inn (☎ 874-3388; www.stikine inn.com; 107 Stikine Ave; s/d $130/160; ▣) Wrangell's largest motel is on the waterfront near the ferry dock and underwent a major renovation in 2008 that included its bar, lobby and many of the 33 rooms. The waterside rooms are now among the best in town while there's also an onsite restaurant, saloon and gift shops.

EATING

Jitterbugs (☎ 874-3350; 309 Front St; ◴ 5:30am-2pm Mon-Sat) An early-morning espresso stand proffering lattes, cappuccinos and Italian sodas with an attitude and a dash of humor. Signs above the outside tables range from 'Friends Don't Let Friends Drink Starbucks' to 'Jitterbugs parking only. Violators will be decaffeinated.'

Hungry Beaver Pizza (☎ 874-3005; Shakes St; pizzas $17-23; ☽ 4-10pm) Adjoining the Marine Bar, this Beaver serves up Wrangell's favorite pie: a taco pizza with seasoned hamburger, refried beans and cheese, baked and then loaded with lettuce, tomatoes, salsa and sour cream. It comes with the fantasy of spending the winter in Mexico.

Alaskan Sourdough Lodge (☎ 874-3613; 1104 Peninsula St; dinner $19-24) If you call ahead, it allows you to join its guests for home-style meals that include a salad bar and often crab, halibut and salmon during the summer.

GETTING THERE & AROUND

Daily northbound and southbound flights are available with **Alaska Airlines** (☎ 874-3308, 800-426-0333). Many claim the flight north to Petersburg is the 'world's shortest jet flight,' since the six- to 11-minute trip is little more than a takeoff and landing.

Alaska Marine Highway (☎ 874-3711) services run almost daily both northbound and southbound from Wrangell in summer. To the north is Petersburg ($33, three hours) via the scenic, winding Wrangell Narrows, to the south Ketchikan ($37, six hours). The **Inter-Island Ferry Authority** (☎ 866-308-4848; www.interislandferry.com) operates the new MV *Stikine* between Coffman Cove on Prince of Wales Island and Wrangell ($37, three hours) on Friday, Saturday and Sunday. On the same days the boat connects Wrangell with the south end of Mitkof Island ($26, one hour), where Petersburg is 25 miles away by road.

PETERSBURG

pop 3120

From Wrangell, the Alaska Marine Highway Ferry heads north to begin one of the Inside Passage's most scenic sections. After crossing over from Wrangell Island to Mitkof Island, the vessel threads through the 46 turns of Wrangell Narrows, a 22-mile channel

ERNEST MANEWAL

MV *Columbia*, Alaska Marine Highway, Petersburg

that is only 300ft wide and 19ft deep in places. So winding and narrow is the channel that locals call it 'pinball alley.' Others refer to it as 'Christmas tree lane' because of the abundance of red and green navigational lights.

At the other end of this breathtaking journey lies Norwegian-influenced Petersburg, one of Southeast Alaska's hidden gems. Peter Buschmann arrived in 1897 and found a fine harbor, abundant fish and a ready supply of ice from nearby LeConte Glacier. He built a cannery in the area, enticed his Norwegian friends to follow him here, and gave his first name to the resulting town. Today, a peek into the local phone book reveals the strong Norwegian heritage that unifies Petersburg.

STEFAN WACKERHAGEN / IMAGEBROKER
Hiker, Klondike Gold Rush National Historical Park (p130)

The waterfront of this busy little fishing port is decorated with working boats and weathered boathouses, while tidy homes and businesses – many done up with distinctive Norwegian rosemaling, a flowery Norwegian art form – line the quiet streets.

The town lies across Frederick Sound from a spectacular glaciated wall of alpine peaks – including the distinctive Devil's Thumb – that form a skyline of jagged snowcapped summits. Nearby LeConte Glacier discharges icebergs to the delight of visitors.

SIGHTS

Clausen Memorial Museum (☎ 772-3598; 203 Fram St; adult/child $3/free; ☸ 10am-5pm Mon-Sat) holds an interesting collection of artifacts and relics, mostly related to local fishing history. Exhibits include the largest king salmon ever caught (126lb), a giant lens from the old Cape Decision lighthouse, a Tlingit dugout canoe and the 30-minute film, *Petersburg; The Town Fish Built.* Outside is *Fisk,* the intriguing fish sculpture that was commissioned in 1967 to honor the Alaska Centennial.

Heading south, Harbor Way passes Middle Boat Harbor and turns into **Sing Lee Alley**. This was the center of old Petersburg, and much of the street is built on pilings over Hammer Slough. On the alley, **Sons of Norway Hall** is the large white building with the colorful rosemaling built in 1912 and the center for Petersburg's Norwegian culture. Come on down and play bingo at 7pm on Saturday; 'O-32,' ja shore you betcha.

Also along Sing Lee Alley is **Bojer Wikan Fishermen's Memorial Park**. This deck of a park is built on pilings over Hammer Slough and features an impressive statue of a fisher that honors all his fellow crew members lost at sea. Also on display is the *Valhalla,* a replica of a Viking ship that was built in 1976 and purchased by Petersburg two years later.

The **North-Boat Harbor** (Excel St at Harbor Way), is the best one for wandering the docks, talking to crews and possibly even scoring some fresh fish. Begin at the Harbormaster Office where a wooden deck provides a picturesque overview of the commercial fleet and has a series of interpretive panels that will teach you the difference between purse seine and a long-liner. Continue north along the waterfront to see **Petersburg Fisheries** (Dolphin St at Nordic Dr), the original outfit founded by Peter Buschmann in 1900; today it's a subsidiary of Seattle's Icicle Seafoods.

From downtown, Nordic Dr heads north on a scenic route that ends at **Sandy Beach Recreation Area**, a beautiful day-use area 2 miles from downtown. There are 2000 year-old Tlingit fish traps snaking the mud flats and a rock with petroglyphs carved on it. Both the traps and the carvings are hard to spot but the **USFS Petersburg Ranger District office** (☎ 772-3871; 12 N Nordic Dr; ✆ 8am-5pm Mon-Fri) organizes guided interpretive walks to them during the summer here. Call for times.

ACTIVITIES
HIKING
Within town is the 0.7-mile **Hungry Point Trail** that begins at the ball field at the end of Excel St and cuts across muskeg. The gravel path keeps your feet dry, but surrounding you are stunted trees so short you have a clear view of Petersburg's mountainous skyline. The trail ends at Sandy Beach Rd and by heading right a quarter-mile you reach **Outlook Park**, a marine wildlife observatory with free binoculars to search

Frederick Sound for humpbacks, orcas and sea lions.

The 4-mile **Raven Trail** begins at the water tower on the airport's southeast side (accessible from Haugen Dr). It crosses muskeg areas on a boardwalk, then climbs to beautiful open alpine areas at 2000ft. Some sections are steep and require a little scrambling. The trail eventually leads to the USFS **Raven's Roost Cabin** (☎ 877-444-6777, 515-885-3639; www.recreation.gov; cabins $35). The cabin is above the treeline, providing easy access to good alpine hiking and spectacular views of Petersburg, Frederick Sound and Wrangell Narrows.

On Kupreanof Island, the 3.5-mile a **Trail** climbs to the top of Petersburg Mountain (2750ft), which offers views of Petersburg, the Coast Mountains, glaciers and Wrangell Narrows. Plan on five hours for the round-trip. To get across the channel, go to the skiff float at the North Boat Harbor and hitch a ride with somebody who lives on Kupreanof Island. On the Kupreanof side, head right on the overgrown road toward Sasby Island. You can also call **Tongass Kayak Adventures** (☎ 772-4600; www.tongasskayak.com), which runs hikers across the channel for $25 per person.

Petersburg Lake Trail is a 10.5-mile trail located deep in the Petersburg Creek-Duncan Salt Chuck Wilderness on Kupreanof Island. The trail leads to the USFS **Petersburg Lake Cabin** (☎ 877-444-6777, 515-885-3639; www.recreation.gov; cabin $35).

At Mile 14.5 of the Mitkof Hwy is the mile-long **Blind River Rapids Boardwalk** that winds through muskeg to the rapids, a scenic area and busy in June for king salmon fishing.

Along Three Lakes Rd, a USFS road heading east off Mitkof Hwy at Mile 13.6

and returning at Mile 23.8, are **Three Lakes Loop Trails**, a series of four short trails that total 4.5 miles. At Mile 14.2 is a 3-mile loop with boardwalks leading to Sand, Crane and Hill Lakes, all known for good trout fishing. Sand Lake has a free-use shelter. From the Sand Lake Trail, a 1.5-mile trail leads to Ideal Cove on Frederick Sound.

PADDLING

Kayak rentals are available from **Tongass Kayak Adventures** (☎ 772-4600; www. tongasskayak.com; s/d $55/65), which also offers kayak transfers and guided tours, including a four-hour paddle up Petersburg Creek ($85). Its best outing, however, begins with boat transport to LeConte Glacier for a day spent whale watching and paddling among the icebergs ($225).

LECONTE GLACIER

The most spectacular paddle in the region is to LeConte Glacier, 25 miles east of Petersburg. It's North America's southernmost tidewater glacier. From town, it takes one to two days to reach the frozen monument, including crossing Frederick Sound north of Coney Island. The crossing should be done at slack tide, as winds and tides can cause choppy conditions. If the tides are judged right, and the ice is not too thick, it's possible to paddle far enough into LeConte Bay to camp within view of the glacier.

THOMAS BAY

Almost as impressive as LeConte Glacier is Thomas Bay, 20 miles from Petersburg and north of LeConte Bay on Frederick Sound's east side. The bay has a pair of glaciers, including Baird Glacier, where many paddlers go for day hikes.

WHALE WATCHING

In recent years, whale watching has become a popular trip out of Petersburg. From mid-May to mid-September humpback whales migrate through, and feed in, Frederick Sound 45 miles northwest of Petersburg, with the peak feeding period in July and August. Other wildlife that can be spotted includes Steller's sea lions, orcas and seals.

A handful of charter-boat operators offer six- to eight-hour whale-watching tours that range from $275 to $325 per person. Among them are **Kaleidoscope Cruises** (☎ 772-3736, 800-868-4373; www. petersburglodgingandtours.com), run by Barry Bracken, a marine biologist who focuses on eco-education, and **Whale Song Cruises** (☎ 772-9393, 772-3724; http://whalesongcruises .com), which is equipped with a hydrophone so you can listen to the whales as well as see them.

TOURS

For a large selection of area tours, head to **Viking Travel** (☎ 772-3818, 800-327-2571; 101 N Nordic Dr), which acts as a clearinghouse for just about every tour in town. Possibilities include a four-hour boat tour to LeConte Glacier ($170), an eight-hour whale-watching tour ($270) and a helicopter flightseeing tour with a glacier walk ($305).

Most of the charter operators that do whale watching also have sightseeing trips to view LeConte Glacier, and that includes Kaleidoscope Cruises, whose five-hour tour is $190 per person. **Pacific Wing Air Charters** (☎ 772-4258; www. pacificwing.com) offers a 45-minute flightseeing trip to the glacier ($165).

Also available, either through Viking or directly, is a combination rainforest hike and LeConte Glacier cruise with **Tongass**

Kayak Adventures (☎ 772-4600; www. tongasskayak.com; per person $180).

SLEEPING

Heron's Rest (☎ 772-3373; www. heronsrestalaska.com; 613 Rambler St; d $70-120; ✗ 🖥) Reached from a private road and tucked away in a personal forest, this elegant B&B is closer to the ferry terminal than downtown. Separated from the main house are three spacious bedrooms and a comfortable living room featuring a flat panel TV, wet bar and a full breakfast in the morning served to a view of the mountains. Completing this Southeast Alaska setting are stacks of crab pots outside (the couple fish commercially) and herons occasionally resting in the surrounding trees.

Waterfront B&B (☎ 772-9300, 866-772-9301; www.waterfrontbedandbreakfast.com; 1004 S Nordic Dr; r $95-105; ✗ 🖥) The closest accommodation option to the ferry terminal – it's practically next door. It has an outdoor hot tub where you can soak while watching the ferry depart. Five bright and

comfortable rooms have private bath and share a living room that overlooks the Petersburg Shipwrights. For many guests, watching a boat being repaired on dry dock is far more interesting than whatever is on TV.

Sea Level B&B (☎ 772-3240; www. sealevelbnb.com; 913 N Nordic Dr; r $95-125; ✗ 🖥) A B&B built on pilings over the Wrangell Narrows, making it look more like a boathouse than a home. Two guestrooms have private bath and large picture windows filled with the boat traffic cruising past Mt Petersburg. On the outside deck there are chairs and rod holders so you can catch your dinner when the tides are in.

Scandia House (☎ 772-4281, 800-722-5006; www.scandiahousehotel.com; 110 Nordic Dr; s/d $110/120, ste $195; 🖥) The most impressive place in town, this hotel has 33 bright and modern rooms, some with kitchenettes, and a main-street location. Rates include courtesy shuttle service from the airport/ferry and muffins and coffee in the morning, though it's hard

THOMAS SBAMPATO / IMAGEBROKER

Humpback whales

to pass up the jolting espresso in the adjoining Java Hus.

EATING

Emily's (☎ 772-4555; 1000 S Nordic Dr; ⏱ 7am-5pm Mon-Fri) If you're catching a morning ferry, stop by Petersburg's best bakery for a cup of coffee and something that just came out of the oven. Even the day-old bread is better than anything else in town.

ourpick **Coastal Cold Storage** (☎ 772-4177; 306 N Nordic Dr; breakfast $4-6, lunch $9-12; ⏱ 7am-3pm) You're in Petersburg, you have to indulge in what they catch. At the very least, stop at this processor/seafood store/carryout restaurant for a shrimp burger, salmon-halibut chowder or the local specialty, halibut beer bits. Or purchase whatever is swimming

Bojer Wikan Fishermen's Memorial Park (p104)

in the tanks; steamer clams, oysters or Dungeness crab. Need a beer with those bits? It'll deliver your order next door to the Harbor Bar.

Beachcomber Inn (☎ 772-3888; 384 Mitkof Hwy; dinner $15-30; ⏱ bar 5-11pm Sun-Thu, to midnight Fri & Sat, restaurant 5:30-9pm) Built on pilings over the sea, this rambling inn is all restaurant and bar. Every seat has a fabulous maritime-and-mountain view but the small tables on the covered outdoor deck are an especially nice place to kick back. The inn is 4 miles south of town but runs a free shuttle van. So even if you don't want to feast on smoked black cod or a bowl of halibut ceviche, come for a drink as an excuse to gather in the view while chatting up the locals.

GETTING THERE & AROUND
There are daily northbound and southbound flights with **Alaska Airlines** (☎ 772-4255, 800-426-0333). The airport is on Haugen Dr, a quarter mile east of the post office.

The Alaska Marine Highway Ferry **terminal** (☎ 772-3855) is a mile south of downtown.

The new MV *Stikine* of the **Inter-Island Ferry Authority (IFA;** ☎ 866-308-4848; www. interislandferry.com) departs from the south end of Mitkof Island for Wrangell ($26, one hour) and Coffman Cove on Prince of Wales Island ($49, five hours) on Friday, Saturday and Sunday. The IFA terminal is 25 miles from Petersburg but **South Mitkof Express** (☎ 772-3818) provides transport ($25). Call to reserve a seat in advance.

Zoom Bike Shop (☎ 772-2546; www. zoombikeshop.com; 400 N Nordic Dr; ⏱ 10am-5:30pm Tue-Sat) is a bike shop downtown that rents mountain and road bicycles for $25 a day.

NORTHERN PANHANDLE

SITKA

pop 8805

Fronting the Pacific Ocean on Baranof Island's west shore, Sitka is a gem in a beautiful setting. Looming on the western horizon, across Sitka Sound, is the impressive Mt Edgecumbe, an extinct volcano with a graceful cone similar to Japan's Mt Fuji. Closer in, myriad small, forested islands out in the Sound turn into beautiful ragged silhouettes at sunset, competing for attention with the snowcapped mountains and sharp granite peaks flanking Sitka on the east. And in town, picturesque remnants of Sitka's Russian heritage lurk around every corner.

SIGHTS

ST MICHAEL'S CATHEDRAL

Two blocks west of the Centennial Building is the cathedral (☎ 747-8120; Lincoln St; donation $2; ❂ 9am-4pm Mon-Fri). Built between 1844 and 1848, the church stood for more than 100 years as Alaska's finest Russian Orthodox cathedral. When a fire destroyed it in 1966, the church was the oldest religious structure from the Russian era in Alaska. Luckily the priceless treasures and icons inside were saved by Sitka's residents, who immediately built a replica of their beloved church.

CASTLE HILL & TOTEM SQUARE

Continue west on Lincoln St for the walkway to Castle Hill. Kiksadi clan houses once covered the hilltop site, but in 1836 the Russians built 'Baranov's Castle' atop the hill to house the governor of Russian America. It was here, on October 18, 1867, that the official transfer of Alaska from Russia to the USA took place. The castle burned down in 1894.

More Russian cannons and a totem pole can be seen in Totem Square, near the end of Lincoln St. Across Katlian St from the square is the prominent, yellow Alaska Pioneers Home. Built in 1934 on the old Russian Parade Ground, the home is for elderly Alaskans.

RUSSIAN BISHOP'S HOUSE

East of downtown along Lincoln St, the Russian Bishop's House (☎ 747-6281; Lincoln St at Monastery St; adult/child $4/free; ❂ 9am-5pm) is the oldest intact Russian building in Sitka. Built in 1843 out of Sitka spruce, the two-story log house is one of the few surviving examples of Russian colonial architecture in North America. The National Park Service (NPS) has renovated the building to its condition in 1853, when it served as a school, Bishop's residence and chapel. Tours are on the hour and half-hour until 4:30pm.

SHELDON JACKSON MUSEUM

Further east along Lincoln St on the former campus of Sheldon Jackson College is Sheldon Jackson Museum (☎ 747-8981; 104 College Dr; adult/child $4/free; ❂ 9am-5pm). The college may be gone but this fine museum survived because the state of Alaska purchased it in 1983. The unusual building, built to look like a tribal community house, is home to a small but excellent collection of indigenous artifacts gathered from 1888 to 1898 by Dr Sheldon Jackson, a minister and federal education agent in Alaska.

SHELDON JACKSON AQUARIUM

Just past the campus on Lincoln St is the Sheldon Jackson Aquarium (☎ 747-3824; 801 Lincoln St; admission by donation; ❂ 8:30am-5:30pm when volunteers are available). The aquarium, a working hatchery, was once the home of the college's hatchery

JUNEAU & SOUTHEAST ALASKA

NORTHERN PANHANDLE

SITKA

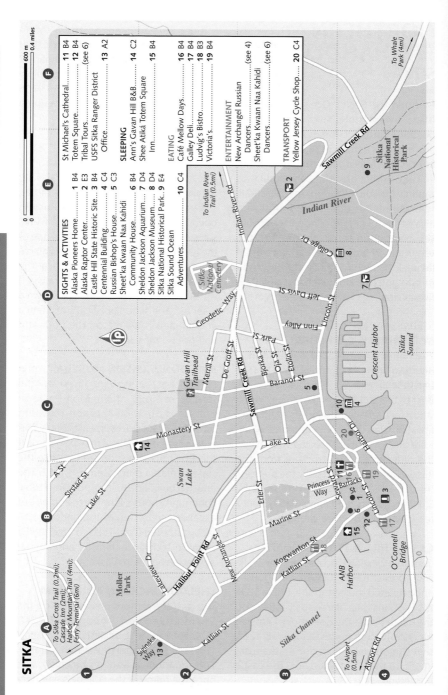

SIGHTS & ACTIVITIES

Alaska Pioneers Home.....	**1** B4
Alaska Raptor Center.....	**2** E3
Castle Hill State Historic Site..	**3** B4
Centennial Building.....	**4** C4
Russian Bishop's House.....	**5** C3
Sheet'ka Kwaan Naa Kahidi Community House.....	**6** B4
Sheldon Jackson Aquarium.....	**7** D4
Sheldon Jackson Museum.....	**8** D4
Sitka National Historical Park..	**9** E4
Sitka Sound Ocean Adventures.....	**10** C4
St Michael's Cathedral.....	**11** B4
Totem Square.....	**12** B4
Tribal Tours.....	(see 6)
USFS Sitka Ranger District Office.....	**13** A2

SLEEPING

Ann's Gavan Hill B&B.....	**14** C2
Shee Atiká Totem Square Inn.....	**15** B4

EATING

Café Mellow Days.....	**16** B4
Galley Deli.....	**17** B4
Ludvig's Bistro.....	**18** B3
Victoria's.....	**19** B4

ENTERTAINMENT

New Archangel Russian Dancers.....	(see 4)
Sheet'ka Kwaan Naa Kahidi Dancers.....	(see 6)

TRANSPORT

Yellow Jersey Cycle Shop.....	**20** C4

program and was saved from closure by volunteers. Hopefully it will remain a summer attraction where children come to view an 800-gallon 'Wall of Water' aquarium filled with sea anemones, rockfish and starfish or get their hands wet in three touch tanks, examining huge starfish or the coarse shell of an abalone.

SITKA NATIONAL HISTORICAL PARK
To the east Lincoln St ends at this 113-acre park, Alaska's smallest national park, at the mouth of Indian River. The park preserves the site where the Tlingits were finally defeated by the Russians in 1804 after defending their wooden fort for a week. It was only when the Tlingits ran out of gunpowder and flint, and slipped away at night, that the Russians were able to enter the deserted fort.

Begin at the park's **visitors center** (☎ 747-0110; adult/child $4/free; ☽ 8am-5pm), where Russian and indigenous artifacts are displayed and a 12-minute video in the theater will provide an overview of the battle. Outside, carvers will be work-

ing on a totem while nearby is Totem Trail, a mile-long path that leads you past 18 totems first displayed at the 1904 Louisiana Exposition in St Louis and then moved to the newly created park. It is these intriguing totems, standing in a beautiful rainforest setting by the sea and often enveloped in mist, that have become synonymous with the national park and even the city itself.

ALASKA RAPTOR CENTER
For an eye-to-eye encounter with an eagle, head to this **raptor center** (☎ 747-8662, 800-643-9425; www.alaskaraptor.org; 1101 Sawmill Creek Rd; adult/child $12/6; ☽ 8am-4pm Mon-Fri), reached by turning right on the first gravel road after crossing Indian River. The 17-acre center treats 200 injured birds a year, with its most impressive facility being a 20,000-sq-ft flight-training center that helps injured eagles, owls, falcons and hawks regain their ability to fly. In the center eagles literary fly past you only 2ft or 3ft away at eye level, so close you can feel the wind from their beating wings – amazing.

PATRICK ENDRES / ALASKASTOCK.COM

Visitor with eagle, Alaska Raptor Center

ACTIVITIES

HIKING

Sitka offers superb hiking in the beautiful but tangled forest surrounding the city. A complete hiking guide is available from the **USFS Sitka Ranger District office** (☎ 747-6671, recorded information 747-6685; 204 Siginaka Way at Katlian St; ⊗ 8am-4:30pm Mon-Fri). **Sitka Trail Works** (☎ 747-7244; www.sitkat-railworks.org), a nonprofit group that raises money for trail improvements, arranges hikes throughout the summer, and **Shore to Summit** (☎ 747-7244; www.shoretosummit. org; per person $50) offers two guided walks daily that include transportation.

INDIAN RIVER TRAIL

This easy trail is a 5.5-mile walk along a clear salmon stream to Indian River Falls, an 80ft cascade at the base of the Three Sisters Mountains. The hike takes you through typical Southeast rainforest, and offers the opportunity to view brown bears, deer and bald eagles. The trailhead, a short walk from the town center, is off Sawmill Creek Rd, just east of Sitka National Cemetery.

GAVAN HILL TRAIL

Also close to town is this trail, which ascends almost 2500ft over 3 miles to Gavan Hill peak. The trail offers excellent views of Sitka and the surrounding area. From the trail's end, the adventurous hiker can continue to the peaks of the Three Sisters Mountains.

SITKA CROSS TRAIL

Rather than leading up out of town, this easy, well-used 2.2-mile trail runs roughly parallel to civilization, from one end of town to the other. The west end starts by the water tower at the intersection of Charteris St and Georgeson Loop, but you can pick it up behind the baseball field at the end of Kimsham St, beside the hostel. The trail leads east from there, crossing Gavan Hill Trail and ending at Indian River Trail. Along the way you'll pass peat bogs and old-growth forests.

HARBOR MOUNTAIN TRAIL

This trail is reached from Harbor Mountain Rd, one of the few roads in the Southeast providing access to a subalpine area. Head 4 miles northwest from Sitka on Halibut Point Rd to the junction with Harbor Mountain Rd. A parking area and picnic shelter are 4.5 miles up the rough dirt road.

MT EDGECUMBE TRAIL

The 6.7-mile trail begins at the USFS **Fred's Creek Cabin** (☎ 877-444-6777, 518-885-3639; www.recreation.gov; cabin $35), reservations required, and ascends to the crater of this extinct volcano. Views from the summit are spectacular on a clear day. About 3 miles up the trail is a free-use shelter (no reservations required).

Mt Edgecumbe (3201ft) is on Kruzof Island, 10 miles west of Sitka, and can only be reached by boat because large swells from the ocean prevent floatplanes from landing.

PADDLING

Sitka also serves as the departure point for numerous blue-water trips along the protected shorelines of Sitka Sound, Baranof and Chichagof Islands. You can rent kayaks in town at **Sitka Sound Ocean Adventures** (☎ 747-6375; www.ssoceanadventures. com), which operates from a blue bus in the parking lot near the main harbor. Kayaks are available (single/double $55/65 per day) with discounts for multiday rentals. Guided trips are also available, indicated by the company motto on the side of the bus, 'Tip Your Guide, Not Your Kayak!'

KATLIAN BAY

This 45-mile round-trip from Sitka Harbor to scenic Katlian Bay (on Kruzof Island's north end) and back is one of the area's most popular paddles. The route follows narrow straits and well-protected shorelines in marine-traffic channels, making it an ideal trip for less experienced bluewater paddlers.

WHALE WATCHING

our pick **Sitka's Secrets** (☎ 747-5089; www. sitkasecret.com) runs its 27ft boat to St Lazaria Island and carries only six passengers for a far more personal adventure. Its three-hour cruise ($120 per person) to view seabirds and whales is operated by a married couple, both degreed biologists and former national wildlife refuge managers.

If you can't afford a wildlife cruise, try **Whale Park** (**Sawmill Creek Rd**), 4 miles south of town, which has a boardwalk and spotting scopes overlooking the ocean. Fall is the best time to sight cetaceans; as many as 80 whales have been known to gather in the waters off Sitka from mid-September to the end of the year.

TOURS

Sitka Tours (☎ 747-8443) If you're only in Sitka for as long as the ferry stopover, don't despair: Sitka Tours runs a bus tour (two hours, adult/child $12/6) just for you. The tour picks up and returns passengers to the ferry terminal, making brief visits to Sitka National Historical Park and St Michael's Cathedral.

Tribal Tours (☎ 747-7290, 888-270-8687; www.sitkatribe.org) A wide array of local tours with a Native Alaskan perspective. Its 2½-hour bus tour (adult/child $44/34) includes Sitka National Historical Park, Sheldon Jackson College and a Tlingit Native dance performance. It also has a 2½-hour coach and hiking tour that includes driving out to Old Historic Sitka and hiking Starrigavan Trail ($50).

SLEEPING

our pick **Ann's Gavan Hill B&B** (☎ 747-8023; www.annsgavanhill.com; 415 Arrowhead St; s/d $75/95; ✕ 🖳) An easy walk from downtown is this lovely Alaskan home with a wrap-around deck that includes two hot tubs. The delightful proprietor is a former

BRENT WINEBRENNER

Hiking in the mountains surrounding Sitka

commercial fisherwomen and still an avid hunter, the reason for the bear skin and marine charts on the walls.

Cascade Inn (☎ 747-6804, 800-532-0908; www.cascadeinnsitka.com; 2035 Halibut Point Rd; r $115-140; ☒ 🖵) Perched right above the shoreline, all 10 rooms in this inn face the ocean and have a private balcony overlooking it. Sure you're 2.5 miles north of town but the inn's oceanfront deck with its sauna and BBQ is worth waiting for a downtown bus.

ourpick Shee Atiká Totem Square Inn (☎ 747-3693, 866-300-1353; www.totemsquareinn. com; 201 Katlian St; r $140-179; ☒ 🖵) Extensively renovated, this is Sitka's finest hotel with 68 large, comfortable rooms featuring the traditional (Native Alaskan art and prints on the walls) and the modern (flat-screen TVs, hairdryers and wi-fi). Its best feature, however, is still the view from the rooms, overlooking either the historic square or a harbor bustling with boats bringing in the day's catch.

EATING

Galley Deli (☎ 747-9997; 2A Lincoln St; sandwiches $7-8; ☽ 10am-3pm Mon-Fri, 11am-3pm Sat; ☒) If you can find this deli in the back of the Raven Radio Building then you can create your own sandwich on homemade breads like Kalamata olive and feta or buttermilk dill and enjoy it on a pleasant outdoor porch.

Café Mellow Days (☎ 747-6000; 315 Lincoln St; breakfast $6-10, lunch $7-12; ☽ 6:30am-6:30pm; ☒) Brightly colored walls, splashy art and new-age music will mellow you out here and put you in the mood for the just-baked breads, muffins and quiches. For lunch be healthy and start with a salad or veggie wrap and finish with a strawberry and cream smoothie.

Victoria's (☎ 747-9301; 118 Lincoln St; breakfast $8-13, lunch $9-14, dinner $15-24; ☽ 4:30am-

10pm; ☒) Sitka's early morning breakfast joint. If you're a late riser come back in the evening for a good selection of seafood, from cedar plank salmon and steamed clams to pan fried oysters.

ourpick Ludvig's Bistro (☎ 966-3663; 256 Katlian St; dinner $20-32; ☽ 2-10pm; ☒) Sitka's boldest restaurant is steadily becoming known as the Southeast's best. Too bad it's so quaint. Ludvig's is as colorful as the commercial fishing district that surrounds it but there are only seven tables and a handful of stools at its brass-and-blue-tile bar. But an evening here is well worth the wait or even a reservation. The menu is described as 'rustic Mediterranean fare' and almost everything is local, even the sea salt. The Katlian Special is whatever the local boats catch that day then pan-seared with a hint of smoke from Sitka alder.

ENTERTAINMENT

New Archangel Russian Dancers (☎ 747-5516; adult/child $8/4) Whenever a cruise ship is in port, this troupe of more than 30 dancers in Russian costumes takes the stage at Centennial Building for a half-hour show. A schedule is posted at the hall.

Sheet'ka Kwaan Naa Kahidi Dancers (☎ 747-7290; www.sitkatribe.com; 200 Katlian St; adult/child $8/4) Not to be outdone, these dancers perform traditional Tlingit dances at the eponymous Tlingit Clan House, next to the Pioneers' Home.

GETTING THERE & AWAY
AIR
Sitka is served by **Alaska Airlines** (☎ 966-2926, 800-426-0333; www.alaskaair.com) and its airport is on Japonski Island, 1.8 miles west, or a 20-minute walk, of downtown. The white **Airport Shuttle** (☎ 747-8443) minibus (one way/round-trip $8/10) meets all jet flights in summer.

BRENT WINEBRENNER

Mountainside near Sitka

BOAT

The Alaska Marine Highway Ferry terminal (☎ 747-8737) is 6.5 miles northwest of
town; ferries depart in both directions
almost daily to Juneau ($39, nine hours),
Angoon ($31, six hours), Petersburg ($39,
11 hours) and Tenakee Springs ($31, nine
hours).

Ferry Transit Bus (☎ 747-8443; one way/
round-trip $8/10), operated by Sitka Tours,
meets all ferries year-round for the trip
to and from town. You can also catch a
Community Ride bus Monday through
Friday.

GETTING AROUND
BICYCLE

Yellow Jersey Cycle Shop (☎ 747-6317; 329
Harbor Dr; per 2hr/day $15/25), across the street
from the library, rents quality mountain
bikes.

BUS

Sitka's public bus system, Community
Ride (☎ 747-7103; adult/child $2/1; ⏱ 6:30am-
6:30pm Mon-Fri), has expanded significantly

in recent years and now offers hourly
service from downtown to as far south as
Whale Park and as far north as the ferry
terminal.

TENAKEE SPRINGS
pop 102

Tenakee Springs is a secondary port that
sits on the ferry route between Sitka and
Juneau. Since its period in the late 19th
century as a winter retreat for fishers and
prospectors, it has evolved into a rustic
village known for its slow and relaxed
pace. On the east side of Tenakee Inlet, the
settlement is basically a ferry dock, a row
of houses on pilings and the hot springs –
the main attraction – which bubble out
of the ground at 108°F.

Tenakee's alternative lifestyle centers
around the free public bathhouse at the
end of the ferry dock. The building en-
closes the principal spring, which flows
through the concrete bath at seven gallons
per minute. Bath hours, separate for men
and women, are posted; most locals take
at least one good soak per day, if not two.

SLEEPING & EATING

Opposite the bathhouse, at the foot of the ferry dock, is **Snyder Mercantile Co** (☎ 736-2205; ◷ 9am-4pm Wed-Mon). Founded by Ed Snyder, who arrived in a rowboat full of groceries in 1899, the store has been in business ever since and sells limited supplies and groceries. For food, there's **Rosie's Blue Moon Café** (◷ 10am-6pm) and the **Bakery & Giftshop** (☎ 736-2262; ◷ 8am-2pm Tue-Sat), both on Tenakee Ave.

Finding lodging is a little more challenging than finding a meal in Tenakee Springs. **Tenakee Hot Springs Lodge** (☎ 736-2400, 364-3640; s/d $90/150; ✗ ▯) features six rooms, a communal kitchen and a great view from its deck. Or you can pitch a tent at the rustic campground a mile east of town, at the mouth of the Indian River.

GETTING THERE & AWAY

The ferry MV *Le Conte* stops at Tenakee Springs roughly once a week, connecting it to Hoonah and Juneau northbound and to Angoon and Sitka (and occasionally Kake and Petersburg) southbound. Study the ferry schedule carefully to make sure you don't have to stay in town longer than you want. The one-way fare from Tenakee Springs to Juneau or Sitka is $35.

Alaska Seaplane Service (☎ 888-350-8277, Juneau 789-3331; www.akseaplanes.com) has scheduled service charging $125 one way.

JUNEAU

pop 31,000

Welcome to America's strangest state capital. It's the most geographically secluded state capital in the country, the only one that cannot be reached by car – only boat or plane.

But Juneau is also the most beautiful city in Alaska and arguably the nation's most scenic capital. The city center, which hugs the side of Mt Juneau and Mt Roberts, is a maze of narrow streets running past a mix of new structures, old storefronts and slanted houses, all held together by a network of staircases. The waterfront is bustling with cruise ships, fishing boats and floatplanes buzzing in and out. High above the city is the Juneau Ice Field, covering the Coastal Range and sending glaciers down between the mountains like marshmallow syrup on a sundae.

For visitors who come to Alaska for outdoor adventure, what really distinguishes the state capital from other Alaskan towns – and certainly other state capitals – is the superb hiking. Dozens of great trails surround the city; some begin downtown, just blocks from the capitol.

SIGHTS
ALASKA STATE MUSEUM

The outstanding **Alaska State Museum** (☎ 465-2901; www.museums.state.ak.us; 395 Whittier St; adult/child $5/free; ◷ 8:30am-5:30pm) is near Centennial Hall and on its 1st floor features artifacts from Alaska's six major indigenous groups. The most intriguing exhibit, 'Art of Survival,' shows how Native Alaskans have turned living in a hostile land into an art form with a display of items ranging from waterproof gut parkas and a century-old umiaq skin boat to tom cod fishing rods.

JUNEAU-DOUGLAS CITY MUSEUM

This **museum** (☎ 586-3572; 114 W 4th St; adult/child $4/free; ◷ 9am-5pm Mon-Fri, from 10am Sat & Sun) focuses on gold, with interesting mining displays and the video *Juneau: City Built On Gold*. If you love to hike in the mountains, the museum's 7ft-long relief map is the best overview of the area's rugged terrain other than a helicopter ride.

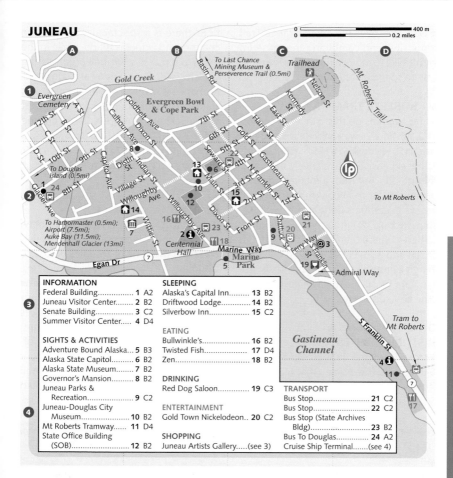

JUNEAU

INFORMATION	
Federal Building	1 A2
Juneau Visitor Center	2 B2
Senate Building	3 C2
Summer Visitor Center	4 D4

SIGHTS & ACTIVITIES	
Adventure Bound Alaska	5 B3
Alaska State Capitol	6 B2
Alaska State Museum	7 B2
Governor's Mansion	8 B2
Juneau Parks & Recreation	9 C2
Juneau-Douglas City Museum	10 B2
Mt Roberts Tramway	11 D4
State Office Building (SOB)	12 B2

SLEEPING	
Alaska's Capital Inn	13 B2
Driftwood Lodge	14 B2
Silverbow Inn	15 C2

EATING	
Bullwinkle's	16 B2
Twisted Fish	17 D4
Zen	18 B2

DRINKING	
Red Dog Saloon	19 C3

ENTERTAINMENT	
Gold Town Nickelodeon	20 B2

SHOPPING	
Juneau Artists Gallery	(see 3)

TRANSPORT	
Bus Stop	21 C2
Bus Stop	22 C2
Bus Stop (State Archives Bldg)	23 B2
Bus To Douglas	24 A2
Cruise Ship Terminal	(see 4)

ALASKA STATE CAPITOL

Next to the City Museum is the **Alaska State Capitol** (☎ 465-3800; 120 4th St; ⏰ 8am-5pm Mon-Fri, from 9am Sat). Built between 1929 and 1931 as the territorial Federal Building, the capitol looks like an overgrown high school. Stuffed inside are legislative chambers, the governor's office, and offices for the hundreds of staff members who arrive in Juneau for the winter legislative session. Free 30-minute tours are held every half-hour and start from the visitor desk in the lobby; a self-guided tour pamphlet is also available.

LAST CHANCE MINING MUSEUM

Amble out to the end of Basin Rd, a beautiful half-mile walk from the north end of Gastineau Ave, to the intriguing **Last Chance Mining Museum** (☎ 586-5338; 1001 Basin Rd; adult/child $4/free; ⏰ 9:30am-12:30pm & 3:30-6:30pm). The former Alaska-Juneau Gold Mining Company complex is now a museum where you can view the remains of the compressor house and examine tools of what was once the world's largest hard-rock goldmine. There is also a re-created mining tunnel and a 3D glass map of shafts that shows just how large

JUNEAU & SOUTHEAST ALASKA

NORTHERN PANHANDLE

it was. Nearby is the Perseverance Trail (opposite), and combining the museum with a hike to more mining ruins is a great way to spend an afternoon.

MT ROBERTS TRAMWAY

As far as trams go this **tramway** (☎ 463-3412, 888-461-8726; www.goldbelttours.com; 490 S Franklin St; adult/child $25/13.50; ⏰ 9am-9pm) is rather expensive for a relatively short five-minute ride. But from a marketing point of view, its location couldn't be better. It whisks passengers right from the cruise-ship dock up 1800ft to the treeline of Mt Roberts, where there is a restaurant, gift shops and a small theater with a film on Tlingit culture. Or skip all that and just use the tram for access to day hikes in the alpine area (opposite).

OTHER MUSEUMS & HISTORICAL SITES

Across from the Juneau-Douglas City Museum is the **State Office Building** (400 Willoughby Ave), known locally as the SOB. From the outdoor court on the 8th floor there is a spectacular view of the channel and Douglas Island, while in the lobby is a massive Kimball organ dating back to 1928. Every Friday at noon a performance is given, a good reason to join state workers for a brown-bag lunch. West of the SOB along 4th Ave is the pillared **Governor's Mansion** (716 Calhoun Ave). Built and furnished in 1912 at a cost of $44,000, the mansion is not open to the public.

ACTIVITIES
CYCLING

Bike paths run between Auke Bay, Mendenhall Glacier and downtown, and from the Juneau-Douglas Bridge to Douglas.

Cycle Alaska (☎ 321-2453; 3172 Pioneer Ave, Douglas Island; per 4/8hr $25/35) rents out good quality road and mountain bikes along with children's bikes and tandems, and will deliver them. The company offers Bike & Brew, a four-hour bicycle tour that includes Auke Bay, Mendenhall Glacier and finishes off at the Alaskan Brewing Co.

DON PITCHER

Mt Roberts Tramway

HIKING
GUIDED WALKS
our pick **Juneau Parks & Recreation** (☎ 586-5226, recorded information 586-0428; www.juneau.org/parksrec; 155 S Seward St) offers volunteer-led hikes every Wednesday (adults) and Saturday (kids OK) in 'rain, shine or snow.' Call or check the website for a schedule and the trails.

CITY CENTER TRAILS
Perseverance Trail off Basin Rd is Juneau's most popular and in 2008 received a $890,000 facelift. The trail is a path into Juneau's mining history but also provides access to two other popular treks, **Mt Juneau Trail** and **Granite Creek Trail**, and together the routes can be combined into a rugged 10-hour walk for hardy hikers, or an overnight excursion into the mountains surrounding Alaska's capital city.

Mt Roberts Trail is a 4-mile climb up Mt Roberts that begins at a marked wooden staircase at the northeast end of 6th St. It starts with a series of switchbacks, then breaks out of the trees at Gastineau Peak and comes to the tram station. From here it's a half-mile to the Cross, where you'll have good views of Juneau and Douglas. The Mt Roberts summit (3819ft) is still a steep climb through the alpine brush. If you hike up, you can ride down the Mt Roberts Tramway to S Franklin St for $5.

MENDENHALL GLACIER TRAILS
East Glacier Loop is one of many trails near Mendenhall Glacier, a 3-mile round-trip providing good views of the glacier from a scenic lookout at the halfway point. Pick up the loop along the **Trail of Time**, a half-mile nature walk that starts at the Mendenhall Glacier Visitor Center.

West Glacier Trail is one of the most spectacular hikes in the Juneau area. The 3.4-mile trail begins off Montana Creek Rd past Mendenhall Lake Campground and hugs the mountainside along the glacier, providing exceptional views of the icefalls and other glacial features.

JUNEAU AREA TRAILS
Point Bishop Trail is at the end of Thane Rd, 7.5 miles southeast of Juneau. This 8-mile trail leads to Point Bishop, a scenic spot overlooking the junction of Stephens Passage and Taku Inlet. The trail is flat but can be wet in many spots, making waterproof boots the preferred footwear. The hike makes for an ideal overnight trip, as there is good camping at Point Bishop.

Montana Creek Trail and **Windfall Lake Trail** connect at Windfall Lake and can be combined for an interesting 11.5-mile overnight hiking trip. It is easier to begin at the trailhead at Montana Creek and follow the Windfall Lake Trail out to the Glacier Hwy.

Herbert Glacier Trail extends 4.6 miles along the Herbert River to Herbert Glacier, a round-trip of four to five hours. The trail is easy with little climbing, though wet in places, and begins just past the bridge over Herbert River at Mile 28 of Glacier Hwy.

PADDLING
Day trips and extended paddles are possible out of the Juneau area in sea kayaks. Rentals are available from **Alaska Boat & Kayak** (☎ 789-6886, 364-2333; www.juneaukayak.com; 11521 Glacier Hwy; single/double $50/70; ☺ 9am-6pm), which is based in the Auke Bay Harbor and offers transport service and multiday discounts. The company also offers half-day and full-day guided paddles.

MENDENHALL LAKE
This lake at the foot of Mendenhall Glacier is an excellent paddling destination. Alaska Boat & Kayak has a self-guided package

to Mendenhall Lake ($95), which includes kayaks, transport and a waterproof map, and leads you on a route among the icebergs in this relatively calm body of water.

AUKE BAY
The easiest trip is to paddle out and around the islands of Auke Bay. You can even camp on the islands to turn the adventure into an overnight trip.

BERNERS BAY
At the western end of Glacier Hwy, 40 miles from Juneau, is Echo Cove, where kayakers put in for paddles in the protected waters of Berners Bay. The bay, which extends 12 miles north to the outlets of the Antler, Lace and Berners Rivers, is ideal for an overnight trip or longer excursions up Berners River.

WHALE WATCHING
The whale watching in nearby Stephens Passage is so good that some tour operators will refund your money if you don't see at least one.

our pick Orca Enterprises (☎ 789-6801, 888-733-6722; www.alaskawhalewatching.com; adult/child $114/84) Uses a 42ft jet boat, that is fully disabled-accessible, to look at sea lions, orcas and harbor seals as well as humpback whales.

ZIPLINING
our pick Alaska Zipline Adventures (☎ 321-0947; www.alaskazip.com; adult/child $139/99) Located at beautiful Eaglecrest Ski Area on Douglas Island, this course includes five ziplines and a sky bridge that zig-zag across Fish Creek Valley. Transportation is included.

JUNEAU FOR CHILDREN
The best attraction for kids visiting Juneau is the Macauley Salmon Hatchery (☎ 463-4810, 877-463-2486; www.dipac.net; 2697 Channel Dr; adult/child $3.25/1.75; ☒ 10am-6pm), 3 miles northwest of downtown. The hatchery has huge seawater aquariums loaded with local marine life, from tanner crabs to octopus, while the interpretive displays explaining the life cycle of

RALPH HOPKINS

Mendenhall Glacier (p124)

salmon are museum quality. Or rent a rod and reel at the adjacent Go Fish Grill ($10 per hour) and try your luck.

The City of Juneau maintains a wonderful system of parks including **Twin Lakes Park** (Old Glacier Hwy), just past the hospital, which is stocked with king salmon and equipped with a fishing pier. There's also a solar-system trail around the lake that provides a realistic idea of how far each planet is from the sun.

TOURS
CITY & GLACIER
Gray Line (☎ 586-3773, 800-544-2206; www.graylineofalaska.com) Has several tours including the standard city–Macauley Salmon Hatchery–Mendenhall Glacier tour. The daily three-hour tour is adult/child $44/22.

Juneau Steamboat Co (☎ 723-0372; www.juneausteamboat.com) Uses a unique 30ft, 16-passenger steamboat to give you a view of Juneau and the surrounding gold mines from the middle of the Gastineau Channel on this hour-long tour (per person $49).

JUNEAU ICE FIELD
The hottest tour in Juneau is a helicopter ride to the Juneau Ice Field for a 20-minute ride in the basket of a dogsled. **ourpick NorthStar Trekking** (☎ 790-4530; www.glaciertrekking.com) Skip the dogsled and strap on the crampons. NorthStar offers several glacier treks that first begin with a helicopter ride and includes all equipment and training. On its two-hour glacier trek ($379) you cross two miles of frozen landscape riddled with crevasses for a hike that is as stunning as it is pricy.

Wings of Alaska (☎ 586-6275; www.wingsofalaska.com) The 40-minute glacier flightseeing adventure (adult/child

$170/140) is the most affordable way to get into the air for a peek at the ice field.

TRACY ARM
This steepsided fjord, 50 miles southeast of Juneau, has a pair of tidewater glaciers and a gallery of icebergs floating down its length. You're almost guaranteed to see seals inside the arm, and you might spot whales on the way there. **Adventure Bound Alaska** (☎ 463-2509, 800-228-3875; www.adventureboundalaska.com; adult/child $140/90) is the longtime tour operator to Tracy Arm and uses a pair of boats that leave daily from the Juneau waterfront.

SLEEPING
Driftwood Lodge (☎ 586-2280, 800-544-2239; www.driftwoodalaska.com; 435 Willoughby Ave; r $94-100, ste $125; ✗ 🖳) Near the Alaska State Museum, this lodge is the best value accommodations downtown. The 63 rooms are clean and updated regularly, the motel offers 24-hour courtesy transportation to the airport and the ferry and it's hard to top the location, unless you're willing to spend twice as much.

Auke Lake B&B (☎ 790-3253, 800-790-3253; www.admiraltytours.com; 11595 Mendenhall Loop Rd; r $125-165; ✗ 🖳) Located 10 minutes from Mendenhall Glacier, this Valley B&B has three rooms, a huge deck and a hot tub that overlooks Auke Lake. Each room has a private bath, phone, TV/VCR, refrigerator and coffeemaker while guests have use of a paddleboat, canoes or kayak.

ourpick Silverbow Inn (☎ 586-4146, 800-586-4146; www.silverbowinn.com; 120 2nd St; r $138-228; ✗) A boutique inn on top of the best (and only) bagel shop downtown. The 11 rooms as well as the inn itself are filled with antiques but come with private bath, king and queen beds and flat panel TVs. A 2nd-floor deck features a hot tub with a view of the mountains of Douglas Island. Breakfast is served in the morning, wine-and-cheese in the evening.

Alaska's Capital Inn (☎ 907-586-6507, 888-588-6507; www.alaskacapitalinn.com; 113 W 5th St; r $175-$305; ✕ ▣) Political junkies will love this place, it's across the street from the state capitol. In the gorgeously restored home of a wealthy gold-rush-era miner, who obviously found color, the inn has seven rooms with private bath, phone and TV/VCR, and feature hardwood floors covered by colorful Persian rugs. The backyard doesn't have a blade of grass; rather multiple decks, gardens and a secluded hot tub that even the governor can't spy on. In the morning there's a full breakfast, in the evening wine and cheese is served on the back deck, which overlooks the city.

EATING

Bullwinkle's (☎ 586-2400; 318 Willoughby Ave; medium pizza $12-18; ⏱ 11am-11pm Mon-Thu, to midnight Fri & Sat, noon-11pm Sun) There's been a moose and a flying squirrel pitching pizza in Juneau for 35 years. The beerhall-like restaurant has changed little in that time and neither has the pizza, it's as tasty as ever. Bullwinkle's also has good sandwiches and a decent little salad bar for the veggie deprived. Enjoy a pitcher of beer and free popcorn while waiting for your garlic chicken pizza.

ourpick Island Pub (☎ 364-1595; 1102 2nd St; pizza $13-18; ⏱ 4-10pm) Across the channel from the Capital City, this relaxing, unhurried restaurant serves firebrick-oven focaccia and gourmet pizza to a mountainous view. Don't worry about a Red Dog Saloon mob scene. You're on Douglas Island.

Twisted Fish (☎ 463-5033; 550 S Franklin St; dinner $15-22; ✕) Beef be gone. Located between Taku Smokeries and a wharf where commercial fishermen unload their

catch, this restaurant is about local seafood, from its menu to the large colorful salmon hanging from the ceiling.

Zen (☎ 586-5074; Goldbelt Hotel, 51 Egan Dr; breakfast $5-12, dinner $20-30) Zen calls itself an Asian fusion restaurant, taking what's readily available, Alaska seafood, and infusing it with an Asian touch. You end up with entrees like ginger halibut, black-cod stir fry or shrimp Alfredo made with jumbo udon noodles.

Thane Ore House (☎ 586-3442; 4400 Thane Rd; dinner $21; ✕) Found 4 miles south of town, this is the best. The all-you-can-eat dinner of grilled salmon, halibut and ribs includes a salad bar, corn, baked beans and more. There is a courtesy bus that departs nightly from the downtown area.

DRINKING

Nightlife centers on S Franklin and Front Sts, a historic, quaint (but not quiet) main drag attracting locals and tourists alike.

Red Dog Saloon (☎ 463-3658; 200 Admiral Way at S Franklin St) A sign at the door says it all – Booze, Antiques, Sawdust Floor, Community Singing – and the cruise-ship passengers love it! Most don't realize, much less care, that this Red Dog is but a replica of the original, a famous Alaskan drinking hole that was across the street until 1987.

ENTERTAINMENT

ourpick Gold Town Nickelodeon (☎ 586-2876; www.goldtownnick.110mb.com; 171 Shattuck St; ⏱ Thu-Sun) This delightful art house theater presents small budget, foreign films and documentaries. On Thursday the popcorn is free.

SHOPPING

The situation between the cruise-ship stores and local shops has become tense in recent years, the reason you see signs like 'Open All Year' or 'An Alaskan Family Owns This Store.'

One of the best downtown is the **Juneau Artists Gallery** (☎ 586-9891; www.juneauartistsgallery.com; Senate Bldg at 175 S Franklin St; ☼ 9am-9pm), a co-op of 26 local artists who have filled the store with paintings, etchings, glass work, jewelry, pottery and quilts. Out in the Valley, near Nugget Mall, is the **Rie Munoz Gallery** (☎ 789-7449; 2101 Jordan Ave; ☼ 9am-5:30pm) featuring a large selection of Rie Munoz prints as well as Dale DeArmond, Byron Birdsall and several other noted Alaskan artists.

GETTING THERE & AWAY
AIR
Alaska Airlines (☎ 800-252-7522; www.alaskaair.com) offers scheduled jet service to Seattle, all major Southeast cities, Glacier Bay, Anchorage and Cordova daily in summer.

Wings of Alaska (☎ 789-0790; www.wingsofalaska.com; 8421 Livingston Way) flies to Angoon ($90), Gustavus ($93), Haines ($105), Hoonah ($69) and Skagway ($114).

BOAT
Alaska Marine Highway (☎ 465-3941, 800-642-0066; www.ferryalaska.com) ferries dock at Auke Bay Ferry Terminal, 14 miles from downtown.

GETTING AROUND
TO/FROM THE AIRPORT & FERRY
A taxi to/from the airport costs around $25. The city bus express route runs to the airport, but only from 7:30am to 5:30pm Monday to Friday. On weekends and in the evening, if you want a bus you'll need to walk 10 minutes to the nearest 'regular route' stop on the backside of Nugget Mall.

Unbelievable but true nonetheless: no buses or regularly scheduled shuttles go to the ferry terminal in Auke Bay, an ungodly long 14-mile distance from downtown. One way to save a few dollars out to the ferry is to take the bus to the airport, where there are usually cabs stationed, and then catch a taxi the rest of the way.

DON PITCHER / ALASKASTOCK.COM

Red Dog Saloon

SUNNY K. AWAZAHURA-REED / ALASKASTOCK.COM

Alaskan Brewing Company

BUS
Juneau's sadistic public bus system, Capital Transit (☎ 789-6901), stops well short of the ferry terminal and a mile short of the Mendenhall Glacier Visitor Center.

AROUND JUNEAU
ALASKAN BREWING COMPANY
Alaska's largest brewery (☎ 780-5866; www.alaskanbeer.com; 5429 Shaune Dr; ☷ 11am-7pm) also makes some of its best beer. Established in 1986, the brewery is in the Lemon Creek area and reached from Anka St, where the city bus will drop you off, by turning right on Shaune Dr. The tour includes viewing the small brewery, free sampling of lagers and ales plus an opportunity to purchase beer in the gift shop, even five-gallon party kegs ($55).

MENDENHALL GLACIER
The most famous of Juneau's ice floes, and the city's most popular attraction, is Mendenhall Glacier, Alaska's famous drive-in glacier. The river of ice is 13 miles

from downtown, at the end of Glacier Spur Rd.

Near the face of the glacier is the USFS Mendenhall Glacier Visitor Center (☎ 789-0097; adult/child $3/free; ☷ 8am-7:30pm), which houses various glaciology exhibits, a large relief map of the ice field, an observatory with telescopes and a theater that shows the film *Magnificent Mendenhall*.

Outside you'll find six hiking trails, ranging from a 0.3-mile photo-overlook trail to a trek of several miles up the glacier's west side. For many the most interesting path is the mile-long Moraine Ecology Trail, which leads to a salmon-viewing platform overlooking Steep Creek. This is Southeast Alaska's most affordable bear-viewing site.

GLACIER TREKKING
One of the most unusual outdoor activities in Juneau is glacier trekking: stepping into crampons, grabbing an ice axe and roping up to walk on ice 1000 years or older. The scenery and the adventure is

like nothing you've experienced before as a hiker. The most affordable outing is offered by **Above & Beyond Alaska** (☎ 364-2333; www.beyondak.com). Utilizing a trail to access Mendenhall Glacier, it avoids expensive helicopter fees on its guided six-hour outing. The cost is $185 per person and includes all mountaineering equipment and transportation.

SHRINE OF ST THERESE

At Mile 23.3 Glacier Hwy is the Shrine of St Therese, a natural stone chapel on an island connected to the shore by a stone causeway. As well as being the site of numerous weddings, the island lies along the Breadline, a well-known salmon-fishing area in Juneau. The island is perhaps the best place to fish for salmon from the shore.

GLACIER BAY NATIONAL PARK & PRESERVE

Eleven tidewater glaciers that spill out of the mountains and fill the sea with icebergs of all shapes, sizes and shades of blue have made Glacier Bay National Park and Preserve an icy wilderness renowned worldwide.

Glacier Bay is the crowning jewel in the itinerary of most cruise ships and the dreamy destination for anybody who has ever paddled a kayak.

SIGHTS & ACTIVITIES
GLACIERS

The *Fairweather Express* operated by **Glacier Bay Lodge & Tours** (☎ 264-4600, 888-229-8687; www.visitglacierbay.com) is a high-speed catamaran that departs at 7:30am for an eight-hour tour into the West Arm and returns by 4pm, in time for the Alaska Airlines flight back to Juneau.

For a more personal and leisurely experience there's the *Kahsteen,* operated by **Gustavus Marine Charters** (☎ 697-2233; www.gustavusmarinecharters.com). The 42ft yacht heads up with four to six passengers, a pair of kayaks, a skiff for shore excursions and Mike Nigro, a former back-country ranger, as your captain.

PADDLING

our pick **Glacier Bay Sea Kayaks** (☎ 697-2257; www.glacierbayseakayaks.com; per day single/double $45/50) rents kayaks as well as leads guided trips to the Beardslee Islands (half/full day $90/140).

WHALE WATCHING

our pick **Woodwind Sailing Adventures** (☎ 697-2282; http://sailglacierbay.homestead. com) has a spacious 40ft sailing catamaran that offers a whale-watching trip to Icy Point ($160) and an excellent kayaking-with-the-whales day trip to Pt Adolphus ($260).

TOURS

Glacier Bay Lodge & Tours (☎ 264-4600, 888-229-8687; www.visitglacierbay.com) Has a weekend kayak package that includes round-trip ferry transport Auke Bay–Bartlett Cove, a night at Glacier Bay Lodge and kayak drop-off and pick-up for a night up the bay. The cost is $400 per person but does not include kayak rental.

Gray Line (☎ 586-3773, 800-544-2206; www. graylineofalaska.com) Offers a three-day package from Juneau that includes round-trip flights to Gustavus, two nights at Glacier Bay Lodge and a boat tour of the West Arm ($875 per person).

SLEEPING & EATING
BARTLETT COVE

Glacier Bay Lodge (☎ 697-2225, 888-229-8687; www.visitglacierbay.com; 199 Bartlett Cove Rd; r $160-185; ✗) This is the only hotel and restaurant in Bartlett Cove. The lodge has

55 rooms, a crackling fire in a huge stone fireplace and a dining room that usually hums in the evening with an interesting mixture of park employees, backpackers and locals from Gustavus. Nightly slide presentations, ranger talks and movies held upstairs cover the park's natural history.

GUSTAVUS

Bear's Nest Café & Cabin Rentals (☎ 697-2440; 2 White Dr; cabin $110-139, r $135; ☺ noon-8pm; ✗) This small restaurant off of Wilson Rd features organic produce and local seafood with daily vegetarian offerings but is best known for its live music on Friday and Saturday. It's so packed with locals and park workers some evenings, people are sitting on the floor.

Annie Mae Lodge (☎ 697-2346, 800-478-2346; www.anniemae.com; Grandpa's Farm Rd; s $115-145, d $160-190; ✗ 🖥) A large rambling lodge with wrap-around porches and 11 rooms, most with private bath. On the 2nd level all seven rooms have a private entrance off the porch, while a large dining room and common area is where a continental breakfast is served in the morning; dinners are available in the evening for an additional charge.

GETTING THERE & AROUND

Alaska Airlines (☎ 800-252-7522; www.alaaskaair.com) offers the only jet service but its rarely the cheapest airfare, with a round-trip ticket running $225 for the daily 25-minute trip from Juneau to Gustavus. **Wings of Alaska** (☎ Juneau 789-0790, Gustavus 697-2201; www.wingsofalaska.com) offers scheduled flights for $93/186 one way/round-trip, as does **Air Excursions** (☎ 697-2375; www.airexcursions.com), which is usually a few dollars cheaper. Both maintain a counter at Juneau Airport.

Glacier Bay Lodge & Tours operates the **Glacier Bay Ferry** (☎ 264-4600, 888-229-8687; www.visitglacierbay.com; one way adult/child $75/38) on Friday and Sunday with the boat departing Bartlett Cove at 4pm and Auke Bay at 7:30pm for the return trip.

Glacier Bay National Park & Preserve (p125)

HAINES

pop 2257

Heading north of Juneau on the state ferry takes you up Lynn Canal, North America's longest and deepest fjord. Along the way, Eldred Rock Lighthouse stands as a picturesque sentinel, waterfalls pour down off the Chilkoot Range to the east, and the Davidson and Rainbow Glaciers draw 'oohs' and 'aahs' as they snake down out of the jagged Chilkat Mountains to the west. You end up in Haines, a scenic departure point for Southeast Alaska and a crucial link to the Alaska Hwy.

You'll immediately notice that this town is different from what you've experienced elsewhere in the Southeast. The town isn't especially well developed for tourism: you won't find a salmon bake here and, no doubt for many travelers, that's part of its charm.

SIGHTS

The **Hammer Museum** (☎ 766-2374; 108 Main St; adult/child $3/free; ☺ 10am-5pm Mon-Fri) is a monument to Dave Pahl's obsession with hammers. He's got a zillion of them (well, actually 1500) on display and several hundred more in storage. In Pahl's museum you learn world history through the development of the hammer, from one less than one-quarter of an ounce to another weighing more than 40lb. You can't miss the museum, there is a 20ft-high hammer outside.

Fort Seward, reached by heading uphill (east) at the Front St–Haines Hwy junction, was Alaska's first permanent army post. Built in 1903 and decommissioned after WWII, the fort is now a national historical site with a handful of restaurants, lodges and art galleries utilizing the original buildings. A walking-tour map of the fort is available at the visitors center, or you can

RALPH HOPKINS

Haines

just read the historical panels that have been erected there. Within the parade ground is **Totem Village**. Although not part of the original fort, the village includes two tribal houses and totem poles and is the home of the **Chilkat Dancers Storytelling Theater Show** (☎ 766-2540; adult/child $12/6; ☺ 4:30pm Mon-Fri), an hour-long performance of Alaska Native dramatization.

Dalton City, the movie set for *White Fang* that was relocated to the Southeast Alaska State Fairgrounds, is a beacon for beer lovers. Among the false-front buildings and wooden sidewalks is the **Haines Brewing Company** (☎ 766-3823; Fair Dr; ☺ 1-7pm Mon-Sat), the maker of such beer as Dalton Trail Ale, Elder Rock Red and Black Fang.

ACTIVITIES
HIKING
MT RIPINSKY TRAIL

The trip to the 3563ft summit of Mt Ripinsky (also known as the South Summit) offers a sweeping view of the landscape from Juneau to Skagway. The route, which includes Peak 3920 and a descent from 7 Mile Saddle to Haines Hwy, is either a strenuous 10-hour journey for experienced hikers or an overnight trip.

BATTERY POINT TRAIL

This 2-mile trail is a flat walk along the shore to Kelgaya Point, where you can cut across to a pebble beach and follow it to Battery Point for excellent views of Lynn Canal. The trail begins a mile beyond Portage Cove Recreation Site at the end of Beach Rd. Plan on a two-hour round-trip.

MT RILEY TRAILS

This climb to a 1760ft summit is considerably easier than the one to Mt Ripinsky, but it still provides good views in all directions, including vistas of Rainbow and Davidson Glaciers. One trail up the mountain begins at a junction 2.2 miles up the Battery Point Trail out of Portage Cove Recreation Site. From here, you hike 3 miles over Half Dome and up Mt Riley.

SEDUCTION POINT TRAIL

This trail begins at Chilkat State Park Campground and is a 6.5-mile, one-way hike to the point separating Chilkoot and Chilkat Inlets. The trail swings between forest and beaches, and provides excellent views of Davidson Glacier.

TOURS
Alaska Nature Tours (☎ 766-2876; www.alaskanaturetours.net; 109 2nd Ave) Offers excellent environmentally focused tours with knowledgeable guides for activities that range from birding and bear watching to easy hikes to Battery Point. Its Twilight Wildlife Watch is a 2½-hour tour (adult/child $65/50) that departs at 6:15pm and heads up the Chilkoot River, stopping along the way to look for eagles, mountain goats and brown bears who emerge at dusk to feed on spawning salmon.

Haines-Skagway Fast Ferry (☎ 766-2100, 888-766-2103; www.hainesskagwayfastferry.com; Beach Rd) If you don't have time for Skagway, the Fast Ferry has a Rail & Sail Tour (adult/child $155/78) that includes round-trip transport to the Klondike city and the Summit Excursion on the White Pass & Yukon Railroad.

SLEEPING

Hotel Halsingland (☎ 766-2000, 800-542-6363; www.hotelhalsingland.com; 13 Fort Seward Dr; r $69-119; ⊠) The grand dame of Haines hotels is the former bachelor officers' quarters and overlooks the Fort Seward's parade ground. A National Historic Landmark, the hotel is a little worn around the edges but some rooms still have fireplaces and classic claw-foot bathtubs.

Fort Seward Lodge (☎ 766-2009, 877-617-3418; www.ftsewardlodge.com; 39 Mud Bay Rd; s/d $95/110, without bath $75; ⊠) Under new ownership, the former Post Exchange of Fort Seward is now one of Haines' best places to spend a night.

Fort Seward B&B (☎ 766-2856, 800-615-6676; r $95-145; ⊠) Haines' first B&B occupies the restored former home of the army's surgeon; a mammoth three-story Victorian house with seven guestrooms, five with shared bath, two with private bath. A wide porch overlooks the parade grounds and Lynn Canal beyond. If the view alone isn't worth the room rate then innkeeper Norm Smith's wonderful sourdough pancakes are. Guests also enjoy free use of bikes and kites.

EATING

Chilkat Restaurant & Bakery (☎ 766-3653; Dalton St at 5th Ave; breakfast $5-8, sandwiches $6-8; ⏰ 7am-3pm Mon-Sat; ✗) A local favorite that has been baking goodies and serving breakfast for 25 years. For a nice break from eggs and potatoes, try the homemade granola with blueberries... but first you have to get past that display case filled with the daily offering of muffins and pastries.

our pick **Mosey's Cantina** (☎ 766-2320; 31 Tower Rd; lunch $8-15, dinner $14-18; ⏰ 11:30am-2:30pm & 5:30-8:30pm Mon-Sat; ✗) A cute and cozy Mexican restaurant with only seven tables inside and a few more outside. The tamales, halibut-stuffed burritos and enchiladas are very good. Best of all it serves the local beer.

Fireweed Restaurant (☎ 766-3838; 37 Blacksmith St; sandwiches $12-15, pastas $11-15, pizza $11-21; ⏰ 4:30-9pm Tue, 11:30am-3pm and 4:30-9pm Wed-Sat; ✗) This clean, bright and laid-back bistro looks like it belongs in California not Haines. On its menu are words like 'organic', 'veggie' and 'grilled' as opposed to 'deep fried' and 'captain's special.' Vegetarians actually have a choice here (try the veggie baked ziti); everybody else can indulge in sandwiches, burgers and the town's best pizza, all washed down with beer served in icy mugs.

Fort Seward Lodge Restaurant (☎ 766-2009; 39 Mud Bay Rd; dinner $17-28; ⏰ 5-9:30pm Wed-Mon; ✗) In what used to be Fort Seward's Post Exchange is now one of Haines' best restaurants. The two-level restaurant has a small bar that's a refreshing break from the smoky, main-street watering holes and a menu that includes the standards of halibut, crab and salmon but also some diversions from the sea like the excellent bourbon baby back ribs. Dangling from the ceiling in the middle is the original red velvet swing that ladies swung to the delight of the soldiers.

EMILY RIDDELL

Arriving in Haines

Commander's Room (☎ 766-2000; 13 Fort Seward Dr; dinner $22-28; ⏰ 5:30-9pm; ✗) Located in Hotel Halsingland is Haines' most upscale restaurant. Begin the evening with a drink in its cozy Officer's Club Lounge and then venture into Commander's Room where you'll find white tablecloths, a fine wine list and a chef who has a herb garden out back. Try the Moroccan spiced braised lamb shank or seared salmon that's topped with a rhubarb-ginger chutney.

SHOPPING

Despite a lack of cruise-ship traffic, or maybe because of it, Haines supports an impressive number of artists and has enough galleries to fill an afternoon of wandering.

Sea Wolf Art Studio (☎ 766-2558; www. tresham.com; Ft Seward Parade Ground; ⏰ 10am-4:30pm)

ourpick **Extreme Dreams Fine Arts** (☎ 766-2097; www.extremedreams.com; Mile 6.5 Mud Bay Rd; ⏰ 10am-6pm)

GETTING THERE & AROUND
AIR
There is no jet service to Haines, but **Wings of Alaska** (☎ 766-2030; www. wingsofalaska.com) has daily flights to Juneau ($110) and Skagway ($60).

BOAT
State ferries, including the high-speed catamaran MV *Fairweather,* depart daily from the **ferry terminal** (☎ 766-2111; 2012 Lutak Rd) north of town heading for Skagway ($31, one hour) and Juneau ($37, 5½ hours). **Haines Shuttle** (☎ 766-3138) meets all the ferries and charges $20 for the 4-mile trip into town. It also departs Haines 30 minutes before each ferry arrival, after stopping at various hotels around town.

Haines-Skagway Fast Ferry (☎ 766-2100, 888-766-2103; www.hainesskagwayfastferry. com; Beach Rd) uses a speedy catamaran to cruise down Taiya Inlet to Skagway in 35 minutes. The 80ft cat departs Haines from the Fast Ferry shuttle dock at 6am, 11am and 5pm and more often if cruise ships are packing Skagway. One-way fares are adult/child $31/16, round trip $62/32.

SKAGWAY
pop 846

Much of Skagway is within Klondike Gold Rush National Historical Park, which comprises downtown Skagway, the Chilkoot Trail, the White Pass Trail corridor and a Seattle visitors center. Beginning in 1897, Skagway and the nearby ghost town of Dyea were the starting places for more than 40,000 gold-rush stampeders who headed to the Yukon primarily by way of the Chilkoot Trail. The actual stampede lasted only a few years but it produced one of the most colorful periods in Alaskan history, that of a lawless frontier town controlled by villainous 'Soapy' Smith who was finally removed from power in a gun fight by town hero Frank Reid.

SIGHTS
KLONDIKE GOLD RUSH NATIONAL HISTORICAL PARK VISITOR CENTER
Your first stop of the day should be this **NPS center** (☎ 983-9223; www.nps.gov/klgo; Broadway St at 2nd Ave; ⏰ 8am-6pm) in the original 1898 White Pass & Yukon Route depot. The center features displays – the most impressive being a replica of the ton of supplies that every gold miner had to carry over the Chilkoot Pass – as well as ranger programs and a small bookstore.

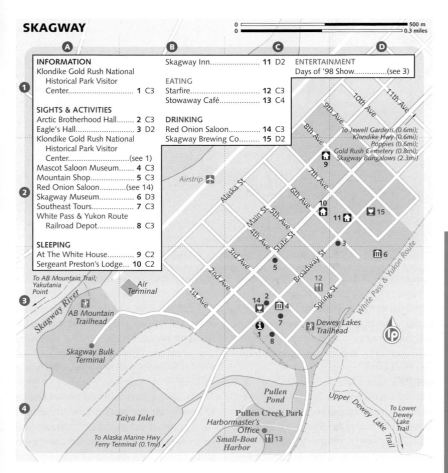

SKAGWAY

INFORMATION
Klondike Gold Rush National
  Historical Park Visitor
  Center..........................**1** C3

SIGHTS & ACTIVITIES
Arctic Brotherhood Hall........**2** C3
Eagle's Hall..........................**3** D2
Klondike Gold Rush National
  Historical Park Visitor
  Center.............................(see 1)
Mascot Saloon Museum.......**4** C3
Mountain Shop.....................**5** C3
Red Onion Saloon.............(see 14)
Skagway Museum.................**6** D3
Southeast Tours..................**7** C3
White Pass & Yukon Route
  Railroad Depot.................**8** C3

SLEEPING
At The White House............**9** C2
Sergeant Preston's Lodge...**10** C2

Skagway Inn.....................**11** D2

EATING
Starfire..............................**12** C3
Stowaway Café.................**13** C4

DRINKING
Red Onion Saloon..............**14** C3
Skagway Brewing Co.........**15** D2

ENTERTAINMENT
Days of '98 Show...............(see 3)

To Jewell Gardens (0.6mi);
  Klondike Hwy (0.6mi);
  Poppies (0.6mi);
Gold Rush Cemetery (0.8mi);
  Skagway Bungalows (2.3mi)

Airstrip

Skagway River

AB Mountain Trailhead

To AB Mountain Trail;
Yakutania Point

Air Terminal

Skagway Bulk Terminal

Taiya Inlet

To Alaska Marine Hwy
Ferry Terminal (0.1mi)

Pullen Pond

Pullen Creek Park
Harbormaster's Office
Small-Boat Harbor

Dewey Lakes Trailhead

Upper Dewey Lake Trail

To Lower Dewey Lake Trail

0 ___ 500 m
0 ___ 0.3 miles

SKAGWAY MUSEUM
Skagway Museum (☎ 983-2420; 7th Ave at Spring St; adult/child $2/1; ☽ 9am-5pm Mon-Fri, 10am-5pm Sat, 10am-4pm Sun) is not only one of the finest in a town filled with museums but one of the finest in the Southeast.

MASCOT SALOON MUSEUM
This is the only saloon in Alaska that doesn't serve beer, wine or a drop of whiskey – but it did during the gold rush, and plenty of it. Built in 1898, the **Mascot** (Broadway St at 3rd Ave; admission free; ☽ 8am-6pm) was one of 70 saloons during

Skagway's heyday as 'the roughest place in the world.' The park service has since turned it into a museum that looks into the vices – gambling, drinking, prostitution – that followed the stampeders to the goldfields, encouraging visitors to belly up to the bar for a shot of sinful history.

ARCTIC BROTHERHOOD HALL
The most outlandish building of the seven-block historical corridor along Broadway St, and possibly the most photographed building in Alaska, is

IMAGEBROKER/STEFAN WACKERHAGEN

Skagway

this now-defunct **fraternal hall**, which is home to the Skagway Convention & Visitors Bureau.

ACTIVITIES
HIKING
The 33-mile Chilkoot Trail is Southeast Alaska's most popular hike, but other good trails surround Skagway. There is no USFS office in Skagway, but the NPS Visitor Center has a free brochure entitled *Skagway Trail Map*. You can also find backcountry information and any outdoor gear you may need (including rentals) at the excellent **Mountain Shop** (☎ 983-2544; www.packerexpeditions.com; 355 4th Ave).

DEWEY LAKES TRAIL SYSTEM
This series of trails leads east out of Skagway to a handful of picturesque alpine and subalpine lakes, waterfalls and historic sites. From Broadway, follow 3rd Ave southeast to the railroad tracks. On the east side of the tracks you'll find the trailheads to Lower Dewey Lake

(0.7 miles), Icy Lake (2.5 miles), Upper Reid Falls (3.5 miles) and Sturgill's Landing (4.5 miles).

YAKUTANIA POINT & AB MOUNTAIN TRAILS
The Skagway River footbridge, reached by following 1st Ave west around the airport runway, leads to two trails of opposite caliber. For an easy hike to escape the cruise-ship crowds turn left from the bridge and follow the mile-long trail to picnic areas and lovely views at Yakutania Point and Smugglers Cove.

Nearby on Dyea Rd is AB Mountain Trail, also known as the Skyline Trail. This route ascends 5.5 miles to the 5100ft summit of AB Mountain, named for the 'AB' that appears on its south side when the snow melts every spring.

RAFTING
Skagway Float Tours (☎ 983-3688; www.skagwayfloat.com) offers a three-hour tour of Dyea that includes a 45-minute float down the placid Taiya River (adult/child

$75/55). Its Hike & Float Tour ($85/65) is a four-hour outing that includes hiking 1.8 miles of the Chilkoot Trail then some floating back.

TOURS

SUMMIT & CITY TOUR

This is the standard tour in Skagway and includes Gold Rush Cemetery, White Pass Summit and Skagway Overlook, including a lively narration that might be historically accurate.

Frontier Excursions (☎ 983-2512, 877-983-2512; www.frontierexcursions.com)

Skagway Tour Co (☎ 983-2168, 866-983-2168; www.skagwaytourco.com)

our pick **Southeast Tours** (☎ 983-2990; www.southeasttours.com; 2990 French Alley)

OTHER TOURS

A couple of cruise tourist-oriented attractions are located a short way out the Klondike Hwy.

Red Onion Saloon (☎ 983-2222; cnr Broadway St & 2nd Ave) Skagway's beloved saloon was once a house of sin, the reason for its tours of the upstairs bedrooms, now a brothel museum.

Klondike Gold Dredge Tours (☎ 983-3175, 877-983-3175; www.klondikegolddredge.com; Mile 1.7 Klondike Hwy; adult/child $45/35) Runs two-hour tours of a former working gold dredge that was in Dawson before being moved to Skagway where it has hit the mother lode. Tours include trying your hand at gold panning.

SLEEPING

MIDRANGE

our pick **Sergeant Preston's Lodge** (☎ 983-2521, 866-983-2521; www.sgt-prestonslodgeskagway.com; 370 6th Ave; s $75-110, d $90-120; ⊠ 💻) Recently updated, this motel is the best bargain in Skagway. All 38 rooms are modern, clean and equipped with TVs, small refrigerators, microwaves and private bath. Other amenities include free internet access, courtesy transportation and very accommodating proprietors.

Skagway Bungalows (☎ 983-2986; www.aptalaska.net/~saldi; Mile 1 Dyea Rd; cabin $125, $99 for 3 nights or longer) These two classic log cabins are situated among the trees on top of rock outcroppings as if Frank Lloyd Wright was here for the summer. Each cabin has a bath, a kitchenette and a small covered deck with a view of Reid Falls across the Skagway River.

Skagway Inn (☎ 983-2289, 888-752-4929; www.skagwayinn.com; Broadway St at 7th Ave; r $119-189; ⊠ 💻) In a restored 1897 Victorian that was originally one of the town's brothels – what building still standing in Skagway wasn't? – the inn is downtown and features 10 rooms with or without baths. All are small but filled with antique dressers, iron beds and chests, and a full breakfast is included.

TOP END

At the White House (☎ 983-9000; www.atthewhitehouse.com; 475 8th Ave at Main St; r $120-160; ⊠ 💻) A very comfortable 10-room inn filled with antiques, remembrances of the Klondike and colorful comforters on every bed. Rooms are spacious and bright even on a rainy day and feature private bath, cable TV and phone. In the morning you wake up to a breakfast of fresh-baked goods and fruit served in a sun-drenched dining room.

EATING

RESTAURANTS

our pick **Starfire** (☎ 983-3663; 4th Ave at Spring St; lunch $12-15, dinner $14-19; 🕑 11am-10pm Mon-Fri, 4-10pm Sat & Sun; ⊠) Skagway's restaurants are among the best in the Southeast, so why wouldn't its Thai be authentic and good? Order pad thai or spicy

STEFAN WACKERHAGEN / IMAGEBROKER

White Pass & Yukon Route Railroad

⬊ WHITE PASS & YUKON ROUTE RAILROAD

Without a doubt the most spectacular tour from Skagway is a ride aboard the historic railway of the White Pass & Yukon Route. Two different narrated sight-seeing tours are available; reservations are required for both.

The premier trip is the Yukon Adventure (8½ hours, 135 miles round-trip). At Skagway's railroad depot you board parlor cars for the trip to White Pass on the narrow-gauge line built during the 1898 Klondike Gold Rush. This segment is only a small portion of the 110-mile route to Whitehorse, but it contains the most spectacular scenery, including crossing Glacier Gorge and Dead Horse Gulch, viewing Bridal Veil Falls and then making the steep 2885ft climb to White Pass, only 20 miles from Skagway. You make a whistle stop at the historic 1903 Lake Bennett Railroad Depot for lunch and then board the train to follow the shoreline of stunning Lake Bennett to Carcross. At this small Yukon town, buses take you back to Skagway. The Yukon Adventure departs from Skagway Sunday through Friday and the fare is $229/115 per adult/child. Note that Lake Bennett is across the border in British Columbia, Canada, so passengers will need to carry passports or other proof of citizenship.

Things you need to know: ☎ 983-2217, 800-343-7373; www.whitepassrailroad.com; depot on 2nd Ave

drunken noodle and enjoy it with a beer on the outdoor patio, so pleasant and secluded you would never know Skagway's largest hotel is across the street.

Poppies (☎ 983-2012; Klondike Hwy; dinner $15-23; ◔ 5:30-9:30pm Thu-Sun; ✗) Located within Jewell Gardens, this restaurant has the best salads in town because

the greens are grown just outside and probably picked that afternoon. Mains range from boneless Colorado lamb leg to marinated chicken breast stuffed with sun-dried tomatoes, pine nuts and feta cheese.

Stowaway Café (☎ 983-3463; 205 Congress Way; dinner $18-27; ◔ 4-10pm; ✗) Just past the harbormaster's office, this place is fun, funky and fantastic. Outside, is a beautiful mermaid and the restaurant's artfully cluttered front and back yards. The small cafe has a handful of tables, a view of the boat harbor, and excellent fish and Cajun-style steak dinners. Skagway's best dish is Stowaway's wasabi salmon.

DRINKING & ENTERTAINMENT

Red Onion Saloon (☎ 983-2200; Broadway St at 2nd Ave) Skagway's beloved brothel at the turn of the century is now its most famous saloon. The 'RO' is done up as a gold-rush saloon, complete with mannequins leering down at you from the 2nd story to depict pioneer-era working girls. When bands are playing here, it'll be packed, noisy and rowdy.

Skagway Brewing Co (☎ 983-2739; Broadway St at 7th Ave) Skagway's microbrew offers you Klondike Gold (a wheat ale) and Chilkoot Trail IPA among others. In the fine spirit of Juneau's Red Dog Saloon there's a Brewpub Gift Shop next door.

ourpick **Days of '98 Show** (☎ 983-2545; Eagle's Hall; 598 Broadway at 6th Ave; adult/child $18/9) Southeast Alaska's best and longest-running melodrama. The evening show begins with 'mock gambling,' moves onto Robert Service poetry and then climaxes with an entertaining show covering the town's gold-rush days and focusing on Soapy and his gang.

GETTING THERE & AWAY
AIR
Regularly scheduled flights from Skagway to Juneau, Haines and Glacier Bay are available from **Wings of Alaska** (☎ 983-2442; www.wingsofalaska.com). Expect to pay $120 to $130 one way to Juneau, $65 to Haines and $205 to Gustavus.

BOAT
There is a daily run of the **Alaska Marine Highway** (☎ 983-2229, 800-642-0066; www.ferryalaska.com) from Skagway to Haines ($31, one hour) and Juneau ($50, 6½ hours) and back again. In Skagway, the

CHRISTIAN HANDL / IMAGEBROKER

Red Onion Saloon

Skagway

IMAGEBROKER/CHRISTIAN HANDL

ferry departs from the terminal and dock at the southwest end of Broadway St.

Haines-Skagway Fast Ferry (☎ 888-766-2103; www.hainesskagwayfastferry.com) provides speedy transport on a catamaran to Haines. The boat departs from the Skagway small boat harbor at 8am, noon and 6pm Monday through Thursday in summer, with additional trips if needed by the cruise ships. The round-trip/one-way fare is $61/31.

BUS
Yukon-Alaska Tourist Tours (☎ 866-626-7383, Whitehorse 867-668-5944; www.yukonalaskatouristtours.com) offers a minibus service three times daily to Whitehorse, departing the train depot in Skagway at 8:45pm, 1:30pm and 3pm. One way is $55 for the first two runs and $40 for the 3pm departure.

Alaska Direct Bus Line (☎ 800-770-6652, Whitehorse 867-668-4833; www.alaskadirectbusline.com) runs a bus on Sunday, Wednesday and Friday from Whitehorse for either Anchorage ($220) or Fairbanks ($190).

GETTING AROUND
BUS
From May 1 to September 30, the city runs the SMART bus on two different routes. The regular route ($1.50) runs from the docks up to 8th Ave; the long route ($2.50) runs from 8th Ave to Jewell Gardens. Buses run whenever there are cruise ships in town, which in Skagway is almost always.

RICHARD CUMMINS

Sailing through Glacier Bay National Park & Preserve (p125)

PRINCE WILLIAM SOUND

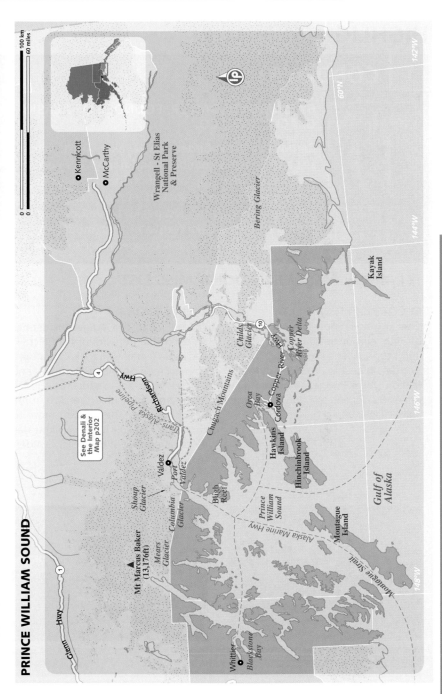

See Denali & the Interior Map p202

PRINCE WILLIAM SOUND

HIGHLIGHTS

HIGHLIGHTS

1 CORDOVA

BY LAUREN PADAWER, FOUNDER OF ALASKA GLACIAL MUD CO.

Cordova calls the birder, sea kayaker, artist, deep-sea and fly fisher, biologist and hunter. It's nestled within a slender strip of mountainous rainforest and wetlands, and is cloaked with glaciers, rivers and snow-capped rugged peaks. I love Cordova's fishing culture, Alaska Native history, mountain springwater, clean air and Copper River salmon.

↘ LAUREN PADAWER'S DON'T MISS LIST

❶ COPPER RIVER DELTA

Check out salmon-fishing, hiking, birding, glacier-trekking, river rafting and berry-picking. You can drive the Copper River Hwy (p155) out to the Million Dollar Bridge, and camp near Childs Glacier and just downriver from Miles Glacier.

❷ DAY HIKING

The USFS Cordova Ranger District has an extensive network of hiking trails and cabin rentals – Mt Eyak/Crater Lake, Power Creek, Sheridan Mountain and Glacier, Haystack, Saddlebag, Heney Ridge and Eyak River are just some of my favorites, but there's more to choose from. Make it an overnight stay by booking one of the USFS's wilderness cabins.

Clockwise from top right: A family views Childs Glacier (p155); Worker at salmon cannery; Chugach Mountains, Copper River Delta (p155)

❸ EATING FRESH SEAFOOD

I love the fish tacos at **Baja Taco** (p154). Fresh Windy Bay oysters are available throughout the summer at the **Alaskan Hotel & Bar** (p154), while the **Reluctant Fisherman** (p154) has a five-star menu and an outstanding view.

❹ ICEWORM FESTIVAL

Cordovans know how to celebrate the end of winter and keep attitudes bright. This quirky winter **festival** (p46) has it all, from survival suit races to an oyster-shucking competition to a varied and impressive downtown parade. You can catch it mid-February.

❺ GLACIER GAWK

Don't miss **Childs Glacier** (p155) at the end of the Copper River Hwy, a truly unique glacier that calves into a river and can be viewed from the opposite shore like an ampitheater. Sheridan Glacier is highly accessible for hiking, but do so with caution.

⬐ THINGS YOU NEED TO KNOW

Transport Tip If you want to explore the Copper River Delta, it's best to rent a car in Cordova. Driving onto the ferry is expensive, so you'll save money by walking or biking onto the boat. **For full details on Cordova, see p152**

HIGHLIGHTS

2

⬆ RIDE THE ALASKA FERRY

Taking the Alaska Marine Highway is the most scenic and least expensive way to travel around Prince William Sound. There's a palpable feeling of community on the boat ride, where locals catch up with each other and exchange gossip. You'll also have a good chance of spotting Dall porpoises, whales, and eagles through the large windows.

3

⬆ TAKE IN THE GLACIERS

Some of Alaska's most accessible and scenic glaciers lie in this region. Outside Valdez, Columbia Glacier (p150) has been releasing chunks over a mile long since 2007, while along the Copper River Hwy you can see a number of stunning rivers of ice. Childs Glacier (p155) gets the most attention for its loud calving and its just-across-the-river location.

4

⬨ EXPERIENCE SMALL TOWN LIVING

Prince William Sound is home to three small towns separated from the rest of Alaska by water, mountains, or long, winding roads. The tiniest, Whittier (p156), houses almost all of its 159 residents under one roof in the cinder-block Begich Towers (p157). Sample life in the community with a night at June's B&B (p158).

5

⬨ SPIN DOWN THE HIGHWAY

The magnificent Copper River Hwy (p155) runs 50 miles outside of Cordova, ending at the Million Dollar Bridge. You can make the drive out (and back) in a lovely day-trip, with stops for bird-watching, hiking, cycling or fishing, or raft one of the many glacial rivers with Alaska River Rafters (p153).

6

⬨ TAKE OUT A KAYAK

Prince William Sound is encircled by glacier-carved fjords, quiet inlets and forest-clad islands. Remote yet accessible, the Sound is an (albeit drizzly) Eden for paddlers. Hook up with an outfitter to take you outside Whittier (p156) to Blackstone Bay or College Fjord, or to Shoup Bay (p150) in Valdez. In Cordova, Orca Inlet (p149) is the place to float your boat.

2 Experiencing the Alaska Marine Highway; **3** Columbia Glacier (p150); **4** Whittier (p156); **5** Copper River Highway (p155); **6** Kayaking, near Columbia Glacier (p150)

PRINCE WILLIAM SOUND

BEST...

BEST...

↘ BIG GLACIERS

- **Childs** (p155) A Cordova favorite that makes waves by calving into a river.
- **Miles** Just across from Childs, massive Miles has been in retreat for years.
- **Columbia** (p150) Outside Valdez, stunning Columbia Glacier releases chunks of ice up to a kilometer wide.

↘ KAYAKING BAYS

- **Shoup Bay** (p150) A protected state marine park outside of Valdez.
- **Orca Inlet** (p149) Paddle to this pristine bay near Cordova.
- **Blackstone Bay** (p157) With two major glaciers, this trip from Whittier is worth the water-taxi ride.

↘ DAY HIKES

- **Portage Pass Trail** (p157) Hike from downtown Whittier up this gentle trail for views of Portage Glacier.
- **Heney Ridge Trail** (p152) A Cordova favorite, this trail follows a bay and then climbs above tree line for spectacular views.
- **Goat Trail** (p150) The oldest path in Valdez, this trail was originally an Alaska Native trade route.

↘ PLACES TO SLEEP

- **Brookside Inn B&B** (p151) A historic home that's been moved three times across Valdez.
- **Northern Nights Inn** (p153) This Cordova house is painted the historic Kennecott Red.
- **June's B&B** (p158) Experience local life in Whittier's Begich Towers.

From left: Childs Glacier (p155); Kayaking, Prince William Sound

THINGS YOU NEED TO KNOW

⬆ VITAL STATISTICS

- **Population** 6800
- **Best time to visit** April through September

⬆ LOCALITIES IN A NUTSHELL

- **Valdez** (p148) The end of the pipeline and a popular winter destination.
- **Cordova** (p152) Charming fishing village backed by North America's largest continuous wetland.
- **Whittier** (p156) A WWII-era town, where almost everyone lives under the one roof.

⬆ ADVANCE PLANNING

- **Two months ahead** Book your accommodation.
- **One month ahead** Buy your ferry tickets.
- **One week ahead** Purchase binoculars.

⬆ RESOURCES

- **Valdez Visitor Information Center** (Map p149; ☎ 835-2984; www.valdezalaska.com; 200 Fairbanks Dr; ☺ 8am-7pm Mon-Sat, noon-7pm Sun) Has free maps and a courtesy phone for booking accommodations.

- **Crooked Creek Information Site** (Map p149; ☎ 835-4680; Mile 0.9 Richardson Hwy, Valdez) Staffed by US Forest Service (USFS) naturalists who offer great advice about outdoorsy activities.
- **USFS Visitor Center** (Map p153; ☎ 424-7661; 612 2nd St, Cordova; ☺ 8am-5pm Mon-Fri) This excellent office has the latest on trails, campsites and wildlife in the Copper River Delta.

⬆ GETTING AROUND

- **Air** Flights service both Cordova and Valdez.
- **Car** A rental car is your best bet if you want to explore Cordova's Copper River Hwy; Valdez and Whittier are on the road systems.
- **Ferry** The Alaska Marine Highway Ferry stops in all three towns and is the best form of transport.

⬆ BE FOREWARNED

- **Calving glaciers** Use caution in a kayak; underwater bergs have been known to suddenly pop up.
- **Bears** Prince William Sound has 'em; put on your bear bells!
- **Hypothermia** Make sure you're prepared for cold water temps when you're out on a boat.

PRINCE WILLIAM SOUND

THINGS YOU NEED TO KNOW

PRINCE WILLIAM SOUND ITINERARIES

CORDOVA Three Days

If you have three days to spend in Prince William Sound, you should spend them around **(1) Cordova** (p152). This down-to-earth place offers small-town charm and superb outdoor activities. Lay your head at the one of the historical homes that has turned into a B&B; many of these homes have views of the Sound. Spend a day wandering the small-boat harbor and taking in a couple of museums that explore the effects of the *Exxon Valdez* oil spill (p150). The next day, drive along the Copper River Hwy and stop to bird-watch and photo-op along the **(2) Copper River Delta** (p155). You'll reach the end of the drivable road at **(3) Childs Glacier** (p155) where you can spend an afternoon watching the active glacier calve into the river. Spend your third day rafting or glacier trekking with one of Cordova's tour companies out on the Delta.

CITY HIGHLIGHTS Five Days

With five days you can visit all three of Prince William Sound's towns, all of which are blessed with magnificent scenery and its own distinct personality. First, approach **(1) Whittier** (p156) through the Anton Anderson Memorial Tunnel, which, at 2.5 miles, is the longest highway tunnel in North America. This dark approach is appropriate for the WWII-created town, which is tucked in a fjord that is almost always shrouded in clouds. Once there, explore the **(2) Begich Towers** (p157), the cinder-block building where most residents live, or hike Portage Pass.

From Whittier you'll take the Alaska Marine Highway Ferry over to **(3) Cordova** (p152), a scenic ride where you'll likely see porpoises or whales. Spend a couple of days hiking, rafting and birding in this outdoorsy town.

Board the ferry again, and set sail for **(4) Valdez** (p148). The Trans-Alaska Pipeline's terminus is here, and Valdez is definitely an oil town. However, the North Slope isn't the only influence in town: Mama Nature's slopes dominate as well. Take a day to enjoy the excellent hiking out the Richardson Hwy, and wander the city's small-boat harbor.

PADDLING AROUND THE SOUND One Week

With a week you'll be able to spend time kayaking the magnificent bays near Prince William Sound's communities. Begin in Valdez, with a water-taxi drop-off near the superactive **(1) Columbia Glacier** (p150). A package tour is a good way to explore the dramatic bays; several companies in town offer multiday trips in the area.

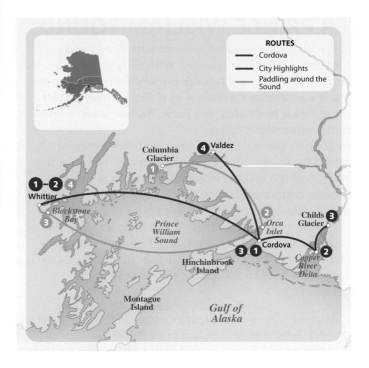

From Valdez, head south to Cordova's (2) Orca Inlet (p149). This pristine body of water is north of town and a favorite local's spot. After tooling around Cordova's mellow waters, head over to Whittier's (3) Blackstone Bay (p157), where you can spend days exploring tidewater glaciers and a kittiwake rookery. The excellent (4) Prince William Sound Kayak Center (p157) will rent you boats or take you out for daylong trips. If a multiday camping trip isn't your thing, spend your nights in town inside the Begich Towers, where you can get a taste of local Whittier life. And if your arms are tired from all that paddling, consider a glacier tour from Whittier – you'll have the chance to spot more than two dozen glaciers.

DISCOVER PRINCE WILLIAM SOUND

Enclosed in a jagged-edged circle and infused with fjords and glaciers, Prince William Sound is a stunner. With only three cities, the 15,000 sq mile region is mostly wilderness packed with quiet coves and rainy islands. It's a paddler's dream – as if the scenery wasn't enough, Ma Nature threw in whales, sea lions, harbor seals, eagles, Dall sheep, mountain goats and bears.

Prince William Sound's three cities couldn't be more different. Valdez is dominated by slopes, including near-vertical crags, luring outdoor extremists, and the distant North Slope, from which the Trans-Alaska Pipeline originates. Earthy Cordova is defiant in its refusal to sell out. Isolated from roads, cruise ships and oil money, Cordovans are doing just fine. In contrast, Whittier is a living relic of WWII: a small town created solely as a military hideout. Practically overshadowed by the mountains that kept it safe during the war, Whittier is accessible by ferry or by a 2.5-mile tunnel.

VALDEZ

pop 4498

Despite its natural attractions, Valdez is not primarily a tourist mecca. Nor, despite its proximity to the Sound, is it mainly a fishing village. On August 1, 1977, when the first tanker of oil issued forth from the Trans-Alaska Pipeline Terminal across the bay, Valdez became an oil town.

Valdez is still one of Alaska's prettiest spots, with glaciers galore, wildlife running amok and a Norman Rockwell–style harbor cradled by some of the highest coastal mountains (topping 7000ft) in the world.

SIGHTS

VALDEZ MUSEUM

This fairly gargantuan museum (☎ 835-2764; www.valdezmuseum.org; 217 Egan Dr; adult/child $7/free; ☼ 9am-5pm) includes an ornate, steam-powered antique fire engine, a 19th-century saloon bar and the ceremonial first barrel of oil to flow from the Trans-Alaska Pipeline.

'REMEMBERING OLD VALDEZ' ANNEX

Operated by the Valdez Museum, this annex (☎ 835-5407; 436 Hazelet Ave; admission free with Valdez Museum ticket; ☼ 9am-5pm) is dominated by a scale model of the Old Valdez township. Each home destroyed in the Good Friday earthquake has been restored in miniature, with the family's name in front. Other exhibits on the earthquake and subsequent tsunamis and fires are moving, but none are as heartwrenching as the recordings of ham-radio operators communicating across the Sound as the quake wore on.

MAXINE & JESSE WHITNEY MUSEUM

This high-quality museum (☎ 834-1690; 303 Lowe St; admission free; ☼ 9am-7pm) has a brand-new home at the Prince William Sound Community College. The center is devoted to Alaska Native culture and Alaskan wildlife, and features ivory and baleen artwork, moose-antler furniture, and natural-history displays, including some very creative taxidermy.

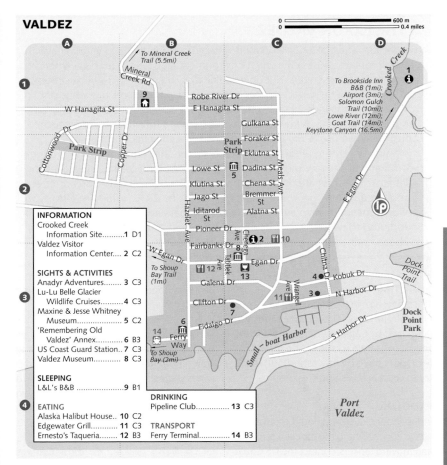

VALDEZ

PRINCE WILLIAM SOUND

VALDEZ

INFORMATION
Crooked Creek
  Information Site..........**1** D1
Valdez Visitor
  Information Center.... **2** C2

SIGHTS & ACTIVITIES
Anadyr Adventures........ **3** C3
Lu-Lu Belle Glacier
  Wildlife Cruises..........**4** C3
Maxine & Jesse Whitney
  Museum.................... **5** C2
'Remembering Old
  Valdez' Annex............ **6** B3
US Coast Guard Station.. **7** C3
Valdez Museum............ **8** C3

SLEEPING
L&L's B&B **9** B1

EATING
Alaska Halibut House.. **10** C2
Edgewater Grill............ **11** C3
Ernesto's Taqueria........ **12** B3

DRINKING
Pipeline Club.............. **13** C3

TRANSPORT
Ferry Terminal.............. **14** B3

ORCA INLET

Easily accessed from town, **Orca Inlet** is a popular kayaking destination because of its pristine and smooth waters. A number of kayaking companies guide trips to the inlet.

ACTIVITIES
HIKING
DOCK POINT TRAIL

Not so much a hike as an enjoyable stroll through Dock Point Park beside the small-boat harbor, this 1-mile loop offers views of the peaks and the port, proximity to eagle nests, as well as salmonberry and blueberry picking.

SHOUP BAY TRAIL

This verdant stunner has views of Port Valdez, Shoup Glacier and the impressive Gold Creek delta.

SOLOMON GULCH TRAIL

A mile past the Solomon Gulch Fish Hatchery on Dayville Rd, this 1.7-mile trail is a steep uphill hike that quickly leads to splendid views of Port Valdez and the city below.

⬅ THE EXXON VALDEZ

Two decades after the *Exxon Valdez* left Valdez' Trans-Alaska Pipeline Terminal with a tippled captain, causing the worst environmental disaster in modern American history, the damage lingers. Not only can oil from the 1989 spill still be collected from just beneath the surface of beaches throughout the Sound, but, while certain fisheries have rebounded, herring stocks haven't recovered at all. The Dungeness crab population remains low and many pink-salmon runs have been eliminated. Loons, harlequin ducks, otters and seals still suffer the effects of the spill.

Thankfully, other legacies of the disaster are more inspiring. Long-recommended security measures have finally been enacted at oil-processing facilities across the nation. Double-hulled tankers, once a pipe dream of environmentalists, will be a pipeline requirement by 2015; some are already in service. Tugs must once again escort tankers passing through Prince William Sound. And the *Exxon Valdez* itself, now renamed the *SeaRiver Mediterranean*, has been banned from ever returning to Valdez.

GOAT TRAIL

The oldest hike in the area is the Goat Trail, originally an Alaska Native trade route and later used by Captain Abercrombie in his search for safe passage to the Interior. A few spots have been washed out; don't try to cross any rushing streams.

PADDLING

Independent kayakers should be aware of no-go zones around the pipeline terminal and moving tankers; contact the **US Coast Guard** (☎ 835-7222; 105 Clifton Dr) for current regulations.

our pick **Anadyr Adventures** (☎ 835-2814, 800-865-2925; www.anadyradventures.com; 225 N Harbor Dr) rents kayaks to (very) experienced paddlers (single/double $45/65, discounts for multiple days) and offers guided trips, ranging from a day at Columbia Glacier ($199) to a week on the water aboard the 'mothership' (from $2700).

SHOUP BAY

Protected as a state marine park, this bay off Valdez Arm makes for a great over-night kayaking trip. You must enter the bay two hours before the incoming tide to avoid swift tidal currents.

COLUMBIA GLACIER

A mile wide and rising 300ft from the waterline at its face, this is the largest tidewater glacier in Prince William Sound, and a spectacular spot to spend a few days kayaking and watching seals and other wildlife.

TOURS

Lu-Lu Belle Glacier Wildlife Cruises (☎ 835-5141, 800-411-0090; www.lulubelletours.com; Kobuk Dr) The dainty and ornately appointed MV *Lu-Lu Belle* is all polished wood, leather and oriental rugs. Cruise into Columbia Bay where, unless winds have cleared away the ice, wildlife is more the attraction than glacier-calving.

SLEEPING

L&L's B&B (☎ 835-4447; www.lnlalaska.com; 533 W Hanagita St; r without bath $75-85; ☒ ☐) Located in a big, airy suburban home, this B&B has two bicycles at your disposal.

our pick **Brookside Inn B&B** (☎ 835-9130, 866-316-9130; www.brooksideinnbb.com;

1465 Richardson Hwy; r $125, ste $160; )
This 100-year-old home originated in Ft
Liscum, was moved to Old Valdez, and
then to its present location after the earthquake. Original floors and arched windows
create cozy ambience, and the homemade
breakfast is served on a large sunporch.

EATING

Edgewater Grille (☎ 835-3212; 107 N Harbor
Dr; breakfast $6-17, lunch & dinner $9-30; ⏱ 6am-
10pm, bar to 11pm) While this joint grills
burgers and serves them up on homemade buns, the more creative dishes –
we like the blackened salmon fajita – are
quite tasty, too.

Alaska Halibut House (☎ 835-2788;
208 Meals Ave; fish $4-10; ⏱ 11am-9pm Mon-Sat,
to 8pm Sun) Frying up fresh local fish, this
place is what every fast-food joint should
be. The halibut basket is delish.

ourpick Ernesto's Taqueria (☎ 835-2519;
328 Egan Dr; meals $7-9; ⏱ 5:30-9:30pm) This
place serves large portions of serviceable
Mexican food on the cheap, and also has
a cold selection of Mexican beer.

DRINKING & ENTERTAINMENT

Pipeline Club (☎ 835-2788; 112 Egan Dr) If
you've ever hugged a tree, this crowd may
not be for you. This smoky lounge is the
watering hole where Captain Hazelwood
had his famous scotch-on-the-rocks before
running the *Exxon Valdez* aground.

GETTING THERE & AROUND
AIR
There are flight services with **ERA
Aviation** (☎ 835-2636, 800-843-1947; www.
flyera.com) three times daily between
Anchorage and Valdez.

BICYCLE
Bikes can be rented through **Anadyr
Adventures** (☎ 835-2814, 800-865-2925; www.
anadyradventures.com; 225 N Harbor Dr; per half/
full day $15/25).

BOAT
Within Prince William Sound, the **Alaska
Marine Highway Ferry** (☎ 835-4436, 800-
642-0066; www.ferryalaska.com) provides daily
services from Valdez to Cordova ($50) and
Whittier ($89).

PRINCE WILLIAM SOUND

VALDEZ

Kayaking, Valdez (p150)

MICHAEL DEYOUNG / ALASKASTOCK.COM

CORDOVA

pop 2126

Cut off from Alaska's road system (for now), Cordova is slightly inconvenient and somewhat expensive to get to. That's all the more reason to visit.

Visitors will also be enthralled by what lies beyond the town limits. Just outside the city along the Copper River Hwy is one of the largest wetlands in Alaska, with more than 40 miles of trails threading through spectacular glaciers, alpine meadows and the remarkable Copper River Delta.

SIGHTS

CORDOVA MUSEUM

Adjacent to the Cordova Library, this museum (622 1st St; admission by donation; 10am-6pm Mon-Fri, to 5pm Sat, 2-4pm Sun) is a small, grassroots collection worth seeing. Displays cover local marine life, relics from the town's early history – including a captivating lighthouse lens – and a three-seater *bidarka* (kayak) made from spruce pine and 12 sealskins.

ILANKA CULTURAL CENTER

This excellent museum (☎ 424-7903; 110 Nicholoff Way; admission free; 10am-5pm Mon-Fri), operated by local Alaska Natives, has a small but high-quality collection of Alaska Native art from all over the state. Don't miss the intact killer-whale skeleton – one of only five in the world – with flippers that could give you quite a slap. Also on display is artist Mike Webber's *Shame Pole*, a totem pole that tells the grim tale of the oil spill, spitting back Exxon's then-top official Don Cornett's famous words, 'We will make you whole again.'

SMALL-BOAT HARBOR

Unsurprisingly, the harbor is the community's heart, humming throughout the season as fishers frantically try to meet their quota before the runs are closed. The fishing fleet is composed primarily of seiners and gillnetters, with the method used by the fishers determining the species of salmon they pursue.

ACTIVITIES
HIKING
HENEY RIDGE TRAIL

Cordova's most popular trail – as it's accessible without a car – is this scenic, fairly easy 3.7-mile route beginning at Mile 5.1 of Whitshed Rd. The first stretch winds around Hartney Bay, followed by a mellow 2-mile climb through forests and wildflowers (and, in rainy weather, lots of mud – rubber boots are recommended) to the treeline. It's another steep mile up to the ridge, where you'll enjoy a gorgeous view.

CRATER LAKE & POWER CREEK TRAILS

The 2.4-mile Crater Lake Trail begins on Eyak Lake, about half a mile beyond the municipal airport, across from Skater's Cabin. The trail ascends steeply but is easy to follow as it winds through lush forest.

BIRDING

The Copper River Delta and the rich waters of Prince William Sound attract an astonishing number and variety of birds. Spring migration is the busiest, and that is when the town hosts the Copper River Delta Shorebird Festival (p46). Stop at the USFS Visitor Center (☎ 424-7661; 612 2nd St; 8am-5pm Mon-Fri) for a birding checklist and advice about where to break out the binoculars.

PADDLING

Alaska River Rafters (☎ 424-7238, 800-776-1864; www.alaskarafters.com; Mile 13 Copper River Hwy) operates rafting trips at Sheridan

PRINCE WILLIAM SOUND

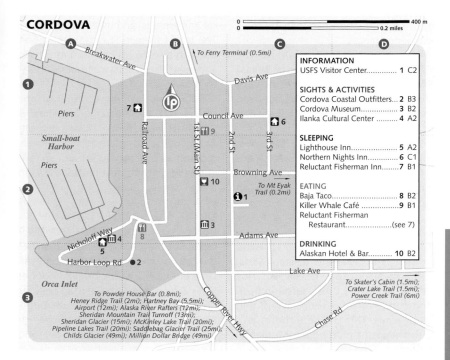

CORDOVA

0 — 400 m
0 — 0.2 miles

INFORMATION	
USFS Visitor Center	1 C2
SIGHTS & ACTIVITIES	
Cordova Coastal Outfitters	2 B3
Cordova Museum	3 B2
Ilanka Cultural Center	4 A2
SLEEPING	
Lighthouse Inn	5 A2
Northern Nights Inn	6 C1
Reluctant Fisherman Inn	7 B1
EATING	
Baja Taco	8 B2
Killer Whale Café	9 B1
Reluctant Fisherman Restaurant	(see 7)
DRINKING	
Alaskan Hotel & Bar	10 B2

CORDOVA

Glacier, on the Copper River and elsewhere in the area; guided half-day trips start from $95/75 per adult/child, ranging up to $1275/675 per adult/child for a six-day multisport adventure including rafting, kayaking and hiking.

If the ocean is more your speed, **Cordova Coastal Outfitters** (☎ 424-7424, 800-357-5145; www.cdvcoastal.com; Harbor Loop Rd; kayaks per day single/double $45/65), located in a cabin just behind the AC Value Center, rents kayaks and arranges guided tours in placid, pristine Orca Inlet north of town.

TOURS
Guided daylong driving tours of the delta are conducted by **Alaska River Rafters** (☎ 424-7238, 800-776-1864; www.alaskarafters. com; Mile 13, Copper River Hwy). The trips run to Million Dollar Bridge and Childs Glacier,

and cost $85 per person with a six-person minimum. You can add a flightseeing excursion for another $100.

SLEEPING
BUDGET
Skater's Cabin (☎ 424-7282; cabin 1st/2nd/3rd night $25/35/50) On Eyak Lake with a nice gravel beach and a woodstove, this place can be booked through the Bidarki Recreation Center. The escalating prices are to deter multiday use so more people can enjoy it.

MIDRANGE & TOP END
our pick **Northern Nights Inn** (☎ 424-5356; www.northernnightsinn.com; cnr 3rd St & Council Ave; r from $85; ✕ 🖳) In a 100-year-old house painted Kennecott red, rooms range from basic to suites with kitchenettes. Some have peek-a-boo views of the

PRINCE WILLIAM SOUND

CORDOVA

bay, and all are furnished with antiques and period pieces.

Reluctant Fisherman Inn (☎ 424-3272; www.reluctantfisherman.com; cnr Railroad & Council Aves; r $135-185; ✕ 💻) As close to luxurious as Cordova gets, this place overhangs Orca Inlet and has a restaurant and lounge.

Lighthouse Inn (☎ 424-7080; www.cordovalighthouseinn.com; 203 Nicholoff Way; r $145; ✕ 💻) This inn has brilliant views of the small-boat harbor from its small, plush rooms, all with baths.

EATING

Killer Whale Café (☎ 424-7733; 1st St; breakfast $5-10, sandwiches & burgers $8-10; 🕑 6:30am-3pm Mon-Sat, to 1pm Sun) This cafe serves hearty breakfasts and fresh (sometimes organic) soups, wraps and sandwiches. This is where the town's lefties hang out, plotting environmental strategy.

Baja Taco (☎ 424-5599; Harbor Loop Rd; fast food $6-10; 🕑 8am-9pm) Graft a bus onto a cabin, add flowers, cattle skulls and nauti-cal implements, and what do you have? The best fish-taco stand north of San Diego. It also serves beer and espressos and great Mexican-flavored breakfasts – try the migas.

Reluctant Fisherman Restaurant (☎ 424-3272, 800-770-3272; cnr Railroad & Council Aves; meals $8-35; 🕑 11:30am-midnight) At lunchtime this place fills with locals digging into hearty all-American fare and taking in the best harbor views in town.

DRINKING & ENTERTAINMENT

Powder House Bar (☎ 424-3529; Mile 2 Copper River Hwy; dinner $8-20; 🕑 10am-late Mon-Sat, from noon Sun) Overlooking Eyak Lake on the site of the original Copper River & Northwestern Railroad powder house, this is a fun place with live music, excellent beer, soup and sandwiches for lunch, and quality steak and seafood dinners.

Alaskan Hotel & Bar (☎ 424-3299; 600 1st St) This raucous fishers' bar offers wine tastings from 5pm to 7pm on Wednesday.

IMAGEBROKER/BERND ZOLLER

Childs Glacier

↘ DETOUR: COPPER RIVER HIGHWAY

Constructed on the old railroad bed to the Kennecott mines, the highway was once destined to connect Cordova with Interior Alaska. Construction was interrupted after the 1964 Good Friday earthquake knocked out the fourth span of the Million Dollar Bridge. Today, the road is gravel past Mile 13, difficult to hitchhike, pricey to arrange transportation, but worth every hassle. Before departing, visit the USFS Visitor Center in Cordova, which has maps and info on roadside attractions.

Copper River Delta

The Copper River Hwy begins as 1st St downtown. Barely 5 miles on, the mountains take a dramatic step back and you emerge, miraculously, into the open-skied 700,000-acre Copper River Delta, a 60-mile arc formed by six glacier-fed river systems.

Millions of birds and waterfowl stop here during the spring and fall, including seven million western sandpipers and the entire population of West Coast dunlins. Other species include Arctic terns, dusty Canada geese, trumpeter swans, great blue herons and bald eagles. There's also a chance you'll spot moose, brown bears, beavers and porcupines.

The delta, which crosses Chugach National Forest, has numerous hiking trails and rafting opportunities.

Childs Glacier

A common malaise affecting tourists in Alaska could be called 'glacier fatigue.' But no matter how jaded you've become, Childs will blow your mind.

At the end of the Copper River Hwy, the 0.6-mile Copper River Trail takes you to the observation deck for Childs Glacier. It's probable, however, that you'll hear the glacier before you see it. A rarity in Alaska, Childs is advancing some 500ft a year, perpetually dumping bergs into Copper River. The thunderous calvings are particularly frequent in late spring and summer, when the water's high.

Million Dollar Bridge

Just beyond the recreation area is this four-span trestle, created during the winter of 1909-10 but put out of commission by the 1964 earthquake. In 2004, fearing the damaged fourth span would fall into the river, the state spent $18 million to return the bridge to a passable condition.

GETTING THERE & AROUND
AIR
ERA Aviation (☎ 800-866-8394; www.flyera.com) flies twice daily between Anchorage and Cordova's Merle K 'Mudhole' Smith Airport; an advance-purchase ticket is $166/332 one way/round-trip. Alaska Airlines (☎ 800-252-7522; www.alaskaair.com) comes here on a milk run from Anchorage to Yakutat and Juneau once per day.

BOAT
The Alaska Marine Highway Ferry (☎ 424-7333, 800-642-0066; www.ferryalaska.com) runs ferries daily to Valdez ($50, four hours) and Whittier ($89, 6½ hours).

JIM D. BARR / ALASKASTOCK.COM

Sheridan Glacier

⇘ IF YOU LIKE...

If you like driving the **Copper River Hwy** (p155), consider walking some of the hiking trails along the road to get you even closer to the scenery.

- **McKinley Lake & Pipeline Lakes Trails** The 2.5-mile McKinley Lake Trail begins at Mile 21.6 of the Copper River Hwy and leads to the head of the lake and the remains of the Lucky Strike gold mine. Departing from the midway point of the McKinley Lake Trail is the Pipeline Lakes Trail, which loops back to the Copper River Hwy at Mile 21.4.
- **Sheridan Mountain Trail** This trail starts near the picnic tables at the end of Sheridan Glacier Rd, which runs 4.3 miles from the turnoff at Mile 13 of Copper River Hwy. For the most part, the 2.9-mile route is a moderate climb, which passes through mature forests before breaking out into an alpine basin.
- **Saddlebag Glacier Trail** You reach this trail via a firewood-cutting road at Mile 25 of Copper River Hwy. It's an easy 3-mile walk through cottonwoods and spruce, emerging at Saddlebag Lake.

WHITTIER

pop 159

You can see glaciers and brown bears, even mountains taller than Denali, without ever once visiting Alaska. But you will never, in a lifetime of searching, find another place that quite compares to Whittier.

The army maintained Whittier until 1968, leaving behind not only the Buckner Building, now abandoned, but also the 14-story-tall Begich Towers, where, it seems, some 80% of Whittiots now reside. A labyrinth of underground tunnels connects the complex with schools and businesses, which certainly cuts down on snow-shoveling time.

The town's main attraction for travelers is its impossibly remote location, which provides access to an almost unspoiled wilderness of water, ice and granite.

SIGHTS

Whittier's dystopian townscape is perversely intriguing, and thus well worth a stroll. Start at **Begich Towers**, visible from anywhere in town, where the 1st, 14th and 15th floors are open to nonresidents.

The **Buckner Building** dominates the otherwise picture-postcard view. Once the largest structure in Alaska, the 'city under one roof' looms dismal and abandoned above town; the use of asbestos in the structure has complicated attempts to remodel or tear down the eerie edifice.

From here, walk along the **Shotgun Cove Trail** (right), which winds through blueberry and salmonberry thickets to First Salmon Run Picnic Area, and then head a quarter mile down the road to your right (northeast) to get to **Smitty's Cove**. At low tide you can comb the beach westward, following the water's edge past the ferry terminal to the Triangle.

This clutter of restaurants, tour outfits and quirkier-than-average gift shops is fun; don't miss **Log Cabin Gifts** (☎ 472-2501; The Triangle; ⏰ 11am-6pm), Whittier's best stab at adorable. The knickknacks, including lots of high-quality leatherwork, are handmade by owner Brenda Tolman, but the live reindeer outside are the real crowd pleasers.

Twenty miles outside Whittier is **Blackstone Bay fjord**, which thunders from calving glaciers. You can paddle from Whittier if you have time for a multiday trip, or have a water taxi drop you off. A guided tour is another option; see right.

ACTIVITIES
HIKING
PORTAGE PASS TRAIL

Whittier's sole USFS-maintained trail is a superb afternoon hike, providing good views of Portage Glacier, Passage Canal and the surrounding mountains and glaciers.

The Portage Pass Trail is along an old roadbed and is easy to follow. To reach it, head west of town toward the tunnel, then follow the signs leftward onto a road crossing the railroad tracks.

SHOTGUN COVE TRAIL

This 0.8-mile walk along a dirt road leads to the First Salmon Run Picnic Area, so named because of the king and silver salmon runs during June and late August. The forest and mountains en route are scenic but, in true Whittier fashion, the roadsides are debris-strewn and the picnic area is in disrepair.

PADDLING

Prince William Sound Kayak Center (☎ 472-2452, 877-472-2452; www.pwskayakcenter.com; Eastern Ave; ⏰ 7am-7pm) is a well-run organization that rents kayaks (single/double $50/80, discounted for multiple days) and runs guided tours, including three-hour paddles to the kittiwake rookery (per person $160) and daylong excursions to Blackstone Bay (for two people $425; hefty discount if you can get six folks together).

Alaska Sea Kayakers (☎ 472-2534, 877-472-2534; www.alaskaseakayakers.com; The Triangle; ⏰ 7am-7pm) rents kayaks ($40 to $75 per day), arranges water-taxis and takes various multiday tours to places like Harriman Fjord, Nellie Juan Glacier and Whale Bay. It has two booking offices (the second at Lot 11, Harbor View Rd) and both will set you up with whatever you need.

DIVING

Whittier is a top spot for (involuntary shiver) Alaskan scuba diving – it's one of the wildest places easily accessible to human beings. The best time to dive is March through June.

Lazy Otter Charters (☎ 694-6887, 800-587-6887; www.lazyotter.com; Harbor View Rd) can provide water-taxi service to the best underwater locations. It charges a minimum of $185 for the boat plus additional fees that are based on mileage.

TOURS

Major Marine Tours (☎ 800-764-7300, 274-7300; www.majormarine.com; Harbor Loop Rd) Has a USFS ranger on every cruise. It does a five-hour tour of glacier-riddled Blackstone Bay for $107/53 (plus tax) per adult/child.

Phillips Tours (☎ 472-2416, 800-544-0529; www.26glaciers.com; Harbor View Rd) Packs in 26 glaciers on a speedy boat ride for adult/child $139/79.

SLEEPING

June's B&B (☎ 472-6001; www.breadnbutter charters.com; Lot 7, Harbor View Rd; condos $145-450; ✕) This business offers an insight into the local lifestyle, putting you up in comfortable, homey suites atop Begich Towers.

Inn at Whittier (☎ 472-3200; www.innatwhittier.com; Harbor Loop Rd; r $169-299; ☐ ✕) Rooms are bland but the view isn't – make sure you spend the $20 extra for a water view. Rates are considerably less from mid-April to mid-May.

EATING

Tunnel's End Café & Espresso (☎ 472-3000; 12 Harbor Loop Rd; mains $4-13; ☽ 7:30am-7pm Wed-Sun, to 4pm Mon) Breakfast is nothing fancy, but it's cheap. For later, there are grilled salmon sandwiches and fried halibut.

Café Orca (☎ 472-2549; The Triangle; light meals $8-12; ☽ 11am-7pm) The vegetable sandwiches, lattes and homemade desserts here aren't cheap, but it's a restful place with a great little waterfront deck.

GETTING THERE & AROUND
BOAT
The **Alaska Marine Highway Ferry** (☎ 800-642-0066; www.ferryalaska.com) sails three times per week direct to Valdez ($89, 3½ to seven hours), and another three times per week direct to Cordova for the same price.

BUS
Magic Bus (☎ 230-6773; www.themagicbus. com) has a daily bus between Anchorage and Whittier (one way/round-trip $40/50, 1½ hours), which leaves Anchorage at 10:30am and departs Whittier for the return trip at 5:30pm. Note that if you're making an Alaska Ferry connection, the arrival time is too late for the 12:45pm ferry.

Whittier Shuttle (☎ 783-1900; www.whit tieralaskashuttle.com) coordinates with the cruise ships' schedules, running shuttles from Whittier to Anchorage at 10am and 3pm, with one trip from Anchorage at 12:25pm (adult/child one way $55/45).

CAR
Whittier Access Rd, also known as Portage Glacier Access Rd, leaves the Seward Hwy at Mile 79, continuing to Whittier through the claustrophobic Anton Anderson Memorial Tunnel, which at 2.7 miles long is the longest 'railroad-highway' tunnel in North America. Eastbound and westbound traffic alternate every 15 minutes, with interruptions for the Alaska Railroad.

TRAIN
The **Alaska Railroad** (☎ 265-2494, 800-544-0552; www.akrr.com) operates the *Glacier Discovery* train between Anchorage and Whittier (one way/round-trip $60/74, 2½ hours) daily from May through to September.

KENAI PENINSULA, KATMAI & KODIAK ISLAND

KENAI PENINSULA, KATMAI & KODIAK ISLAND

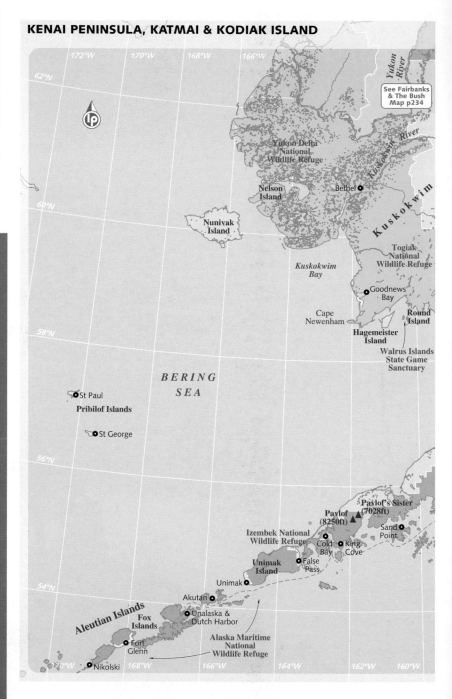

See Fairbanks
& The Bush
Map p234

Yukon River

Kuskokwim River

Yukon Delta National Wildlife Refuge

Nelson Island

Bethel

Kuskokwim

Nunivak Island

Togiak National Wildlife Refuge

Kuskokwim Bay

Goodnews Bay

Cape Newenham

Round Island

Hagemeister Island

Walrus Islands State Game Sanctuary

BERING SEA

St Paul

Pribilof Islands

St George

Pavlof's Sister (7028ft)

Pavlof (8250ft)

Sand Point

Izembek National Wildlife Refuge

Cold Bay

King Cove

Unimak Island

False Pass

Unimak

Akutan

Aleutian Islands

Fox Islands

Unalaska & Dutch Harbor

Fort Glenn

Alaska Maritime National Wildlife Refuge

Nikolski

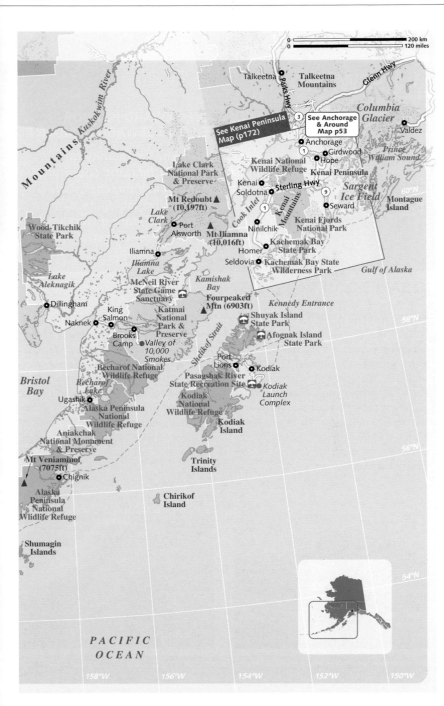

0   200 km
0   120 miles

Kuskokwim River

Mountains

Talkeetna

Parks Hwy

Talkeetna
Mountains

Glenn Hwy

Columbia
Glacier

Valdez

See Kenai Peninsula
Map (p172)

See Anchorage
& Around
Map p53

3

Anchorage

1

Girdwood
Hope

Prince
William Sound

Lake Clark
National Park
& Preserve

Kenai National
Wildlife Refuge

Kenai Peninsula

Kenai

Soldotna

Sterling Hwy

Sargent
Ice Field

Montague
Island

Mt Redoubt ▲
(10,197ft)

Lake
Clark

Port
Alsworth

Mt Iliamna ▲
(10,016ft)

Cook Inlet

1

Kenai
Mountains

9

Seward

Kenai Fjords
National Park

60°N

Iliamna

Iliamna
Lake

Ninilchik

Homer

Kachemak Bay
State Park

Seldovia

Kachemak Bay State
Wilderness Park

Gulf of Alaska

Wood-Tikchik
State Park

Lake
Aleknagik

Dillingham

MeNeil River
State Game
Sanctuary

Kamishak
Bay

Fourpeaked
Mtn (6903ft) ▲

Kennedy Entrance

58°N

King
Salmon

Naknek

Katmai
National
Park &
Preserve

Shuyak Island
State Park

Afognak Island
State Park

Brooks
Camp

Valley of
10,000
Smokes

Shelikof Strait

Port
Lions

Kodiak

Bristol
Bay

Becharof National
Wildlife Refuge

Becharof
Lake

Pasagshak River
State Recreation Site

Kodiak
Launch
Complex

Ugashik

Alaska Peninsula
National
Wildlife Refuge

Kodiak
National
Wildlife Refuge

Kodiak
Island

56°N

Aniakchak
National Monument
& Preserve

Trinity
Islands

Mt Veniaminof
(7075ft) ▲

Chignik

Alaska
Peninsula
National
Wildlife Refuge

Chirikof
Island

Shumagin
Islands

54°N

PACIFIC
OCEAN

158°W   156°W   154°W   152°W   150°W

HIGHLIGHTS

1 SEWARD

BY KARI ANDERSON, SEWARD HARBOR-MASTER AND LIFE-LONG SEWARD RESIDENT

Seward is a scenic maritime community on Resurrection Bay. There are fantastic opportunities to experience the marine environment: whale-watching, charter fishing, and sailing, to name a few. I grew up in Seward and started working on boats when I was 16. I've never missed a summer here, and I'm proud to call it home.

⬎ KARI'S DON'T MISS LIST

❶ KAYAKING A TIDEWATER GLACIER

Seward is known as the gateway to the **Kenai Fjords National Park** (p180). This national park is one of the few places in the world where you can get up close and personal with glaciers as they meet the ocean. The perspective from a kayak is unbeatable. The crackling berg bits, the seals swimming around you…I can only describe it as epic.

❷ ALASKA SEALIFE CENTER

The **SeaLife Center** (p176) is one of northern-most marine research facilities in the world, and has beautiful public exhibits. Meet the staff and listen to their stories of rehabilitating injured marine mammals and conducting scientific research. I recommend taking a behind-the-scenes tour to interact with seals, puffins or an octopus!

Clockwise from top left: Exit Glacier (p180); Kayaking, Resurrection Bay (p177); Boy meets sea lion, Alaska SeaLife Center (p176); Lost Lake (p175), Kenai Fjords National Park

CLOCKWISE FROM TOP: BRENT WINEBRENNER; EDDIE BRADY; DAVID TIPLING; GRANT DIXON

❸ SEWARD SMALL-BOAT HARBOR

An evening stroll near the **harbor** (p175) is one of my favorite activities when I have guests in town. Seward has a rich maritime history and there is a variety of vessels that have their home port in this scenic harbor. It's a great spot to take photos of fishers cleaning their catch, and playful otters swimming between the boats.

❹ EXIT GLACIER

There is something for everyone here; an accessible, paved trail leads up to the **glacier** (p180), while the more adventurous can hike up to the **Harding Ice Field** (p180). National Park Service interpreters will point out wildlife and tell you about the flora, fauna, and geology of this area. I like to bike out to the glacier, and stop off at a restaurant for a beer along the way.

❺ LOST LAKE TRAIL

This scenic **trail** (p175) is a local favorite, and is used year-round. You can hike the 16-mile traverse, or just up to the lake and back. The views above Seward are breathtaking, and there are great berries late in the summer.

↘ THINGS YOU NEED TO KNOW

Transport Tip Exit Glacier is the only road-accessible site in Kenai Fjords National Park; take Exit Glacier Guides' (p176) recycled-veggie-oil shuttle **Best photo op** Standing in front of the glacier, with a wall of ice as your backdrop **For full details on Kenai Fjords National Park, see p180**

HIGHLIGHTS

2

⬂ GET CLOSE TO GRIZZLIES

You can't rub noses with these guys, but you'll almost be close enough to. Brooks Camp in **Katmai National Park & Preserve** (p199) is *the* prime viewing spot for brown bears in Alaska. Three spots offer great views, but the best is at the falls, where bears stand on top of the water waiting to catch salmon jumping upstream. Polish your camera lens and wow everyone back home.

3

⬂ HIT THE TRAILS

The area is nothing if not rich with excellent hiking. North of Seward, the **Ptarmigan Lake Trail** (p178) is a rewarding 3.5-mile hike to an alpine lake, while down on Kodiak Island you can take a quick hike for spectacular views up **Barometer Mountain** (p195). Across from Homer in Kachemak Bay is the **Glacier Lake Trail** (p191),which has amazing views of Grewingk Glacier.

4

◢ PADDLE AROUND

Between **Kenai Fjords National Park** (p180) and **Kachemak Bay State Park** (p191), kayaking opportunities abound. Narrow fjords, tidewater glaciers and the occasional whale are all sights you can expect to come across.

5

◢ EXPERIENCE 'COMBAT'

Combat fishing, that is. When the salmon are running, anglers stand shoulder-to-shoulder on some of the state's richest salmon rivers: the **Russian** (p182) and the **Kenai** (p182). Wander past fishers crowded together in an otherwise unpopulated wilderness and you'll begin to understand the rules of engagement.

6

◢ ISLAND HOP

The US's second-largest island, **Kodiak** (p192), is not only home to the famous (or infamous?) Kodiak brown bear, but also to a vibrant community that relies more on fishing than it does tourism. Opportunities abound for hiking and kayaking, and you could spend your entire vacation exploring the quiet coves and deep valleys of the island.

2 MARK NEWMAN; 3 JEFF SCHULTZ; 4 BILL SCOTT; 5 BRENT WINEBRENNER; 6 GRAEME CORNWALLIS

2 Brown bear cubs; 3 Grace Ridge Trail (p194), Kachemak Bay State Park; 4 Kayakers, Kachemak Bay State Park (p191); 5 Combat fishermen; 6 Kodiak Island (p192)

BEST...

⤴ HIKING TRAILS

- **Harding Ice Field** (p180) Get beyond the glaciers to this ice age remnant.
- **Caines Head State Recreation Area** (p176) A six-mile beach walk to WWII bunkers.
- **Glacier Lake Trail** (p191) In Kachemak Bay State Park, with amazing views of Grewingk Glacier.
- **Barometer Mountain** (p195) A popular climb with great views of Kodiak and southern bays.

⤴ GLACIERS

- **Exit Glacier** (p180) Kenai Fjords' only glacier accessible by land.
- **Grewingk Glacier** (p191) Visible from Homer and a great day hike.
- **Holgate Glacier** (p181) A tidal glacier that calves into the waters of Kenai Fjords National Park.

⤴ WATERING HOLES

- **Salty Dawg Saloon** (p187) On the Homer Spit, housed in an old lighthouse.
- **Thorn's Showcase Lounge** (p179) Has a Jim Beam bottle collection worth $100,000.
- **Seaview Café** (p173) A great place to hear live music in Hope.

⤴ RESTAURANTS

- **Henry's Great Alaskan** (p198) Combines local seafood and Cajun spice.
- **Bowman's Bear Creek Lodge** (p173) A menu that changes nightly in a tiny Hope venue.
- **Smoke Shack** (p179) Biscuits and gravy, and pulled pork in a small rail car in Seward.
- **Fat Olives** (p185) Upper-scale bistro in an old Homer bus barn.

From left: Exit Glacier (p180); Downtown Hope (p171)

THINGS YOU NEED TO KNOW

⬗ VITAL STATISTICS

- **Best time to visit** April to September

⬗ LOCALITIES IN A NUTSHELL

- **Seward** (p173) Mountain-lover's hub surrounded by Kenai Fjords National Park.
- **Homer** (p182) Artsy town with great dining, perched along Kachemak Bay.
- **Kodiak Island** (p192) One of the biggest islands in the US houses giant grizzlies.
- **Katmai National Park & Preserve** (p199) Best known for its awesome bear watching.

⬗ ADVANCE PLANNING

- **Two months ahead** Book your accommodation, especially in Katmai.
- **One month ahead** Strengthen your fishing arm and shutter finger.
- **One week ahead** Book fishing or kayaking charters.

⬗ RESOURCES

- **Kenai Fjords National Park Visitor Center** (Map p174; ☎ 224-3175; ⏲ 8am-6pm) Beside the small-boat harbor in Seward.
- **USFS Ranger Station** (Map p174; ☎ 224-3378; 334 4th Ave, Seward; ⏲ 8am-5pm Mon-Fri) Has maps and information about Seward's outstanding selection of trails, cabins and campgrounds.

- **Homer Visitor Center** (Map p186; ☎ 235-7740; www.homeralaska.org; 201 Sterling Hwy; ⏲ 9am-7pm Mon-Fri, 10am-6pm Sat & Sun) Has countless brochures; it's operated by the chamber of commerce, however, and only provides info on members.
- **Katmai National Park Headquarters** (☎ 246-3305; ⏲ 8am-4:30pm Mon-Fri) In King Salmon Mall.
- **Kodiak Island Visitor Center** (☎ 486-4782, 800-789-4782; www.kodiak.org; 100 Marine Way; ⏲ 8am-7pm Mon & Tue, 9am-5pm Wed & Thu, 8am-7pm Fri,10am-2pm & 5-9pm Sat, noon-5pm Sun)

⬗ GETTING AROUND

- **Bus and motorcoach** Several companies have services between Homer and Seward to points north.
- **Train** Rails run to Seward.
- **Air** Jets travel to major hubs, while bush planes will take you beyond.
- **Ferry** Runs between Homer and Kodiak Island.

⬗ BE FOREWARNED

- **Bears** Take extra precaution at twilight and when salmon are running.
- **Wilderness** Be prepared; don't go for a hike without food, water and extra clothing.

KENAI PENINSULA, KATMAI & KODIAK ISLAND ITINERARIES

END OF THE ROADS Three Days

The Kenai Peninsula is small enough to explore in a long weekend, but wild enough to allow you to enjoy the freedom of the open road. Follow this itinerary to hit a few of the main towns and roads.

Drive south out of Anchorage on the Seward Hwy. At mile 56.7, turn onto the Hope Hwy. This two-lane road winds 16.5 miles before ending at **(1) Hope** (p171), where you can stay a night at **(2) Bowman's Bear Creek Lodge** (p173) – and be sure to sample their daily menu. The next morning, hike up to **(3) Hope Point** (p172), before driving back out to the Seward Hwy. Continue south until you hit the end (or the beginning): at mile 0 is namesake **(4) Seward** (p173). Turn onto Herman Leirer Rd and at the end you'll find **(5) Exit Glacier** (p180). Spend your evening walking around the outwash plain. The next day you'll backtrack 35 miles to the Sterling Hwy and, just past Cooper Landing, the mountains open up to flatter lands and bigger skies. Again, you'll drive until the end of road, stopping at **(6) Homer** (p182). Take time to meander along the **(7) Homer Spit** (p183) or take a look at some of the town's many art galleries. Finish up with dinner at **(8) Fat Olives** (p185).

BEAR WATCHING Five Days

If you have a long weekend, go see some bears. You'll likely pass through **(1) King Salmon** (p198), a good base for exploring Katmai National Park & Preserve. Originally created to preserve a giant ash-flow deposited in 1912 during the biggest volcanic eruption of the 20th century, Katmai is now best known for its grizzly-bear watching; it features the world's largest population of protected brown bears.

Mosey on over to **(2) Brooks Camp** (p199), *the* spot for photographing these giant mammals. You can follow a path that will lead you through the **(3) Valley of 10,000 Smokes** (p199), which, despite its evocative name, is no longer smoking. It's still a sight to behold; a sort of moonscape surrounded by green mountains.

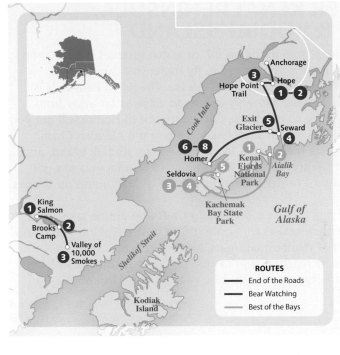

BEST OF THE BAYS One Week

With one week, you have plenty of time to explore the main Peninsula towns as well as the excellent public parks. Give yourself a couple of days to explore (1) Kenai Fjords National Park (p180). You can arrange a single- or multiday excursion to (2) Aialik Bay (p181), where seven glaciers promise to awe you.

After working your arms through the Kenai Fjords, take a day to drive to the other side of the Peninsula to the Homer area. Catch a boat across the bay to scenic (3) Seldovia (p189) and wander the tiny streets. Don't miss a night or three at (4) Across the Bay Tent & Breakfast (p190), a unique lodging option 8 miles down the road. Hire a water taxi to drop you off in (5) Kachemak Bay State Park (p191), where you can hike up to the 'wow!'-inducing Grewingk Glacier.

DISCOVER KENAI PENINSULA, KATMAI & KODIAK ISLAND

Gawk at Dall sheep from inside an RV, or watch grizzlies snap salmon from streams so remote you'll have to fly there: you can choose your own adventure in these parts of Alaska. The Kenai Peninsula is an accessible wilderness, allowing visitors to edge as far away from civilization as they're comfortable. But a ferry out of Homer will get you to Southwest Alaska, which stretches out along the Aleutian Chain.

Southwest boasts the world's largest bears, on Kodiak Island, and Alaska's richest salmon runs, in Bristol Bay. In Katmai you can get within 60ft of a bruin catching flying salmon as they jump up Brooks Falls.

On the Peninsula are yet more hiking trails and alpine lakes, and the jagged coastline makes for some of the best kayaking you'll find, with waters full of marine mammals, birds and fish.

Remote or easily reached, you're sure to fill your camera with images of a stereotypical Alaska: big, beautiful and bountiful.

SEWARD HIGHWAY

The Seward Hwy is a road-trip-lovers de-light, with smooth, winding turns through mountains that have you craning your neck around every corner. The 127 miles of highway is all Scenic Byway, and there are plenty of turn-offs for gawking and snapping photos. Keep in mind that the mileposts along the highway show distances from Seward (Mile 0) to Anchorage (Mile

MATT HAGE / ALASKASTOCK.COM

Traveling the Seward Hwy

127). The first section of this road – from Anchorage to Portage Glacier (Mile 79) – is covered in the Anchorage chapter (p72).

TURNAGAIN PASS & AROUND

After it departs Turnagain Arm, Seward Hwy heads for the hills. Near Mile 68 it begins climbing into the alpine region of **Turnagain Pass**, where there's a roadside stop with garbage cans and toilets. In early summer, this area is a kaleidoscope of wildflowers.

Bertha Creek Campground (Mile 65 Seward Hwy; campsites $10), just across the Bertha Creek Bridge, is understandably popular – site No 6 even has a waterfall view. You can spend a day climbing the alpine slopes of the pass here, or head to Mile 64 and the northern trailhead of both the 23-mile **Johnson Pass Trail** and the paved **Sixmile Bike Trail**, which runs 8 miles – not six – along the highway.

The Hope Hwy junction and south trailhead for the Sixmile Bike Trail are both at Mile 56.7. From here, the Hope Hwy heads 16 miles north to the small hamlet of Hope.

The Seward Hwy continues south of this junction to Upper Summit Lake, surrounded by neck-craning peaks. The lakeside **Tenderfoot Creek Campground** (Mile 46 Seward Hwy; campsites $14) has 27 sites that are open enough to catch the view but wooded enough for privacy.

Within walking distance of the campground is **Summit Lake Lodge** (☎ 244-2031; www.summitlakelodge.com; Mile 45.8 Seward Hwy; d $90; ✗), with basic rooms, an espresso/gift shop and a bustling **restaurant** (lunch $7-14, dinner $11-23; ✓ 8am-11pm).

The **Devil's Pass Trail** (Mile 39.4 Seward Hwy) is a very well-signed, difficult, 10-mile hike over a 2400ft gap to the Resurrection Pass Trail.

At **Tern Lake Junction** (Mile 37 Seward Hwy) is the turnoff for the Sterling Hwy (p182), running 143 miles to Homer.

HOPE

pop 147

Hope has beautiful views of Turnagain Arm surrounded by snowcapped mountains; a quaint and historic downtown; wonderful restaurants and gold rush-era relics; and incredible camping and hiking opportunities within easy access from Anchorage by car.

Somehow, the moose-nugget jewelry purveyors have passed this place by, perhaps missing the turnoff at Mile 56.7 of the Seward Hwy, or failing to follow the winding Hope Hwy the 16.5 miles necessary to reach this rustic hamlet. Don't make the same mistake.

SIGHTS & ACTIVITIES
HOPE-SUNRISE MINING MUSEUM
This small **log cabin** (☎ 782-3740; Old Hope Rd; admission free; ✓ noon-4pm) preserves relics from early miners and homesteaders with a great deal of respect. Creaky buildings give a feel for life at the turn of the 20th century; a quick guided tour is worth the tip for history buffs and anyone with a little extra time.

GOLD PANNING
There are about 125 mining claims throughout the Chugach National Forest. Some of the more serious prospectors actually make money, but most are happy to take home a bottle with a few flakes of gold in it.

The Hope area provides numerous opportunities for the amateur panner, including a 20-acre claim that the US Forest Service (USFS) has set aside near the Resurrection Pass trailhead for recreational mining. Out at the claim there are usually some regulars who don't mind showing newcomers how to swirl the pan. You'll find other panning areas at Sixmile Creek, between Mile 1.5 and Mile 5.5 of the Hope Hwy, as well as many of the creeks along the Resurrection Pass Trail.

HIKING

The **Gull Rock Trail** is a flat 5-mile, four- to six-hour walk to Gull Rock, a rocky point 140ft above the Turnagain shoreline. The trail follows an old wagon road built at the turn of the 19th century, and along

the way you can explore the remains of a cabin and sawmill.

Hope Point is steeper and a bit more difficult, following an alpine ridge 5 miles for incredible views of Turnagain Arm. Begin at an unmarked trail along the right-hand side of the small Porcupine Creek. Except for an early-summer snowfield, you'll find no water after Porcupine Creek.

PADDLING

Sixmile Creek is serious white water, with thrilling – and dangerous – rapids

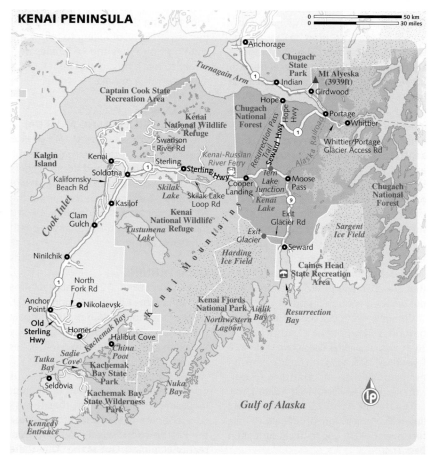

KENAI PENINSULA

through deep gorges that survivors describe as 'the best roller coaster in Alaska.'

Chugach Outdoor Center (☎ 277-7238; www.chugachoutdoorcenter.com; Mile 7.5 Hope Hwy) guides trips down Sixmile twice daily during summer. The two-canyon run is $99 per person; if you want to defy death on all three canyons it's $149 per person.

Nova River Runners (☎ 800-746-5753; www.novalaska.com) also does twice-daily trips down the river, at $90 for the Class IV canyons, and $135 for the Class V.

SLEEPING & EATING

ourpick Bowman's Bear Creek Lodge (☎ 782-3141; www.bowmansbearcreeklodge. com; Mile 15.9 Hope Hwy; cabins $150, Sun brunch $20, dinner $10-24; ☺ restaurant 4-10pm Tue-Sun, 10am-2pm Sun; ✗) This place has five hand-hewn, log cabins surrounding a beautiful pond and burbling creek, as well as a fabulous menu that changes daily, with homemade desserts, seafood specials and a friendly, intimate dining room.

Tito's Discovery Café (☎ 782-3274; Mile 16.5 Hope Hwy; breakfast $6-10, wraps $11-12, dinners $12-16; ☺ 7am-9pm) This is a very popular eatery, that serves homemade soups, seafood wraps, and local gossip.

Seaview Café (☎ 782-3300; B St; mains $10-20; ☺ noon-9pm Sun-Wed, to 11pm Thu-Sat) Serves up good beer and chowder with views of the Arm. There's always live music on weekends.

GETTING THERE & AWAY

Hope remains idyllic in part because of its isolation. Though the **Seward Bus Line** (☎ 224-3608) and **Homer Stage Line** (☎ 224-3608; www.homerstageline.com) will drop you off at the junction of the Hope and Seward Hwys, the only way to get to the town proper is by driving, hitching, pedaling or plodding.

Seward marina

RICHARD CUMMINS

SEWARD

pop 2661

Seward is an unpolished gem, rewarding visitors with small-town charm and phenomenal access to the mountains and sea. Located at the terminus of both the Alaska Railroad and the Seward Hwy, and a final stop on many cruises, the town is easily accessible from Anchorage. Travelers flock to kayak, hike, fish, whale watch and glacier-view.

SIGHTS

BENNY BENSON MEMORIAL

This humble **monument** at the corner of the Seward Hwy and Dairy Hill Lane honors Seward's favorite son, Benny Benson. In 1926 the orphaned 13-year-old Alaska Native boy submitted his design for the

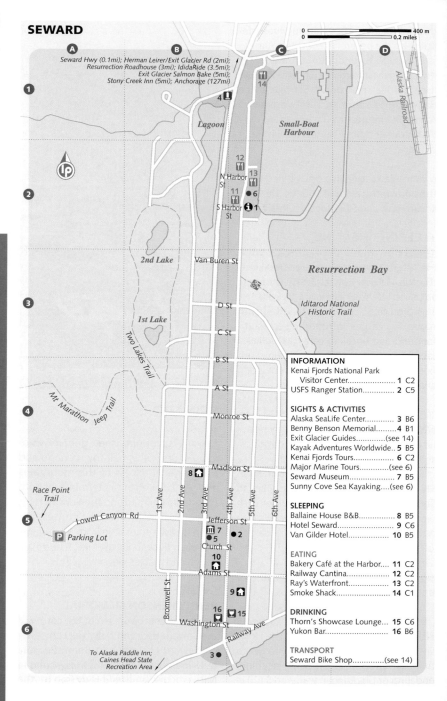

SEWARD

Seward Hwy (0.1mi); Herman Leirer/Exit Glacier Rd (2mi);
Resurrection Roadhouse (3mi); IdidaRide (3.5mi);
Exit Glacier Salmon Bake (5mi);
Stony Creek Inn (5mi); Anchorage (127mi)

Lagoon

Small-Boat Harbour

Alaska Railroad

N Harbor St

S Harbor St

2nd Lake

Van Buren St

Resurrection Bay

1st Lake

Two Lakes Trail

D St

Iditarod National Historic Trail

C St

B St

A St

Mt Marathon Jeep Trail

Monroe St

Madison St

1st Ave

2nd Ave

3rd Ave

4th Ave

5th Ave

6th Ave

Race Point Trail

Lowell Canyon Rd

Jefferson St

P *Parking Lot*

Church St

Adams St

Bromwell St

Washington St

Railway Ave

To Alaska Paddle Inn;
Caines Head State
Recreation Area

INFORMATION
Kenai Fjords National Park
  Visitor Center.....................**1** C2
USFS Ranger Station.............**2** C5

SIGHTS & ACTIVITIES
Alaska SeaLife Center.............**3** B6
Benny Benson Memorial.........**4** B1
Exit Glacier Guides.............(see 14)
Kayak Adventures Worldwide..**5** B5
Kenai Fjords Tours..................**6** C2
Major Marine Tours............(see 6)
Seward Museum....................**7** B5
Sunny Cove Sea Kayaking....(see 6)

SLEEPING
Ballaine House B&B...............**8** B5
Hotel Seward.........................**9** C6
Van Gilder Hotel.................**10** B5

EATING
Bakery Café at the Harbor....**11** C2
Railway Cantina...................**12** C2
Ray's Waterfront.................**13** C2
Smoke Shack.......................**14** C1

DRINKING
Thorn's Showcase Lounge...**15** C6
Yukon Bar...........................**16** B6

TRANSPORT
Seward Bike Shop..............(see 14)

Alaska state flag, arguably the loveliest in the Union. His stellar design (you can see one of his first at the library) includes the North Star, symbolizing the northern-most state, the Great Bear constellation for strength, and a blue background for both the sky and the forget-me-not, Alaska's state flower. Seward will never forget.

SEWARD MUSEUM
This eclectic, if a bit dusty, **museum** (☎ 224-3902; 336 3rd Ave; adult/child $3/1; ⏲ 9am-5pm) has an excellent Iditarod exhibit; a rare 49-star US flag; and relics of Seward's Russian era, the 1964 Good Friday earthquake, and the 1989 oil spill. There are also lots of amusing antiques, including an ancient electric hair-curling machine and a 'cow raincoat' designed for the oft-drenched cattle at the now-defunct Seward dairy. The staff are en-thusiastic and knowledgeable, and worth engaging. The museum has eventual plans to move to a new site next to the library.

SMALL-BOAT HARBOR
The **small-boat harbor**, at the northern end of 4th Ave, hums during the sum-mer with fishing boats, charter vessels, cruise ships and a number of sailboats. Radiating outward from the docks are seasonal restaurants, espresso bars, tourist offices, hotels and almost any other service the visitor might want. There are also picnic tables and a free sighting scope overlooking the harbor and the bay.

ACTIVITIES
HIKING
MT MARATHON TRAIL
According to (rather suspect) local leg-end, grocer Gus Borgan wagered $100 in 1909 that no-one could run Mt Marathon in an hour, and the race was on. The 3.1-mile suffer-fest quickly became a cel-ebrated Fourth of July event and today is Alaska's most famous footrace, pitting runners from all over the world against the 3022ft-high peak. In 1981 Bill Spencer set the record at 43 minutes, 23 seconds. Many runners take twice as long, and each year several end up with bloody knees or broken bones after tumbling during the hell-bent descent.

At the end of Monroe St, the so-called Jeep Trail provides easier (though not drivable) access to the peak and a heav-enly bowl behind the mountain. The run-ner's trail is painful – think Stairmaster with a view – and every summer several tourists who didn't know what they were in for are rescued.

TWO LAKES TRAIL
This easy 1-mile loop circumnavigates pleasant Two Lakes Park (cnr 2nd Ave & C St), through woods and picnic grounds, across a salmon-spawning creek and around the two promised lakes at the base of Mt Marathon. Unsatisfied hikers can access the Jeep Trail nearby, which climbs Mt Marathon, for a much more intense climb.

LOST LAKE TRAIL
This challenging 7-mile trail to an alpine lake is one of the most scenic hikes the Kenai Peninsula has to offer in midsum-mer. The final 2 miles are above the treeline, making the shores of Lost Lake a wondrous place to pitch a tent for the night.

If you'd rather not return the same way, continue around the east side of Lost Lake to the **Primrose Trail**, an 8-mile alpine trek ending at Primrose Campground at Mile 17.2 of the Seward Hwy (see p170).

Visitors and sea lion, Alaska SeaLife Center

↘ ALASKA SEALIFE CENTER

A fitting legacy of the *Exxon Valdez* oil spill settlement, this $56-million **marine center** is more than just one of Alaska's finest attractions. As the only coldwater marine-science facility in the Western Hemisphere, it serves as a research and educational center and provides rehabilitation for injured marine animals; for $6 on top of the admission fee you can tour the labs at 9am and 12:30pm daily.

Amazing enough for most folks are the regular exhibits, such as oil-spill displays and the Alaska Waters Gallery, with aquariums holding colorful fish and gossamer jellyfish. Kids will love the tidepool touch tank, where you can hold sea anemones and starfish.

Without a doubt the highlight, however, is a series of two story-deep, glass-sided tanks: upstairs you get the above-water view of seabird rookeries and recuperating harbor seals, while below deck you'll be eyeball-to-eyeball with prowling sea lions and puffins diving for dinner.

Things you need to know: Map p174; ☎ 224-6300, 800-224-2525; www.alaskasealife.org; 301 Railway Ave; adult/child $20/10; ☉ 8am-7pm

CAINES HEAD STATE RECREATION AREA

This 6000-acre preserve, 5.5 miles south of Seward on Resurrection Bay, contains WWII military facilities (bring a flashlight for exploring), a 650ft headland, the Coastal Trail, and two public-use cabins. If you're not up for an overnight backpacking excursion, the hike to Tonsina Point is an easy 3-mile round-trip. In 2006, however, floods washed out the Tonsina Creek bridge, making it necessary for hikers to trek along the creek to the shore and cross the stream where it braids. Beyond that you will need to time your passage with low tide; hikers have gotten stranded and even drowned after being caught by the rising waters.

GLACIER TREKKING

Exit Glacier Guides (☎ 224-5569; www.exitglacierguides.com) For those not satisfied with merely gazing up at Seward's backyard glacier, Exit Glacier Guides gives you the chance to tread upon it. The company's five-hour ice-hiking trip costs $120 per person. It gears you up with all the necessary equipment including ice-axes and crampons, and then ascends part-way up the Harding Ice Field Trail and out onto the glacier for crevasse exploration as well as interpretive glaciology.

PADDLING

Kayaking right outside Seward in Resurrection Bay can still make for a stunning day on the water. Both **Sunny Cove Sea Kayaking** (☎ 224-8810, 800-770-9119; www.sunnycove.com; small-boat harbor) and **Kayak Adventures Worldwide** (☎ 224-3960; www.kayakak.com; 328 3rd Ave) guide half- and full-day trips in the bay.

SLED-DOG MUSHING

Hey, this is where the Iditarod started. Why not meet the dogs?

IdidaRide (☎ 800-478-3139; www.ididaride.com; Exit Glacier Rd; adult/child $59/29) is cheesy, but it's more like Stilton than Velveeta: after touring Iditarod veteran Mitch Seavey's kennels and hearing junior mushers discuss their experiences with subzero sleep deprivation, delicate doggy feet and cutthroat competition, you'll be strapped in for a 20-minute training run in a cart hitched behind a team of huskies.

Godwin Glacier Dog Sled Tours (☎ 224-8239, 888-989-8239; www.alaskadogsled.com; adult/child $430/390) goes one better, transporting you by helicopter to an alpine glacier, where you'll be met by lots of dogs and a genuine snow-sledding adventure, even in July.

➘ THE JESSE LEE HOME

Off to the side of the Seward Hwy on the lagoon sits the fairly unremarkable Benny Benson Memorial. Benson is well-known in Alaska as the young orphan who beat out 700 other contestants with his design for the Alaska state flag, but lesser known and visited is his old home.

Just over a half-mile from the memorial sits the deteriorating Tudor hulk of the Jesse Lee Home, an orphanage that serviced mainly Alaska Native children orphaned by tuberculosis or influenza. It was started in 1890 in Unalaska and moved to Seward in 1925, when several of the home's original buildings were constructed.

The 1964 earthquake heavily damaged the building, and it was abandoned shortly after as childcare trends shifted away from group homes to the foster care system. Today the buildings are fenced in on a 2½ acre site that makes a great photography subject (ask any high school photography student in town). The view of Resurrection Bay, while not as striking as from atop Mt Marathon, is easily attained and pleasant.

Though there have been several movements to restore the home before it deteriorates any more, no plans have been set.

To reach the home, walk south one block from the Benny Benson Memorial and turn left on Phoenix Rd. The home – you can't miss it – is a half-mile up Phoenix.

SLEEPING

Ballaine House B&B (☎ 224-2362; www.super
page.com/ballaine/; 437 3rd Ave; s $65-75, d $90;
☒) Raved about by readers, this place –
one of the original Seward homes –
does cook-to-order breakfasts and offers
a wealth of advice on what to do around
town.

Stoney Creek Inn (☎ 224-3940; www.
stoneycreekinn.net; Stoney Creek Ave; d $95-85)
This secluded place comes complete
with a fantastic sauna and hot tub just
next to a deliciously icy-cold salmon
stream. Rates include a continental
breakfast.

Upper Winner Creek Trail

↘ IF YOU LIKE...

If you like the mellow **Winner Creek
Trail** (p73), we think you'll like these
two hikes near Seward:

- **Ptarmigan Lake Trail** Leads 3.5
  miles from the campground to
  Ptarmigan Lake. Here you'll find
  turquoise, trout-filled waters
  that reflect the mountains that
  cradle it.
- **Grayling Lake Trail** Accessed
  from a parking lot at Mile 13.2,
  leads two pleasant miles to
  Grayling Lake, a beautiful spot
  with views of Snow River and
  (surprise!) excellent fishing for
  grayling. This is a nice hike for
  kids.

ourpick Alaska Paddle Inn (☎ 362-2628;
www.alaskapaddleinn.com; 13745 Beach Dr; r from
$179) Two custom-built rooms overlook
the beach and bay on Lowell Point.
Arched ceilings, walk-in tiled show-
ers, and gas fireplaces make this place
both one of the coziest and classiest in
Seward.

Van Gilder Hotel (☎ 800-204-6835;
www.vangilderhotel.com; 307 Adams St; d $119-
209) Gossips say poltergeists plague the
1st floor of this landmark, which dates
from 1916. If you dare to spend the night
here, however, you'll find elegant suites
with antique furnishings, as well as some
affordable European pensions without
baths.

Hotel Seward (☎ 224-8001, 800-440-
2444; www.hotelsewardalaska.com; 221 5th Ave;
r $89-450) The 'historic' side was recently
remodeled and has affordable shared-
bath rooms; the new wing makes for
an excellent splurge with grand views
of Resurrection Bay. An old-time saloon
serves up appetizers, but the lobby is
definitely overdoing it in the taxidermy
department.

EATING
RESTAURANTS

Exit Glacier Salmon Bake (☎ 224-2204;
Exit Glacier Rd; lunch $6-10, dinner $18-22; ☺ 5-
10pm) Its motto – 'cheap beer and lousy
food' – is wrong on the second count.
Locals are particularly fond of the salmon
sandwich, which you can adorn with
pickles from a barrel.

Resurrection Roadhouse (☎ 224-
2223; Exit Glacier Rd; lunch $9-14, dinner $18-46;
☺ 6am-2pm & 5-10pm) This local favorite is
home to the 'Buddha Belly' pizza, sweet
potato fries worth traveling for, and the
best deck in town. It also has a vast range
of on-tap brews, and the bar is open until
midnight.

EDDIE BRADY

View of Seward from the Mt Marathon Trail (p175)

Ray's Waterfront (☎ 224-5606; breakfast & lunch $10-16, dinner $19-31; ⏰ 11am-10pm) This is Seward's culinary high point, with attentive service, picture-postcard views and the finest seafood above water.

CAFES & QUICK EATS

Bakery Café at the Harbor (☎ 224-6091; 1210 4th Ave; breakfast & lunch $3-6, dinner $5-10; ⏰ 5am-7pm) This busy joint is a bargain: breakfast is delish, and dinner includes half-pound burgers on homemade buns. Also sells box lunches for those going out on the bay for the day.

ourpick Smoke Shack (☎ 224-7427; 411 Port Ave; breakfast & lunch $6-11; ⏰ 6am-8pm) Housed in a rail car, this tiny joint oozes blue collar atmosphere. It has the best breakfast in town, with biscuits and gravy made from scratch.

Railway Cantina (☎ 224-8226; light meals $4-8; ⏰ 11am-8pm) Near the small-boat harbor; offers unorthodox quesadillas, burritos and tacos. Try the 'black-n-blue' quesadilla, with blackened chicken and blue cheese.

DRINKING & ENTERTAINMENT

Yukon Bar (☎ 224-3063; 201 4th Ave) There are hundreds of dollars pinned to this bar's ceiling and almost nightly live music. It's festive.

Thorn's Showcase Lounge (☎ 224-3700; 208 4th St; mains $14-18) This saloon serves the strongest drinks in down – try its White Russians. The Jim Beam collection is valued at thousands of dollars; can you spot the pipeline bottle?

GETTING THERE & AROUND
BICYCLE

You can rent bikes through **Seward Bike Shop** (☎ 224-2448; 411 Port Ave; per half-/full-day cruisers $14/23, mountain bikes $21/38; ⏰ 9:30am-6:30pm Mon-Sat, 11am-4pm Sun).

BUS

The **Seward Bus Line** (☎ 224-3608; www.sewardbuslines.net) departs at 9:30am daily en route to Anchorage ($50).

Homer Stage Line (☎ 868-3914; www.homerstageline.com) runs daily from Seward to Homer ($55) and Anchorage ($55).

↘ DAY TRIP TO EXIT GLACIER

The marquee attraction of Kenai Fjords National Park is Exit Glacier, named by explorers crossing the Harding Ice Field who found the glacier a suitable way to 'exit' the ice and mountains. Now 3 miles long, it's believed the river of ice once extended all the way to Seward.

From the Exit Glacier Nature Center, the **Outwash Plain Trail** is an easy half-mile walk to the glacier's alluvial plain – a flat expanse of pulverized silt and gravel, cut through by braids of grey meltwater. The **Overlook Loop Trail** departs the first loop and climbs steeply to an overlook at the side of the glacier before returning; don't skip the short spur to Falls Overlook, a scenic cascade off the upper trail. Both trails make for a short hike, not much more than a mile in length; you can return along the half-mile **nature trail** through cottonwood forest, alder thickets and old glacial moraines before emerging at the ranger station.

The **Park Connection** (☎ 800-266-8625; www.alaskacoach.com) has a daily service from Seward to Denali Park (one way $135) via Anchorage (one way $56).

TRAIN
From May to September, the **Alaska Railroad** (☎ 265-2631, 800-544-0552; www.akrr.com; 408 Port Ave; one way/round-trip $69/110) offers a daily run to Anchorage. It's more than just public transportation; it's one of the most famous rides in Alaska, complete with glaciers, steep gorges and rugged mountain scenery.

TROLLEY
The **Seward Trolley** (☎ 224-4378; one way adult/child $5/3) runs between the ferry terminal and downtown every half-hour from 10am to 7pm daily.

KENAI FJORDS NATIONAL PARK
Seward is the gateway to Kenai Fjords National Park, created in 1980 to protect 587,000 acres of Alaska's most awesome, impenetrable wilderness. Crowning the park is the massive Harding Ice Field; from

it, countless tidewater glaciers pour down, carving the coast into dizzying fjords.

Road-accessible Exit Glacier is its highlight attraction, drawing more than 100,000 tourists each summer.

SIGHTS & ACTIVITIES
HIKING
RANGER-LED HIKES
At 10am, 2pm and 4pm daily, rangers at the Exit Glacier Nature Center lead free one-hour hikes to the face of the glacier, providing information on the wildlife and natural history of the area.

HARDING ICE FIELD TRAIL
This strenuous and extremely popular 4-mile trail follows Exit Glacier up to Harding Ice Field. The 936-sq-mile expanse remained undiscovered until the early 1900s, when a map-surveying team discovered that eight coastal glaciers flowed from the exact same system.

Today you can rediscover it via a steep, roughly cut and sometimes slippery ascent to 3500ft; for reasonably fit trekkers, that's a good three- or four-hour trip.

PADDLING

ourpick **Kayak Adventures Worldwide** (☎ 224-3960; www.kayakak.com) is a highly respected operation that guides educationally-based half- and full-day trips ($70 to $125). It also arranges a two-day trip with Exit Glacier Guides (p176) for a day of kayaking and a day of glacier hiking.

AIALIK BAY

With several glaciers to visit, many people hire water-taxis to drop them near Aialik Glacier, then take three or four days to paddle south past Pedersen Glacier and into Holgate Arm, where they're picked up.

NORTHWESTERN LAGOON

This fjord is more expensive to reach but much more isolated. The wildlife is excellent, especially the seabirds and sea otters, and more than a half-dozen glaciers can be seen.

TOURS

Kenai Fjords Tours (Map p174; ☎ 224-8068, 877-777-2805; www.kenaifjords.com) goes the farthest into the park (Northwestern Fjord; per adult/child $159/79.50) and offers the widest variety of options, including an all-inclusive overnight on Fox Island at the Kenai Fjords Wilderness Lodge (per person $359 based on double occupancy).

Although it has fewer options, **Major Marine Tours** (Map p174; ☎ 224-8030, 800-764-7300; www.majormarine.com) is cheaper and includes a national park ranger on every boat.

GETTING THERE & AROUND

To reach the coastal fjords, you'll need to take a tour or a water-taxi.

Getting to Exit Glacier is a bit easier. If you don't have a car, **Exit Glacier Guides** (☎ 224-5569) runs an hourly shuttle to the glacier in its recycled-vegetable-oil van between 9:30am and 5pm. The van departs from the Holiday Inn Express at the small-boat harbor and costs $10 roundtrip. Otherwise, there are cabs: **Glacier Taxi** (☎ 224-5678) charges $50 for as many people as you can squeeze in.

EDDIE BRADY

Harding Ice Field Trail

STERLING HIGHWAY

COOPER LANDING & AROUND

pop 353

The picturesque outpost, named for Joseph Cooper, a miner who worked the area in the 1880s, is best known for its rich and brutal combat salmon fishing along the Russian and Kenai Rivers (see the boxed text, p67). While rustic log-cabin lodges featuring giant fish freezers are still the lifeblood of this town, the trails and white-water rafting opportunities attract a very different sort of tourist.

ACTIVITIES

FISHING

Most of the fishing on the Upper Kenai is for rainbow trout, Dolly Varden, and silver and sockeye salmon.

Alaska River Adventures (☎ 595-2000, 888-836-9027; www.alaskariveradventures.com; Mile 47.9 Sterling Hwy)

Alaska Rivers Company (☎ 595-1226; www.alaskariverscompany.com; Mile 49.9 Sterling Hwy)

OTHER ACTIVITIES

Alaska River Adventures (☎ 595-2000, 888-836-9027; www.alaskariveradventures.com; Mile 48 Sterling Hwy) runs scenic three-hour floats on the Kenai (per person $49). The coolest trip, however, is the Paddle Saddle ($179), which combines a float trip with gold panning and a two-hour horseback ride.

our pick Alaska Horseman Trail Adventures (☎ 595-1806; www.alaskahorsemen.com; Mile 45 Sterling Hwy) is the place to feel like a cowboy or girl. It offers horseback rides along Quartz and Crescent Creeks (per half-/full day $130/175) and pricier guided overnight trips that include rafting and/or flightseeing.

SLEEPING & EATING

Hutch B&B (☎ 595-1270; www.arctic.net/~hutch; Mile 48.5 Sterling Hwy; r $89-119, cabins $225; ⊠ ⌨) In a three-story, balcony-ringed lodge, the big, simple, clean rooms are the best deal in town, and its minimess hall the cutest.

Gwin's Lodge (☎ 595-1266; www.gwinslodge.com; Mile 52 Sterling Hwy; cabins & chalets $109-299, breakfast $5-15, lunch $9-14, dinners $17-25) This classic 1952 log-cabin lodge is a fish-frenzied madhouse when the sockeyes are running. It's got a 24-hour restaurant, a salmon-bake, and a round-the-clock grocery store that books everything from fishing charters to flightseeing. It's a landmark. It's food is hearty American fare, with items such as salmon omelets, salmon chowder, salmon salad, grilled salmon – even salmon-stuffed halibut.

GETTING THERE & AROUND

If you're without wheels, your best option for reaching Cooper Landing is **Homer Stage Line** (☎ 868-3914; www.homerstageline.com).

HOMER

pop 5384

Lucky is the visitor who drives into Homer on a clear day. As the Sterling Hwy descends into town, a panorama of mountains sweeps in front of you. The Homer Spit slowly comes into view, jutting into a glittering Kachemak Bay, and just when you think the view might unwind forever it ends with the dramatic Grewingk Glacier.

And then there's the vibe: the town is a magnet for radicals, artists and folks disillusioned with mainstream society, who've formed a critical mass here, dreaming up a sort of utopian vision for their city, and striving – with grins on their faces – to enact it. Because of that, this is the arts capital of Southcentral Alaska, with great galleries,

BILL SCOTT

View of Homer Spit, Kachemak Bay & Kenai Mountains

museums, theater and music. As well, it's a culinary feast, with more wonderful eateries than most places 10 times its size.

SIGHTS
HOMER SPIT

The **Spit** throbs all summer with tourists who mass here in unimaginable density, gobbling fish-and-chips, quaffing specialty coffees, getting chair massages, purchasing alpaca sweaters, arranging bear-watching trips, watching theatrical performances, and – oh yeah – going fishing in search of 300lb halibut. The hub of all this activity is the **small-boat harbor**, one of the best facilities in Southcentral Alaska and home to more than 700 boats. Close by is the **Seafarer's Memorial**, which, amid all the Spit's hubbub, is a solemn monument to residents lost at sea.

PRATT MUSEUM

This recently renovated **museum** (☎ 235-8635; www.prattmuseum.org; 3779 Bartlett St; adult/child $8/4; ⏰ 10am-6pm) is fantastic – so much so, it has loaned exhibits to the Smithsonian.

Light-hearted and whimsical, and perhaps the coolest aspect of the museum, is the Forest Ecology Trail, where artists can contribute to the 'Facing the Elements' exhibit. Paths wind through the trees, and you'll stumble upon small exhibits, be they mirrors, rocks, or pottery. A must-do.

ACTIVITIES
HIKING
BISHOP'S BEACH TRAIL

This hike is a 7-mile waterfront trek from north of Homer back into town (you could do it in reverse, but you're likely to miss the turnoff to the highway). The views of Kachemak Bay and the Kenai Mountains are superb, while the marine life that scurries along the sand at low tide is fascinating.

HOMESTEAD TRAIL

This 6.7-mile trek from Rogers Loop Rd to the City Reservoir, just off Skyline Dr on Crossman Ridge Rd, is a 2½-mile walk to Rucksack Dr, which crosses Diamond Ridge Rd. Along the way you pass through open meadows, with panoramic

↘ DETOUR: NIKOLAEVSK

Tucked inconspicuously down a winding road from Anchor Point sits one of several Russian Old Believer Villages on the Kenai Peninsula. The Old Believers are members of a sect that split from mainstream Russian Orthodoxy in the 1650s, defending their 'old beliefs' in the face of what they considered heretical reforms. Long considered outcasts in Russia, they fled communism in 1917, ending up in Brazil, then Oregon, and then – in 1968 – Alaska, where they finally felt they could enjoy religious freedom while avoiding the corruptive influences of modernity.

Nowadays, Alaska's Old Believers number at most 3000. They're hardcore traditionalists, speaking mainly Russian, marrying in their teens, raising substantial broods of children, and living simply. The men – usually farmers or fishermen – are forbidden from trimming their beards; the women typically cover their hair and are garbed in long dresses.

To get there, head 10 miles east on North Fork Rd, which departs the Sterling Hwy in the heart of Anchor Point and winds through hillbilly homesteads and open, rolling forest.

At first, you may be disappointed. Apart from the dress and language of the inhabitants (who are often nowhere to be seen), the community appears downright Alaskan: wooden prefab homes, rusting pickup trucks, gardens with gargantuan produce. Look hard, though, and you'll notice subtle Russian touches – the ornate scrollwork on a porch railing, for instance. Impossible to miss is the village's house of worship, the Church of St Nikolas, built in 1983 and sporting an elaborately painted façade and a white-and-blue onion dome.

But to really get into the heart of Nikolaevsk, you must follow the signs to the **Samovar Café & B&B** (☎ 235-6867; www.russiangiftsnina.com; mains $5-12, r $39-79, campsites/RV sites $15/29; ☼ cafe 10am-10pm Mon-Fri, to 8pm Sat), which has more than simply the best Russian food on the peninsula, and more than a wonderful collection of cheap and colorful (and pretty basic) accommodations. Nina, the proprietor, is an electrical engineer, writer, and force of nature. She'll offer you two dining choices: in the sun room, where she'll simply serve your meal, or inside, where you can 'dine in Russia.' This choice gets you an inside seat, borscht, cream puffs and delicious *pelimeny* (Siberian dumplings), Nina's stories, and a photo session where she'll dress you up in traditional Orthodox gear.

views of Kachemak Bay, and Mt Iliamna and Mt Redoubt on the other side of Cook Inlet.

HALIBUT FISHING

There are more than two dozen charter captains working out of the Spit, and they charge anywhere from $200 to $400 for a halibut trip.

WHALE WATCHING

Whenever you are out in the bay there is a chance of spotting whales – sometimes you can even spot orcas from the tip of the Spit. However, only the MV *Rainbow Connection,* which is operated by **Rainbow Tours** (☎ 235-7272; Homer Spit Rd), runs a dedicated whale-watching tour.

SLEEPING

Room at the Harbor (☎ 299-6767, 299-6868; Homer Spit Rd; s/d $85/100; ✗) This establishment has one beautiful room upstairs from Spit Sisters. Though the shower is in the room, one of the beds is in its own nook overlooking the town's boat harbor.

ourpick **Old Town B&B** (☎ 235-7558; www.oldtownbeadandbreakfast.com; 106 W Bunnell Ave; d $95-115; ✗ 🖳) There are beautiful rooms with wood floors, great views, fresh flowers and cookies, and lots of antiques. Breakfast is served in a lovely little sitting room.

Bear Creek Lodging (☎ 235-8484; www.bearcreekwineryalaska.com; Bear Creek Dr; d $245; ✗) On a stunning hillside at the Bear Creek Winery, this place has two posh, romantic suites (each with a kitchenette), a hot tub overlooking the fruit vineyard and koi pond, and a complimentary bottle of vino beside each bed.

Land's End Resort (☎ 800-478-0400; www.lands-end-resort.com; r $140-245; ✗) Located at the end of the Spit; it's considered a luxury hotel for its grand views and storied ambience, but only the pricier rooms really fit that description.

EATING
RESTAURANTS

ourpick **Fat Olives** (☎ 235-8488; 276 Olson Lane; dinner $16-29; ☯ 11am-9:30pm) Housed in the old 'bus barn,' this chic and hyper-popular pizza joint/wine bar serves affordable appetizers like prosciutto-wrapped Alaska scallops and delicious mains like wood-oven-roasted rack of lamb. You can also grab a huge slice of pizza to go ($4).

Homestead (☎ 235-8723; Mile 8.2 E End Rd; dinner $26-32; ☯ 5-9pm) Considered the best – and perhaps the most delicious – restaurant in Homer, with mains such as cranberry duck ($28) and teriyaki rockfish ($29). Though the waiters wear black ties, patrons can come as they are (hey, this is Homer, after all). Reservations are recommended.

CAFES

Fresh Sourdough Express (☎ 235-7571; 1316 Ocean Dr; breakfast $6-10, lunch & dinner $6-11; ☯ 7am-9pm) This is the first official 'green' restaurant in Alaska, and you can taste it. Almost everything on offer here is organic and as much as possible locally raised or grown. Come here for breakfast – you'll be served a small bakery sweet while you wait for your 'howling hotcakes.'

Spitfire Grill (☎ 235-9379; Homer Spit Rd; mains $8-14; ☯ noon-9:30pm) With a unique menu that includes local sausage, a chicken apple sandwich, and raved-about brisket, this small eatery actually gets locals down to the Spit.

QUICK EATS

Two Sisters Bakery (☎ 235-2280; 233 E Bunnell Ave; light meals $3-8; ☯ 7am-8pm Mon-Sat, 9am-4pm Sun) A beloved Homer institution with espresso and great fresh-baked bread, plus quiche, soups, salads and pizza by the slice.

Fritz Creek General Store (☎ 235-6521; Mile 8.2 East End Rd; quick eats $3-8; ☯ 7am-9pm Mon-Sat, 10am-6pm Sun) What is an excellent deli doing all the way out on East End Rd? Serving some of the best take-out food in Homer. It's worth the drive out here for the veggie burritos alone, but make sure you don't leave without dessert.

Mermaid Café (☎ 235-7649; 3487 Main St; breakfast & lunch $5-12; ☯ 9am-3pm Tue-Fri, to 2pm Sat, to 1pm Sun) This sunny spot has all the basics such as soups, salad and sandwiches, and all the bread is house-baked. Don't miss the French toast.

KENAI PENINSULA, KATMAI & KODIAK ISLAND

STERLING HIGHWAY

HOMER

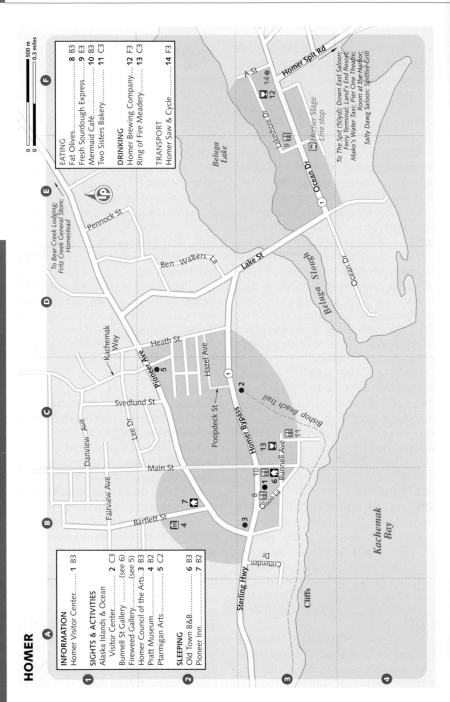

0 — 500 m
0 — 0.3 miles

INFORMATION
Homer Visitor Center.........**1** B3

SIGHTS & ACTIVITIES
Alaska Islands & Ocean
  Visitor Center.................**2** C3
Bunnell St Gallery.............(see 6)
Fireweed Gallery..............(see 5)
Homer Council of the Arts...**3** B3
Pratt Museum...................**4** B2
Ptarmigan Arts.................**5** C2

SLEEPING
Old Town B&B...................**6** B3
Pioneer Inn......................**7** B2

EATING
Fat Olives.........................**8** B3
Fresh Sourdough Express....**9** E3
Mermaid Café....................**10** B3
Two Sisters Bakery...........**11** C3

DRINKING
Homer Brewing Company....**12** F3
Ring of Fire Meadery..........**13** C3

TRANSPORT
Homer Saw & Cycle...........**14** F3

To The Spit (50yd); Down East Saloon;
Ferry Terminal; Land's End Resort;
Mako's Water Taxi; Pier One Theatre;
Room at the Harbor;
Salty Dawg Saloon; Spitfire Grill

Homer Spit Rd
A St
Lakeshore Dr
Homer Stage
Line stop
Ocean Dr

To Bear Creek Lodging;
Fritz Creek General Store;
Homestead

Pennock St

Beluga
Lake

Ben Walters La

Lake St

Beluga Slough

Ocean Dr

Kachemak
Way

Heath St

Hazel Ave

Pioneer Ave

Svedlund St

Poopdeck St

Homer Bypass

Bishop Beach Trail

Danview Ave

Lee Dr

Main St

Bunnell Ave

Fairview Ave

Bartlett St

Olson La

Sterling Hwy

Crittenden Dr

Cliffs

Kachemak
Bay

DRINKING & ENTERTAINMENT

Salty Dawg Saloon (Homer Spit Rd) Perhaps the most storied bar on the Kenai Peninsula, the Salty Dawg Saloon is one of those places that's famous for being famous. In the evenings every square foot of its wood-shaving-laden floor is packed with tourists singing along to sea shanties, rubbing elbows with the occasional fisherman and paying 50% more for beer than they would elsewhere in town.

Homer Brewing Company (☎ 399-8060; 1411 Lakeshore Dr; ✆ noon-7pm Mon-Sat, to 5pm Sun) Isn't a bar, but it does offer 'tours' with free samples of fresh beer – try the broken birch bitter ale, and then grab a growler to go.

Ring of Fire Meadery (☎ 235-2656; 178 E Bunnell Ave; ✆ noon-6pm) Like the brewery, this isn't a bar, but there's a tasting room where you can sample the excellent mead, made with locally grown berries and fruit. It's unique and highly recommended.

Down East Saloon (☎ 235-6002; 3125 E End Rd) This spacious bar is where locals head to listen to live music. The view is a killer, but you'll likely be paying more attention to whichever Homer talent is on stage.

Pier One Theater (☎ 235-7333; Homer Spit Rd; admission $16) Live drama and comedy is performed in a 'come-as-you-are' warehouse next to the Fishing Hole on the Spit. Shows start at 8:15pm Friday and Saturday, and 7:30pm Sunday during summer.

CHRIS AREND, USFWS

Visitors at Alaska Islands & Ocean Visitor Center

⚓ ALASKA ISLANDS & OCEAN VISITOR CENTER

More a research facility and **museum** than a visitors center, this impressive new place has numerous cool interactive exhibits, perhaps the best of which is a room that's a replica seabird colony, complete with cacophonous bird calls and surround-view flocking. There's also a decent film about ship-based marine research, a hands-on discovery lab, and a slate of daily educational programs and guided walks.

Things you need to know: ☎ 235-6961; www.islandsandocean.org; 95 Sterling Hwy; admission free; ✆ 9am-6pm

GETTING THERE & AROUND

AIR

The contract carrier for Alaska Airlines, **ERA Aviation** (☎ 235-7565, 800-426-0333; www.flyera. com) provides daily flights between Homer and Anchorage from Homer's airport, 1.7 miles east of town on Kachemak Dr.

Smokey Bay Air (☎ 235-1511; www.smokeybayair.com; 2100 Kachemak Dr) offers flights to Seldovia for $47 each way.

BICYCLE

Homer Saw & Cycle (☎ 235-8406; www. homersaw.com; 1532 Ocean Dr; ☺ 9am-5:30pm Mon-Fri, 11am-5pm Sat) rents mountain bikes ($25 per day).

BOAT

The Alaska Marine Highway provides thrice-weekly service from Homer to Seldovia ($33, 1½ hours) and Kodiak ($74, 9½ hours), with connecting service to Seward as well as the Aleutians. Homer's **ferry terminal** (☎ 235-8449; www.ferryalaska.com) is located at the end of Homer Spit.

Rainbow Tours (☎ 235-7272; Homer Spit Rd; one way/round-trip $30/45) offers the inexpensive Rainbow Connection shuttle from Homer to Seldovia. It departs at 9am, gets to Seldovia an hour later, and then returns to take you back to Homer at 5pm. It'll transport your bike for $5 and your kayak for $10.

Many water-taxi operations shuttle campers and kayakers between Homer and points across Kachemak Bay. Though the companies are good and work closely together, the most respected by far is **Mako's Water Taxi** (off Map p186; ☎ 235-9055; www.makoswatertaxi. com; Homer Spit Rd). Mako's usually charges $75 (which includes the state park fee) per person round-trip, and it has a two-person minimum.

BUS

The **Homer Stage Line** (☎ 868-3914; www.homerstageline.com) runs daily from Homer to Anchorage (one way/round-trip $65/120), Seward ($55/100) and all points in between.

HOMER ART GALLERIES

This is just the tip of the iceberg – grab a free *Downtown Homer Art Galleries* flyer at the visitors center with many more gallery listings, or stop by the **Homer Council of the Arts** (☎ 235-4288; www.homerart.org; 355 W Pioneer Ave; ☺ 9am-6pm Mon-Fri), with its own awesome gallery and information on various tours.

- **Bunnell Street Gallery** (☎ 235-2662; www.bunnellstreetgallery.org; 106 W Bunnell Ave; ☺ 10am-6pm Mon-Sat, noon-4pm Sun) An avant-garde place with the priciest and most experimental offerings – definitely the star of the show.
- **Fireweed Gallery** (☎ 235-3411; 475 E Pioneer Ave; ☺ 10am-6pm Mon-Sat, 11am-5pm Sun) Has a more statewide representation than most of the other galleries. It's got photography, metalwork, oil paintings, jewelry, and is also home to the Kachemak Bay Watercolor Society.
- **Ptarmigan Arts** (☎ 235-5345; 471 E Pioneer Ave; ☺ 10am-7pm Mon-Sat, 10am-6pm Sun) An artist-owned and operated co-op featuring mostly works from the Kenai Peninsula, including jewelry, textiles, Alaska Native pieces, and Homer spruce ash-glaze pottery.

JOHN R. DELAPP / ALASKASTOCK.COM

Fishermen, Seldovia

SELDOVIA

pop 284

If the tourist-thronged towns of the Kenai Peninsula have left you frazzled, catch a boat to Seldovia, on the south side of Kachemak Bay and in a world of its own.

SIGHTS & ACTIVITIES

SELDOVIA VILLAGE TRIBE VISITOR CENTER

This **visitors center** (☎ 234-7898; www. svt.org; cnr Airport Ave & Main St; ⊗ 10am-5pm; 🖳), opened in 2005, attempts to showcase Seldovia's Alaska Native heritage – a unique blend of Alutiiq (Eskimo) and Tanaina (Indian) cultures. Though enjoyable (especially on a rainy day), the displays are a hodge-podge, featuring artifacts like arrowheads and stone knives dredged up from nearby waters, a series of old photos of Seldovia, and an exhibit about the intricacies of seal hunting.

ST NICHOLAS ORTHODOX CHURCH

Seldovia's most popular attraction is this onion-domed **church** (⊗ 1:30-3:30pm Mon-

Sat), which overlooks the town from a hill just off Main St. Built in 1891 and restored in the 1970s, the church is open on afternoons, when you can see the exquisite icons inside. Note the chandelier, made from old barrel staves.

HIKING

The **Otterbahn Trail** was famously created by local high school students, who dubbed it the 'we-worked-hard-so-you-better-like-it trail.' Lined with salmonberries and affording great views of Graduation Peak, it skirts the coastline most of the way and reaches Outside Beach in 1.5 miles. Make sure you hike it at tides below 17ft, as the last stretch runs across a slough that is only passable (legally – property above 17ft is private) when the water is out.

Two trails start from Jakolof Bay Rd. You can either hike down the beach toward the head of Seldovia Bay at low tide, or you can follow a 4.5-mile logging road to reach several secluded coves. There is also the **Tutka/Jakolof Trail**, a 2.5-mile trail to a campsite on the Tutka Lagoon, the site of a state salmon-rearing facility. The posted trail departs from Jakolof Bay Rd about 10.5 miles east of town.

The town's newest hike is the rigorous **Rocky Ridge Trail**, where 800ft of climbing will be rewarded with remarkable views of the bay, the town and Mt Iliamna. The trail starts (or ends) on Rocky St and loops back to the road near the airport, covering about 3 miles.

PADDLING

Kayak'Atak (☎ 234-7425; www.alaska. net/~kayaks/; kayaks 1st day single/double $50/80, subsequent days $35/50) rents kayaks and can help arrange transportation throughout the bay. It also offers various guided tours starting from $80, some including a 'gourmet lunch.'

SLEEPING

our pick **Across the Bay Tent & Breakfast** (☎ summer 235-3633, winter 345-2571; www. tentandbreakfastalaska.com; tent cabins per person $75; ✂) Located 8 miles from town on Jakolof Bay, this is something a little different. Its cabinlike tents include a full breakfast, and for $110 per day you can get a package that includes all your meals – and dinner could consist of fresh oysters, beach-grilled salmon or halibut stew with a side of garden-grown greens.

Bridgekeeper's Inn B&B (☎ 234-7535; www.thebridgekeepersinn.com; r $140-150) A cozy place with private baths and full breakfasts; one room has a balcony overlooking the salmon-filled slough.

Seldovia Rowing Club B&B (☎ 234-7614; www.seldoviarowingclub.net; 343 Bay St; r $135) Also located on the Old Boardwalk, this place – the first B&B in Southcentral Alaska – has homey suites decorated with quilts, antiques and owner Susan Mumma's watercolors. She serves big breakfasts and often hosts music concerts.

EATING

Tidepool Café (☎ 234-7502; 267 Main St; breakfast $6-11, lunch $9-16, dinner $16-30; ☻ 7am-3pm daily, plus 5:30-9pm Wed-Sun) In a sunny space overlooking the harbor,

Seldovia Rowing Club B&B

DON PITCHER

this eclectic eatery serves great wraps, sandwiches and espressos, and has dinner offerings like drunken mussels ($13) and sweet-chili salmon ($23). You'll need reservations for dinner.

Mad Fish (☎ 234-7676; 221 Main St; lunch $9-11, dinner $13-29; ☺ 11:30am-9pm) The only white-tablecloth venue in Seldovia is a bit overpriced but serves adequate croissant sandwiches and chowder. Its bread is fresh-baked.

GETTING THERE & AROUND
BICYCLE
If you didn't bring your two-wheeler over from Homer, the Boardwalk Hotel rents **mountain bikes** (per hr guests/nonguests $20/30).

BOAT
Alaska Marine Highway ferries provide twice-weekly service between Homer and Seldovia ($33, 1½ hours), with connecting service throughout the peninsula and the Aleutians. The **Seldovia ferry terminal** (☎ 234-7886, www.ferryalaska.com) is at the north end of Main St.

Rainbow Tours (☎ 235-7272; drop-off at Homer Spit Rd; one way/round-trip $30/45) offers the inexpensive Rainbow Connection shuttle from Homer to Seldovia.

Mako's Water-taxi (☎ 235-9055; www.makoswatertaxi.com; drop-off at Homer Spit Rd; round-trip $135) offers an excellent tour that takes you by boat, car, and plane. Mako's drops you off at Jakolof Bay, from which you'll be driven to Seldovia. You return to Homer via a short flightseeing trip.

PLANE
Smokey Bay Air (☎ 235-1511; www.smokeybayair.com; 2100 Kachemak Dr; one way $47) offers a scenic 12-minute flight from Homer, over the Kenai Mountains and Kachemak Bay to Seldovia.

Homer Air (☎ 235-8591; www.homerair.com; one way/round-trip $45/90) flies to Seldovia hourly.

KACHEMAK BAY STATE PARK
Stand on Homer Spit and look south, and an alluring wonderland sprawls before you: a luxuriantly green coastline, sliced by fjords and topped by sparkling glaciers and rugged peaks. This is Kachemak Bay State Park, which, along with Kachemak Bay State Wilderness Park to the south, includes 350,000 acres of idyllic wilderness accessible only by bush plane or boat.

SIGHTS & ACTIVITIES
HIKING
GLACIER LAKE TRAIL
The most popular hike in Kachemak Bay State Park is this 3½-mile, one-way trail that begins at the Glacier Spit trailhead, near the small Rusty Lagoon Campground. The level, easy-to-follow trek proceeds across the glacial outwash and ends at a lake with superb views of Grewingk Glacier. At Mile 1.4 you can connect to the 6½-mile **Grewingk Glacier Trail**, with a hand-tram and access to the face of the glacier.

PADDLING
A tiny family-run outfit, **Seaside Adventures** (☎ 235-6672; www.seasideadventure.com; trips incl water-taxi half-/full day $110/150) will show you the bay on kayak, complete with running commentary about local flora and fauna.

True North Kayak Adventures (☎ 235-0708; www.truenorthkayak.com), based on Yukon Island, runs half-day paddles amid the eagles overhead and otters for $99, water-taxi included.

Glacier Lake Kayaking & Hiking (☎ 888-777-0930, 235-0755; www.threemoose.com) offers kayaking on Glacier Lake, inside

Kachemak Bay State Park, combined with guided hikes ($175).

GETTING THERE & AROUND

Mako's Water-taxi (☎ 235-9055; www.makoswatertaxi.com) is the most respected of Homer's water-taxi services, famed for making timely pickups even in foul weather – and for dropping off beer to unsuspecting campers.

Other good outfits include **Smoke Wagon Water-taxi & Charter** (☎ 235-2947, 888-205-2947; www.homerwatertaxi.com) and **Tutka Bay Taxi** (☎ 399-1723; www.tutkabaytaxi.com).

KODIAK ISLAND

Stretching across 3670 sq miles and more than 100 miles long, Kodiak is Alaska's largest island and the US's second largest, after the Big Island of Hawaii. It's fitting then that its most famous residents are the world's largest terrestrial carnivores.

The vast majority of this island is a green and jagged wilderness that was so deeply carved by glaciers, no point on land is more than 15 miles from the ocean.

KODIAK

pop 13,574

Kodiak sits at the crossroads of some of the most productive fishing grounds in the world and is home to Alaska's largest fishing fleet – 650 boats, including the state's largest trawl, longline and crab vessels.

This is the real Alaska: unaltered, unassuming and not inundated by tourism. Arrive for the scenery, stay to enjoy outdoor adventures that range from kayaking to photographing a 1000lb bear.

SIGHTS

BARANOV MUSEUM

Housed in the oldest Russian structure in Alaska is **Baranov Museum** (☎ 486-5920; 101 Marine Way; adult/child $3/free; ☼ 10am-4pm Mon-Sat, from noon Sun), across the street from the visitor center. The museum fills the Erskine House, which the Russians built in 1808 as a storehouse for precious sea-otter pelts. Today it holds many items

GRAEME CORNWALLIS

Baranov Museum

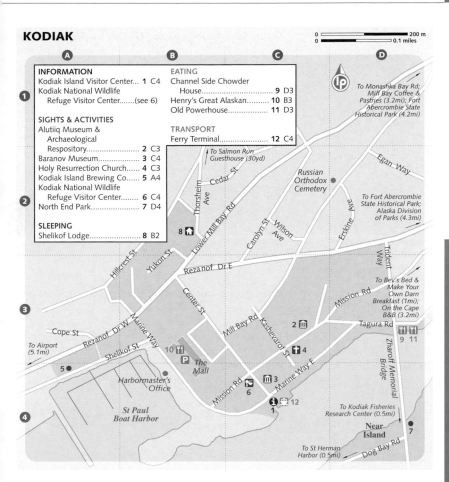

KODIAK

| 0 | 200 m |
| 0 | 0.1 miles |

INFORMATION
Kodiak Island Visitor Center... **1** C4
Kodiak National Wildlife
   Refuge Visitor Center.......(see 6)

SIGHTS & ACTIVITIES
Alutiiq Museum &
   Archaeological
   Repository....................... **2** C3
Baranov Museum.................. **3** C4
Holy Resurrection Church...... **4** C3
Kodiak Island Brewing Co...... **5** A4
Kodiak National Wildlife
   Refuge Visitor Center........ **6** C4
North End Park.................... **7** D4

SLEEPING
Shelikof Lodge..................... **8** B2

EATING
Channel Side Chowder
   House............................... **9** D3
Henry's Great Alaskan.......... **10** B3
Old Powerhouse................. **11** D3

TRANSPORT
Ferry Terminal.................... **12** C4

To Monashka Bay Rd;
Mill Bay Coffee &
Pastries (3.2mi); Fort
Abercrombie State
Historical Park (4.2mi)

To Salmon Run
Guesthouse (30yd)

Russian
Orthodox
Cemetery

To Fort Abercrombie
State Historical Park;
Alaska Division
of Parks (4.3mi)

Thorsheim Ave

Cedar St

Egan Way

Erskine Ave

Trident Way

Hillcrest St

Yukon St

Rezanof Dr E

Lower Mill Bay Rd

Carolyn St

Wilson Ave

To Bev's Bed &
Make Your
Own Darn
Breakfast (1mi);
On the Cape
B&B (3.2mi)

Mission Rd

Tagura Rd

Cope St

Rezanof Dr W

Marine Way

Center St

Mill Bay Rd

Kashevarof St

Zharoff Memorial
Bridge

To Airport
(5.1mi)

Shelikof St

The
Mall

Harbormaster's
Office

Mission Rd

Marine Way E

To Kodiak Fisheries
Research Center (0.5mi)

St Paul
Boat Harbor

Near
Island

Dog Bay Rd

To St Herman
Harbor (0.5mi)

---

from the Russian period of Kodiak's history, along with fine examples of Alutiiq basketry and carvings. The gift shop is particularly interesting, offering a wide selection of *matreshkas* (nesting dolls), samovars and other Russian crafts.

HOLY RESURRECTION CHURCH
Near the Alutiiq museum on Mission Rd is **Holy Resurrection Church** (☎ 486-5532; **385 Kashevarof St**), which serves the oldest Russian Orthodox parish in the New World, established in 1794. The present church, marked by its beautiful blue onion

domes, was built in 1945 and is the third one to occupy this site. You are free to join tours that are staged when a cruise ship is in.

KODIAK NATIONAL WILDLIFE REFUGE VISITOR CENTER
This new **visitor center** (☎ 487-2600; **402 Center St;** 9am-5pm) focuses on the Kodiak brown bear, the most famous resident of the refuge, and it features an exhibit room that's especially well suited for children, a short film on the bears and a bookstore.

MICHAEL DEYOUNG

Hiker, Kodiak Island

➤ IF YOU LIKE...

If you like getting of the beaten path, we think you'll like to explore the following trails; the first two originate on the **Glacier Lake Trail** (p191):

- **Alpine Ridge Trail** At the high point of the mile-long Saddle Trail, an offshoot of the Glacier Lake Trail, you will reach the posted junction for this 2-mile climb to an alpine ridge above the glacier.
- **Lagoon Trail** Also departing from the Saddle Trail is this 5½-mile route that leads to the ranger station at the head of Halibut Cove Lagoon.
- **Emerald Lake Trail** This steep, difficult 6.4-mile trail begins at Grewingk Glacial Lake and leads to Portlock Plateau. At Mile 2.1 a spur trail reaches the scenic Emerald Lake, and there are great views of the bay from the plateau.
- **Grace Ridge Trail** This is a 7-mile trail that stretches from a campsite at Kayak Beach trailhead to deep inside Tutka Bay in the state park. Much of the hike runs above the treeline along the crest of Grace Ridge, where, needless to say, the views are stunning.

ALUTIIQ MUSEUM & ARCHAEOLOGICAL REPOSITORY

Preserving the 7500-year heritage of Kodiak's indigenous Alutiiq people is the **Alutiiq Museum & Archaeological Repository** (☎ 486-7004; www.alutiiqmuseum. com; 215 Mission Rd; adult/child $5/free; ⏱ 9am-5pm Mon-Fri, from 10am Sat). The exhibits display one of the largest collections of Alutiiq artifacts in the state, ranging from a kayaker in his waterproof parka of seal gut to a 19th-

century spruce-root hat and the corner of a sod house. Take time to explore 'Sharing Words,' an intriguing interactive computer program that uses village elders to teach Alutiiq words and songs in an attempt to save the indigenous language.

FORT ABERCROMBIE STATE HISTORICAL PARK

This military **fort**, 4.5 miles northeast of Kodiak, off Monashka Bay Rd, and its pair of 8in guns, were built by the US Army during WWII for a Japanese invasion that never came. In the end, Kodiak's lousy weather kept the Japanese bombers away from the island. The fort is now a 186-acre state historical park, sitting majestically on the cliffs above scenic Monashka Bay. Between the guns is Ready Ammunition Bunker, which stored 400 rounds of ammunition during the war. Today the park contains the small **Kodiak Military History Museum** (☎ 486-7015; adult/child $3/free; ⊙ 1-4pm Fri-Mon).

KODIAK ISLAND BREWING CO

This is another one of Alaska's fantastic one-man microbreweries. Behind the counter, pouring the suds, at **Kodiak Island Brewing Co** (☎ 486-2537; 338 Shelikof St; ⊙ noon-7pm) is brewmaster, owner and tour guide Ben Millstein. He'll be more than happy to give you a short tour (after all, it's only a one-room operation) or to simply let you taste the five beers he brews onsite.

ACTIVITIES
HIKING

The best source of hiking information is the **Alaska Division of Parks** (☎ 486-6339) or the excellent *Kodiak Audubon's Hiking & Birding Guide* (sold at various places around town including the Kodiak National Wildlife Refuge Visitor Center for $13), a large waterproof topographical map with notes on the trails and birds.

Plant-lovers might consider **Backwoods Botany** (☎ 486-5712, ext 201; tours $25; ⊙ 1pm Mon-Fri) and its 3-hour plant-identification hiking tour of the island.

BAROMETER MOUNTAIN

This popular hiking trail is a steep climb and a 4-mile round-trip to the 2452ft summit. The trek, which begins in thick alder before climbing the hogback ridge of the mountain, provides spectacular views of Kodiak and the bays south of the city.

TERMINATION POINT

Another popular hike, this 5-mile loop starts at the end of Monashka Bay Rd

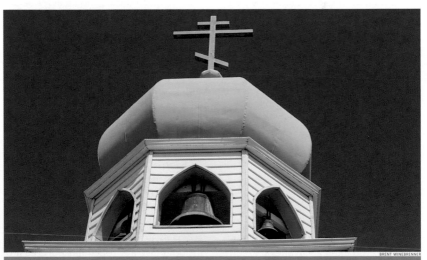

BRENT WINEBRENNER

Russian Orthodox Church, Kodiak Island

Fishing boats, Kodiak Island

JAMES MARSHALL

and branches into several trails near Termination Point, a spectacular peninsula that juts out into Narrow Strait.

NORTH SISTER MOUNTAIN
Starting 150ft up a creek bed a mile before the end of Monashka Bay Rd, this trail (find it on the left side of the creek bed) first leads up steeply through dense brush, but then levels off on alpine tundra.

PYRAMID MOUNTAIN
Two trails, both starting on Anton Larsen Bay Rd, lead to the top of Pyramid Mountain (2401ft).

ANTON LARSEN PASS
This 5-mile loop is a scenic ridge walk and a far easier alpine hike than Barometer Mountain.

PADDLING
With its many bays and protected inlets, scenic coastline and offshore rookeries, much of Kodiak is a kayaker's dream. Unfortunately, there is nowhere in Kodiak

to rent a kayak. A number of outfitters do offer fully equipped tours.

ourpick **Orcas Unlimited** (☎ 539-1979; www.orcasunlimited.com; 1 day $200-240, 2 day $720-860) has a full-day paddle looking for marine wildlife around islands near Kodiak, utilizing a mother ship with a dive platform to make this outing ideal for beginner kayakers. It also has a two-day kayak adventure.

Alaska Wilderness Adventures (☎ 487-2397; www.akwildadventures.com; full day $145-160) specializes in whale watching, along with seeing other marine wildlife like sea otters and puffins, from kayaks. Destinations depend on where the wildlife is.

KODIAK FOR CHILDREN
Kodiak Fisheries Research Center (☎ 481-1800; Trident Way; ⊙ 8am-4:30pm Mon-Fri) Opened in 1998 to house the fisheries research being conducted by various agencies, it has an interesting lobby that includes displays, touch tanks and a large aquarium.

North End Park (Trident Way) This small park is laced with forested trails that converge at a stairway heading to the shoreline. At low tide you can search the tidal pools for starfish as well as other marine life.

St Herman Harbor (Dog Bay Rd) A great place to look for sea lions, which often use the Dog Bay Breakwall as a haul-out, while eagles are usually perched in the trees onshore.

TOURS

Galley Gourmet (☎ 486-5079, 800-253-6331; www.kodiak-alaska-dinner-cruises.com; brunch/dinner $110/135) Along with their whale watching and harbor cruises, Marty and Marion Owen offer a delightful dinner cruise onboard their 42ft yacht.

Kodiak Tours (☎ 486-3920; www.kodiaktours.com; half-/full-day $55/95) The best operator of tours on land.

SLEEPING

our pick Bev's Bed & Make Your Own Darn Breakfast (☎ 486-8217; www.bevsbedandbreakfast.com; 1510 Mission Rd; r $85-110; ☒ ▢) The name of this B&B is misleading. Bev no longer runs it and the new host often brings down muffins and fresh-baked breads for breakfast.

Shelikof Lodge (☎ 486-4141; www.shelikoflodge.com; 211 Thorsheim Ave; s/d $100/111; ☒ ▢) The Shelikof Lodge has the nicest rooms downtown for what you pay, plus a good restaurant and a lounge that's not the smokiest in town. A bonus is the airport shuttle service.

Salmon Run Guesthouse (☎ 486-0091; www.salmonrunguesthouse.com; 410 Hillside Dr; r with/without bath $110/150; ☒) It maybe a bit of an uphill climb to this downtown B&B, but it's worth every step.

On the Cape B&B (☎ 486-4185; www.onthecape.net; 3476 Spruce Cape Rd; r $135-160; ☒ ▢) This is a beautiful home located between downtown and Fort Abercrombie, with three rooms whose windows are filled with the ocean and boats motoring by.

EATING

our pick Mill Bay Coffee & Pastries (☎ 486-4411; 3833 E Rezanof Dr; breakfast $5-7, lunch $8-10; ☺ 7am-6pm Mon-Sat, 8am-5pm Sun; ☒) What on earth is a French chef doing in Kodiak? Joel Chenet's love of hunting is the reason this city is blessed with the best pastries in Alaska, hands down. A warning – get there early: the case is empty of tortes, éclairs and apple pies by midafternoon.

MICHAEL DEYOUNG

Hikers, Pyramid Mountain

Old Powerhouse (☎ 481-1088; 516 Marine Way; lunch special $8-10, dinner $15-22; 🕙 11:30am-2pm & 5-9pm Tue-Thu, 11:30am-2pm & 5-10pm Fri & Sat, 5-9pm Sun; ✖) Kodiak's best dining experience is this historic power plant that has been beautifully renovated into a superb Japanese seafood restaurant.

Henry's Great Alaskan (☎ 486-8844; 512 Marine Way; sandwiches $9-13, dinner $16-33; 🕙 11:25am-10pm Mon-Thu, to 10:30pm Fri & Sat, noon-9:30pm Sun) Where else in Kodiak can you order crawfish pie or Henry's bouillabaisse: a bowl of clams, mussels, halibut and Cajun sausage in a rich seafood broth?

Channel Side Chowder House (☎ 486-4478; 450 E Marine Way; fish 'n' chips $9-15; 🕙 7am-7:30pm Mon-Thu, 7am-8pm Fri, 8am-8pm Sat, 9am-6pm Sun; ✖) You just know the fish is superfresh at this busy chowder house, which is located right in the middle of a boat harbor.

GETTING THERE & AWAY

Both **Alaska Airlines** (☎ 487-4363, 800-252-7522) and its contract carrier **ERA Aviation** (☎ 487-4363, 800-866-8394; www.eraaviation.com) fly to Kodiak daily. Fares range between $300 and $350.

Alaska Marine Highway's MV *Tustumena* (see the boxed text, p268) stops at **Kodiak Ferry Terminal** (☎ 486-3800; 100 Marine Way) several times a week, coming from Homer (one way $74, 9½ hours), and stopping twice a week at Port Lions, a nearby village on Kodiak Island. Once a month the 'Trusty Tusty' continues west to Unalaska and Dutch Harbor (costing $293 one way departing from Kodiak). Several times a month the MV *Kennicott* sails to Kodiak from Homer and Whittier (one way $91, 10 hours).

ALASKA PENINSULA

The Alaska Peninsula's most popular attraction, Katmai National Park & Preserve, has turned King Salmon into the main access point. Two other preserves – McNeil River State Game Area and Lake Clark National Park & Preserve – also attract the interest of travelers; while the Alaska Marine Highway stops at four small communities along the peninsula before it snakes its way into the Aleutians.

KING SALMON
pop 426

Just under 300 air miles from Anchorage, King Salmon is the air-transport hub for Katmai National Park & Preserve (see opposite). Most visitors see little more than the airport terminal and the float dock from where they catch a flight into the park.

SLEEPING & EATING

King Ko Inn (☎ 246-3377, 866-234-3474; www.kingko.com; 100 Airport Rd; cabins s/d $195/215; 💻) Friendly, comfortable and adjacent to the airport terminal. It offers 16 cabins with private baths; eight of them also have kitchenettes. The King Ko is also home to the liveliest bar in town.

The King Ko Inn has a full-service restaurant, or you might try **Eddie's Fireplace Inn** (☎ 246-3435; Airport Rd; breakfast $11-14, dinner $20-32; 🕙 7am-10pm), across the street, with an atmospheric bar and a kitchen that is open all day.

GETTING THERE & AWAY

Alaska Airlines (☎ 800-252-7522; www.alaskaair.com) flies up to six times daily between Anchorage and King Salmon during the summer.

↘ BEAR WATCHING

Katmai has the world's largest population of protected brown bears (more than 2000).

Brooks Camp has three established viewing areas. From the lodge, a dirt road leads to a floating bridge over the river and the first observation deck – a large platform dubbed 'Fort Stevens' by rangers, for the Alaskan senator who secured the funding for it. From here you can see the bears feeding in the mouth of the river or swimming in the bay.

Continue on the road to the Valley of 10,000 Smokes, and in half a mile a marked trail winds to Brooks Falls. Two more viewing platforms lie along this half-mile trail. The first sits above some riffles that occasionally draw sows trying to keep their cubs away from aggressive males at the falls.

The last deck, at the falls, is the prime viewing area, where you can photograph the salmon making spectacular leaps or a big brownie at the top of the cascade waiting with open jaws to catch a fish. At the peak of the salmon run, there might be eight to 12 bears here, two or three of them atop the falls themselves. The observation deck holds 40 people, and in early to mid-July it will be crammed with photographers, forcing rangers to rotate people on and off.

KATMAI NATIONAL PARK & PRESERVE

In June 1912 Novarupta Volcano erupted violently and, with the preceding earthquakes, rocked the area now known as Katmai National Park & Preserve. The wilderness was turned into a dynamic landscape of smoking valleys, ash-covered mountains and small holes and cracks fuming with steam and gas. Only one other eruption in documented historic times, on the Greek island of Santorini in 1500 BC, displaced more ash and pumice.

The fumaroles no longer smoke and hiss and today the park is best known for bears. In July, at the peak of bear viewing, throngs of visitors arrive to watch brown bears, snagging salmon in midair, just 30yd away.

TOURS
PACKAGE TOURS

Because of the logistics of getting there and the need to plan and reserve so much in advance, many visitors arrive in Katmai as part of a one-call-does-it-all package tour.

ourpick Hallo Bay Bear Camp (☎ 235-2237, 888-535-2237; www.hallobay.com) This ecofriendly camp is on the outside coast of Katmai National Park and is designed exclusively for bear viewing. The cabins are simple but comfortable and the camp can handle only 12 guests at a time. In such an intimate setting, the bear watching can be surreal at times. Packages include airfare from Homer, lodging, meals and guides and begin at $1200 per person for two nights.

Katmailand (☎ 243-5448, 800-544-0551; www.katmailand.com) Offers packages that are geared for either anglers or bear watchers. Its one-day tour to see the bears of Brooks Falls is $589 per person. A three-night angler's package which includes all transportation, lodging and meals is $1542 to $1849 per person based on double-occupancy.

Katmai National Park & Preserve

IMAGEBROKER/BERND ZOLLER

SLEEPING & EATING

Brooks Lodge (Katmailand; ☎ 243-5448, 800-544-0551; www.katmailand.com) The lodge has 16 basic, but modernized, cabin-style rooms, each with two bunk beds and a private bath with shower. Cabins are rented as part of package tours that include transportation from Anchorage, and in July there is a three-night maximum stay. A three-night package is $1497 per person, a three-night stay outside of the prime bear-viewing period is $920 to $1190.

A store at Brooks Camp sells limited supplies of freeze-dried food, white gas (for camp stoves), fishing equipment, flies, and other odds and ends…such as beer.

GETTING THERE & AWAY

Most visitors to Katmai fly into King Salmon on **Alaska Airlines** (☎ 800-252-7522; www.alaskaair.com). Once you're in King Salmon, a number of air-taxi companies offer the 20-minute floatplane flight out to Brooks Camp. **Katmai Air** (☎ 243-5448, 800-544-0551; www.katmailand.com/air-services), the Katmailand-affiliated company, charges $176 for a round-trip.

DENALI & THE INTERIOR

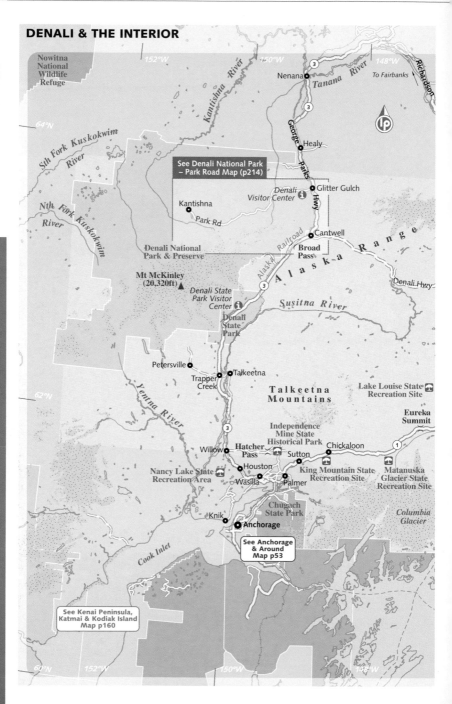

Nowitna National Wildlife Refuge

Kantishna River

152°W

150°W

148°W

Richardson

Tanana River

Nenana

To Fairbanks

64°N

Sth Fork Kuskokwim River

George Parks Hwy

Healy

See Denali National Park – Park Road Map (p214)

Denali Visitor Center

Glitter Gulch

Nth Fork Kuskokwim River

Kantishna

Park Rd

Denali Hwy

Cantwell

Denali National Park & Preserve

Alaska Railroad

Broad Pass

A l a s k a   R a n g e

Mt McKinley (20,320ft)

Denali State Park Visitor Center

Denali Hwy

Susitna River

Denali State Park

Petersville

Talkeetna

Trapper Creek

T a l k e e t n a
M o u n t a i n s

Lake Louise State Recreation Site

62°N

Yentna River

Eureka Summit

Independence Mine State Historical Park

Chickaloon

1

Willow

Hatcher Pass

Sutton

Nancy Lake State Recreation Area

Houston

King Mountain State Recreation Site

Matanuska Glacier State Recreation Site

Wasilla

Palmer

Knik

Chugach State Park

Columbia Glacier

Anchorage

See Anchorage & Around Map p53

Cook Inlet

See Kenai Peninsula, Katmai & Kodiak Island Map p160

60°N

152°W

150°W

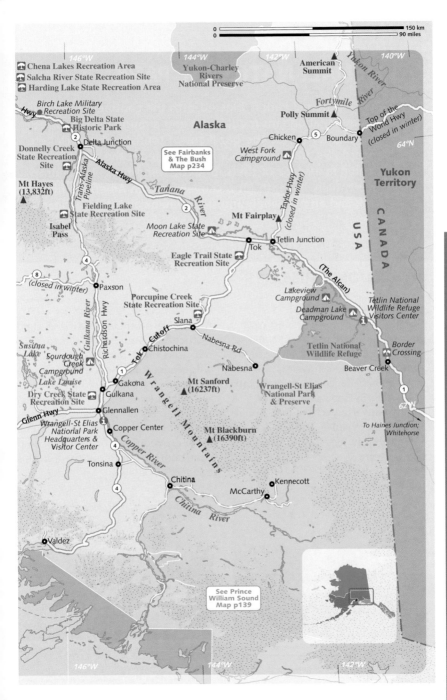

HIGHLIGHTS

1 DENALI NATIONAL PARK

Denali National Park is blessed with the continent's mightiest mountain, abundant megafauna and enough untrammeled backcountry to flee the gazillions of tourists who flock here aboard RVs, trains and tour buses. You get the massive arching landscape of the sub-Arctic wilderness, which drops reverentially beneath Mt McKinley – North America's highest peak and an overwhelming sight when caught on a clear day.

↘ OUR DON'T MISS LIST

❶ PARK ROAD

The 92 miles of the **Park Rd** (p212) pierces the heart of Denali National Park. Closed to vehicle traffic at Mile 14, the road offers travelers the unmatched experience of venturing into true wilderness by park shuttle – a comfy, converted school bus. You're likely to spot wildlife, and can hop on and off the shuttles for day hikes and photography.

❷ THE BACKCOUNTRY

A massive protected area plus rigid restrictions (you even have to pack out used toilet paper) equals a true wilderness experience in Denali's **backcountry**. The park has 87 units, but only around half of those are accessible to backpackers, and even then the limit is four to six people per unit. Strap on your bear bells and lace up your boots; it's wild out there in this trail-free wilderness.

Clockwise from top: Mt McKinley (p213); Brown bears alongside tour buses; Denali National Park (p212)

❸ BUZZING THE SUMMIT

More than 20,000 feet high, the summit of Mt McKinley is unlike anything most people will ever see. The mighty slab of rock and ice begins at 2000 feet, making for a vertical rise of 18,000 dramatic feet. A flightseeing tour (p218) past the summit, especially with a glacier landing, is the perfect way to appreciate just how huge this iconic mountain is.

❹ DENALI VISITOR CENTER

A large facility whose size mirrors that of the park and its namesake mountain, the Denali Visitor Center (p209) showcases a giant table-top relief map giving you the lay of the land, while downstairs there are museum-quality displays on the area's natural and human history. Every half hour in the theater the beautifully photographed, unnarrated film *Heartbeats of Denali* provides a peek at the park's wildlife and scenery.

↘ THINGS YOU NEED TO KNOW

Best photo op If you're lucky enough to visit on a clear day, take a park shuttle bus to Wonder Lake Campground, at Mile 84 of Park Rd. Here you can see the mountain reflected in the still waters of the lake, and it's especially breathtaking at sunset **For full details about Denali National Park, see p212**

HIGHLIGHTS

2

↘ RIDE THE RAILS

For a truly unique and local experience, hop on Alaska Railroad's **Hurricane Turn** (p226), allegedly the last flag-stop train in the US. Running from Talkeetna to Hurricane Gulch, the older rail cars carry fishers, hikers and weekend cabin vacationers. It's a scenic route and well worth a simple day trip just for the experience, or you can pitch a tent for a night and flag the train down the next day.

3

↘ EXPLORE THE PARKS

Your opportunities to experience massive wilderness are only limited by your time. Huge expanses of wild, protected lands cover the region, from **Denali National Park** (p212) to **Wrangell-St Elias National Park** (p228). Hubs nearby, such as Talkeetna and Kennecott, offer amenities and tour options. Take a simple walk from your lodge or a plane to a remote glacier; either way, you'll be in the wild.

4

◥ PHOTOGRAPH THE WILDLIFE

Denali National Park is home to the Denali herd of caribou and around 350 grizzly bears, as well as wolves, moose, bears and wolverines. Hop on a park bus or take a tour down the **Park Rd** (p212), where you're practically guaranteed to spot an animal in the wild.

5

◥ RUN THE RIVERS

There are about as many rivers as there are glaciers in the area – and that's a lot. In Denali National Park, floating the **Nenana River** (p218) is one of the most popular activities, while in **Talkeetna** (p223), you'll find rafting companies to can take you on a mellow float of the Talkeetna River.

6

◥ WALK ON A GLACIER

There are few things cooler (literally) than standing on a river of ice thousands of years old. How you get on the glacier is your pick: take a helicopter to a glacier on **Mt McKinley** (p218), try your hand at ice climbing on the **Matanuska Glacier** (p228) or just hike on up to the **Root Glacier** (p230).

2 IMAGEBROKER/JAN RICHTER; 3 ROB BLAKERS; 4 MARK NEWMAN; 5 DON PITCHER / ALASKASTOCK.COM; 6 GRANT DIXON

2 Alaska Railroad; 3 Autumn trees, Talkeetna (p223); 4 Dall sheep, Denali National Park (p212); 5 Rafting, Nenana River (p218); 6 Ski plane, Denali National Park (p212)

BEST...

⇘ RIVERS TO FLOAT

- **Nenana** (p218) A Class III river that's tourist-friendly.
- **Talkeetna** (p223) You'll stay dry on this placid two-hour float.
- **Kennicott** (p231) Run the glacial meltwater in Wrangell-St Elias.

⇘ WILDERNESS ESCAPES

- **Kantishna** (p219) Deep in the heart of Denali National Park.
- **McCarthy** (p229) You can't drive into this mountain town; walk across a footbridge instead.
- **Carlo Creek** (p220) A great place for independent travelers to stay while visiting Denali National Park.

⇘ LODGES & ROADHOUSES

- **Kantishna Roadhouse** (p220) This place sits on a creek at the end of the Park Rd.
- **Kennicott Glacier Lodge** (p231) A sprawling place with upscale dining.

- **Sheep Mountain Lodge** (p227) Great views, a sauna and a bunkhouse make for a fun stay.
- **Talkeetna Roadhouse** (p224) A climbers' favorite, built in 1917.

⇘ HIKING TRAILS

- **Savage River Loop** (p216) In Denali, you can wander past the wheelchair-accessible path and head into the backcountry.
- **Polychrome Pass Circuit** (p217) This 8-mile hike through colorful volcanic rock is one of the most scenic day hikes in the Park.
- **Bonanza Mine Trail** (p230) A challenging hike to a view of mining ruins.
- **Byers Lake Loop Trail** (p222) In Denali State Park; a nice 4.8-mile loop around the lake.

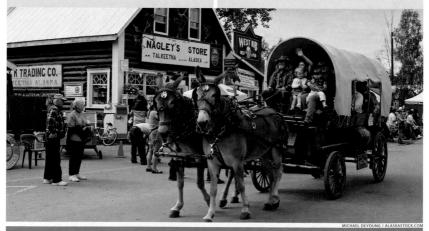

MICHAEL DEYOUNG / ALASKASTOCK.COM

Talkeetna Moose Dropping Festival (p48)

THINGS YOU NEED TO KNOW

⬐ VITAL STATISTICS
- **Best time to visit** April to September

⬐ LOCALITIES IN A NUTSHELL
- **Denali National Park & Around** (p212) Glitter Gulch, Healy, Carlo Creek and Kantishna all have lodging and dining available.
- **Wrangell-St Elias** (p228) The US's largest national park, with massive peaks, valleys, glaciers and ice fields.
- **Talkeetna** (p223) Headquarters for mountain climbers heading up Denali.

⬐ ADVANCE PLANNING
- **Two months ahead** Start exercising your quadriceps.
- **One month ahead** Reserve your accommodations.
- **Two weeks ahead** Plan rafting, flightseeing and bus tours.

⬐ RESOURCES
- **Backcountry Information Center** (Map p219; BIC; ☎ 683-9510; Mile 0.5 Park Rd; ☽ 9am-6pm) If you want to overnight in Denali's backcountry you'll need to come to the BIC.
- **Wilderness Access Center** (Map p219; WAC; ☎ 683-9274; Mile 0.5 Park Rd; ☽ 5am-8pm) The WAC's main function is as the park's transport hub and campground reservation center.

- **Denali Visitor Center** (Map p219; ☎ 683-2294; www.nps.gov/dena; Mile 1.5 Park Rd; ☽ 8am-6pm) This 14,000-sq-ft, $5-million facility is the place to come for an executive summary of Denali National Park.
- **Wrangell-St Elias National Park Headquarters & Visitor Center** (☎ 822-5234; www.nps.gov/wrst; Mile 106.8 Richardson Hwy; ☽ 8am-6pm)

⬐ GETTING AROUND
- **Bus** Several companies travel from both Anchorage and Fairbanks.
- **Train** You can hop on from Anchorage, Talkeetna or Fairbanks.
- **Air** Bush planes are the mode of transport for any place off the road or rails.

⬐ BE FOREWARNED
- **Getting lost** This is a real, life-threatening danger. Always let people know your plans.
- **Wildlife encounters** Grizzlies live here, and mosquitoes and black flies are abundant.
- **Glacier travel** Always go with a guide if you don't know how to self-arrest or perform a crevasse rescue.
- **Weather** Denali creates its own weather patterns, and glacier landings are often cancelled due to clouds.

DENALI & THE INTERIOR ITINERARIES

THE GREAT ONE Three Days

This tour sends you after the best view of Mt McKinley, the tallest mountain in North America. To get face to face with Denali, take a flightseeing tour. Several companies out of **(1) Denali National Park** (p212) will buzz the mountain and the more adventurous can land on a glacier or visit base camp via helicopter. Flights that go over the summit even require oxygen masks. It's worth noting that you can't actually see the mountain from the park headquarters, but must travel up Park Rd or take an air tour.

From Denali, ride the **(2) Alaska Railroad** (p222) south. As you head past Hurricane Gulch, you'll begin to spot the bright white top of the mountain peeking over closer ridges; this is the closest the train and Parks Hwy will get to it. Glide on into **(3) Talkeetna** (p223), the headquarters for mountaineers heading up to or returning from a summit attempt. While Talkeetna has some of the best options for flightseeing tours, it also claims breathtaking views from land. On a clear day, Denali looms over the foothills, looking like a cardboard cut-out. Hanging out on the sandy banks of the Susitna River in bright July sunshine, gazing at the lofty peak, is one of the more amazing experiences you're likely to have in a lifetime.

EXPLORE DENALI Five Days

With five days in **(1) Denali National Park** (p212) you'll be able to go backpacking or get in a lot of day hiking. Your first venture, however, should be on a shuttle down the Park Rd to **(2) Kantishna** (p215). You can hop on and off for hiking and photography, and are likely to spot some serious wildlife. Spend a night or two down at the end of the road, taking photos of Wonder Lake and its surrounds, and then catch the shuttle back in.

If you tire of the tundra, take a raft trip down the Nenana River to **(3) Healy** (p216). No trip to the park is complete without stopping by the **(4) Backcountry Information Center** (p209), where you can either plan your own overnight excursion into the park, or watch other hikers meticulously plan their trips across the park's grids.

INTERIOR NATIONAL PARKS One Week

Interior Alaska is crammed full of massive peaks. Mt McKinley gets most of the credit (deservedly), but don't forget about the others in the area. With a week, you'll have enough time to travel across the Interior. You might want to book a massage, however; you might get a cramp from looking up so much.

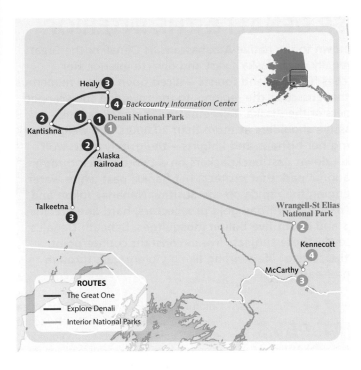

DENALI & THE INTERIOR

DENALI & THE INTERIOR ITINERARIES

Begin by spending some time in (1) Denali National Park (p212); you can follow the Explore Denali itinerary.

From Denali National Park, roll east across the Denali Hwy, down the Richardson, and on over to (2) Wrangell-St Elias National Park (p228). The biggest National Park in the United States is an impressive array of giant mountains, seemingly infinite glaciers and rivers, and hardly any people. Make (3) McCarthy (p229) your base, taking day hikes into the wilderness from here. A trip to the end of the road isn't complete without visiting (4) Kennecott (p229), with an abandoned mine that looks like the perfect place for a ghost.

DISCOVER DENALI & THE INTERIOR

Mt McKinley, known to the native Athabascans as Denali or the Great One, presides regally over Alaska's vast and diverse interior. Her dominion stretches from lowland forests – sliced open by the numerous braided rivers that crisscross the region – to the towering snowcapped peaks and glaciers of the Alaska, Talkeetna and Wrangell ranges.

From her massive shoulders at more than 20,000ft, she weighs her strategy, sending her bishops and knights – the grizzly bear, wolf, coyote and fox – down past backpackers on a two-day trek through the gigantic national park that protects her flanks; past white-water paddlers challenging the rapids on the Susitna, Nenana, Yukon and Tanana Rivers; past modern-day gold prospectors, hard-line greenies, hunters, fishers and about five billion mosquitoes. Beneath Denali's ever-watching eyes, these subjects live in constant counterpoint, constant flux: the cycle of life swirling like a violent gale through this massive stretch of earth.

DENALI NATIONAL PARK

For many travelers, Denali National Park is the beginning and end of their Alaskan adventure. And why shouldn't it be? This is probably your best chance in the Interior (if not in the entire state) of seeing a grizzly bear, a moose, a caribou, and maybe even a fox or wolf.

The best thing is that here in Denali, unlike most wilderness areas in the country, you don't have to be a backpacker to view this wildlife – people who never sleep in a tent have excellent, once-in-a-lifetime opportunities to get a close look at these magnificent creatures roaming free in their natural habitat.

SIGHTS & ACTIVITIES
PARK ROAD
The Park Rd begins at George Parks Hwy and winds 92 miles through the heart of the park, ending at Kantishna, an old mining settlement and the site of several wilderness lodges. With few exceptions,

motorists can drive only to a parking area along the Savage River at Mile 14, a mile beyond the Savage River Campground. To venture further along the road you must walk, bike, be part of a concessionaire-run tour, or, most popularly, take a park shuttle or camper bus.

If you're planning to spend the day riding the buses (it's an eight-hour round-trip to the Eielson Visitor Center – the most popular day trip in the park), pack plenty of food and drink.

SHUTTLE BUSES
Shuttle buses are aimed at wildlife watchers and day hikers. They aren't fancy, comfortable, high-tech wonders but big, clunky school-bus-style affairs. On board, passengers armed with binoculars and cameras scour the terrain for animals, most of which are so accustomed to the rambling buses that they rarely run and hide.

Day hikers don't need a backcountry permit and can get off shuttle buses anywhere along Park Rd. After hiking, produce your bus-ticket stub and flag down the next bus that comes along. (Due to space considerations, you might have to wait a bus or two during peak season.) Many park visitors hop on and off buses several times in one day.

Certain buses head into the park as early as 5:30am; the last ones are back by around 10:35pm. It's wise to reserve a seat as far in advance as possible. Before showing up in Denali you can book shuttles (and campsites) through the **Denali National Park Reservation Service** (☎ 272-7275, in the USA 800-622-7275; www. reservedenali.com). Payment is by credit card. You can reserve online for the following year beginning December 1; phone reservations start February 15 for the same year.

POINTS OF INTEREST

Mt McKinley is not visible from the park entrance or the nearby campgrounds and hotel. Your first glimpse of it comes between Mile 9 and Mile 11 of Park Rd, if you're blessed with a clear day. While the 'Great One' might not be visible for most of the first 15 miles, this is the best stretch to spot moose because of the proliferation of spruce and especially willow, the animal's favorite food.

From **Savage River (Mile 14)** – which has an established trail alongside the river – the road dips into the **Sanctuary and Teklanika River valleys**, and Mt McKinley disappears behind the foothills. Both these rivers are in excellent hiking areas, and three of the five backcountry campgrounds lie along them. **Sanctuary River Campground (Mile 22)** is the most scenic, and it's a good base camp for hiking up Primrose Ridge.

The **Igloo Creek Campground (Mile 34)** lies among some spruce woods along the creek, and is the unofficial beginning

of 'bear country.' From here you can make an easy day hike into the Igloo and Cathedral Mountains to spot Dall sheep, and maybe even wolves.

After passing through the canyon formed by the Igloo and Cathedral Mountains, the road ascends to 3880ft **Sable Pass (Mile 38.5)**. The canyon and surrounding mountains are excellent places to view Dall sheep, while the pass is known as a prime habitat for Toklat brown bears. Given the prevalence of brown bear, the area around Sable Pass was closed to hikers and backpackers when this book went to press. From here, the road drops to the bridge over the **East Fork Toklat River (Mile 44)**. Hikers can trek from the bridge along the riverbanks both north and south.

Polychrome Pass Overlook (Mile 47) is a rest stop for the shuttle buses. This scenic area, at 3500ft, has views of the Toklat River to the south. The alpine tundra above the road is good for hiking, as you can scramble up ridges that lead north and south of the rest-stop shelter.

Folks on the shuttle bus normally stop at the **Toklat Ranger Station (Mile 53;** ✦ 9am-7pm) on the way back. There are a few displays and some books for sale, as well as scopes to check out Dall sheep on the neighboring hills.

On the far side of Thorofare Pass (3900ft), **Eielson Visitor Center (Mile 66;** ✦ 9am-7pm) is the most common turning-around point for day-trippers taking the shuttle or tour bus to visit the park by wheel (an eight-hour round-trip affair). The 7400-sq-ft facility cost around $9.2 million to build, and features several 'green' design elements – solar and hydroelectric power, transplanted tundra mats on the roof deck and a low-slung architectural profile that blends well with the landscape. Finished in 2008, this remote outpost has some interesting exhibits on natural history of the region, a massive panorama of Mt McKinley to give you an idea of the mountain's topography, and ginormous windows for viewing the mountain herself. There are toilets here, but no food.

Past Eielson, Park Rd drops to the valley below, passing a sign for **Muldrow Glacier** (Mile 74.4). At this point, the glacier lies about a mile to the south, and the terminus of the 32-mile ice floe is clearly visible, though you might not recognize it because the ice is covered with a mat of plant life. If the weather is cloudy and Mt McKinley and the surrounding peaks are hidden, the final 20 miles of the bus trip will be a ride through rolling tundra and past numerous small lakes known as kettle ponds. Study the pools of water carefully to spot beavers or waterfowl.

Wonder Lake Campground (Mile 84) is a place where the beauty of Mt McKinley is doubled on a clear day, with the mountain's reflection on the lake's surface.

Ironically, the heavy demand for the 28 sites at Wonder Lake and the numerous overcast days caused by Mt McKinley itself prevent the majority of visitors from ever seeing this remarkable panorama. If you do experience the reddish sunset on the summit reflecting off the still waters of the lake, cherish the moment.

The campground is on a low rise above the lake's south end and is only 26 miles from the mountain. Those who come on the early buses can gain another hour at the lake by getting off and picking up a later bus for the trip back. Keep in mind that those famous McKinley-reflected-in-the-lake photos are taken along the

DENALI NATIONAL PARK – PARK ROAD

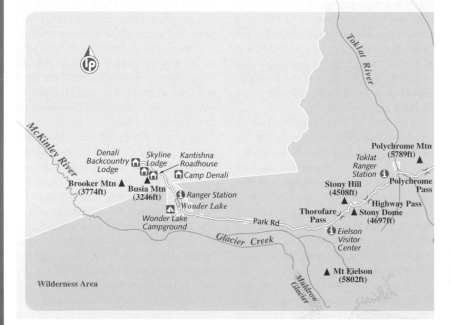

northeast shore, 2 miles beyond the campground, so you might want to save some time for hiking.

Kantishna (Mile 90) is mainly a destination for people staying in the area's private lodges. The buses turn around here, and begin the long trip back to the Wilderness Access Center.

WILDLIFE WATCHING

Because hunting has never been allowed in the park, professional photographers refer to animals in Denali as 'approachable wildlife.' That means bear, moose, Dall sheep and caribou aren't as skittish here as in other regions of the state. For this reason, and because Park Rd was built to maximize the chances of seeing wildlife by traversing high open ground, the national park is an excellent place to view a variety of animals.

Anywhere between 1000 and 1800 moose roam the north side of the Alaska Range within the park, and the most spectacular scene in Denali comes in early September, when the bulls clash their immense racks over breeding rights to the cows.

All the park's caribou belong to the Denali herd – one of 32 herds in Alaska – which presently numbers around 2000 animals. Caribou are easy to spot, as the rack of a bull often stands 4ft high and appears to be out of proportion with the rest of his body.

Consider yourself lucky if you spot a wolf in the park. Denali is home to a fluctuating population of the animals, with approximately 100 wolves living in 18 packs. Probably your best shot at sighting a wolf is along the Park Rd, or near Igloo Campground

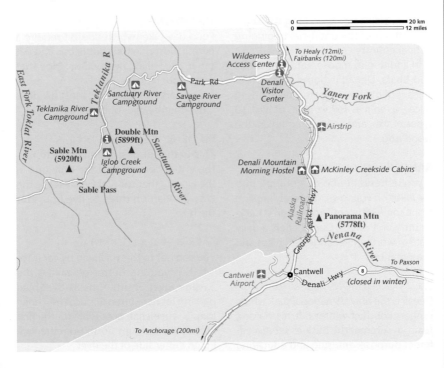

North of the Alaska Range, the park holds an estimated 350 grizzly bears, usually inhabiting tundra areas. South of here, the bear density should arguably go up, as there are more salmon streams to support a bigger population, but no hard-and-true statistics are available. The black bears tend to stick to the forested areas, and avoid the grizzlies. Park biologists estimate there to be 200 black bears within the park's boundaries. Since most of Denali's streams are fed by glaciers, the fishing is poor, and bears must rely on vegetation for 85% of their diet. This accounts for their small size. Most male grizzlies here range from only 300lb to 600lb while their cousins on the salmon-rich coasts can easily top 1000lb. While there is no guarantee of seeing a grizzly in the park, your chances are pretty darned good. Most park bus drivers say that they see around five to eight grizzlies per day along the road. Mile 34 marks the unofficial beginning of bear country.

In addition to moose, caribou, wolves and bears, Denali is home to 35 other species of mammal – from wolverines to mice – as well as 167 varieties of bird, 10 types of fish, and a lone amphibian, the wood frog.

RANGER-LED ACTIVITIES

If you're hesitant about venturing into the wilds on your own, or merely looking to kill some time until your desired back-country unit opens, Denali offers a daily slate of worthwhile ranger-led hikes and presentations.

SLED-DOG DEMONSTRATIONS

Denali is the only US national park where rangers conduct winter patrols via dog team. In summer the huskies serve a different purpose: amusing and educating the legions of tourists who sign up for the park's free daily tours of the sled-dog kennels, and dog demonstrations. The 40-minute show also takes place daily at Park Headquarters at 10am, 2pm and 4pm.

ENTRANCE-AREA HIKES

To join a ranger on an easy, guided stroll (ranging from a half hour to 2½ hours) along the park's entrance area trails, check out the schedule at the visitor center and show up ready to hike at the appointed departure time.

DISCOVERY HIKES

These are moderate-to-strenuous, three- to five-hour hikes departing from Park Rd. The location varies from day to day; you can find out the schedule at the visitor center.

DAY HIKING

For a day hike (which doesn't require a permit), just ride the shuttle bus and get off at any valley, riverbed or ridge that grabs your fancy.

The park has few trails; most hiking is cross-country over open terrain.

MT HEALY OVERLOOK TRAIL

This is the longest maintained trail in the entrance area, and the only one in the vicinity that truly lets you escape the crowds. Plan on three to five hours for the hike.

SAVAGE RIVER LOOP TRAIL

You can get to this trailhead by car (Mile 14), but you are better off taking the Savage River Shuttle Bus as the small parking lot here often fills up. The 2-mile loop is wheelchair accessible for the first half a mile and runs north from the Park Rd on either side of the river.

GRANT DIXON

Ranger, Denali National Park

↘ IF YOU LIKE...

If you like Denali's **ranger-led hikes** (opposite), consider following some of these mellow trails near the park entrance.

- **Horseshoe Lake Trail** A leisurely 1½-mile walk along a wide gravel path to an oxbow lake. Access the trail at Mile 1.2 of the Park Rd.
- **Taiga Loop Trail** Turns west from the Horseshoe Lake Trail and leads to both Mt Healy Overlook Trail and Rock Creek Trail.
- **Rock Creek Trail** This 2.3-mile trail leads west to the park headquarters and dog kennels. It's far easier hiking this trail downhill from the headquarters end, where the trail begins just before Park Rd.
- **McKinley Station Trail** A 2.6-mile loop that takes you from the visitor center to the Wilderness Access Center and back again, and provides an easy route to Glitter Gulch.

POLYCHROME PASS CIRCUIT

One cross-country route you might consider off Park Rd is Polychrome Pass Circuit, an 8-mile trek that will challenge fit, experienced day hikers. (Less studly souls might want to do it as an overnight, which requires a permit.) This hike traverses one of the park's most scenic areas.

The brilliantly colored rocks of Polychrome Pass are the result of volcanic action some 60 million years ago. Today the multicolored hills and mountains, including Polychrome Mountain (5789ft)

and Cain Peak (4961ft), are a stunning sight in the low-angle light of a clear Alaskan summer day.

BACKPACKING

For many, the reason to come to Denali is to escape into the backcountry for a truly Alaskan experience. Unlike many parks in the Lower 48, Denali's rigid restrictions ensure you can trek and camp in a piece of wilderness all your own, even if it's just for a few days.

Obtain permits at the BIC, where you'll find wall maps with the unit outlines and a quota board indicating the number of vacancies in each unit.

For an overview of the different units in the park, check out the BIC's copy of *Backcountry Companion for Denali National Park* by Jon Nierenberg (Alaska National History Association), which is now out of print.

Regardless of where you're headed, remember that 5 miles is a full-day trip for the average backpacker in Denali's backcountry.

BIKING

No special permit is needed to cycle on Park Rd, but biking off-road is prohibited. Camper buses will carry bikes, but only two at a time and only if you have a reservation. Many cyclists ride the bus in and bike back out, carrying their gear and staying at campsites they've reserved along the way. It's also possible to take an early-morning bus in, ride for several hours and catch a bus back the same day.

You can rent bikes at **Denali Outdoor Center** (☎ 683-1925, 888-303-1925; www. denalioutdoorcenter.com; Mile 240.5 and Mile 247 George Parks Hwy). Each location charges $8 per hour (minimum two-hour rental) or $40 for a full day. Rates include a helmet, water bottle, tools and lock.

TOURS
PARK ROAD

The park shuttle buses are the most common 'tours' along Park Rd, but there are others. None of these are especially noteworthy, and you're probably better off saving some money by simply taking the park bus.

Park co-concessionaire **Aramark** (☎ 272-7275, 800-622-7275; www.reservedenali.com) offers a five-hour Natural History Tour (adult/child 14 and under $55/28) to Primrose Ridge, a four- to five-hour Teklanika Tundra Wilderness Tour (adults/child 14 and under $60.50/30.25) to the Teklanika River Overlook, and a six- to eight-hour Tundra Wildlife Tour (adults/child 14 and under $93.50/46.75) to Toklat River. All include narration, hot drinks and a snack or box lunch.

The other co-concessionaire, Doyon, runs **Kantishna Roadhouse** (☎ 800-230-7275; www.seedenali.com), which offers a one-day bus tour (adults/child 14 and under $139/69.50) along Park Rd to Kantishna.

FLIGHTSEEING

Most flightseeing around Denali leaves from Talkeetna, but some companies also operate out of the park area.

Denali Air (☎ 683-2261; www.denaliair. com) charges around $325/$165 per adult/ child for a narrated flight of about an hour around the mountain. Flights leave from the company's airstrip at Mile 229.5 of George Parks Hwy.

Era Helicopters (☎ 550-8625, 800-843-1947; www.eraflightseeing.com; Mile 238 George Parks Hwy) will take you up on a 50-minute Mt McKinley tour ($320) or a 75-minute flight that includes a glacier landing ($415). Heli-hiking trips are also available. The helipad is on the north side of the Nenana River bridge, at the south end of Glitter Gulch.

Fly Denali (☎ 683-2899, 866-733-7768; www. flydenali.com) is based in Healy and has tours of various durations and routes. Its 2½-hour flight ($439) includes the only glacier landing available from the park entrance.

RIVER RAFTING

Thanks to Denali Park tourists, the Nenana River is the most popular white-water rafting area in Alaska. The river's main white-

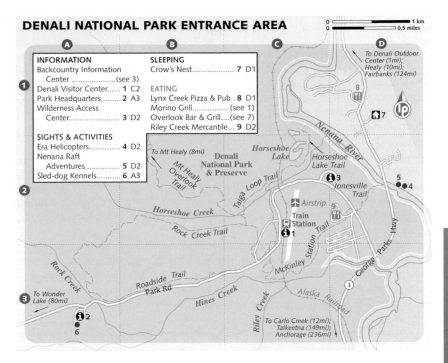

DENALI NATIONAL PARK ENTRANCE AREA

water stretch begins near the park entrance and ends 10 miles north, near Healy.

Denali Outdoor Center (☎ 683-1925, 888-303-1925; www.denalioutdoorcenter.com; Mile 240.5 & Mile 247 George Parks Hwy), with two locations, is universally considered the finest rafting outfit, with good equipment, a safety-first philosophy and friendly guides.

Nenana Raft Adventures (☎ 800-789-7238; www.raftdenali.com; Mile 238 George Parks Hwy) offers trips and dips on the upper Nenana ($85), Nenana Gorge ($85) and a short afternoon Class IV paddle ($70), as well as pricier oar-boat trips for families with young ones.

SLEEPING & EATING
INSIDE THE PARK

Morino Grill (Mile 1.5 Park Rd; mains $8-9; ☯ 11am-7pm) This cafeteria-style establishment in a barnlike structure beside the visitor center is the only eatery within the park. It has burgers, paninis and small pizzas, as well as seafood chowder and reindeer stew.

Riley Creek Mercantile (☎ 683-9246; Mile 0.2 Park Rd; ☯ 7am-11pm) Next to the Riley Creek Campground, it has a few groceries, as well as espressos, deli sandwiches and wraps.

KANTISHNA

Skyline Lodge (☎ 683-1223; www.katair.com; r with continental breakfast $255, full meal plan $40 per person) This small, solar-powered, three-room place serves as Kantishna Air Taxi's base of operations. Guests have use of a kitchen, dining area, bath, shower and decks overlooking the Kantishna Valley.

Denali Backcountry Lodge (☎ 376-1992, 877-233-6254; www.denalilodge.com; per person $450-530) The last lodge on this end

A MOUNTAIN BY ANY OTHER NAME

The Athabascans called it Denali or the 'Great One'; their brethren to the south in the Susitna Valley called it Doleika, the 'Big Mountain'; and the Aleuts referred to it as Traleika. So why do we largely know North America's highest peak by the name McKinley?

This white-washed moniker was not even the first European name to be bestowed upon the mountain. While McKinley was first sighted by European eyes in 1794 by explorer George Vancouver, it remained unnamed until a prominent Russian administrator, Ferdinand von Wrangell, marked it on a map as Tenada. Later, during the gold-rush days, it would change names again, first to Densmore's Mountain in honor of a local prospector, and soon thereafter to Mt McKinley after William McKinley, an Ohioan who would soon become president of the United States. And so the name remained for many years, at least on our maps.

But the name 'Denali' slowly began creeping back into people's minds, and finally made the maps in 1980 when the park was re-designated as Denali National Park and Preserve and the Alaskan Geographic Board officially renamed the mountain Denali. Given that William McKinley never even visited Alaska, and Europeans lagged behind the first native 'explorers' by thousands of years, it seems like a good idea.

of the road, this is a great-looking place on the banks of Moose Creek with comfortable modern cabins and common areas. Transport, meals and guided activities are included, and you can save some duckets by coming here in the 'shoulder' season.

Kantishna Roadhouse (☎ 800-942-7420; www.kantishnaroadhouse.com; per person $415) Owned by park co-concessionaire Doyon, Kantishna Roadhouse has clean, modern cabins, a beautiful dining room, a bar and guided activities.

Camp Denali (☎ 683-2290; www.campdenali. com; cabin 3-night minimum per person $1425) Verging on legendary, Camp Denali has been the gold standard among Kantishna lodges for the last half-century. Widely spread across the ridgeline, the camp's simple, comfortable cabins elegantly complement the backcountry experience while minimizing impact on the natural world. Think of it as luxury camping, with

gourmet meals, guided hikes, killer views of the mountain, and staff so devoted to Denali that you'll come away feeling like the beneficiary of a precious gift. You can only arrive or depart on Monday or Friday, so you'll need to plan accordingly.

CARLO CREEK

Located 12 miles south of the park entrance (Mile 224), this is one of the best places to stay near Denali Park, especially for independent travelers looking for a chilled out experience.

our pick **Denali Mountain Morning Hostel** (☎ 683-7503; www.hostelalaska.com; dm $32, d $75-95; 🖳) Perched lovingly beside the gurgling Carlo Creek, this is the area's only true hostel. And, lucky for indie travelers, it is one of the best in all Alaska. Only open during the summer months, the hostel features a hotchpotch of tent-cabins, log cabins and platform tents.

McKinley Creekside Cabins (☎ 683-2277, 888-533-6254; www.mckinleycabins.com; cabins $139-199; ☐) Ask ahead of time for a creekside cabin at this well-maintained spot across from the hostel. The cabins aren't right on the water, but you'd be able to hear the burbling creek as you loll off to dreamland.

GLITTER GULCH

Glitter Gulch (Mile 238.5) contains the mangy lion's share of park lodgings.

Crow's Nest (☎ 683-2723, 888-917-8130; www.denalicrowsnest.com; Mile 238.5 George Parks Hwy; cabins $186-197; ☐) Old pictures add a welcome touch of home to these modern log cabins up on the hill behind the gas station. The rooms are pleasant enough with TVs and private baths, and, if you can ignore the highway noise, you have pretty good views of the surrounding wilderness.

Lynx Creek Pizza & Pub (☎ 683-2547; Mile 238.6 George Parks Hwy; pizza slices $4.50; ☉ 11am-midnight) Owned by Princess, this Glitter Gulch fixture has a small pub with log-cabin atmosphere and a nice outdoor patio. The pizza wedges are sizable and the taste is tolerable.

Overlook Bar & Grill (☎ 683-2641; Mile 238.5 George Parks Hwy; sandwiches & burgers $9-18; ☉ 11am-11pm) Way up on the hill over Glitter Gulch, the 'Big O' does steak, seafood, pasta and poultry. It's a good nightlife spot and gets raves for its view and beer list, but razzes for slow and haphazard service.

GETTING THERE & AROUND
BUS

Both northbound and southbound bus services are available from Denali National Park.

Alaska/Yukon Trails (☎ 479-2277, 800-770-7275; www.alaskashuttle.com) has southbound buses that pick up at the Park Mart Store, Visitor Center and WAC around noon, reaching Anchorage ($65 one way) by 6:30pm. Northbound buses leaving Denali around noon as well and arrive in Fairbanks ($46 one way) at 4pm ($7 extra will get you to the airport).

Road to Kantishna (p215)

MICHAEL KRABS

Denali National Park

↘ IF YOU LIKE...

If you liked hiking the trails in **Denali National Park** (p212), we think you might enjoy the solitude of the **Denali State Park**. At 325,240 acres, Denali State Park is the fourth-largest state park in Alaska and is roughly half the size of Rhode Island. On a clear day the panorama of Mt. McKinley is amazing, and there are some great day hikes. Here are a few of them:

- **Byers Lake Loop Trail** An easy 4.8-mile trek around the lake. It begins at Byers Lake Campground and passes six hike-in campsites on the other side, 1.8 miles from the posted trailhead.
- **Little Coal Creek Trail** Departs from Mile 163.8 of George Parks Hwy, ascending to the alpine areas of Kesugi Ridge.
- **Ermine Hill Trail** A short day-hike (3 miles one way) accessed from the trailhead at Mile 156.5 George Parks Hwy.

Park Connection (☎ 800-266-8625; www.alaskacoach.com) runs to and from Fairbanks ($56 one way) and to and from points south, including Anchorage ($79 one way) and Seward ($135 one way). It leaves Anchorage at 7am and 3pm for Denali; Fairbanks at 9am down to Denali; and from Denali north to Fairbanks at 2pm and south to Anchorage at 2pm.

TRAIN

The most enjoyable way to arrive or depart from the park is aboard the **Alaska Railroad** (☎ 265-2494, 800-544-0552; www.

alaskarailroad.com), with its viewing-dome cars that provide sweeping views of Mt McKinley and the Susitna and Nenana River valleys along the way.

PLANE

Talkeetna Aero Services (☎ 683-2899, 888-733-2899; www.talkeetnaaero.com), based in Talkeetna, offers air transportation to/from Talkeetna.

Kantishna Air Taxi (☎ 683-1223; www.katair.com) offers high-priced charters (around $1495 for up to five people) to and from Anchorage.

COURTESY BUSES & SHUTTLES

The free Riley Creek Loop Bus makes a circuit through the park entrance area, picking up at the visitor center every half hour and stopping at the Horseshoe Lake trailhead, WAC and Riley Creek Campground.

TALKEETNA

pop 850

This peppery little town at the end of the road (and at times toward the edge of reality) was once the quintessential off-the-grid Alaskan community. Once a gold-mining center, Talkeetna's biggest draw today is its proximity (at least by air) to the Alaska Range. Among alpinists, the community is famed as the staging area for ascents of Mt McKinley, Mt Foraker, the Moose's Tooth and other dizzying summits, the very names of which jumpstart the saliva glands of mountaineers the world over.

SIGHTS

TALKEETNA HISTORICAL SOCIETY MUSEUM

A block south of Main St is this **museum** (☎ 733-2487; adult/child $3/free; ☻ 10am-6pm), a small complex of restored buildings. But the most fascinating building by far is the Section House. Inside you will discover a 12ft by 12ft relief model of Mt McKinley surrounded by Bradford Washburn's famous mural-like photos of the mountain.

MOUNTAINEERING RANGER STATION

Whether you're intrigued by high-altitude alpinism or boggled by it, this **ranger station** (☎ 733-2231; cnr 1st & B Sts; ☻ 8am-6pm) provides an excellent window into that rarefied world. In addition to coordinating the numerous expeditions to Mt McKinley during the spring and summer, the station functions as a visitor center, with maps,

books, photos and video presentations about the Alaska Range, as well as climbing-club flags from around the world and signed ice axes from successful ascents.

ARTISAN MARKET

Alaskans are crafty people – after all, they spend half their year indoors – and the local crafts just north of the Sheldon Hangar at Talkeetna's **Artisan Market** (☻ 10am-6pm Sat-Mon) are pretty good.

TOURS

FLIGHTSEEING

When in Talkeetna, it's pretty much mandatory to go flightseeing around Mt McKinley. It's not cheap, but on a clear day it's so worthwhile that it's one of the best bargains in this expensive state (and you're gonna save a buck by flying from here rather than from within Denali NP).

Hudson Air Service (☎ 733-2321, 800-478-2321; www.hudsonair.com)

K2 Aviation (☎ 733-2291, 800-764-2291; www.flyk2.com)

Talkeetna Aero Services (☎ 733-2899, 888-733-2899; www.talkeetnaaero.com)

Talkeetna Air Taxi (☎ 733-2218, 800-533-2219; www.talkeetnaair.com)

TOWN & RIVER TOURS

Alaska Nature Guides (☎ 733-1237; www.alaskanatureguides.com) offers several nature walking tours in the area ($49 to $94), and can arrange for custom trips, focusing mainly on birding. It also offers a quick walking tour of town for groups only (minimum of six people, $19 per person).

To get out onto Talkeetna's many nearby waterways, sign up with **Talkeetna River Guides** (☎ 733-2477; www.talkeetnariverguides.com; Main St), who'll put you in a raft for a two-hour float on the Talkeetna River ($69) or a four-hour float on the Chulitna River, through Denali State Park ($115).

DENALI & THE INTERIOR

TALKEETNA

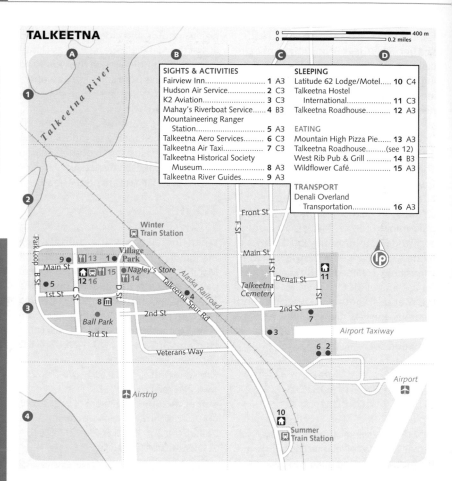

TALKEETNA

SIGHTS & ACTIVITIES		
Fairview Inn	**1**	A3
Hudson Air Service	**2**	C3
K2 Aviation	**3**	C3
Mahay's Riverboat Service	**4**	B3
Mountaineering Ranger Station	**5**	A3
Talkeetna Aero Services	**6**	C3
Talkeetna Air Taxi	**7**	C3
Talkeetna Historical Society Museum	**8**	A3
Talkeetna River Guides	**9**	A3

SLEEPING		
Latitude 62 Lodge/Motel	**10**	C4
Talkeetna Hostel International	**11**	C3
Talkeetna Roadhouse	**12**	A3

EATING		
Mountain High Pizza Pie	**13**	A3
Talkeetna Roadhouse	(see 12)	
West Rib Pub & Grill	**14**	B3
Wildflower Café	**15**	A3

TRANSPORT		
Denali Overland Transportation	**16**	A3

Fishing around Talkeetna is absurdly good, with runs of every species of Pacific salmon plus grayling, rainbow trout and Dolly Varden. **Mahay's Riverboat Service** (☎ 800-736-2210; www.mahaysriverboat.com; **Spur Rd**) will equip you with fishing gear and take you where the fish are biting.

SLEEPING

Talkeetna Hostel International (☎ 733-4678; www.talkeetnahostel.com; I St; campsites/dm/s/d/tr $12/22/50/65/75; 🖳) This well-loved hostel even has a converted VW van ($35) you can sleep in – you can't get much more hippie than that. Popular with climbers and backpackers alike, this is the best hostel in town, with a cool host, large common area and kitchen, laundry, free internet, and the occasional fire for swapping tales and fighting the mosquitoes.

Talkeetna Roadhouse (☎ 733-1351; www.talkeetnaroadhouse.com; Main St; dm $21, s/d from $57/68, cabins $110) This place is the real Alaskan deal. It dates from 1917 and hosts scores of climbers in season. It has seven small private rooms without bath, a bunkroom and cute cabins out back, also without baths.

Latitude 62 Lodge/Motel (☎ 733-2262; Mile 13.5 Talkeetna Spur Rd; s/d $78/99) If downtown Talkeetna is just too hippie-dippy for you, there's always this place, with hunting-lodge decor that includes plenty of pelts and skulls, as well as a fairly friendly bar and beer garden.

EATING & DRINKING

Mountain High Pizza Pie (☎ 733-1234; Main St; pizza slices $3.50, sandwiches $5-11; ☽ 11:30am-11pm) This arty, airy downtown establishment makes fabulous pizzas with names such as 'the Yentna' and 'the Grizzly.' It's also got lots of microbrews available.

Talkeetna Roadhouse (☎ 733-1351; Main St; breakfast $7-13, sandwiches $7; ☽ 7am-9pm) This venerable, colorful establishment has the best breakfast in town. Half-orders are adequate; fulls are mountain-sized. The restaurant also doubles as a bakery, cooking up giant cinnamon rolls in the morning.

West Rib Pub & Grill (☎ 733-3354; Main St; burgers & sandwiches $9-13; ☽ 11:30am-2am) Located at the back of Nagley's Store, this is a terrific place to soak in Talkeetna's live-and-let-live vibe, rubbing shoulders with visitors and locals alike. It's got burgers, salmon and halibut, plenty of craft brews, and, if it's sunny, outdoor seating.

Wildflower Café (☎ 733-2694; Main St; sandwiches $14, mains $22-32; ☽ 11am-9pm) Despite the circumspect service, this new entrant to the Talkeetna culinary scene is doing well for itself. The yummy burgers and large wholesome mains are served on the large deck, a perfect perch for people watching. Unfortunately, when the rain hits, things can get a bit cramped inside.

GETTING THERE & AROUND
AIR

You can stay in Talkeetna and get a ride up to Denali National Park with **Talkeetna Aero Services** (☎ 733-2899, 888-733-2899; www.talkeetnaaero.com). The company offers a day-trip package from Talkeetna to Denali National Park ($395) that includes round-trip flights, a McKinley tour (not to the summit), lunch and a bus tour in the park.

DENALI & THE INTERIOR

TALKEETNA

IMAGEBROKER/EGMONT STRIGL

Mountain range, Talkeetna (p223)

POISON YOURSELF AT THE FAIRVIEW INN

Though not an official museum, the Fairview Inn (☎ 733-2423; Main St; ◷ noon-late) might as well be. Founded in 1923 to serve as the overnight stop between Seward and Fairbanks on the newly constructed Alaska Railroad, the inn is listed on the National Register of Historic Places. One corner holds Talkeetna's only slot machine; another is devoted to President Warren G Harding. When the railroad was finished in 1923, Harding arrived in Alaska and rode the rails to the Nenana River, where he hammered in the golden spike. Talkeetna locals swear (with grins on their faces) that he stopped at the Fairview Inn on the way home, was poisoned, and wound up dying in San Francisco less than a week later.

BUS

In the climbing (which starts in spring) and summer season, Denali Overland Transportation (☎ 733-2384, 800-651-5221; www.denalioverland.com; Main St in the Denali Dry Goods Store) runs shuttles to Denali ($75 per person, based on a four person minimum) and Anchorage ($75 per person, based on a four person minimum).

Alaska/Yukon Trails (☎ 479-2277, 800-770-7275; www.alaskashuttle.com) plies the whole George Parks Hwy, leaving Anchorage daily at around 7am, getting to downtown Talkeetna around 10:15am and continuing northbound through Denali Park to Fairbanks.

TRAIN

The Alaska Railroad (☎ 265-2494, 800-544-0552; www.alaskarailroad.com) runs a couple of trains that stop in Talkeetna. From mid-May to mid-September, the *Denali Star* stops daily on its run between Anchorage and Fairbanks.

America's Last Flagstop Train, sometimes called the 'Local' or the 'Bud Car,' provides a local rural service from Thursday through Sunday in the summertime. It's a flag-stop train, departing Talkeetna at 12:15pm for the trip north to Hurricane Gulch, where it turns around and heads back the same day. This 'milk run' takes you within view of Mt McKinley and into some remote areas (see boxed text, p72).

GLENN HIGHWAY

The quickest path from the Alcan to Anchorage, the paved Glenn Hwy offers some of the best hiking, boating and scenery-gawking in the state. The rugged 328-mile route is graced by both the Wrangell and Chugach Mountains, and is among Alaska's most jaw-dropping drives.

The Glenn runs 189 miles from Richardson Hwy at Glennallen through the Chugach Range to Anchorage, merging with George Parks Hwy just after Palmer. Appropriately, most of this corridor has been declared a National Scenic Byway.

TOLSONA CREEK TO MATANUSKA GLACIER

West of Glennallen, Glenn Hwy slowly ascends through woodland into wide-open high country, affording drop-dead views of the Chugach and Talkeetna Mountains, and limitless hiking opportunities.

A lookout marks the trailhead for the Mae West Lake Trail, a short hike away from Mile 169.3 of Glenn Hwy. This mile-long trail leads to a long, narrow lake fed by Little Woods Creek. The trailhead for the **Lost Cabin Lake Trail** is at another pull-out on the south side of the highway at Mile 165.8. The trail winds 2 miles to the lake and is a berry-picker's delight from late summer to early fall.

At Mile 160, a 19-mile spur road runs north to scenic **Lake Louise State Recreation Area** (campsites $15), which has 52 sites in two campgrounds and is popular among Alaskans keen on swimming, boating and angling for grayling and trout. A few lodges and numerous private cabins are on the lake as well.

Little Nelchina State Recreation Site (Mile 137.4 Glenn Hwy; campsites free), just off Glenn Hwy, has 11 campsites but, due to state budget cuts, no services.

From Little Nelchina River, Glenn Hwy begins to ascend, and Gunsight Mountain comes into view (you have to look hard to see the origin of its name). From Eureka Summit you can see both Gunsight Mountain and the Chugach Mountains to the south, the Nelchina Glacier spilling down in the middle and the Talkeetna Mountains to the northwest. This impressive, unobstructed view extends to the west, where the highway drops into the river valley that separates the two mountain chains. **Eureka Summit** (Mile 129.3 Glenn Hwy) is the highway's highest point (3322ft).

Just after the summit, at Mile 126.4, lies one of numerous trailheads for the old **Chickaloon-Knik-Nelchina Trail**, a gold miner's route used before the Glenn Hwy was built. Today it's an extensive trail system extending to Palmer and beyond. The system is not maintained regularly, and hikers attempting any part of it should have extensive outdoor experience and the appropriate topographic maps. You will have to share the trail with off-road vehicles.

The trailhead for the **Belanger Pass Trail** (Martin Rd at Mile 123.3 Glenn Hwy), is signposted. Usually miners and hunters in off-road vehicles use it to travel into the Talkeetna Mountains. The views from Belanger Pass, a 3-mile hike, are excellent and well worth the climb. From the 4350ft pass, off-road-vehicle trails continue another 3.5 miles north to Alfred Creek, then eventually lead around the north side of Syncline Mountain past active mining operations.

Sheep Mountain Lodge (☎ 745-5121, 877-645-5121; www.sheepmountain.com; Mile 113.5 Glenn Hwy; cabins $149-189) is among the finest and most scenically situated lodges along Glenn Hwy, featuring a cafe, a bar, a sauna, cabins and bunkrooms without bath. The restaurant has the area's best eating.

CHRIS AREND / ALASKASTOCK.COM

Glenn Highway

DENALI & THE INTERIOR

GLENN HIGHWAY

Four miles down the road are the idyllic **Tundra Rose Guest Cottages** (☎ 745-5865, in Alaska 800-315-5865; www.tundrarosebnb.com; Mile 109.5 Glenn Hwy; cottages $128-138), in a glacier-view setting that's as pretty as the name implies.

MATANUSKA GLACIER TO PALMER

One of Alaska's most accessible ice tongues, Matanuska Glacier nearly licks Glenn Hwy, stretching 27 miles from its source in the Chugach Mountains. Some 18,000 years ago it was way bigger, covering the area where the city of Palmer is today.

You can get to the glacier via **Glacier Park Resort** (☎ 745-2534; Mile 102 Glenn Hwy; campsites $15), which charges $15 (children six and under free) to follow its private road to a parking lot at the terminal moraine. From there, a self-guided trail will take you a couple of hundred yards onto the gravel-laced ice itself; to go further, duck into the nearby office of **MICA Guides** (☎ 800-956-6422; www.micaguides.com), where you'll be outfitted with a helmet, crampons and trekking poles, and led on a 1½-hour glacier tour ($45), a three-hour trek ($70) or a six-hour ice-climbing excursion ($130). If you haven't been ice-climbing before it's worth the splurge: it is both terrifying and intoxicating at the same time.

For lower-key fun – perhaps a picnic and a stroll through the clovers – try the **Alpine Historical Park** (☎ 745-7000; Mile 61 Glenn Hwy; admission free; ☺ 9am-7pm), encountered just before passing through Sutton. The park contains several buildings, including the Chickaloon Bunkhouse and the original Sutton post office, which now houses a museum.

Almost 12 miles beyond Sutton is the junction with the Fishhook-Willow Rd, which provides access to Independence Mine State Historical Park. The highway then descends into the agricultural center of Palmer.

From Palmer, Glenn Hwy merges with George Parks Hwy and continues south to Anchorage, 43 miles away.

WRANGELL-ST ELIAS NATIONAL PARK

One of the world's few remaining stands of 'absolute wilderness,' Wrangell-St Elias National Park is the closest you're going to get to 'the wild as God imagined it' in all of Alaska.

Wildlife in the park is more diverse and plentiful than in any other Alaskan park. Species include moose, black and brown bear, Dall sheep, mountain goat, wolf, wolverine, beaver and three of Alaska's 32 caribou herds.

This area is a veritable crossroads of mountain ranges. To the north are the Wrangell Mountains; to the south, the Chugach Mountains; and thrusting from the Gulf of Alaska and clashing with the Wrangell Mountains are the St Elias Mountains.

Spilling out from the peaks are extensive ice fields and more than 100 major glaciers, including some of the world's largest and most active.

The Bagley Ice Field, near the coast, is 127 miles long, making it the largest subpolar mass of ice in North America.

SIGHTS & ACTIVITIES

MCCARTHY ROAD

Edgerton Hwy and McCarthy Rd combine to provide a 92-mile route into the heart of Wrangell-St Elias National Park, ending at the footbridge across the Kennicott River to McCarthy.

The 32-mile Edgerton Hwy, fully paved, begins at Mile 82.6 of Richardson Hwy. If you want to camp before reaching the park, the best bet is lovely **Liberty Falls State Recreation Site** (Mile 24 Edgerton Hwy; campsites $10), where the cascade sends its waters rushing past several tent platforms.

At Chitina, the McCarthy Rd begins, auspiciously enough, by passing through a single-lane notch blasted through a granite outcrop. From here 60 miles eastward you'll be tracing the abandoned Copper River & Northwest Railroad bed that was used to transport copper from the mines to Cordova.

At Mile 14.5 you'll reach the access road to the trailheads for the **Dixie Pass**, **Nugget** and **Kotsina Trails**, across from the Strelna airstrip.

At Mile 17 of McCarthy Rd sits the one-lane, 525ft-long **Kuskulana River Bridge**, long known as 'the biggest thrill on the road to McCarthy.' Built in 1910, this historic railroad span is a vertigo-inducing 238ft above the bottom of the gorge.

After rattling through another 43 miles of scrubby brush and thick forest – with few good mountain vistas and not many diversions en route – the road ends at the **Kennicott River**. If you're driving in, that's as far as you can go; to get into McCarthy, you cross the river on a footbridge and walk a short distance into the tiny town.

On the other side, a **shuttle** (☎ 554-4411; one way $5; 🕑 9am-7:30pm) can take you to McCarthy (half a mile) or Kennecott (4.5 miles), or you can hoof or bike it.

MCCARTHY & KENNECOTT
pop 54

A funky renegade mountain hamlet just half a mile past the end of the road, **McCarthy** exudes the spirit of the Alaskan frontier like few can. Facing the Kennicott Glacier's terminal moraine and just a stone's throw from the river, the tiny community is a car-free idyll, where the handful of gravel roads wind past rotting cabins and lovingly restored boomtown-era buildings.

DENALI & THE INTERIOR

WRANGELL-ST ELIAS NATIONAL PARK

ERNEST MANEWAL

Willow Lake, Wrangell-St Elias National Park

Once you've crossed the Kennicott River on the footbridge, follow the road across another footbridge and about half a mile further to the unstaffed **McCarthy-Kennecott Historical Museum**, an old railroad depot featuring historical photographs, a few mining artifacts and a model of McCarthy in its heyday (donations are appreciated). At the museum, the road bends back 500ft into downtown (such as it is) McCarthy, or continues toward Kennecott, 4.5 miles up the road.

Historically, the two towns have always been different. **Kennecott** was a company town, self-contained and serious. McCarthy, on the other hand, was created in the early 1900s for miners as a place of 'wine, women and song.' The spirit remains lively today, and McCarthy is definitely the best spot to stay for indie travelers.

HIKING & BIKING

You can buy US Geological Society (USGS) topographic maps at **Fireweed Arts & Crafts** (☎ 554-4500; ☽ 9:30am-6:30pm), on the main drag in Kennecott. If you just want to wander through Kennecott on your own, stop at the visitor center and pick up a copy of the *Walking Tour of Kennecott* ($3).

Beginning from Kennicott Glacier Lodge, the **Root Glacier Trail** is a 3-mile round-trip route past the mine ruins to the sparkling white-and-blue ice.

You can climb the glacier, but use extreme caution if you're inexperienced or lack proper equipment (crampons, ice ax etc). A safer alternative is to follow the rough trail up the lateral moraine. The path continues another 2.5 miles, providing excellent views of the ice. For this trek, you'll need the USGS topographic maps *McCarthy B-6* and *McCarthy C-6*.

Another excellent hike from Kennecott is the alpine **Bonanza Mine Trail**. It's a round-trip of almost 8 miles and a steep uphill walk all the way. Plan on three to five hours to hike up if the weather is good and half that time to return. The trail is actually a rough dirt road to the treeline and starts just north of town at a junction

IMAGEBROKER/JIM WEST

Hikers, Wrangell-St Elias National Park

that makes a sharp 180-degree turn up the mountain. Once above the treeline the view is stunning, and you can clearly see the mountain where the mine still sits.

It's fun just to bike around town, but you can also bike 12 miles south of town to the **Nizina River**, a nice spot for an afternoon picnic. You can rent bikes through many of the campgrounds you'll find before the pedestrian bridge.

TOURS
HIKING
St Elias Alpine Guides (☎ 554-4445, 888-933-5427; www.steliasguides.com), with offices in McCarthy (before the river) and on Kennecott's main road, runs the only tours that go inside Kennecott's mine buildings ($25). It can also equip you with crampons for half-day hikes on Root Glacier ($60) or take you on a full-day alpine hike to the mining ruins at the base of Castle Mountain ($95). There's free day parking and cheap overnight parking ($5) at its McCarthy branch.

The other local guiding firm, also extremely experienced, is **Kennicott Wilderness Guides** (☎ 554-4444, 800-664-4537; www.kennicottguides.com), whose offerings include full-day ice-climbing and glacier excursions from $95, summer skiing tours and fly-in hiking trips

RIVER RUNNING
Where there are mountains and melting glaciers, there's sure to be white water. **Copper Oar** (☎ 554-4453, 800-523-4453; www.copperoar.com) has offices in the St Elias Alpine Guides Kennecott location. For a full-day float, it combines the Kennecott with the Nizina and a portion of the Chitina River and returns you to McCarthy by bush plane. The high point is going through the vertical-walled Nizina Canyon.

FLIGHTSEEING
If the day is clear, splurge on a flightseeing tour of the surrounding mountains and glaciers. Both **McCarthy Air** (☎ 554-4440; www.mccarthyair.com) and **Wrangell Mountain Air** (☎ 554-4411, 800-478-1160; www.wrangellmountainair.com), with offices on McCarthy's main drag, have a fantastic reputation, offering a wide range of scenic flights and charging around $95 to $210 per person (two-person minimum) for around 35 to 90 minutes. It can also arrange flights to Chitina ($106 round-trip) and backcountry drops ($135 and up).

SLEEPING
MCCARTHY
our pick **Kennicott River Lodge & Hostel** (☎ 554-4441, 552-2329; www.kennicottriverlodge.com; road's end; dm $30, cabins $100-150) A short walk from road's end is this beautiful two-story log lodge with outlying private and dormitory cabins offering glacier views. There's a great communal kitchen and common room, a bright outhouse and a Finnish sauna.

Currant Ridge Cabins (☎ 554-4424, 877-647-2442; www.currantridgecabins.com; Mile 56.7 McCarthy Rd; cabins $189) On a little mountainside not far from the 'end of the road,' these upscale cabins are the nicest in the area, with hardwood floors and hand-sewn quilts.

KENNECOTT
Kennicott Glacier Lodge (☎ 258-2350, 800-582-5128; www.kennicottlodge.com; s/d from $189/259; 🖳) Built in 1987 as a replica of a historic mining building, the sprawling Kennicott Glacier Lodge has a 'Grande Dame' feel, kind of like Stephen King's Stanley Hotel, only without the crazy girls blurting out 'Redrum, redrum.' Rooms are decorated with old mining artefacts.

EATING & DRINKING

Roadside Potatohead (hotdogs, burgers, burritos $8-12; ☺ 10am-7pm Mon-Wed, 9am-8pm Thu-Sun) Deck out your own Mr Potatohead doll as you dine is this screened-in snack shack just off McCarthy's Main St.

McCarthy Lodge (☎ 554-4402; www. mccarthylodge.com; McCarthy's Main St; dinner $20-45; ☺ 7-10am & 6-10pm) In the heart of McCarthy, this eatery has a surprisingly good wine list. Many of the greens come from the restaurant's greenhouse (ask if you can get a tour) and the rotating menu features everything from halibut to elk.

Kennicott Glacier Lodge (☎ 258-2350, 800-582-5128; www.kennicottlodge.com; Kennecott; breakfast $10-16, lunch $7-15, dinner $29-34; ☺ 7-10am, noon-3pm & 7-10pm) This may be the area's most upscale dining options. You'll need a reservation for the family-style dinners, and there's only one seating: at 7pm. Bag lunches are available for day hikers.

GETTING THERE & AROUND
AIR
Ellis Air (☎ 822-3368, 800-478-3368; www. ellisair.com) departs from Anchorage via Gulkana at 8:30am Wednesdays and Fridays, arriving in McCarthy at 11am and then returning. Fares are $300/600 one way/round-trip from Anchorage or $222/444 from Gulkana.

Wrangell Mountain Air (☎ 554-4400, 800-478-1160; www.wrangellmountainair.com) offers daily scheduled flights between McCarthy and Chitina for around $106 round-trip, as well as flightseeing trips.

BUS
Backcountry Connection (☎ 822-5292, 866-582-5292; www.alaska-backcountry-tours. com) departs Glennallen at 7am daily in summer, reaching Chitina at 8:30am and the McCarthy footbridge at 11:00am. After a four-hour layover – enough time to see McCarthy and the ruins at Kennecott – the van returns to Glennallen, arriving at 8:30pm. You'll need to make a reservation.

McCarthy-Kennicott Community Shuttle (☎ 554-4411; one way $5) runs vans between McCarthy and Kennecott from 9am to 8:30pm daily. Pick-up at the footbridge is on the hour; in downtown Kennecott it's on the half-hour.

FAIRBANKS & THE BUSH

FAIRBANKS & THE BUSH

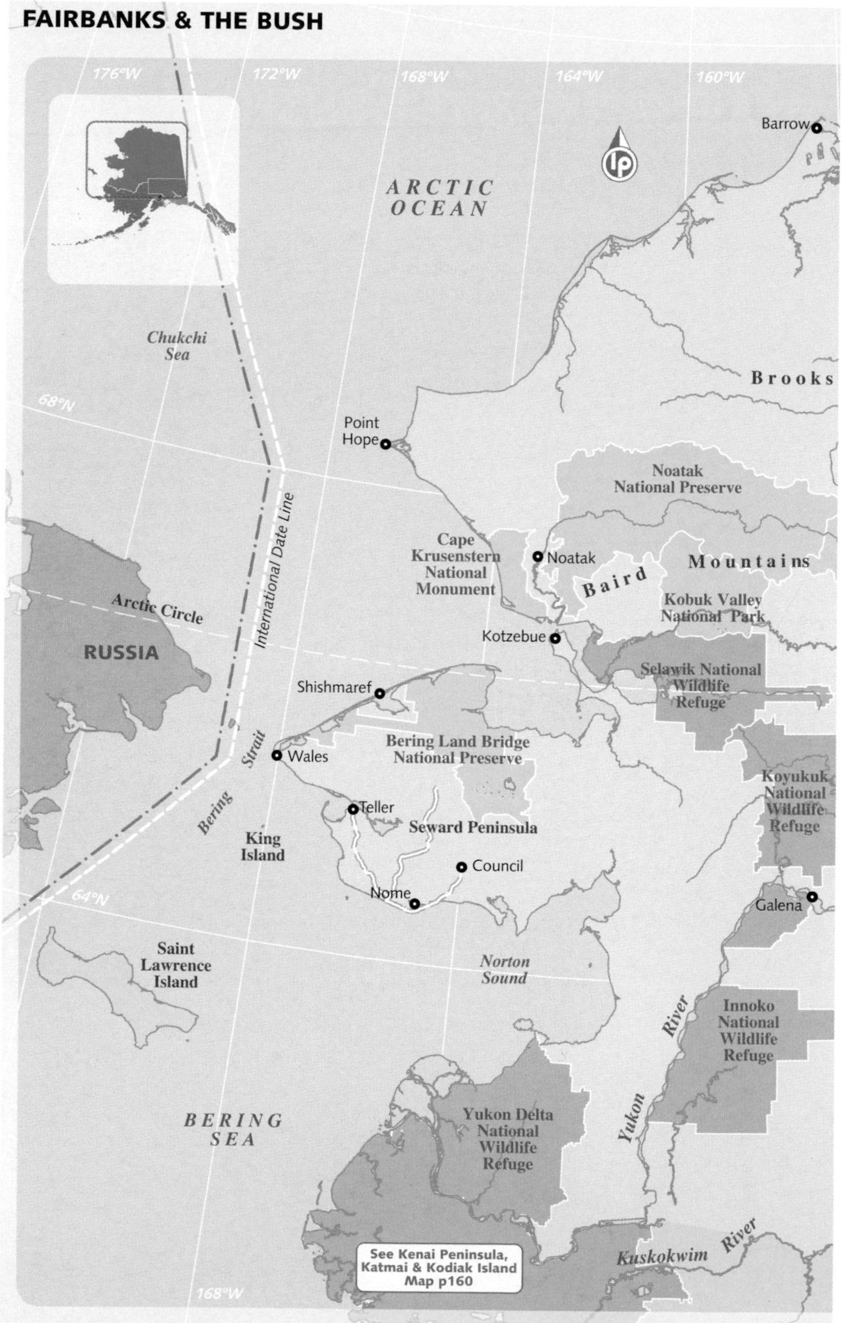

176°W 172°W 168°W 164°W 160°W

ARCTIC OCEAN

Barrow

Chukchi Sea

Brooks

68°N

International Date Line

Point Hope

Noatak National Preserve

Cape Krusenstern National Monument

Noatak

Mountains

Baird

Kobuk Valley National Park

Kotzebue

Selawik National Wildlife Refuge

Arctic Circle

RUSSIA

Shishmaref

Koyukuk National Wildlife Refuge

Bering Strait

Wales

Bering Land Bridge National Preserve

King Island

Teller

Seward Peninsula

Council

Galena

64°N

Nome

Saint Lawrence Island

Norton Sound

Innoko National Wildlife Refuge

Yukon River

BERING SEA

Yukon Delta National Wildlife Refuge

Kuskokwim River

168°W

See Kenai Peninsula, Katmai & Kodiak Island Map p160

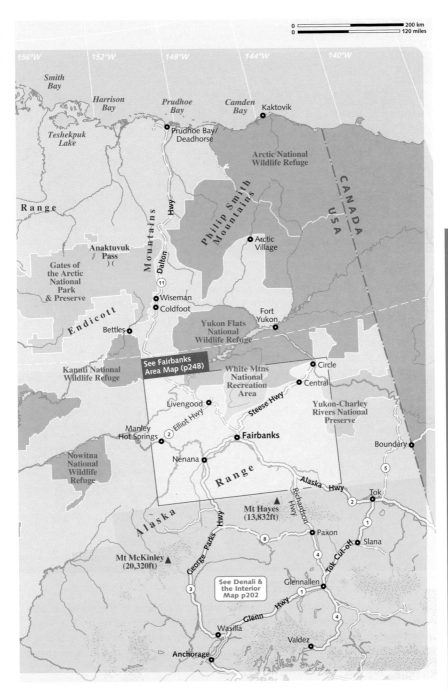

HIGHLIGHTS

1

⬊ GET ON TOP

Of the world, that is. As the northernmost settlement in the US, **Barrow** (p258) is situated 330 miles above the Arctic Circle and is the largest Iñupiat community in Alaska. This is the place to search for polar bears and appreciate the fact that in summer the sun doesn't set for 82 days.

2

⬊ GET ON THE RIVERS

A seemingly endless variety of paddle trips is available in the **Gates of the Arctic National Park & Preserve** (p257). On the Chena River, follow the **Great Fairbanks Pub Paddle** (p245) – a pub crawl without the crawling. If you don't feel like working out, ride the **Riverboat Discovery** (p245), a historic stern-wheeler that tours the waters.

3

↘ SOAK AWAY YOUR WORRIES

The Fairbanks area bubbles over with hot springs. The most accessible is **Chena Hot Springs** (p249), followed by **Manley Hot Springs** (p251). A couple of rural springs are better accessed in winter when the trails are frozen. **Tolovana Hot Springs** (p251) has cabin rentals; **Hutlinana Warm Springs** (p251) is undeveloped.

4

↘ BASK IN THE MIDNIGHT SUN

In Fairbanks in midsummer, the sun sets for barely three hours and residents take advantage of the nighttime sunshine. Whether they're watching the **Goldpanners** (p246) play a late-night ballgame or teeing off at 10pm at the **North Star Golf Club** (p245), Fairbanks residents will be working on their midnight tans. Join them!

5

↘ VISIT NOME

A Wild West settlement full of saloons, the end of Alaska's most famous race, the Iditarod, and home of the most western highway in the US, **Nome** (p251) is a wonderful place to explore. Visit nearby Native villages and mining ruins, or drive out of town and hike on tundra; you'll end up wishing you could stay longer.

1 Barrow (p258); 2 Hiker, Gates of the Arctic National Park & Preserve (p257); 3 Chena Hot Springs (p249); 4 Goldpanners baseball game (p246), Fairbanks; 5 Iditarod, Nome (p251)

BEST...

ANIMALS

- **Musk ox** (p256) Woolly mammals that have changed little since the ice age.
- **Polar bear** (p259) See these massive white bears near Barrow.
- **Reindeer** (p256) Outside Nome, residents of Teller own a herd.
- **Walrus** (p259) You might spot one of these on a flight tour around Barrow.

SCENIC DRIVES

- **Chena Hot Springs Road** (p247) This paved road curves through 56 miles of rolling hills.
- **Elliot Highway** (p250) Drive 152 miles out past great hiking trails, and end at Manley Hot Springs.
- **Nome–Council Road** (p255) Winding 73 miles outside of Nome, this route passes beaches, ghost towns and great birding sites.

SLEEPING & EATING

- **Chena Hot Springs Resort** (p250) This establishment runs almost entirely off of geothermal power.
- **Tanana Valley Farmers Market** (p246) Buy yourself a 20lb cabbage and some Alaskan art at this market; Wednesdays and Saturdays.
- **Silver Gulch Brewery** (p250) Out of town on the Steese Hwy, this place has great beer, good pizza and a buzzy vibe.
- **Pepe's North of the Border** (p260) It's the northernmost Mexican restaurant in the world!

OFF-BEAT ENTERTAINMENT

- **Palace Theatre & Saloon** (p246) Honky-tonk and cancan dancers make for a wild evening.
- **Marlin** (p246) Fairbanks' best live-music venue; sleep in the flophouse upstairs if you can't make it home.
- **Goldpanners** (p246) Catch a baseball game under the midnight sun.

BRENT WINEBRENNER

Mural, Fairbanks (p242)

THINGS YOU NEED TO KNOW

⤳ VITAL STATISTICS

- **Best time to visit** May to September

⤳ LOCALITIES IN A NUTSHELL

- **Fairbanks** (p242) Alaska's second-largest city, featuring the University of Alaska Fairbanks.
- **Chena Hot Springs** (p249) The most-developed of Alaska's hot springs, located down smooth Chena Hot Springs Rd. Take your pick from several different pools.
- **Nome** (p251) A Gold Rush settlement on the Seward Peninsula.
- **Barrow** (p258) The northernmost town in the US.

⤳ ADVANCE PLANNING

- **Two months ahead** Book accommodations at any of the hot springs, as well as remote tours.
- **One month ahead** Research and reserve your rental car; book bush flights.
- **One day ahead** Throw your swimsuit in (or take it out, depending on which hot springs you want to visit…).

⤳ RESOURCES

- **Morris Thomson Cultural & Visitor Center** (Map p243; ☎ 456-5774, 800-327-5774; www.nps.gov/aplic; 101 Dunkel St, Fairbanks; ⏱ 8am-7pm)
- **Fairbanks Daily News-Miner** (www.news-miner.com) Covers the city, the Interior and the Bush.
- **Bering Land Bridge Interpretive Center** (Map p253; ☎ 443-2522, 800-471-2352; www.nps.gov/bela; 179 Front St, Nome; ⏱ 8am-5pm Mon-Fri) This National Park Service center is the best place to go for information on hiking, fishing and wildlife in the area.
- **North Slope Borough Public Information Office** (☎ 852-0215; PO Box 60, Barrow) You can contact this place for information in advance of your trip.

⤳ GETTING AROUND

- **Bus** Several companies travel from both Anchorage and Fairbanks.
- **Train** You can hop on in Anchorage or Talkeetna and end in Fairbanks.
- **Car** Your best option for visiting any of the hot springs or touring outside Nome.
- **Air** Alaska Airlines flies into Fairbanks and Nome; smaller bush planes depart for other locations.

⤳ BE FOREWARNED

- **Gravel roads** If you're headed out of town, make sure your car-rental company allows travel on non-paved roads.
- **Polar bears** You might see one around Barrow, but take the same precaution you would with black and brown bears.
- **Roadside assistance** When driving remote highways, bring enough supplies to be self-sufficient – help is usually far away.
- **Nightlife** Downtown Fairbanks can get a bit seedy; use the same precautions as you wood in a normal US city after dark.

FAIRBANKS & THE BUSH ITINERARIES

THE BEST OF THE CITY One Day

(1) Fairbanks (p242) is a great place to spend a day exploring. Begin at **(2) University of Alaska Fairbanks** (p244), making sure to spend some in the **(3) Museum of the North** (p244).

After your academic morning, lighten things up with a visit to the cheesy but fun **(4) Pioneer Park** (p242), where you can amble through the guts of a dry-docked stern-wheeler or ride a miniature train.

The sun doesn't set until well after midnight in the summer, so have a splashy evening on the Chena River following the **(5) Great Fairbanks Pub Paddle** (p245). If you still have stamina after all your activities, make the most of the midnight sun by attending a late-night baseball game at **(6) Growden Memorial Park** (p246).

NORTHERN BEACHES Three Days

Alaska might be the last place you think of when you're dreaming of beaches, but there are several of them in the state, and at least two of them in the far north. **(1) Nome** (p251) is home to the mile-long **(2) Golden Sands Beach** (p252), which is (as the name indicates) both sandy and a place where folks sluice and dredge in search of gold. You won't find that in Hawaii.

Now, head up north for an entirely different experience. In **(3) Barrow** (p258) you're more likely to see a polar bear than a bikini-clad sunbather. Take a tour up to **(4) Point Barrow** (p258) for a chance to spot not only the big white bears, but also walrus and migrating birds.

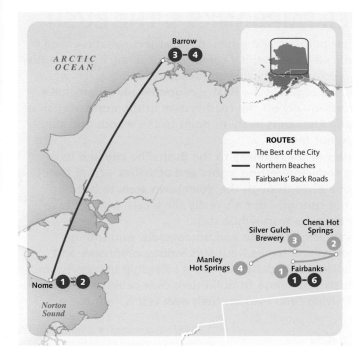

FAIRBANKS' BACK ROADS Five Days

This itinerary starts in (1) Fairbanks (p242). You'll spend a day or two following Chena Hot Springs Rd, driving east and stopping at (2) Chena Hot Springs (p249). Then head west on the Steese Hwy, where you can stop for a pint (or a growler to go) at the (3) Silver Gulch Brewery (p250).

Here the road forks, and you'll head northwest on the Elliot Hwy. You can stop at a couple of very rural hot springs here, both which warrant an overnight camping trip. If you're not feeling up to that, continue on the long but scenic drive to (4) Manley Hot Springs (p251), set in a tropical greenhouse. This is as good a place as any to end your road trip, though options for further travel abound. Better think about it over another soak…

DISCOVER FAIRBANKS & THE BUSH

Mythical in its proportions and untenable vastness, what is called 'the Bush' is difficult to define; it's comprised of small, isolated native villages and sweeping stretches of untracked wilderness.

For this book, we separate the Bush geographically and include places that are essentially off the road system in the northern half of the state. But any Alaskan is likely to point to the woods and simply tell you that it's 'out there.'

Fairbanks serves as the gateway to the Bush. The city and its surrounds have some interesting sights and activities – from paddling the mighty Chena River through the downtown area, to heading out to remote hot springs – but it's really the locals' frontiersman persona that makes it a worthwhile stop.

Here you have businesspeople and bureaucrats, gun-toting conspiracy-theorists and freaked-out survivalists, professors and hygienically-challenged students at Alaska's flagship university, and rugged individuals who chose to build their own cabins and grow their own food, living their lives on their own terms, 'out there.'

FAIRBANKS

A spread-out maze of strip malls, snaking rivers and bleak storefronts, Alaska's second-largest city holds very little attraction for the independent traveler. This said, the people around here can be fascinating, the nightlife moves at a good clip (sometimes even during the day) and there are a few interesting museums.

SIGHTS

DOWNTOWN FAIRBANKS

Begin your downtown tramp at the slated location for the **Old Log Cabin Visitor Center** (☎ 452-7954; www.yukonquest.com; 550 1st Ave at Cushman St; admission free; ☺ 10am-6pm Tue-Sat). Then head out the door into **Golden Heart Plaza**, a pleasant riverside park in the city center. In the middle of the plaza is an impressive bronze statue, *The Unknown First Family*, which depicts an Athabascan family braving the elements. You can follow a river walkway along the

Chena River east from here to Griffin Park and the new Morris Thomson Cultural & Visitor Center (p239).

PIONEER PARK

Fairbanks' guiltiest pleasure is this 44-acre **theme park** (☎ 459-1087; Airport Way at Peger Rd; ☺ stores noon-8pm, park 24hr), formerly known as Alaskaland. It may sound corny, but suspend your cynicism and you'll dig this vacation from your vacation. Best of all: entry is free.

Nearby is the **Pioneer Museum** (admission free), mainly a jumble of antiques ostensibly chronicling the history of Fairbanks. This is also where, six times daily, you can catch the 40-minute **Big Stampede Show** (admission $4), re-enacting gold-rush days.

Across the park, the geodesic **Pioneer Air Transportation Museum** (admission $2) is full of exhibits on the state's aviation history – there's even an experimental gyroplane and a 'flying saucer.'

FAIRBANKS

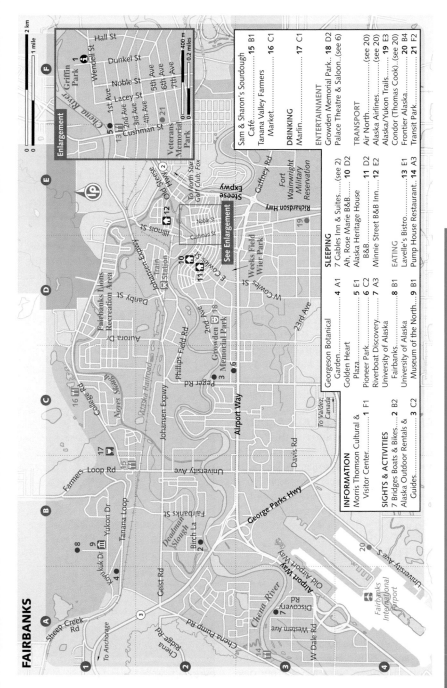

INFORMATION

Morris Thomson Cultural &
Visitor Center...................**1** F1

SIGHTS & ACTIVITIES

7 Bridges Boats & Bikes.....**2** B2
Alaska Outdoor Rentals &
Guides.............................**3** C2
Georgeson Botanical
Garden............................**4** A1
Golden Heart
Plaza..............................**5** E1
Pioneer Park......................**6** C2
Riverboat Discovery............**7** A3
University of Alaska
Fairbanks.........................**8** B1
University of Alaska
Museum of the North.........**9** B1

SLEEPING

7 Gables Inn & Suites.....(see 2)
Ah, Rose Marie B&B...........**10** D2
Alaska Heritage House
B&B................................**11** D2
Minnie Street B&B Inn........**12** E2

EATING

Lavelle's Bistro....................**13** E1
Pump House Restaurant.......**14** A3
Sam & Sharon's Sourdough
Café................................**15** B1
Tanana Valley Farmers
Market.............................**16** C1

DRINKING

Marlin...............................**17** C1

ENTERTAINMENT

Growden Memorial Park......**18** D2
Palace Theatre & Saloon..(see 6)

TRANSPORT

Air North........................(see 20)
Alaska Airlines..................(see 20)
Alaska/Yukon Trails............**19** E3
Condor (Thomas Cook)....(see 20)
Frontier Alaska..................**20** B4
Transit Park.......................**21** F2

FAIRBANKS & THE BUSH

⬊ UNIVERSITY OF ALASKA MUSEUM OF THE NORTH

In an architecturally abstract igloo-and-aurora-inspired edifice near the west end of the campus is one of Alaska's finest museums, the **University of Alaska Museum of the North** (☎ 474-7505; www.uaf.edu/museum; 907 Yukon Dr; adult/child $10/ free; ⏱ 9am-9pm). A recent $42-million overhaul has doubled the facility's size and further amplified its impact. Inside, you'll find the Gallery of Alaska, which examines the geology, history and unusual aspects of each region of the state, and is where you can view the museum's most famous exhibit, Blue Babe: a 36,000-year-old bison found, by Fairbanks-area miners, preserved in the permafrost. In the new wing is a temporary-exhibit space, as well as the permanent Rose Berry Alaska Art Gallery, where northern works, ranging from ancient ivory carvings to contemporary photographs, are intermixed in an egalitarian fashion.

FAIRBANKS

UNIVERSITY OF ALASKA FAIRBANKS
WOOD CENTER & CONSTITUTION HALL

A good place to start exploring the campus is the **Wood Center** (☎ 474-7037; 505 Yukon Dr; ⏱ 7:30am-5:30pm Mon-Fri), where the information desk can provide you with the *UAF Campus Map & Visitors' Guide*, and the latest scoop on university events.

GEORGESON BOTANICAL GARDEN

On the station grounds is the 5-acre **Georgeson Botanical Garden** (☎ 474-1944; www.uaf.edu/salrm/gbg; W Tanana Dr; admission $2, guided tours $5; ⏱ 8am-8pm), a perfect picnicking spot that's a riot of wildflowers, herbs, fruits and gigantic vegetables.

ACTIVITIES
CYCLING

Pick up a free *Bikeways Map* at the Morris Thomson C&V Center.

    Alaska Outdoor Rentals & Guides (☎ 457-2453; www.2paddle1.com; Pioneer Park; ⏱ 10am-7pm) is located on the river behind Pioneer Park and rents mountain bikes for $27 per day.

7 Bridges Boats & Bikes (☎ 479-0751; www.7gablesinn.com; 4312 Birch Lane), at the 7 Gables Inn & Suites, rents bikes for $20 per day.

PATRICK ENDRES / ALASKASTOCK.COM

University of Alaska Museum of the North

PADDLING

The best journey around town is the **Great Fairbanks Pub Paddle**. Start at Alaska Outdoor Rentals & Guides in Pioneer Park and paddle or float down river. Along the way, you can stop for brews, pub grub, horseshoes and games at the Boatel, Pike's Landing and the Pump House. Of course, it's dangerous to paddle while inebriated, so exercise restraint and caution.

Those looking for an overnight – or even longer – paddle, should try a float down the Chena River from Chena Hot Springs Rd, east of Fairbanks, or a pleasant two-day trip down the Tanana River.

TOURS

Fairbanks Historical City Tour (☎ 474-0286, 800-770-3343; www.riversedge.net; 4140 Boat St; adult/child $27/10) Departing from River's Edge RV Park & Campground, this four-hour motorcoach tour leaves daily at 8:30am and visits downtown, the Trans-Alaska Pipeline, and the UAF Museum and Botanical Gardens.

Riverboat Discovery (☎ 479-6673, 866-479-6673; www.riverboatdiscovery.com; 1975 Discovery Dr, Mile 4.5 Airport Way; adult/child

---

⭷ **FAIRBANKS MIDNIGHT SPORTS**

The most revered of the city's wee-hour athletic activities is the **Midnight Sun Baseball Game**, held every solstice since 1906, without artificial light and, thus far, never canceled due to darkness.

North Star Golf Club (☎ 457-4653; www.northstargolf.com; 330 Golf Club Dr; 18 holes $30) is an 18-hole course where visitors can start a round as late as 10pm.

$50/35) Departing at 8:45am and 2pm daily, this 3½-hour tour navigates the Chena River via historic stern-wheeler.

SLEEPING

our pick **Ah, Rose Marie B&B** (☎ 456-2040; www.akpub.com/akbbrv/ahrose.html; 302 Cowles St; s/d $65/90; 🖳) Just west of downtown, this highly recommended B&B has cozy rooms at an amazingly affordable rate. There aren't many rooms in this 80-year-old cottage, so call ahead.

7 Gables Inn & Suites (☎ 479-0751; www.7gablesinn.com; 4312 Birch Lane; r $90-130, apt $120-200) This B&B, just off the Chena River, is entered via a hothouse garden and offers plush rooms, some with Jacuzzis, as well as private apartments. Full breakfasts have an international theme, like eggs in curry sauce or Norwegian farmers' omelettes.

Alaska Heritage House B&B (☎ 456-4100; www.alaskaheritagehouse.com; 410 Cowles St; r $189-220; 🖳) Probably the fanciest B&B in town, Heritage House was built in 1916 by Arthur Williams as a way to lure his future wife up to the Great White North to marry him.

Minnie Street B&B Inn (☎ 456-1802; www.minniestreetbandb.com; 345 Minnie St; r with/without bath $179/139, apt $189-239; 🖳) North of the river from downtown, this spacious B&B provides full breakfasts and bountiful advice on what to do around Fairbanks, and is the nicest midrange spot in town. There's a hot tub here and the condo-like suites are perfect for families.

EATING

Sam & Sharon's Sourdough Café (☎ 479-0523; University Ave at Cameron St; breakfast $6-11, burgers & sandwiches $7-11; ⏰ 6am-10pm) Considered by many to be the town's best diner, this place, just down University Ave from campus, serves up sourdough pancakes all day long.

our pick **Tanana Valley Farmers Market** (☎ 456-3276; www.tvfmarket.com; College Rd at Caribou Dr; ☼ 11am-4pm Wed, from 9am Sat, occasionally open Sun) The market sells fresh produce, baked goods, local handicrafts and more. Come in late August and you can buy a 20lb cabbage. Try the scrumptious falafel at Pita Place; the line's definitely worth it.

Lavelle's Bistro (☎ 450-0555; 575 1st Ave; mains $16-33; ☼ 4:30-9pm Sun & Mon, to 10pm Tue-Sat) Chic, urbane and blessedly devoid of 'Last Frontier' kitsch, Lavelle's has a wine list as long as your arm and mains that include potato-crusted salmon and 'the best meatloaf you've ever had.'

Pump House Restaurant (☎ 479-8452; Mile 1.3 Chena Pump Rd; www.pumphouse.com; dinner $18-36; ☼ 11:30am-2pm & 5-11pm) Located 4 miles from downtown, this is the best place to turn dinner into an evening, or to enjoy a great Sunday brunch. A pump house during the gold-mining era, the

building is now a national historic site. The MACS Blue Line goes by here.

DRINKING & ENTERTAINMENT

Marlin (3412 College Rd) This subterranean dive hosts Fairbanks' edgiest musical acts, most nights of the week.

Palace Theatre & Saloon (☎ 452-7274; www.akvisit.com; adult/child $18/9) At Pioneer Park, this saloon comes alive at night with honky-tonk piano, cancan dancers and other acts in the *Golden Heart Revue*. Showtime is 8:15pm nightly.

The **Goldpanners** (www.goldpanners.com) are Fairbanks' entry in the collegiate-level Alaska Baseball League, which also includes teams from Anchorage, Mat-Su Valley and Kenai Peninsula. Games are played mid-June through July at **Growden Memorial Park** (cnr Wilbur St & 2nd Ave; tickets $10), starting at 7pm. Don't miss the Midnight Sun Baseball Game (see the boxed text, p245) on June 21 – it's a century-old tradition.

PATRICK ENDRES / ALASKASTOCK.COM

Tanana Valley Farmers Market

GETTING THERE & AWAY

AIR

Alaska Airlines (☎ 800-252-7522; www.alaskaair.com) flies direct to Anchorage (where there are connections to the rest of Alaska, the Lower 48 and overseas), Barrow and Seattle. **Frontier Alaska** (☎ 450-7200, 800-478-6779; www.frontierflying.com) is your best way into the Bush. It also visits Anchorage daily, charging $158 (one way) or $209 (round trip). **Air North** (in USA or Canada ☎ 800-661-0407; www.flyairnorth.com) flies to Whitehorse and other Canadian destinations.

In summer, **Condor** (Thomas Cook; in USA & Canada ☎ 800-524-6975, in Germany 01-805-707 202; www.condor.com) operates a weekly service direct to and from Frankfurt, Germany, for about $1900 return.

BUS

Long-distance bus services are available through the **Alaska Direct Bus Line** (☎ 800-770-6652; www.alaskadirectbusline.com), which leaves from the Downtown Transit Park, and makes a Fairbanks to Whitehorse run (one way $180) on Sundays, Wednesdays and Fridays. Along the way the bus will stop at Delta Junction (one way $45), Tok (one way $70), Beaver Creek (one way $95) and Haines Junction (one way $155).

Travel down the George Parks Hwy to Denali National Park, Talkeetna and Anchorage with **Alaska/Yukon Trails** (☎ 800-770-7275; www.alaskashuttle.com).

TRAIN

The **Alaska Railroad** (☎ 458-6025, 800-544-0552; www.alaskarailroad.com) leaves Fairbanks daily at 8:15am from mid-May to mid-September. The new **train station** (🕑 6:30am-3pm) is at the south end of Danby St.

GETTING AROUND

TO/FROM THE AIRPORT

MACS Yellow Line (☎ 459-1011) bus departs eight times a day between 6:30am and 8pm, charging $1.50 and taking you past some Airport Way motels and the Go North Hostel en route to Transit Park, the downtown transfer station.

Alaska Shuttle (☎ 800-770-2267; www.alaskashuttle.com) has a shuttle service from the airport to anywhere in town, for $7, and one-way shuttles within the city limits for $5.

PUBLIC TRANSPORTATION

The **Metropolitan Area Commuter Service** (MACS; ☎ 459-1011; www.co.fairbanks.ak.us/transportation) provides a local bus service in the Fairbanks area from around 6:15am to 7:30pm Monday to Friday, with limited service on Saturday and to noon on Sunday. **Transit Park** (cnr Cushman St & 5th Ave) is the system's central hub – all six bus routes stop here. The fare on all routes is $1.50, or you can purchase an unlimited day pass for $3.

AROUND FAIRBANKS

CHENA HOT SPRINGS ROAD

This fireweed-lined, forest-flanked corridor parallels the languid Chena River 56 miles east off the Steese Hwy, to the Chena Hot Springs Resort, the closest hot springs to Fairbanks and also the most developed. The road is paved and in good condition. From Mile 26 to Mile 51 it passes through **Chena River State Recreation Area**, a 397-sq-mile preserve encompassing the river valley and nearby alpine areas, which is home to some of the Fairbanks area's best hiking, canoeing and fishing.

FAIRBANKS AREA

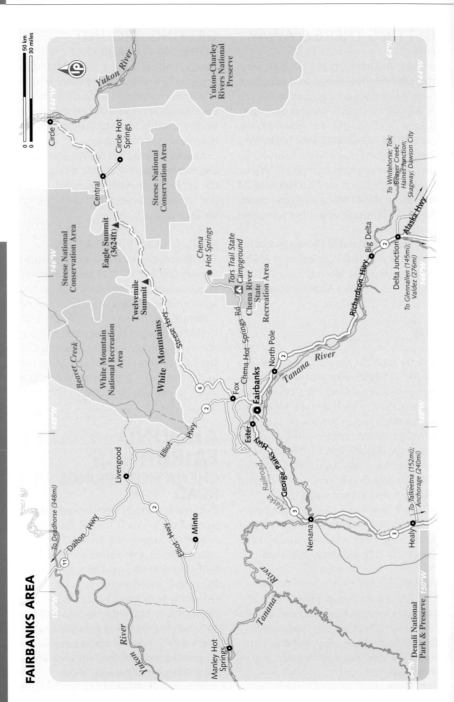

50 km
30 miles

Yukon River

Circle

Circle Hot Springs

Central

Yukon-Charley Rivers National Preserve

Steese National Conservation Area

Eagle Summit (3624ft)

Steese National Conservation Area

Twelvemile Summit

White Mountains

Steese Hwy

Chena Hot Springs

Chena Hot Springs Rd

Tors Trail State Campground

Chena River State Recreation Area

To Whitehorse; Tok; Beaver Creek; Haines Junction; Skagway; Dawson City

Alaska Hwy

Big Delta

Delta Junction

Richardson Hwy

To Glennallen (145mi); Valdez (276mi)

Beaver Creek

White Mountain National Recreation Area

Fox

North Pole

Tanana River

Fairbanks

Ester

George Parks Hwy

Elliot Hwy

Livengood

Alaska Railroad

Minto

To Deadhorse (348mi)

Dalton Hwy

Elliot Hwy

Nenana

Tanana River

To Talkeetna (152mi); Anchorage (240mi)

Healy

Denali National Park & Preserve

Manley Hot Springs

Yukon River

Tanana River

DON PITCHER / ALASKASTOCK.COM

Relaxing at Chena Hot Springs

⬑ CHENA HOT SPRINGS

At the heart of a 40-sq-mile geothermal area, the **Chena Hot Springs**, at Chena Hot Springs Resort (p250), produce a steady stream of water that, at 156°F, must be cooled before you can even think about bathing in it. The facility has several indoor and outdoor tubs, Jacuzzis and pools, including what amounts to a boulder-ringed artificial lake with a fountain at its center. If you've just come to soak it costs adult/child $10/7. Other activities include a visit to the ice museum (adult/child $15/7.50), ice-sculpting classes, mountain biking, hiking, horseback riding, and fishing the local streams for grayling. Guided activities are available. In winter, this is one of the best places in the world to view the aurora.

Things you need to know: ☎ 451-8104; www.chenahotsprings.com; Mile 56.6 Chena Hot Springs Rd; adult/child $10/7; ⊗ 7am-midnight

ACTIVITIES
HIKING

The 15-mile **Granite Tors Trail Loop** – accessed from the Tors Trail State Campground, at Mile 39 of the Chena Hot Springs Rd – provides access into an alpine area with unusual tors: isolated pinnacles of granite rising out of the tundra.

The first set is 6 miles from the trailhead but the best group lies 2 miles further along the trail. The entire trail is a five- to eight-hour trek gaining 2700ft in elevation, with a free-use shelter midway.

Angel Rocks Trail is a 3.5-mile loop trail that leads to Angel Rocks: large granite outcroppings near the north boundary of Chena River State Recreation Area. It's a moderate day-hike; the elevation gain is 900ft and the rocks are less than 2 miles from the road. The trail is also the first leg of the **Angel Rocks–Chena Hot Springs Traverse**, a more difficult 8.3-mile trek that ends at the Chena Hot Springs Resort, at the end of Chena Hot Springs Rd.

The upper trailhead for the most popular hike in the area, **Chena Dome Trail**, is at Mile 50.5 of Chena Hot Springs Rd. The

Angel Rocks Trail (p249)

PATRICK ENDRES / ALASKASTOCK.COM

trail follows the ridge for almost 30 miles in a loop around the Angel Creek drainage area; the first 3 miles to the treeline make an excellent day hike.

SLEEPING & EATING

Chena Hot Springs Resort (☎ 451-8104; www.chenahotsprings.com; Mile 56.6 Chena Hot Springs Rd; campsites & RV sites $20, r $179, cabins & yurts with outhouse $65-249, pool $10) This come-as-you-are complex at the end of Chena Hot Springs Rd is a great spot to unwind for the weekend. Nearly 80% of the hotel's energy is geothermal, and you can take 'green and gassy' tours daily at 6pm. See p249 for more on the springs.

Two Rivers Lodge (☎ 488-6815; Mile 16 Chena Hot Springs Rd; burgers & pub grub $10-17, dinner $14-35; ☒ 5-10pm Mon-Fri, 3-10pm Sat & Sun) The rustic decor at this friendly lodge, complete with bearskin rugs, is in keeping with the natural setting.

GETTING THERE & AWAY

Call the Chena Hot Springs Resort to book its shuttle-van service; round-trip trans-portation from Fairbanks is $90 for one person, or $45 per person for two or more.

STEESE HIGHWAY

The scenic but severely lonely Steese Hwy follows an old miners' trail 162 miles from Fairbanks to the Athabascan village of Circle, on the Yukon River. This hilly and winding road is paved for the first 53 miles, and then has a good gravel base to the mining settlement of Central.

Silver Gulch Brewery (☎ 452-2739; Mile 11 Old Steese Hwy; burgers $11, mains $15-34; ☒ 4-10pm Mon-Fri, from 11am Sat & Sun) is a slightly overdone brewpub making the best beer in the region – the new restaurant and bar are certainly worth the stop. There are free brewery tours Monday, Wednesday and Friday at 3pm.

ELLIOT HIGHWAY

From the crossroad with the Steese Hwy at Fox, just north of Fairbanks, the Elliot Hwy extends 152 miles north and then west to Manley Hot Springs, a small settlement near the Tanana River.

The first half of the highway is paved, the rest is gravel, and there's no gas and few services until you reach the end. Diversions along the way are comparatively few, but the leisurely, scenic drive, coupled with the disarming charms of Manley Hot Springs, make it a worthwhile one- or two-day road trip.

The rustic, privately managed **Tolovana Hot Springs** (☎ 455-6706; www.mosquitonet. com/~tolovana; cabin $30-120) can be accessed via a taxing 11-mile overland hike south from Mile 93. Facilities consist of two plastic tubs bubbling with 125°F to 145°F water, plus, a quarter mile up the valley, two cedar cabins that must be reserved in advance. The trailhead isn't signposted; contact the managers for directions.

At Mile 110 is the paved 11-mile road to the small Athabascan village of **Minto** (pop 180), which isn't known for welcoming strangers.

Hutlinana Creek is reached at Mile 129, and a quarter mile east of the bridge is an 8-mile creekside trail to **Hutlinana Warm Springs**, an undeveloped thermal area with a 3ft-deep pool.

The springs are visited mainly in winter; in summer, the buggy bushwhack seems uninviting.

GETTING THERE & AWAY
Finally, **Warbelow's Air Ventures** (☎ 474-0518, 800-478-0812; www.warbelows.com), in Fairbanks, has regular flights to Manley Hot Springs for $140 round-trip.

MANLEY HOT SPRINGS
pop 72
The town of Manley Hot Springs may be one of the loveliest discoveries you'll make around the Fairbanks area. At the end of a long, lonely road, this well-kept town is full of friendly folks, tidy log homes and luxuriant gardens.

Just before crossing the slough you pass the town's namesake **hot springs** (☎ 672-3231, roadhouse 672-3161; admission $5; ☉ 24hr). Privately owned by famously hospitable Chuck and Gladys Dart, bathing happens within a huge, thermal-heated greenhouse that's a veritable Babylonian garden of grapes, Asian pears and hibiscus flowers.

SLEEPING & EATING
Manley Roadhouse (☎ 672-3161; r with/without bath $120/70, sandwiches $9-11, dinner mains $22-30; ☉ 8am-10pm) Facing the slough, this antique-strewn, century-old establishment has clean, uncomplicated rooms and is the social center of town.

WESTERN ALASKA

A wild region in an already wild state, Western Alaska is home to the Iñupiat, wild-eyed prospectors and some of Alaska's least-seen wilderness. But don't expect a forested wonderland: this is too far north (and too close to the Arctic and Bering Seas) for trees. Instead, you have a naked, harsh landscape carpeted with coral-like tundra grasses and flowers, herds of reindeer and, of course, the region's star Pleistocene-era ungulate, the musk ox.

NOME
pop 3497
Nome is, in so many ways, the Alaskan archetype: a rough-hewn, fun-loving, undying Wild West town, thriving at the utmost edge of the planet. It's even the finish line of that most Alaskan of races, the Iditarod, and during its gold-rush heyday, Wyatt Earp and some 30,000 stampeders called the town home. With America's biggest concentration of non-Natives north of

NIK WHEELER / ALAMY

Aerial view in winter, Nome

the treeline, the town is both comfortably familiar and spectacularly exotic, with paved streets, grassy public squares, many saloons (more than in the rest of Bush Alaska combined) and a palpable gold-rush history.

SIGHTS & ACTIVITIES
CENTRAL NOME
Begin at the **Nome Visitor Center** and pick up a copy of its walking-tour brochure.

Across the street is the **Bering Land Bridge Interpretive Center** in the Sitnasuak Native Corporation Building. The center is dedicated to Beringia, the 1000-mile-wide landmass that linked Alaska and Siberia until about 10,000 years ago.

In a lot next to the city hall is the **Iditarod finish-line arch**. The huge wooden structure, a distinctly bent pine tree with burls, is raised over Front St every March in anticipation of the mushers and their dogsled teams ending the 1049-mile race here.

To the east of the visitors center, on Front St, is **Carrie McLain Museum** (☎ 443-6630; 223 Front St; adult/child $1/0.50; ☼ 9:30am-5:30pm), in the basement of the Kegoayah Kozga Public Library. There are displays on Native culture and local reindeer-cultivation efforts, but the focus is the gold rush and Nome's history in the early 20th century. See the preserved body of Fritz the sled dog, one of the leaders of the famed 1925 race to deliver diphtheria serum to Nome, which inspired the Iditarod.

Among the historic buildings listed in the walking tour is **St Joseph Church**. It overlooks Anvil City Sq at Bering St and 3rd Ave. Built in 1901, when there were 30,000 people living in Nome, this huge church was originally located on Front St, and the electrically lit cross at the top of the building was used as a beacon for seamen.

GOLDEN SANDS BEACH
A very interesting afternoon can be spent at Nome's Golden Sands Beach, stretch-

ing a mile east of town along Front St. At the height of summer a few local children may be seen playing in the 45°F water, and on Memorial Day (in May), more than 100 masochistic residents plunge into the ice-choked waters for the annual **Polar Bear Swim**.

Usually more numerous than swimmers here are gold prospectors, as the beach is open to recreational mining.

HIKING

If you're well prepared and the weather holds, the backcountry surrounding Nome can be a hiker's heaven. Though there are no marked trails in the region, the area's three highways offer perfect access into the tundra and mountains. What's more, the lack of trees and big, rolling topography make route-finding fairly simple: just pick a point and go for it. For those who'd like a little more direction, a seven-page list of suggested day hikes is available from the Nome Visitor Center.

The climb up 1062ft **Anvil Mountain** is the closest hike to Nome and the only one that can be easily pulled off without a car. It's about 1 mile round-trip to the summit, ascending through wonderful wildflower patches. At the top you'll find the giant parabolic antennae of the Cold War–era White Alice Communications System, plus great views of town and the ocean, as well as the Kigluaik Mountains further inland.

TOURS

Bering Air (☎ 443-5464) Offers helicopter tours of the area for around $200 per person (three person minimum).

our pick **Nome Discovery Tours** (☎ 443-2814; discover@cgi.net; tours $125-185) The

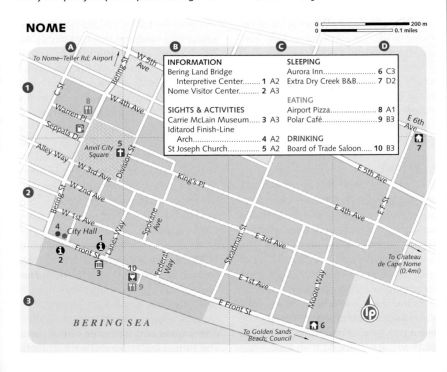

NOME

0 / 200 m
0 / 0.1 miles

INFORMATION		SLEEPING	
Bering Land Bridge		Aurora Inn.................... 6 C3	
Interpretive Center........ 1 A2		Extra Dry Creek B&B......... 7 D2	
Nome Visitor Center......... 2 A3			
		EATING	
SIGHTS & ACTIVITIES		Airport Pizza.................... 8 A1	
Carrie McLain Museum..... 3 A3		Polar Café........................ 9 B3	
Iditarod Finish-Line			
Arch.............................4 A2		DRINKING	
St Joseph Church.............5 A2		Board of Trade Saloon..... 10 B3	

To Nome–Teller Rd; Airport

W 5th Ave
Bering St
W 4th Ave
Warren Pl
Seppala Dr
Alley Way
Anvil City Square
W 3rd Ave
Division St
King's Pl
W 2nd Ave
Bering St
W 1st Ave
Lanes Way
Spokane Ave
City Hall
Front St
Federal Way
Steadman St
E 3rd Ave
E 5th Ave
E 4th Ave
E 6th Ave
E F St
E 1st Ave
Moore Way
E Front St

To Chateau de Cape Nome (0.4mi)

BERING SEA

To Golden Sands Beach; Council

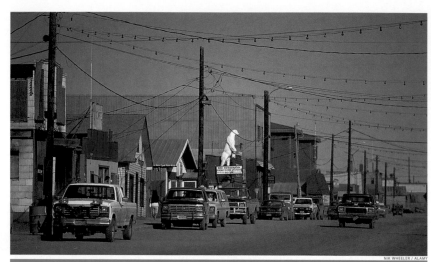

NIK WHEELER / ALAMY

Main St, Nome

most intimate, highly recommended tours are run by Richard Beneville, an old song-and-dance man who decided to hang up his tap shoes to live out in the Alaska wilds. He offers everything from two-hour evening tundra-exploration drives to full-day excursions to Teller, where you'll drop in on an Iñupiat family, or to Council, with fishing along the way. **Wilderness Birding Adventures** (☎ 694-7442; www.wildernessbirding.com) Runs high-priced birding trips in the area.

SLEEPING

Chateau de Cape Nome (☎ 443-2083; cussy@nome.net; 1105 E 4th Ave; r from $100) Spectacularly situated overlooking the tundra on the far eastern edge of town, this is Nome's most colorful inn. The owner 'Cussy' Kauer is a descendant of gold rush-era pioneers and her place is a trove of local history.

Extra Dry Creek B&B (☎ 443-7615; sbabcock@gci.net; 607 E F St; s/d $115/125) More like a rental apartment than a B&B, this pristine suite (named for an apparently desiccated waterway outside of town) has a full kitchen stocked with breakfast fixings that you prepare yourself.

Aurora Inn (☎ 443-3838, 800-354-4606; www.aurorainnome.com; E Front St at Moore Way; d $154-245) Probably the nicest rooms in town – 'rivaling that found in Anchorage' as one employee put it – the Aurora has simple motel-style rooms and all the amenities (but none of the charm) you could ask for.

EATING

Polar Café (☎ 443-5191; Front St; breakfast $7-13, lunch $7-14, dinner $14-24; ☉ 6am-10pm) Nome's only waterfront eating option, this popular eatery serves straightforward food that delivers. It has remarkable views of the Bering Sea, a down-and-out interior and a $9 salad bar that veggies will love.

our pick **Airport Pizza** (☎ 443-7992; 406 Bering St; pub grub $10-17, pizza $20-29; ☉ 7am-10pm) Hands down the best restaurant in town, this pub-tastic joint has the feeling of an airport hangar with corrugated metal walls and propeller ceiling fans. The simple pub grub will send you into the stratosphere with everything from chicken tacos to reindeer-sausage pizza.

DRINKING & ENTERTAINMENT

The **Board of Trade Saloon** (212 Front St), dating back to 1900, claims to be the oldest bar on the Bering Sea and is certainly the most notorious.

GETTING THERE & AROUND

Nome is serviced by **Alaska Airlines** (☎ 443-2288, 800-468-2248; www.alaskaair. com), which offers at least three daily flights from Anchorage for about $500. If you want to fly to Nome from Fairbanks, you can go direct aboard **Frontier Alaska** (☎ 450-7200, 800-478-6779; www.frontierflying. com) for about $440.

AROUND NOME

Radiating east, north and northwest from Nome are its finest features: three gravel roads, each offering passage into very different worlds and each providing a full-day adventure at minimum. While Nome can seem dirty and rundown, the surrounding country is stunning – think sweeping tundra, crystal-clear rivers, rugged mountains and some of the best chances in Alaska to see waterfowl, caribou, bears and musk oxen.

NOME–COUNCIL ROAD

This 73-mile route, which heads northeast to the old mining village of Council, is perhaps the best excursion if you have time for only one of Nome's roads. For the first 30 miles it hugs the glimmering Bering Sea coastline and passes an outstanding, motley array of shacks, cabins, tepees and Quonset huts used by Nome residents as summer cottages and fish camps. On sunny days miles of beaches beckon – but note how far inland autumn storms have tossed driftwood. At Mile

22 the road passes **Safety Roadhouse** (☎ 443-2368; ☿ summer only), a dollar-bill-bedecked dive of a watering hole, and then crosses the birders' wonderland of **Safety Sound**. Ten miles further along is Bonanza Crossing, on the far side of which is the Last Train to Nowhere, a series of locomotives abandoned in the tundra in 1907 by the Council City & Solomon River Railroad. Just to the north is the ghost town of **Solomon**, which was originally established in 1900 and once boasted a population of 1000 and seven saloons.

The road ends at Mile 73 at **Council**. Actually, the road ends at the banks of the Niukluk River and Council is on the other side. Most of the houses here are weekend getaways for people living in Nome, and there are currently no year-round residents.

KOUGAROK ROAD

Also known as Nome–Taylor Rd, Kougarok Rd leads 86 miles north from Nome through the heart of the Kigluaik Mountains. There are a few artifacts from the gold-rush days, and the best mountain scenery and hiking in the Nome area, along the way.

The Kigluaiks spring up almost immediately, flanking the road until around Mile 40 where the free, BLM-operated Salmon Lake Campground is beautifully situated at the north end of the large Salmon Lake.

Just before Mile 54 is Pilgrim River Rd, a rocky lane that heads northwest. Less than 8 miles from Kougarok Rd, Pilgrim River Rd ends at the gate of **Pilgrim Hot Springs**. A roadhouse and saloon was located here during the gold rush, but burnt down in 1908. Today the hot springs are privately owned and somewhat dilapidated, but if you contact caretaker Louie Green (☎ 443-5583) ahead of time you'll likely get permission to walk inside for a soak.

Kougarok Rd crosses Pilgrim River at Mile 60, the Kuzitrin River at Mile 68 and the Kougarok Bridge at Mile 86. This is one of the best areas to look for herds of musk oxen. At all three bridges you can fish for grayling, Dolly Varden and salmon, among other species.

After the Kougarok Bridge the road becomes a rough track impassable to cars. The extremely determined, however, can shoulder a pack and continue overland for a very challenging, boggy, unmarked 30-plus miles to **Serpentine Hot Springs**, inside the Bering Land Bridge National Preserve.

NOME–TELLER ROAD

This road leads 73 miles (a one-way drive of at least two hours) to Teller, a year-round, subsistence Iñupiat village of 256 people. The landscape en route is vast and undulating, with steep climbs across spectacular rolling tundra. Hiking opportunities are numerous, as are chances to view musk oxen and a portion of the reindeer herd communally owned by families in Teller. The huge **Alaska Gold Company dredge**,

which operated until the mid-1990s, lies just north of Nome on the Nome–Teller Rd.

Teller lies at the westernmost end of the westernmost road in North America. This wind-wracked community overlooks the slate waters of the Bering Sea and stretches along a tapering gravel spit near the mouth of Grantley Harbor.

Though Teller is a scenic place – witness the fishnets set just offshore and the salmon hanging from racks on the beach – there's little for a visitor to do.

Still, out of respect for the residents (who are likely tired of drive-by gawkers from Nome), park your car and ask one of the village kids for directions to the tiny community store. Once there, you can buy a snack and perhaps a handmade craft, thereby supporting the Teller economy and facilitating interaction with the locals.

ARCTIC ALASKA

Perhaps the least-visited portion of the state, Alaska's Arctic region is tough and expensive to visit. But for those looking

ANDONI CANELA

Gold Dust Saloon, Nome

for adventure, and strange moonlike dystopian towns, you might have just hit the jackpot. There's also plenty of outdoor stuff to do: paddling the numerous rivers, backpacking in national parks and preserves like Gates of the Arctic and ANWR, or driving the precarious and prodigious Dalton Highway.

GATES OF THE ARCTIC NATIONAL PARK & PRESERVE

The Gates of the Arctic National Park & Preserve is one of the world's finest wilderness areas. Covering 13,125 sq miles, it straddles the ragged spine of the Brooks Range, America's northernmost chain of mountains, and sprawls 800 miles from east to west. The sparse vegetation is mainly made up of shrubbery and tundra; animals include grizzlies, wolves, Dall sheep, moose, caribou and wolverines.

The park contains no visitor facilities, campgrounds or trails, and the NPS is intent upon maintaining its virgin quality.

Unguided trekkers, paddlers and climbers entering the park should be well versed in wilderness travel; they should also check in at one of the ranger stations for a backcountry orientation and updates on river hazards and bear activity.

SIGHTS & ACTIVITIES
HIKING
NOLAN/WISEMAN CREEK AREA
Head west at the Wiseman exit just before Mile 189 of the Dalton Hwy, and hike along Nolan Rd, which passes through Nolan – a hamlet of a few families – and ends at Nolan Creek. You can then reach Wiseman Creek and Nolan Creek Lake, which lies in the valley through which Wiseman and Nolan Creeks run, at the foot of three passes: Glacier, Pasco and Snowshoes.

LOWER HAMMOND RIVER AREA
From Wiseman, go north by hiking along Hammond Rd, which can be followed for quite a way along the Hammond River. From the river you can explore the park by following one of the drainage areas, including Vermont, Canyon and Jenny Creeks.

PADDLING
Floatable rivers in the park include the John, the north fork of the Koyukuk, the Tinayguk, the Alatna and the middle fork of the Koyukuk River from Wiseman to Bettles. The headwaters for the Noatak and Kobuk are in the park.

Of the rivers, the Koyukuk's north fork is especially popular because of the location and challenge – the float starts in the Gates' shadow and goes downstream 100 miles to Bettles through Class I and II waters. Canoes and rafts can be rented in Bettles (see p258) and floated downstream.

UPPER NOATAK
The best-known river, and the most popular for paddlers, is the upper portion of the Noatak, due to the spectacular scenery as you float by the sharp peaks of the Brooks Range and because it's a mild river that many canoeists can handle on an unguided journey.

The most common trip is a 60-mile float that begins near Portage Creek and ends at a riverside lake near Kacachurak Creek, just outside the national park's boundary.

GUIDED TOURS
A few guide companies run extremely spendy trips through the Gates of the Arctic National Park & Preserve. These companies include **ABEC's Alaska Adventures** (☎ 457-8907, 877-424-8907; www.abecalaska.com), **Too-loó-uk River Guides** (☎ 683-1542; www.akrivers.com) and **Arctic Wild** (☎ 479-8203, 888-577-8203; www.arcticwild.com).

FAIRBANKS & THE BUSH

ARCTIC ALASKA

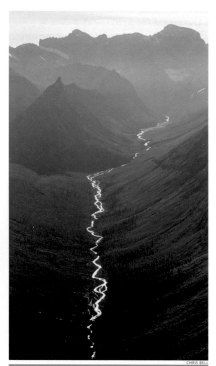

Gates of the Arctic National Park & Preserve

GETTING THERE & AWAY
Access to the park's backcountry is usually accomplished in two steps, with the first being a scheduled flight from Fairbanks to Bettles. Check out **Bettles Air Service** (☎ 800-770-5111, 692-5111), which makes regular flights to Bettles for $335 round-trip. The second step is to charter an air-taxi from Bettles to your desired destination within the park. If you are in Bettles, check with **Brooks Range Aviation** (☎ 692-5444, 800-692-5443; www.brooksrange-alaska-wilderness-trips.com) or Bettles Air Service.

BETTLES
pop 28
This small village serves as the major departure point to the Gates of the Arctic National Park & Preserve.

SLEEPING & EATING
Bettles Lodge (☎ 692-5111, 800-770-5111; www.bettleslodge.com; dm $35; r $175-195; ✕ 🖳) This is a classic Alaskan log lodge with a restaurant, a small tavern and bush pilots constantly wandering through in their hip boots.

GETTING THERE & AROUND
There's no summer road to Bettles – in winter they enjoy an ice road – so you'll need to fly or float here for the most part.

BARROW
pop 4054
Barrow is the northernmost settlement in the USA, the largest Iñupiat community in Alaska and one of the most distinctive places you're ever likely to visit. It's a flat, bleak, fogbound and strangely evocative place patrolled by polar bears and locked in almost perpetual winter.

For tourists, however, Barrow's appeal isn't so much its Iñupiat culture as its novel latitude. They come to see the midnight sun (which doesn't set for 82 days from May to early August) and say they've been at the top of the world.

SIGHTS
The main thing to do at the top of the world is bundle up and stand on the shore of the Arctic Ocean gazing toward the North Pole.

Follow the shore 12 miles northeast of the city and you'll come to **Point Barrow**, a narrow spit of land that's the northernmost extremity of the US (though not, as locals sometimes claim, North America). While you can walk out to the point, it's best to go with an organized tour considering the prevalence of polar bears in the area.

Among Barrow's artificial attractions, by far the most impressive is the **Iñupiaq**

Heritage Center (☎ 852-0422; Ahkovak St; admission $5; ☺ 8:30am-5pm Mon-Fri, 12:30-4pm Sat & Sun). This 24,000-sq-ft facility houses a museum, gift shop and a large multipurpose room where traditional dancing-and-drumming performances take place each afternoon. The show is worth the additional $15, and afterwards local craftspeople assemble in the lobby to sell masks, whalebone carvings and fur garments.

BIRDING & WILDLIFE WATCHING
Barrow is a birder's paradise. At least 185 distinct avian species visit during the summer months. Head west of town to **Freshwater Lake** for some good birding. Along the way you pass the cemetery and are likely to see jaegers, arctic terns, snowy owls and snow buntings. East of Bowerville along the **Cakeater Rd** is another excellent birding spot.

To spot polar bear, you are best taking a tour. But don't get your hopes up too high: they're tough to spot.

TOURS
Arctic Adventure Tours (☎ 852-4512) Offers an intimate two-hour wildlife tour to Point Barrow to look for polar bears, marine life such as walrus and a variety of migrating birds.
Northernmost Tours (☎ 852-5893; www.northernmosttoursbarrow.com; tours $60-100) Daniel Lum, a knowledgeable Iñupiat guide, takes people all the way out to the point. He's a wealth of knowledge when it comes to local cultural and natural history, and this is the best tour in town.

SLEEPING
King Eider Inn (☎ 852-4700, 888-303-4337; www.kingeider.net; 1752 Ahkovak St; r $185-315; ☒ ☐) With a cozy log-cabin feel, wood-post beds and an inviting fireplace in the lobby, the Eider has the nicest rooms in town.

EATING
Barrow is a 'damp' town, so don't expect to be throwing back margs at the local Mexican restaurant.

Brower's Café (☎ 852-3456; 3220 Brower Hill; burgers $8-12; ☺ 11am-11pm Mon-Sat, noon-10pm Sun) This beachfront structure was built in the late 19th century by Charles Brower, an American whaler, and has whaling antiques inside and a whale-jawbone arch out front. Nowadays it's Barrow's best burger joint (with about 10 varieties) and hosts what's almost certainly America's northernmost karaoke night.

Pepe's North of the Border (☎ 852-8200; 1204 Agvik St; mains $8-22; ☺ 6am-10pm Mon-Sat, to 9pm Sun) Attached to the Top of the World Hotel, this 'northernmost Mexican restaurant in the world' has achieved renown thanks to the tireless Barrow-boosting efforts of owner Fran Tate. The food is decent and eclectic, including lobster, flautas and big burritos.

GETTING THERE & AROUND
While you can get to Barrow in the winter by ice road (you'll need a GPS, extra gas, survival gear and some big-ass *cajones*), it's best to fly. **Alaska Airlines** (☎ 852-4653, 800-468-2248; www.alaskaair.com) charges about $500 for a round-trip, advance-purchase ticket from Fairbanks and about $600 from Anchorage.

Such fares make package tours attractive. A same-day excursion, which includes airfare from Fairbanks and a town tour but not meals, is around $520 through Alaska Airlines, or $625 if you want to stay overnight.

↘ ALASKA IN FOCUS

ALASKA IN FOCUS

ALASKAN WILDLIFE

ALASKAN WILDLIFE

MARK NEWMAN

Grizzly bear cubs

With almost three-quarters of its population concentrated in three cities, Alaska is able to boast one of the largest concentrations of wildlife on earth. It's one of the few places in the USA where entire ecosystems are still intact and ancient migratory routes uninterrupted. There are almost twice as many caribou in Alaska as people, and 400 species of birds have been sighted in the state.

LAND MAMMALS

BEARS

There are three species of bear in Alaska – brown, black and polar – but you're most likely to see brown bears, since they have the greatest range.

At one time, brown and grizzly bears were listed as separate species, but now both are classified as *Ursus arctos*. The difference isn't as much genetics as size. Browns live along the coast, where abundant salmon runs help them reach weights exceeding 800lb – with the famed Kodiak brown bear often tipping the scales at 1500lb. Grizzlies are browns found inland, away from the salmon runs. Normally a male weighs from 500lb to 700lb, and females half that. The most common way to identify a brown bear is by the prominent shoulder hump, easily seen behind the neck when it's on all fours.

Black bears live in most forested areas of the state, but not north of the Brooks Range, on the Seward Peninsula or on many large islands, such as Kodiak and Admiralty. The average male weighs 180lb to 250lb. A brown or cinnamon black bear often appears in Southcentral Alaska, leaving many backpackers confused about what the species is.

THE BEST

MARK NEWMAN

Polar bear

PLACES TO SPOT WILDLIFE

- **Denali National Park** (p212)
- **Katmai National Park** (p199)
- **Kenai Fjords National Park** (p180)
- **Turnagain Arm** (p72)
- **Ketchikan** (p90)

ALASKA IN FOCUS

ALASKAN WILDLIFE

Beyond measuring an upper rear molar, look for a straight facial profile to confirm it's a black bear.

Polar bears *(Ursus maritimus)* are fascinating because of their size and white color, but they're not easy to encounter. Polar bears dwell only in the northern hemisphere, and almost always in association with Arctic Sea ice.

MOOSE

The moose is long-legged to the extreme, with a huge rack of antlers and a drooping nose. Standing still, they look uncoordinated – until you watch them run or, better still, swim. They're the world's largest members of the deer family, and the Alaskan species is the largest of all moose. A newborn weighs 35lb and can grow to more than 300lb in five months; cows weigh 800lb to 1200lb; and bulls 1000lb to more than 1600lb, with antlers up to 70in wide.

CARIBOU

Although more than a million caribou live in Alaska's 32 herds, they are difficult to view, as they travel from the Interior north to the Arctic Sea. Caribou range in weight from 150lb to more than 400lb. Some caribou have been known to migrate 3000 miles a year between their calving grounds, rutting areas and winter home. The caribou are crucial to the Iñupiat and other Alaska Natives, who hunt more than 30,000 a year to support their subsistence lifestyle.

Perhaps one of the greatest wildlife events left in the world is the migration of the Western Arctic herd of caribou, the largest such herd in North America, with almost 500,000 animals. The herd uses the North Slope for its calving area, and in late August many of the animals begin to cross the Noatak River on their journey southward.

MOUNTAIN GOATS

Mountain goats are the only North American species in the widespread group of goat antelopes, and are characterized by a fondness for rugged alpine terrain that allows them to avoid predators. More mountain goats are killed by snow slides than by wolves or bears.

Although mountain goats are often confused with Dall sheep, they are easily identified by their longer hair, short black horns and deep chest.

In Alaska mountain goats range through the bulk of the Southeast, fanning out north and west into the coastal mountains of Cook Inlet, as well as the Chugach and Wrangell Mountains.

DALL SHEEP

These are more numerous and widespread than mountain goats – they number close to 80,000 – and live principally in the Alaska, Wrangell, Chugach and Kenai mountain ranges.

It's spectacular to watch rams in a horn-clashing battle, but they're not fighting for a female, just for social dominance. Dall sheep prefer rocky, open, alpine tundra regions. In the spring and fall, however, they move to lower slopes, where the grazing is better. The best time to spot rams, and see them clash, is right before the mating period, beginning in November.

WOLVES

While gray wolves are struggling throughout most of the USA, they inhabit 85% of Alaska, and their numbers are strong despite predator control programs. No animal has been more misunderstood. A pack of wolves is no match for a healthy 1200lb moose; wolves can usually only catch and kill the weak, injured or young, thus strengthening the herd they are stalking.

In total, about 8000 wolves live in packs throughout almost every region of Alaska. Most adult males average 85lb to 115lb, and their pelts can be either grey, black, off-white, brown or yellow, with some tinges approaching red. Wolves travel, hunt, feed and operate in the social unit of a pack.

FISH & MARINE MAMMALS

WHALES

The three most common whales seen in coastal waters are the 50ft-long humpback, with its humplike dorsal fin and long flippers, the smaller bowhead whale and the gray whale. The humpback is by far the most frequently seen whale by visitors on cruise ships and on the state ferries, as they often lift their flukes (tails) out of the water to begin a dive, or blow every few seconds when resting near the surface. Biologists estimate 1000 humpbacks migrate to the Southeast and more than 100 head to Prince William Sound each year.

SEALS

The most commonly seen marine mammals are seals, which often bask in the sun on an ice floe. Six species exist in Alaska, but most visitors will encounter just the harbor seal, the only seal whose range includes the Southeast, Prince William Sound and the rest of the Gulf of Alaska. The average weight of a male is 200lb – achieved through a diet of herring, flounder, salmon, squid and small crabs.

DOLPHINS & PORPOISES

Many visitors also see dolphins and harbor porpoises, even from the decks of the ferries. Occasionally, ferry travelers spot a pod of orcas (killer whales), whose high black-and-white dorsal fins make them easy to identify. Orcas, which can be more than 20ft long, are the largest members of the dolphin family, which also includes the beluga or white whale. Belugas range in length from 11ft to 16ft and often weigh more than 3000lb. The 50,000 belugas that live in Alaskan waters travel in herds of more than 100. Most

MARK NEWMAN

Dall sheep

ALASKA IN FOCUS

ALASKAN WILDLIFE

visitors will spot them in Turnagain Arm, along the Seward Hwy (p170). Beluga Point, at Mile 110, is a popular observation area.

SALMON

Salmon runs are where thousands of fish swim upstream to spawn, and rank among Alaska's most amazing and easiest-to-find sights. From late July to mid-September, many coastal streams are choked with salmon. You won't see just one fish here and there, but thousands – so many, they have to wait their turn to swim through narrow gaps of shallow water.

Five kinds of salmon populate Alaskan waters: sockeye (also referred to as red salmon), king or chinook, pink or humpie, coho or silver, and chum.

BIRDS
BALD EAGLES

The most impressive bird in Alaska's wilderness is the bald eagle – with a white tail and head, and a wingspan that often reaches as much as 8ft – and it has become the symbol of the nation. While elsewhere the bird is on the endangered species list, in Alaska it thrives. It can be sighted almost daily in most of the Southeast, is common in Prince William Sound and is impossible to miss in Dutch Harbor in the Aleutian Islands.

PTARMIGAN

The state bird of Alaska is the ptarmigan, a cousin of the prairie grouse. Three species of the ptarmigan can be found throughout the state, in high treeless country.

SEABIRDS & WATERFOWL

Alaskan seabirds include the playful horned and tufted puffins, six species of auklet and three species of albatross (which boast a wingspan of up to 7ft). The puffin, in particular, is a crowd pleaser, due to its large colorful bill, stout body and red, webbed feet. The optimum way to see puffins and a variety of seabirds is onboard a wildlife cruise to coastal islands used for breeding.

An amazing variety of waterfowl also migrates to Alaska, including trumpeter swans. The trumpeter swan is the world's largest member of the waterfowl family and occasionally weighs 30lb. Other waterfowl include Canada geese, of which more than 130,000 nest in Alaska; all four species of eider; the colorful harlequin duck; and five species of loon *(Gavia)*.

IMAGEBROKER/STEFAN WACKERHAGEN

Ptarmigan

CRUISING IN ALASKA

MARK NEWMAN

Early evening on the Lynn Canal

While many independent travelers will find the strictures of 'cruise life' a bit stifling, there are plenty of reasons to take an Alaskan cruise, namely the two 'Cs': comfort and convenience. And in a state that could take months, if not years, to thoroughly explore, you get a chance to see many of the top sights in one convenient, all-inclusive package.

Most days, you'll get a chance to disembark in port for anywhere from four to eight hours, where you can bop around town, take in a hike or an excursion (which will cost you extra, of course), or even a longer trip inland to Denali National Park, Talkeetna or Eagle. You also get to sit on deck and spot bald eagles hunting, humpback whales breaching and glaciers calving: not a bad little bit of sight-seeing. On the smaller lines, you'll get more wildlife excursions and more stops. And backpackers, independent travelers and spendthrifts can always hop on the Alaska Marine Highway Ferry. You see the same sights, but you don't get a casino, heated pool, hot-tub, B-team comedian, all-you-can-eat buffet or cruise director.

Cruises run May through September.

PICKING YOUR SHIP
CRUISE SHIPS
For the comfort of a floating all-inclusive hotel, you can't beat a large cruise ship. These resorts on the sea do have their limitations, however. Most large cruises stop only in the major ports of call, and generally start from Vancouver or Seattle. Excursions range

ALASKA IN FOCUS

CRUISING IN ALASKA

ALASKA MARINE HIGHWAY: THE INDEPENDENT TRAVELER'S CRUISE JIM DUFRESNE

Travel on the state ferries is a leisurely and delightful experience. The midnight sun is warm, the scenery stunning and the possibility of sighting whales, bald eagles or sea lions keeps most travelers at the side of the ship.

Alaska Marine Highway (☎ 465-3941, 800-642-0066; www.ferryalaska.com) runs ferries equipped with observation decks, food services, lounges and solariums with deck chairs. You can rent a stateroom for overnight trips – these aren't as 'stately' as they may sound, and are downright spartan compared with what you'll get on a cruise liner – but many travelers head straight for the solarium and unroll their sleeping bags on deck chairs.

The ferries are extremely popular during the peak season (June to August). If boarding in Bellingham, you absolutely need reservations for a cabin or vehicle space, and just to be safe you should probably have one even if you're just a walk-on passenger.

from heli-seeing trips and zipline tours to guided hikes, kayaks and day trips to Denali National Park. Cruises cost around $120 a night, but that does not include your flight to the port of embarkation.

Here's how they break down:

Carnival (☎ 888-227-6482; www.carnival.com) Young people rule on these ships.

Celebrity (☎ 877-202-4345; www.celebritycruises.com) Family-friendly and laid back.

Holland America (☎ 877-932-4259; www.hollandamerica.com) A bit more classy.

Norwegian (☎ 866-234-7350; www.ncl.com) Works well for the older crowd.

Princess (☎ 800-774-62377; www.princess.com) Nonroyalty need not apply.

Royal Caribbean (☎ 866-562-7625; www.royalcaribbean.com) Despite the name, it offers more than 50 voyages to Alaska each summer.

SMALL SHIPS

Just 3% of Alaskan cruisers take a small-ship voyage. And while you'll have tighter quarters, bumpier seas and less entertainment options than on the big boys, these vessels offer better chances at seeing wildlife, more land and kayak excursions, onboard naturalists (most of the time), generally better food, a more casual atmosphere (you can leave that blue sports coat at the office where it belongs), and a more intimate portrait of Alaska.

These boats sleep anywhere from eight to 100 and are more likely to depart from Alaska. While this is probably your best bet if you are looking to match comfort with quality and authentic experience, it does come with a steeper price tag: anywhere from $400 to $1200 a night.

SMALL-SHIP CRUISES

Each small cruise ship is different. Here's a breakdown of some of our favorites:

Adventure Life Voyages (☎ 800-244-6118; www.alvoyages.com; number of passengers 62-128;

per person $7599-19,349) Has top-end trips out to the Aleutians, King Island, around the 'Ring of Fire,' through the Northwest Passage, and over to Russia.

ourpick **AdventureSmith Explorations** (☎ 800-728-7825; www.adventuresmithexplorations. com; number of passengers 12-102; per person $1390-4500) This company offsets its carbon emissions and focuses on learning and adventure cruises in Southeast Alaska aboard its fleet of small boats, which range from intimate charters (accommodating just 12 people) to larger cruisers that can take around 100 people. The boats have kayaks and small skiffs for the numerous excursions that include everything from kayaking in Glacier Bay National Park to wildlife watching near Tracy Arm, the ABC Islands, Icy Straight, Misty Fjords and Frederick Sound. Most trips depart from Juneau.

America Safari Cruises (☎ 888-862-8881; www.amsafari.com; number of passengers 12-36; per person $4395-7995) Offers themed cruises that focus on whale watching, Glacier Bay, wildlife watching or adventure travel. The small boats have modern, elegant staterooms, and a naturalist is on board to teach you the ways of the Alaska wilderness. Most trips depart from Juneau, but it has one trip that leaves from Seattle.

Cruise West (☎ 888-851-8133; www.cruisewest.com; maximum passengers 102; per person $3999-18,499) It does cruises up to the Bering Sea, passing Kodiak, Katmai National Park, the Shumagin Islands, Dutch Harbor, the Pribilof Islands, on up to Nome.

Discovery Voyages (☎ 800-324-7602; www.discoveryvoyages.com; maximum passengers 12, cabins 6; per person $3650-15,850) While the quarters are tight on this small boat, Discovery Voyages offer some interesting five- to eight-day options, with trips focusing on whale watching, hiking and kayaking, photography, or wildlife exploration. It also offsets its carbon emissions.

Lindblad Expeditions (☎ 800-397-3348; www.expeditions.com; maximum passengers 62, cabins 31; per person from $7500) Offers kayaking, wilderness walks, onboard naturalists and

EMILY RIDDELL

Enjoying the views from MV *Taku*

Zodiac excursions during eight-day cruises in the Southeast. Many trips include the airfare from Seattle, and take visitors from Juneau through the Inside Passage, past Tracy Arm, Petersburg, Frederick Sound, Chatham Strait, Glacier Bay National Park, Point Adolphus and Inian Pass.

Yukon Queen II (☎ 867-993-5599, 800-544-2206; www.hollandamerica.com; one way $90) This 110-passenger tour boat plies the mighty Yukon between Eagle and Dawson City.

PICKING YOUR CRUISE ROUTE
INSIDE PASSAGE
This is a classic route, which sails from Seattle or Vancouver up through the Inside Passage. Most trips will stop in Ketchikan, which has just about as many bars as people and some very fine totem poles. They then continue to the state capital in Juneau, home to a lovely glacier and some nice heli-seeing tours; Skagway, a gold-rush port with some nice hiking not far out of town; and the granddaddy attraction of Alaska cruises, Glacier Bay, where you'll see 11 tidewater glaciers spilling their icy wares into the sea.

GULF OF ALASKA
This trip includes the Inside Passage, but then continues to the Gulf of Alaska, with stops in Seward, the Hubbard Glacier and Prince William Sound. While you get a broader picture of coastal Alaska on this one-way cruise, it also comes at a price, as you'll generally need to arrange for flights from separate ports.

BERING SEA
These trips are more expensive and generally focus on natural and cultural history. Folks that enjoy learning on their vacations will like this trip, with stops in the Pribilof Islands, Nome and, on the really expensive cruises, King Island.

'CRUISE TOURS'
These trips give you the chance to get off the boat for about half of your trip. Most begin with the Inside Passage cruise, then head out on a tour bus, with stops in Talkeetna, Denali National Park, Fairbanks, Eagle or the Copper River. Most cruise companies have all-inclusive hotels in these destinations (basically cruise ships without the rocking).

ENVIRONMENT

RALPH HOPKINS

Tongass National Forest

Alaska is a place so huge, so wild and so unpopulated, it's incomprehensible to most people until they arrive. Only when they are standing on the edge of a river, watching thousands of salmon spawning upstream and being feasted upon by a pair of 1000lb brown bears, do they begin to understand that Alaska's environment – its land and its wildlife – is special, rare and irreplaceable.

Colliding tectonic plates created three impressive mountain systems that arch across the state. The Coast Range, a continuation of Washington state's Olympic Range, which includes the St Elias Range and the Chugach and Kenai Mountains, sweeps along the southern edge of Alaska before dipping into the sea, southwest of Kodiak Island. The Alaska and Aleutian Ranges parallel the same arc, and the Brooks Range skirts the Arctic Circle.

In between the Alaska Range and the Brooks Range is Interior Alaska: an immense plateau rippled by foothills, low mountains and great rivers, among them the third-longest in the USA, the Yukon River, which runs for 2300 miles. North of the Brooks Range is the North Slope, a tundra that gently descends to the Arctic Ocean.

REGIONS
SOUTHEAST ALASKA
Southeast Alaska is a 500-mile coastal strip extending from north of Prince Rupert to the Gulf of Alaska. In between are the hundreds of islands of the Alexander Archipelago, and a narrow strip of coast, separated from Canada's mainland by the glacier-filled

ALASKA IN FOCUS

ENVIRONMENT

↘THE BEST

View of Mt McKinley (p213)

WILDERNESS LODGES

- Glacier Bay Lodge (p126)
- Camp Denali (p220)
- Brooks Lodge (p200)
- Kennicott River Lodge & Hostel (p231)
- Bettles Lodge (p258)

Coast Mountains. Winding through the middle of the region is the Inside Passage waterway; the lifeline for isolated communities, as the rugged terrain prohibits road building. High annual rainfall and mild temperatures have turned the Southeast into rainforest, broken up by majestic mountain ranges, glaciers and fjords that surpass those in Norway.

PRINCE WILLIAM SOUND & KENAI PENINSULA

Like the Southeast, much of this region (also known as Southcentral Alaska) is a mixture of rugged mountains, glaciers, steep fjords and lush forests. This mix of terrain makes Kenai Peninsula a superb recreational area for backpacking, fishing and boating, and Prince William Sound, home of Columbia Glacier, a mecca for kayakers and other adventurers.

SOUTHWEST ALASKA

Stretching 1500 miles from Kodiak Island to the international date line, Southwest Alaska is an island-studded region that includes the Aleutian Islands, the Alaska Peninsula and Bristol Bay. Home to 46 active volcanoes, Southwest Alaska is also rich in wildlife. It boasts the largest bears in the world, on Kodiak Island, the richest salmon runs in Alaska at Bristol Bay and great opportunities to view marine mammals and birds on the Alaska Marine Highway Ferry run to the Aleutian Islands.

DENALI & THE INTERIOR

Three major highways – the George Parks, Glenn and Richardson Hwys – cut across Alaska's Interior and pass numerous recreational areas, including Denali National Park, Alaska's most noted attraction.

The heartland of Alaska offers warm temperatures in the summer and ample opportunities for outdoor activities in some of the state's most scenic and accessible areas. With the Alaska Range to the north, the Wrangell and Chugach Mountains to the south and the Talkeetna Mountains cutting through the middle, the Interior has a rugged appearance matching that of either Southeast or Southcentral Alaska, but without much of the rain and cloudy weather.

THE BUSH

This is the largest slice of Alaska and includes the Brooks Range, Arctic Alaska, and Western Alaska on the Bering Sea. The remote, hard-to-reach Bush is separated from the rest of the state by mountains, rivers and vast roadless distances, offering a glimpse of a lifestyle unaffected by the state's tourist industry. The main communities are Nome, Barrow, Kotzebue and Bethel, while scattered between are small isolated Native villages.

CLIMATE

The oceans surrounding 75% of the state, the mountainous terrain and the low angle of the sun, give Alaska an extremely variable climate, and daily weather that is infamous for its unpredictability.

In the Interior and up around Fairbanks, precipitation is light, but temperatures can fluctuate by more than 100°F during the year. Fort Yukon holds the record for the state's highest temperature, at 100°F in June 1915, yet it once recorded a temperature of -78°F in winter. Fairbanks regularly has the odd summer's day that hits 90°F and always has nights during winter that drop below -60°F.

The Southeast and much of Southcentral have a temperate maritime climate. Juneau averages 57in of rain or snow annually, and Ketchikan gets 154in a year, most of which is rain as the temperatures are extremely mild.

Shielded from Southcentral Alaska's worst weather by the Kenai Mountains, the Anchorage Bowl receives only 14in of rain annually and enjoys a relatively mild climate: January averages 13°F, July about 58°F.

For visitors, the most spectacular part of Alaska's climate is its long days. At Point Barrow, Alaska's northernmost point, the sun doesn't set for 2½ months from May to August. In other Alaskan regions, the longest day is on June 21 (the summer solstice), when the sun sets for only two hours in Fairbanks and for five hours in the Southeast. Even after sunset in late June, daylight is replaced not by darkness, but by a dusk that still allows good visibility.

ROB BLAKERS

Wrangell-St Elias National Park (p228)

ALASKA IN FOCUS

NATIONAL, STATE & REGIONAL PARKS

Alaska's 15 national parks are the state's crown jewels as far as most travelers are concerned. The park system attracts more than two million visitors a year, with the most popular units being Klondike Gold Rush National Historical Park (☎ 907-983-9221; www.nps.gov/klgo), which draws 850,000 visitors to Skagway, and Denali National Park (☎ 907-683-2294; www.nps.gov/dena), home of Mt McKinley. Other popular units are Glacier Bay National Park (☎ 907-697-2230; www.nps.gov/glba), a highlight of every cruise-ship itinerary in the Southeast, and Kenai Fjords National Park (☎ 907-224-7500; www.nps. gov/kefj) in Seward.

Alaska State Parks oversees 121 units that are not nearly as renowned as most national parks, and are thus far less crowded at trailheads and in campgrounds. The most popular is Chugach State Park (☎ 907-345-5014; www.alaskastateparks.org), the 495,000-acre unit that is Anchorage's after-work playground.

For more pretrip information, contact the Alaska Public Lands Information Center (☎ 907-271-2737; www.nps.gov/aplic/center), a clearinghouse for information on all of Alaska's public lands.

ENVIRONMENT

ENVIRONMENTAL ISSUES

Due to Alaska's size, huge tracts of wilderness and natural resources, its environmental issues are, more often than not, national debates. And the focus of most debates centers on the effects of global warming on Alaska or the push for the extraction of minerals from the wilderness.

Fewer and fewer people argue these days that global warming is not an issue. Alaska's temperatures are rising, causing Arctic sea ice and glaciers to melt at alarming rates. Some scientists now believe Arctic sea ice could disappear entirely by 2040, or even sooner.

SAVING THE POLAR BEAR

Biologists estimate 20,000 to 25,000 polar bears live in the Arctic. That's a healthy population, but the bears' dependence on sea ice for survival makes them vulnerable. Polar bears hunt by waiting near holes in ice for seals, their main source of food, to come up for air. They also travel, mate and sometimes give birth, on the ice. Since 1980, the northern ice cap has been shrinking, according to the National Snow and Ice Data Center, and in 2007 there was a record melt of more than a million acres of Arctic sea ice.

The result is that polar bears are showing up on northern Alaska beaches in increasing numbers during the summer. When bears get stranded on land they can't hunt, and must live off body fat or search for washed-up sea mammal carcasses, until the frigid temperatures of autumn, when prevailing winds push the sea ice closer to shore. In 2007 the US Geological Survey released a study concluding that two-thirds of the world's polar bears could be gone by 2050, due to the loss of ice.

ALASKA IN FOCUS

ENVIRONMENT

ERNEST MANEWAL

Polar bears

Alaska's other environmental issue centers on development versus preservation, and is best symbolized by the debate over drilling for oil in the Arctic National Wildlife Refuge (ANWR). But the ANWR is hardly the only wilderness in contention. The proposed Pebble Mine would be a 2-mile-wide open pit on state land in Southwest Alaska, with copper and gold deposits estimated to be worth a staggering $362 billion. But the minerals would be extracted from near the headwaters of Bristol Bay, streams that support the world's largest run of wild salmon, and that has environmentalists, commercial fishers and Alaska Natives up in arms.

Issues of resources exploitation are not restricted to land. At least four times since 1997, the salmon runs of Bristol Bay and Kuskokwim River have been declared economic disasters, and in 2008, the king salmon run up the Yukon River was so poor that even subsistence gatherers were restricted from catching them.

For more information on environmental issues, contact these conservation organizations:

Alaska Sierra Club (☎ 907-276-4048; www.alaska.sierraclub.org)

Southeast Alaska Conservation Council (☎ 907-586-6942; www.seacc.org)

Wilderness Society (☎ 907-272-9453; www.wilderness.org)

ALASKA IN FOCUS

FAMILY TRAVEL

FAMILY TRAVEL

Hikers, Mendenhall Glacier (p124)

CHRISTOPHER S. MILLER / ALASKASTOCK.COM

Everybody is a kid in Alaska. Whether it's a stream choking with bright red salmon or a bald eagle winging its way across an open sky, nature's wonders captivate five-year-olds just as much as their parents. A fourth grader might not fully appreciate, or even endure, a visit to Wall Street like Dad, but both will be equally stunned when they see the 8-mile-wide face of Hubbard Glacier from the deck of a cruise ship.

Alaska is a young state – the median age is 33 – and very family orientated, so infant needs, such as disposable diapers and formula, are widely available in most cities, towns and villages. Breast-feeding in public is practiced in large cities but not always tolerated in small rural towns.

PRACTICALITIES
THE BASICS

Most chain motels in Alaska have roll-away beds for children and cribs for toddlers. You'll find that many independently owned accommodations and lodges in small towns won't offer such amenities. If you absolutely need a crib at night either check your lodging in advance or bring along a travel crib. The same is true for car seats; many national companies have safety seats for toddlers and young children. The cost is around $10 a day and you should try to reserve them in advance.

Most Alaskan restaurants welcome families and tend to cater to children with high chairs, kids menus of smaller sizes and reduced prices, and waitresses quick with a rag when somebody spills their drink. Upscale places where an infant would be frowned upon are limited to a handful in Anchorage. One of the best places to take children for dinner is to a salmon bake, an outdoor affair that is lively and colorful.

TRANSPORTATION

One of the best ways to see Alaska with toddlers or young children is on a cruise ship (p267). The larger the ship, the more family amenities and activities it will offer. **Carnival Cruises** (www.carnival.com) offers Camp Carnival, an activity-based program for children aged two through 14, and in-cabin babysitting services for those who are younger. Other cruise ship companies have similar programs.

The **Alaska Marine Highway System** (www.ferryalaska.com; p316) is also well suited for families. Children have the space to move around, and large ferries like the MV *Columbia*, MV *Kennicott*, MV *Malaspina* and MV *Matanuska* feature both current movies and ranger programs on marine life, birds and glaciers.

Children also do well on the **Alaska Railroad** (www.akrr.com; p318) as they can walk between passenger carriages and spend time taking in the scenery from special domed viewing cars. You could avoid long drives by flying in and out of Anchorage and Fairbanks and taking the Alaska Railroad from one city to the other, stopping along the way at such popular places as Talkeetna or Denali National Park.

DISCOUNTS

In Alaska families with young children can look forward to a wide range of discounts. Kids aged two through 11 receive a 50% discount on the Alaska Marine Highway, and infants travel free. The same discount and age limits apply to children riding the Alaska Railroad. City bus systems also discount heavily for children.

Museums offer some of the largest discounts, often 50% to 75%, with children under the age of six or seven free. Many tour operators also offer reduced kids rates; the popular **White Pass & Yukon Railroad** (www.whitepassrailroad.com; p134) in Skagway offers a 50% discount to kids three to 12 years old, as does Seward's **Kenai Fjords Tours** (www.kenaifjords.com; p181) on its wildlife boat tours in Kenai Fjords National Park. If more than one company is offering a particular bus or boat tour, it pays to look around in order to secure the best rate for children.

> **THE BEST**

ERNEST MANEWAL

Taking to the slopes

ALASKAN ADVENTURES FOR CHILDREN

- Ride the Alyeska tram, Girdwood (p73)
- Walk on a glacier, Matanuska Valley (p228)
- Paddle Orcas Cove, Ketchikan (p92)
- Take a train to Spencer Glacier, Girdwood (p74)

HEADING OUTDOORS

WILDLIFE WATCHING

Children marvel at seeing wildlife in its natural habitat but may not always have the patience for a long wait before something pops out of the woods. The shuttle buses that travel the Denali National Park Rd (p212) offer one of Alaska's best wildlife viewing opportunities, but the entire trip to Wonder Lake and back is an extremely long day with few opportunities to get out of your seat. With most children it's better to ride only to Eielson Visitor Center, leave the bus for a short hike in the area and then head back.

Marine wildlife boat tours work out better because, let's face it, a boat trip is a lot more fun than a bus ride. Nature tours that are done in vans are also ideal for children as they stop often and usually include short walks. An excellent one for families is offered by Alaska Nature Tours (p128) in Haines, which heads out in the evening along the Chilkoot River to look for eagles, mountain goats and brown bears feeding on salmon.

HIKING & BACKPACKING

The key to any Alaskan adventure is to match the hike to your child's ability and level of endurance. With children in tow, it's equally important to select a hike that has an interesting aspect to it – a glacier, gold mine ruins, waterfalls or a remote cabin to stop for lunch. It is always a highlight for children to spot wildlife while hiking, but it's impossible to know when a moose will pop out of the woods or a handful of Dall sheep will wander over a ridge. In July and August, however, you can count on seeing a lot of fish in a salmon stream, a wide variety of marine life in tidal pools, and bald eagles where the birds are known to congregate to feed, such as Chilkat River in Haines.

When backpacking with children, make sure their pack will hold up in Alaska's weather. This is particularly true with their rain gear, both parka and rain pants. It is also important to pack enough food. After a full day of hiking parents are always shocked to see their children consume twice as much as they would at home.

KAYAKING & CANOEING

Paddling with children involves a greater risk than hiking due to the frigid temperature of most fjords, rivers and lakes in Alaska. You simply don't want to tip at any cost. You need to judge how much paddling experience your child has – and, for that matter, you as well – when considering kayaking and canoeing adventures.

Flat, calm water should be the rule with young children. Choose a place like Auke Bay (p120) near Juneau where you can rent double kayaks to team up a parent with a child and then spend an afternoon paddling around the small islands in the protective

⇘ THE NITTY GRITTY

- **Change facilities** Readily available in airports, ferry terminals and most restaurants
- **Cribs** Available in chains; check and reserve ahead
- **Health** Remote locations have fewer and smaller facilities if at all
- **Highchairs** Readily available in restaurants
- **Diapers** (nappies) Widely available
- **Strollers** Bring your own
- **Car seats** Available in most car-rental agencies; not in taxis

ALASKA IN FOCUS

FAMILY TRAVEL

Kayaking, Resurrection Bay (p177)

EDDIE BRADY

bay. Another excellent choice for a flat-water paddle is to rent canoes at Nancy Lake State Recreation Area in the Denali area, while the Chena River (p245) in the heart of Fairbanks can be paddled upstream almost as easily as downstream. Needless to say all rentals should come with paddles and lifejackets that fit your child.

HISTORY

ALASKA IN FOCUS

HISTORY

GRAEME CORNWALLIS

Bering Sea kayak

Alaska made it to 50, celebrating in 2009 the 50th anniversary of President Dwight Eisenhower's official welcome into the Union. It's been a long, strange road, from being labeled a frozen wasteland to the discovery of the country's largest oil reservoir, and from the persecution of Native Alaskans to creating Native corporations and granting them land, money and subsistence rights that are the envy of other indigenous peoples today.

EARLY ALASKANS

It is believed that the first Alaskans migrated from Asia to North America between 15,000 and 30,000 years ago, during an ice age that lowered the sea level and created a 900-mile land bridge linking Siberia and Alaska. The nomadic groups who crossed the bridge were following animal herds that provided them with food and clothing.

The Tlingits and Haidas also came across the land bridge from Asia and settled throughout the Southeast and British Columbia, while the Athabascans, a nomadic

18,000–13,000 BC	1000 BC	1728
The first Alaskans migrate across the Bering land bridge, following animal herds.	Iñupiat, Yupik and Aleuts are believed to have migrated to Alaska.	Vitus Bering, a Danish navigator, makes the first written record of the state.

tribe, settled in the Interior. The other two major groups were the Iñupiat, who settled the north coast of Alaska and Canada (where they are known as Inuit), and the Yupik, who settled southwest Alaska. The smallest group of Alaska Natives to arrive was the Aleuts of the Aleutian Islands. The Iñupiat, Yupik and Aleuts are believed to have migrated 3000 years ago and were well established by the time the Europeans arrived.

The Tlingit and Haida cultures were advanced; the tribes had permanent settlements, including large clan dwellings that housed related families. These tribes were noted for their excellent wood carving, especially carved poles, called totems. Tlingits were spread across the Southeast in large numbers and occasionally went as far south as Seattle in their huge dugout canoes. Both groups had few problems gathering food, as fish and game were plentiful in the Southeast.

Life was not so easy for the Aleuts, Iñupiat and Yupik. With much colder winters and cooler summers, these people had to develop a highly effective sea-hunting culture to sustain life in the harsh regions of Alaska. Though motorized boats replaced the kayaks and modern harpoons the jade-tipped spears, the whaling tradition still lives on in places such as Barrow.

The indigenous people, despite their harsh environment, were numerous until non-Natives, particularly fur traders and whalers, brought guns, alcohol and disease that destroyed the Alaska Natives' delicate relationship with nature and wiped out whole communities. At one time an estimated 20,000 Aleuts lived throughout the Aleutian Islands. In only 50 years the Russians reduced the Aleut population to less than 2000.

AGE OF EXPLORATION

Spanish Admiral Bartoleme de Fonte is credited by many with making the first European trip into Alaskan waters in 1640, but the first written record of the state was made by Vitus Bering, a Danish navigator sailing for the Russian tsar. In 1728 Bering's explorations demonstrated that America and Asia were two separate continents. Thirteen years later, commanding the *St Peter,* he went ashore near Cordova, becoming the first European to set foot in Alaska. With tales of seal and otter colonies to inspire them, Russian fur merchants wasted little time in overrunning the Aleutian Islands and quickly established a settlement at Unalaska and then Kodiak Island. The peaceful Aleuts, living near the hunting grounds, were almost annihilated through massacres and forced labor.

The British arrived when Captain James Cook began searching the area for the Northwest Passage. Cook sailed north from Vancouver Island to Southcentral Alaska in 1778, anchoring at what is now Cook Inlet for a spell before continuing on to the Aleutian Islands, Bering Sea and Arctic Ocean. The French sent Jean-François Galaup, comte de La Pérouse, who in 1786 made it as far as Lituya Bay, now part of Glacier Bay National Park.

1867	1898	1913
William H Seward signs a treaty to purchase the state for $7.2 million.	Klondike Gold Rush turns Skagway into Alaska's largest city, with a population of 10,000.	Walter Harper, an Alaska Native, and Harry Kartens become the first to summit Mt McKinley.

Having depleted the fur colonies in the Aleutians, Aleksandr Baranov, who headed the Russian-American Company, moved his territorial capital from Kodiak to Sitka in the Southeast, where he built a stunning city, dubbed 'an American Paris in Alaska.' At one point, Baranov oversaw (some would say ruled) an immensely profitable fur empire that stretched from Bristol Bay to Northern California.

SEWARD'S FOLLY

By the 1860s the Russians found themselves badly overextended. The country made several overtures to the USA to purchase Alaska but it wasn't until 1867 that Secretary of State William H Seward, with extremely keen foresight, signed a treaty on October 18, 1867 to purchase the state for $7.2 million – less than 2¢ an acre.

By then the US public was in an uproar over the purchase of 'Seward's Ice Box' or 'Walrussia,' and, on the Senate floor, the battle to ratify the treaty lasted six months before the sale was finally approved.

Though this remote and inaccessible land stayed a dark, frozen mystery to most, eventually its riches were uncovered. First whaling began, then the phenomenal salmon runs, with the first canneries built in 1878 at Klawock on Prince of Wales Island.

CHIP PORTER / ALASKASTOCK.COM

Prince of Wales Island (p95)

1942	1958	1964
During WWII Japan invades the Aleutian Islands, the first enemy occupation of American soil since 1812.	President Dwight D Eisenhower officially proclaims Alaska the 49th state.	The Good Friday earthquake hits, killing more than 100 people.

THE ALASKAN GOLD RUSH

The promise of quick riches and frontier adventures was the most effective lure Alaska has ever had and, to some degree, still has today.

Often called 'the last grand adventure,' the Klondike Gold Rush occurred when the country and much of the world was suffering a severe recession. When the banner headline of the *Seattle Post-Intelligencer* bellowed 'GOLD! GOLD! GOLD! GOLD!' on July 17, 1897, thousands of people quit their jobs and sold their homes to finance a trip through Southeast Alaska to Skagway. From this tent city almost 30,000 prospectors tackled the steep Chilkoot Trail to Lake Bennett, where they built crude rafts to float the rest of the way to the goldfields. An equal number of people returned home along the same route, broke and disillusioned.

The Klondike stampede, though it only lasted from 1896 to the early 1900s, was Alaska's most colorful era and forever earned the state the reputation of being the country's last frontier.

Within three years of the Klondike stampede Alaska's population doubled to 63,592, including more than 30,000 non-Native people.

WORLD WAR II

In June 1942, only six months after their attack on Pearl Harbor, the Japanese opened their Aleutian Islands campaign by bombing Dutch Harbor for two days and then taking Attu and Kiska Islands. Other than Guam, it was the only foreign invasion of US soil during WWII and is often dubbed 'the Forgotten War' because most Americans are unaware of what took place in Alaska. The battle to retake Attu Island was a bloody one. After 19 days and landing more than 15,000 troops, US forces recaptured the plot of barren land, but only after suffering 3929 casualties, including 549 deaths. Of the more than 2300 Japanese on Attu, fewer than 30 surrendered, with many taking their own lives.

THE ALCAN & STATEHOOD

Following the Japanese attack on the Aleutian Islands in 1942, Congress panicked and rushed to protect the rest of Alaska. Large army and air-force bases were set up at Anchorage, Fairbanks, Sitka and Whittier, and thousands of military personnel were stationed in Alaska. But it was the famous Alcan (also known as the Alaska Hwy) that was the single most important project of the military expansion.

The growth brought on by the Alcan, and to a lesser degree the new military bases, pushed Alaska firmly into the 20th century and renewed its drive for statehood. When the US Senate passed the Alaska statehood bill on June 30, 1958, Alaska had made it into the Union and was officially proclaimed the country's 49th state by President Dwight Eisenhower that January.

1968	1971	1973
■	■	■
Oil and natural gas are discovered at Prudhoe Bay on the North Slope.	President Richard Nixon signs the Alaska Native Claims Settlement Act to pave the way for the Trans-Alaska Pipeline.	The first Iditarod Trail Sled Dog Race is held on an old dog team mail route blazed in 1910.

ALASKA IN FOCUS

HISTORY

The most powerful earthquake ever recorded in North America (registering 9.2 on the Richter scale) hit Southcentral Alaska on Good Friday morning in 1964. More than 100 lives were lost, and damage was estimated at $500 million. A tidal wave virtually obliterated the community of Valdez. In Kodiak and Seward, 32ft of the coastline slipped into the Gulf of Alaska, and Cordova lost its entire harbor as the sea rose 16ft.

THE ALASKAN BLACK-GOLD RUSH

In 1968 Atlantic Richfield discovered massive oil deposits underneath Prudhoe Bay in the Arctic Ocean. However, it couldn't be tapped until there was a pipeline to transport it to the warm-water port of Valdez and the pipeline couldn't be built until the US Congress, which still administered most of the land, settled the intense controversy among industry, environmentalists and Alaska Natives over historical claims to the land.

The Alaska Native Claims Settlement Act of 1971 was an unprecedented piece of legislation that opened the way for a consortium of oil companies to undertake the construction of the 789-mile pipeline. The Trans-Alaska Pipeline took three years to build, cost more than $8 billion – in 1977 dollars – and, at the time, was the most expensive private construction project ever undertaken. At the peak of construction, the pipeline employed 28,000 people, doing '7-12s' (seven 12-hour shifts a week).

IMAGEBROKER/STEFAN WACKERHAGEN

Grave, Chilkoot Trail (p132)

1980	1985	1989
President Jimmy Carter signs the Alaska National Interests Lands Conservation Act (ANILCA).	Libby Riddles becomes the first woman to win the Iditarod Trail Sled Dog Race.	The *Exxon Valdez* spills 11 million gallons of oil into Prince William Sound.

ALASKA IN FOCUS

HISTORY

⬎ THE BEST

KEVIN G SMITH / ALASKASTOCK.COM

University of Alaska Museum of the North (p244)

MUSEUMS

- **The Anchorage Museum** (p58)
- **University of Alaska Museum of the North** (p244)
- **'Remembering Old Valdez' Annex** (p148)
- **Skagway Museum** (p132)
- **Pratt Museum** (p183)

The oil began to flow on June 20, 1977, and for a decade oil gave Alaska an economic base that was the envy of every other state, accounting for as much as 80% of state government revenue. In the explosive growth period of the mid-1980s, Alaskans enjoyed the highest per-capita income in the country.

DISASTER AT VALDEZ

Reality hit hard in 1989, when the *Exxon Valdez*, a 987ft Exxon oil supertanker, rammed Bligh Reef outside of Valdez. The ship spilled almost 11 million gallons of North Slope crude into the bountiful waters of Prince William Sound. The spill eventually contaminated 1567 miles of shoreline and killed an estimated 645,000 birds and 5000 sea otters.

Today the oil, like other resources exploited in the past, is simply running out. That pot of gold called Prudhoe Bay began its decline in 1988 and now produces less than half of its 1987 peak of two million barrels a day.

A NEW ALASKA

Alaska was at a low point both financially and politically in 2006 when Sarah Palin, a self-described 'hockey mom' and former mayor of Wasilla, ran for governor. At the time, three former state legislators had been arrested on public corruption charges, while in Washington, DC, longtime Senator Ted Stevens and Representative Don Young were under federal investigation for bribery. Palin crushed incumbent Governor Frank Murkowski in the Republican primary by almost two-to-one. She was then handed the keys to the governor's mansion in the general election by voters tired of their state being dominated by career politicians. In 2008 she stunned the political world even more when presidential candidate John McCain named Palin his running mate on the Republican ticket. McCain lost the historic election to Barack Obama but the campaign vaulted Palin onto the national stage.

In her first year as governor, Palin worked with legislators to dramatically increase Alaska's share of royalties from oil production. When oil began its meteoric rise in price

2006	2008	2010
Sarah Palin, former mayor of Wasilla, becomes Alaska's first female governor and also its youngest.	Palin is catapulted onto the international stage as John McCain's running mate for the presidential election.	Former Senator Ted Stevens dies in a plane crash in Southwest Alaska.

ALASKA IN FOCUS

HISTORY

on the world markets, topping $140 a barrel in 2008, Alaska was carried along for the ride. Oil revenue pumped almost $7 billion into the state treasury that year, giving Alaska a $5 billion surplus during a time when many states couldn't make ends meet.

But the rising price of oil was a double-edged sword for Alaska. The state still has an unemployment rate hovering near 7%, one of the highest in the country, and the high cost of fuel was devastating rural communities where everything has to be shipped in, often by costly air freight. The short-term solution was the state issuing every resident a $1200 energy check along with the annual Permanent Fund check. Between the two, a family of four picked up $13,076 in 2008 for simply living in Alaska.

But many Alaskans believe the long-term solution lies in opening up the Arctic National Wildlife Refuge (ANWR) to drilling, the construction of a natural gas line from the North Slope to the Lower 48, opening new mines, and other major projects designed to extract valuable minerals. Thus the greatest challenge facing Alaskans in the 21st century is convincing a nation, and more importantly Washington, DC, they have a right to make a living from an economy based on removing natural resources from the country's great wilderness areas. With a sky-rocketing price of gas at the pump, it might not be a hard argument to win.

LEE FOSTER

Oil pipeline

NATIVE ALASKA

PETER ARNOLD IMAGES

Alaska Native fisherman

The state is young: Alaska recently turned 50, and its residents are new, the majority having moved here from somewhere else. Yet thanks to its isolation, its spectacular scenery and, yes, its long, dark winters, Alaska has a culture that is vibrant and rich, and a northern lifestyle that is thoroughly unique: whether its Alaska Natives celebrating a successful whale hunt in Barrow; or residents of Juneau staging a folk music festival to help pass an April of daily rain.

While most of Alaska is made up of rural, roadless areas collectively known as the Bush, most Alaskans are urban. Almost 60% of the residents live in the three largest cities: Anchorage, Fairbanks and Juneau. There are also Alaskans maintaining a subsistence lifestyle, gathering and hunting the majority of their food and living in small villages that can only be reached by boat, plane or, in the winter, snowmobile. But the majority live in urban neighborhoods, work a nine-to-five job and head to the supermarket when their cupboards are bare.

Only 30% of the state's population was born in Alaska. Such a transient population creates a melting pot of ideas, philosophies and priorities. What they usually have in common is an interest in the great outdoors: they were lured here to either exploit it or enjoy it, and many residents do a little of both.

LIFESTYLE

Lifestyles in Alaska are as diverse as the state is big. Rural or urban, Alaskans tend to be individualistic, following few outside trends and, instead, adhering to what their harsh

➤THE BEST

BRENT WINEBRENNER

Alaska Native Heritage Center (p61)

PLACES TO LEARN ABOUT NATIVE ALASKA CULTURE

- **Alaska Native Heritage Center** (p61)
- **Alaska State Musuem** (p116)
- **Totem Heritage Center** (p92)
- **Chief Shakes Island** (p99)
- **Alutiiq Museum & Archaeological Repository** (p194)
- **Iñupiaq Heritage Center** (p258)

environment dictates. Mother Nature and those -30°F winter days, not California, are responsible for the Alaskan dress code, even in Anchorage's finest restaurants. In the summer, Alaskans play because the weather is nice and the days are long. In the winter, they linger at the office because the temperature is often below 0°F.

Visitors may find most of the locals they meet in towns and cities have lifestyles similar to their own. They work, they love their weekends, they live in a variety of homes big and small, and they participate in double coupon days at supermarkets. Even in remote villages there are satellite TV dishes, the latest hip-hop CDs and internet access to the rest of the world.

But Alaska also has social ills, spurred on in large measure by the environment. The isolation of small towns and the darkness of winter has contributed to Alaska being one of the top 10 states for binge and heavy drinking, and sixth overall for the amount of alcohol sold per capita. Since the 1980s, Alaska has seen some of the highest per capita use of controlled drugs in the country, while it is second only to Nevada for suicides among women.

To survive this climate and to avoid those demons, you have to possess a passion for the land and an individualistic approach to a lifestyle that few, other than Alaskans, would choose.

POPULATION

Alaska is by far the largest state in the USA but has the fourth-smallest population, making it the most sparse. There is a lot of land but few people, with a density of 1.2 persons per sq mile.

Alaskans are overwhelmingly urban (74%) and white (70%), with 42% of them living in one city, Anchorage. But they are four years younger than the national average: the median age is 33. And along with Nevada, Alaska is still the only other state that has more men (almost 51%) than women. That leads to the most popular saying among Alaskan women: 'the odds are good but the goods are odd.'

MULTICULTURALISM

Military bases and the construction of the Alaska Hwy during WWII spurred Alaska's most rapid period of growth, creating a society that in the 1950s was largely a mix of Alaska Natives and military-minded whites. Since then the percentages of both indigenous people and especially the military, due to base closures, have drastically decreased.

Alaska is still predominantly white (70%), with Alaska Natives now representing less than 16% and African Americans less than 4% of the population. The most significant immigration growth in Alaska has been Asians, now making up 4.2% of the population. This is particularly true in communities connected to the commercial fishing industry; in Unalaska and Dutch Harbor, Asians represent 30% of the residents and outnumber Alaska Natives.

RELIGION

Every religion that mainstream America practices in the Lower 48 can be found in Alaska, but the state's oldest and most enduring is Russian Orthodox. In 1794, after Russian merchants and traders had decimated indigenous populations, particularly the Aleuts, missionaries arrived. The priests not only converted the indigenous people of Southwest, Southcentral and Southeast Alaska to a new religious belief, but also managed to provide Alaska Natives basic privileges, including education and wages.

Ironically, a period that started with brutal hostility ended with a legacy still evident today through Russian family names and active Russian Orthodox congregations in 80 Alaskan communities.

ECONOMY

Since the early 1980s, Alaska's economy has been fueled by oil. Nearly 90% of the state's general fund revenue comes from taxes on oil and gas production. When the price of a barrel is up, as it was in the early 1980s and again in 2008, Alaska is flushed

ALASKA NATIVES

Long before Western colonization, Alaska Natives had established a thriving culture and lifestyle in one of the world's harshest environments. Although they traded and even fought with each other, the tribes inhabited separate regions. The Aleuts and Alutiiqs lived from Prince William Sound to the end of the Aleutian Islands; the Iñupiat and Yupik lived on Alaska's northern and western coasts; the Athabascan populated the Interior; and the Tlingit, Haida and Tsimshian lived along the coasts of Southeast Alaska. Today the ethnic and territorial distinctions have blurred, especially with the growing number of Alaska Natives moving to urban areas.

More than 118,000 indigenous people, half of whom are Iñupiat, live in Alaska but the percentage of the population that is Alaska Native has greatly decreased. Prior to 1940 they were the majority. During WWII they became a minority, and today they represent less than 16%. Even more dramatic has been the shift to the cities. Alaska Natives living in the large urban areas increased from 17% in 1970 to 45% today, and the largest center of indigenous people in Alaska isn't Barrow, but Anchorage, home to 27,000 Alaska Natives.

ALASKA IN FOCUS

with cash. When it isn't, such as the mid-1990s, there are serious budget problems in Juneau because Alaska has the lowest individual tax burden in the country.

For Alaskans it's almost impossible to diversify beyond this boom-and-bust economy based on natural resources. Alaska unfortunately is at the end of an economic highway; raw materials leave the state, finished products come back. Government officials have long argued for in-state processing of raw materials – oil, timber, fish – as a way to stabilize the economy. But this has never been feasible due to high salaries, costly transportation and expensive-to-build infrastructure such as plants and mills.

SPORTS

The state sport of Alaska, officially adopted in 1972, is dog mushing, and its Super Bowl, the biggest spectator sport in the state, is the Iditarod. A 1049-mile dogsled race, the Iditarod retraces the famous 'serum run' that saved the town of Nome from diphtheria in 1925. Over 1000 dogs and their mushers run the 'Last Great Race' in early March. But there are other spectator sports in Alaska that you don't have to bundle up to watch, including the great American pastime: baseball. The **Alaska Baseball League** (www.alaskabaseballleague.org) is made up of six semipro teams of highly regarded college players eyeing the major leagues.

NATIVE ALASKA

The state's most unusual sporting event is the **World Eskimo-Indian Olympics** (www.weio.org) in July, when several hundred athletes converge on Fairbanks. For four days Alaska Natives compete in greased pole walking, seal skinning, blanket toss and other events that display the skills traditionally needed for survival in a harsh environment.

MEDIA

A good read before your trip is **Alaska Magazine** (www.alaskamagazine.com), which has the state's best writers – Nick Jans, Sherry Simpson and Ned Rozell – as regular contributors.

PATRICK ENDRES / ALASKASTOCK.COM

Iñupiat dancers, World Eskimo-Indian Olympics

RALPH HOPKINS

Tlingit art, Haines Totem Village (p127)

The **Anchorage Daily News** (www.adn.com) is Alaska's largest newspaper and a top-rated publication that won the Pulitzer Prize in the 1970s for stories on the Trans-Alaska Pipeline. **Alaska Public Radio Network** (www.akradio.org) has 18 stations in communities as far-flung as Barrow and Fort Yukon.

ARTS
NATIVE ARTS & CRAFTS

Alaska's first artists, its indigenous people, still create some of the state's most impressive work. Alaska Natives are renowned for their ingenious use of natural materials at hand, from roots and ivory tusks to birch bark and grasses, or even seal intestines.

The Iñupiat and Yupik, having the fewest resources to work with, traditionally made their objects out of sea-mammal parts; their scrimshaw work, also known as 'engraved ivory,' is incredibly detailed etching often presenting a vignette of daily life on a whale bone or walrus tusk. They made *mukluks* (knee-high boots) out of sealskin and parkas out of the skins of caribou or ground squirrels.

Athabascans of the Interior had mastered the art of porcupine-quill weaving and embroidery in the 19th century when beads were introduced to Alaska's indigenous peoples by Russian traders, whalers and agents of the Hudson Bay Company. Athabascans quickly adopted these shiny and colorful ornaments to adorn clothing and footwear, and today are renowned for their intricate bead embroidery.

But perhaps no single item represents indigenous art better than Alaskan basketry. Athabascans weave baskets from alder, willow roots and birch bark; the Tlingits use cedar bark and spruce root; the Iñupiat use grasses and baleen, a glossy, hard material that hangs from the jaws of whales; the Yupik often decorate their baskets with sea lion whiskers and feathers.

The Aleuts are perhaps the most renowned basket weavers. Using rye grass, which grows abundantly in the Aleutian Islands, they are able to work the pliable but very tough material into tiny, intricately woven baskets.

LITERATURE

Two of the best-known writers identified with Alaska were not native to the land nor did they spend much time there, but Jack London and Robert Service witnessed Alaska's greatest adventure and turned the experience into literary careers.

Today's contemporary standouts of Alaskan literature are not memorized nearly as much as Service's, but are no less elegant in capturing the spirit of the Far North. Kotzebue author Seth Kantner followed his critically acclaimed first novel, *Ordinary Wolves,* with the equally intriguing *Shopping for Porcupine*, a series of short stories about growing up in the Alaska wilderness. One of the best Alaska Native novels is *Two Old Women* by Velma Wallis, an Athabascan born in Fort Yukon. This moving tale covers the saga of two elderly women abandoned by their migrating tribe during a harsh winter.

Other Alaskans who have captured the soul of the Far North include Nick Jans, whose *The Last Light Breaking* is considered a classic on life among the Iñupiat, and Sherry Simpson, who chronicles living in Fairbanks in the series of wonderful stories, *The Way Winter Comes*. For entertaining fiction using Alaska's commercial fishing as a stage, there's Bill McCloskey, whose three novels have characters ranging from the greenhorn fisherman to the hardnose cannery manager, leaping from one to the next. His first, *Highliners*, is still his best.

MUSIC

Anchorage has the population and the pull to host well-known artists and bands, with most of them playing at Atwood Concert Hall, Sullivan Sports Arena or even Chilkoot Charlie's (p69). If they're in town, **Center-Tix** (☎ 907-263-2787; www.centertix.net) will sell you the ticket. You can also catch nationally known acts, particularly country bands, at the Alaska State Fair Borealis Theatre in Palmer and Fairbanks' Carlson Center. Beyond that a band has to be on the downside of its career before it arrives in towns such as Juneau, Ketchikan or Kodiak.

Homegrown artists, and we're not talking Jewel here, make up an important segment of the Alaskan music scene and are the reason for the state's numerous music festivals.

OUTDOOR ACTIVITIES

DARYL PEDERSON / ALASKASTOCK.COM

Rafters, near Spencer Glacier

What truly unites all Alaskans, young and old, tall and small, is the overwhelming desire to be out in the wilderness. You don't have to scale Mt McKinley to enjoy the Alaskan outdoors – there are plenty of ways to leave the pavement behind because Alaska is, after all, the USA's biggest playground. Now head outside and play!

CABINS

Every agency overseeing public land in Alaska, from the Bureau of Land Management (BLM) and the National Park Service (NPS) to the Alaska Division of Parks, maintains rustic cabins in remote areas. The cabins are not expensive ($25 to $50 per night) but they are not easy to reach either. Most of them are accessed via a floatplane charter. Others can be reached on foot, by boat or by paddling. By arranging a charter and reserving a cabin in advance you can sneak away into the wilderness, with half the effort and time that backpackers or paddlers put in, and reach remote corners of Alaska.

CANOEING & KAYAKING

The paddle is a way of life in Alaska and every region has either canoeing or kayaking opportunities, or both. Both the Southeast and Prince William Sound offer spectacular kayaking opportunities, while Fairbanks and Arctic Alaska are home to some of the best wilderness canoe adventures in the country. For paddling possibilities and rental locations see the regional chapters.

ALASKA IN FOCUS

OUTDOOR ACTIVITIES

CYCLING

With its long days, cool temperatures, a lack of interstate highways and a growing number of paved paths around cities such as Anchorage, Juneau and Fairbanks, Alaska can be a land of opportunity for road cyclists.

Cyclists do have to take some extra precautions in Alaska. Other than cities and major towns, comprehensively equipped bike shops are rare, so it's wise to carry not only metric tools but also a tube-patch repair kit, brake cables, spokes and brake pads. Due to high rainfall, especially in the Southeast, waterproof saddle bags are useful, as are tire fenders.

Some roads do not have much of a shoulder, so cyclists should utilize the sunlight hours to pedal when traffic is light in such areas. It is not necessary to carry a lot of food, as you can easily restock on all major roads.

DOGSLEDDING

If Alaska is too hot or crowded for you in the summer, arrive in the winter and join a dogsled expedition. There are more than two-dozen outfitters from Bettles to Homer that will set you up with a team and then lead you into the winter wilderness. You don't need previous experience with dog teams or mushing but you should be comfortable with winter camping and have cold-weather clothing and gear.

Even if there's no snow around, you can still experience the thrill of the dogs. A growing number of kennels offer summer tours that include playing with the pups, learning about mushers and the Iditarod, and short demonstration rides in wheeled carts. Some will even fly you onto a glacier for the true on-ice experience.

A word of caution: People for the Ethical Treatment of Animals (PETA) feel that dog-sledding – especially the Iditarod and other races – is harmful to dogs. Go to www.peta.org for more information.

JEFF SCHULTZ / ALASKASTOCK.COM

Dogsledding, Willow

FISHING

Many people cling to a 'fish-per-cast' vision of angling in Alaska. They expect every river, stream and lake, no matter how close to the road, to be bountiful, but often go home disappointed when their fishing efforts produce little to brag about. Serious anglers visiting Alaska carefully research the areas to be fished and are equipped with the right gear and tackle. They often pay for guides or book a room at remote camps or lodges where rivers are not fished out by every passing motorist.

A backpacking rod that breaks down into five sections and has a light reel is ideal, and in the Southeast and Southcentral will allow you to cast for cutthroat trout, rainbow trout and Dolly Varden (another type of trout). Further north, especially around Fairbanks, you'll get grayling, with its sail-like dorsal fin, and arctic char. In August, salmon seem to be everywhere.

An open-face spinning reel with light line, something in the 4lb to 6lb range, and a small selection of spinners and spoons will allow you to fish a wide range of waters from streams and rivers to lakes. For fly fishing, a No 5 or No 6 rod with a matching floating line or sinking tip is well suited for Dolly Vardens, rainbows and grayling. For salmon, a No 7 or No 8 rod and line are better choices. You can purchase the locally used lures and flies after you arrive.

You will also need a fishing license. A nonresident's fishing license costs $145 a year, but you can purchase a 7-/14-day license for $55/80; every bait shop in the state sells them. You can also order a license online or obtain other information through the **Alaska Department of Fish & Game** (☎ 907-465-4100; www.state.ak.us/adfg).

Serious anglers should consider a fishing charter. Joining a captain on his boat is $170 to $250 per person for four to six hours on the water, but local knowledge is the best investment to ensure fishing success. Communities with large fleets of charter captains include Homer, Seward, Kodiak and Ketchikan, with halibut most in demand among visitors.

If money is no option, fly-in fishing adventures are available from cities such as Anchorage and Fairbanks. These outings use small charter planes to reach wilderness lakes and rivers for a day of salmon and steelhead fishing.

FLIGHTSEEING

There isn't a bush pilot in Alaska who wouldn't be more than willing to take you on a flightseeing trip. Happy to, in fact. Most flightseeing is done in small planes, holding three to five passengers, with the tour lasting, on the average, one to two hours. A much smaller number are done in helicopters due to the high costs of operating the aircraft. Concerns were raised about the safety of such flights after 15 people died in four flightseeing

---

🔖 DON'T FORGET…

When you're heading outside, even for a short hike or bike, you should always be prepared for inclement weather or getting lost. Wear synthetic or wool clothing, and throw the following in your day pack:

- Woollen hat and gloves
- Water bottle
- High-energy food such as trail mix or protein bars
- Waterproof parka
- Matches
- Map and compass
- Knife

ALASKA IN FOCUS

OUTDOOR ACTIVITIES

Hiking, Denali National Park (p212)

crashes in 2007, two that occurred near Ketchikan. But considering the large number of tours that take place in Alaska every summer, flightseeing is still deemed a safe activity.

Among the most spectacular places to book a flight is Ketchikan to view Misty Fiords National Monument (p96), Haines to view Glacier Bay National Park (p128) and Talkeetna for a flight around Mt McKinley (p223).

GLACIER TREKKING & ICE CLIMBING

Most first-time glacier trekkers envision a slick and slippery surface but in reality the ice is very rough and embedded with gravel and rocks to provide surprisingly good traction. There are several roadside-accessible glaciers, the Matanuska Glacier (p228) being the best known, where you can walk a short distance on the gravel-laced ice in just hiking boots.

Glaciers are also the main destination in Alaska for ice climbers in the summer. Ice falls and faces, where the glacier makes its biggest vertical descents out of the mountains, are where climbers strap on crampons and helmets and load themselves with ropes, ice screws and anchors. Inexperienced climbers should sign up for a one-day ice climbing lesson, where guides lead you to an ice fall and then teach you about cramponing, front pointing and the use of ice tools.

HIKING

Even if you don't have any desire to hoist a hefty backpack, don't pass up an opportunity to spend a day hiking one of the hundreds of well-maintained and easy-to-follow trails scattered across the state.

Keep in mind that even when day hiking you have to be prepared for Alaska's finicky weather. Don't undertake a day hike with little or no equipment and then, three hours from the trailhead, get caught in bad weather wearing only a flimsy cotton jacket. Most day hikes described in regional chapters can easily be walked in lightweight nylon hiking boots made by sporting-shoe companies like Vasque, Lowa or Merrell.

MOUNTAIN BIKING

Alaska has a near-endless supply of dirt roads, miner's two tracks and even hiking trails that a mountain bike's durable design, knobby tires and suspension system are perfect for.

Just remember to pick your route carefully before heading out. Make sure the length of the route and the ruggedness of the terrain are within your capability, and that you have appropriate equipment. Always pack a lightweight, wind and water resistant jacket and an insulating layer because the weather changes quickly in Alaska and so can the terrain. Even when renting a bike, make sure you can repair a flat with the proper spare tube and tools. Water is a must.

If you need a guide and a set of wheels, **Alaska Backcountry Bike Tours** (☎ 866-354-2453; www.mountainbikealaska.com) is a great little company that offers bike adventures from Anchorage, including both day outings and multiday trips.

PADDLING

Both white-water and expedition rafting are extremely popular in Alaska. The Nenana River just outside of Denali National Park is a mecca for white-water thrill seekers with companies like the **Denali Outdoor Center** (☎ 907-683-1925; www.denalioutdoorcenter.com) offering daily raft trips through the summer through Class IV rapids. The season climaxes on the second weekend after the Fourth of July holiday when the **Nenana River Wildwater Festival** (www.nenanawildwater.org) is staged as two days of river races and a wildwater rodeo. Other rivers that attract white-water enthusiasts include the Lowe River near Valdez, Six Mile Creek with its Class V rapids near Hope, the Matanuska River east of Palmer and the Kennicott River at McCarthy.

ROCK CLIMBING & MOUNTAINEERING

Rock climbing has been growing in popularity in Alaska. On almost any summer weekend, you can watch climbers working bolt-protected sport routes just above Seward Hwy along Turnagain Arm. Canyons in nearby Portage are also capturing the attention of rock climbers. Not far from Portage Lake, a short hike leads to the magnificent slate walls of Middle

⇘THE BEST

DOUG DEMAREST / ALASKASTOCK.COM

Mt Marathon Trail (p175)

IN-TOWN HIKES

- **Deer Mountain Trail, Ketchikan** (p92)
- **West Glacier Trail, Juneau** (p119)
- **Williwaw Lakes Trail, Anchorage** (p62)
- **Mt Marathon Trail, Seward** (p175)
- **Dewey Lakes Trail System, Skagway** (p132)

ALASKA IN FOCUS

OUTDOOR ACTIVITIES

ALASKA IN FOCUS

OUTDOOR ACTIVITIES

Canyon. Fairbanks climbers head north of town to the limestone formations known as Grapefruit Rocks.

For climbing equipment and more information in Anchorage, contact **Alaska Mountaineering & Hiking** (☎ 907-272-1811; www.alaskamountaineering.com). In Fairbanks, contact **Beaver Sports** (☎ 907-479-2494; www.beaversports.com) for equipment. The best mountaineering guidebook to the state is *Alaska: A Climbing Guide* by Michael Wood and Colby Coombs.

SKIING & SNOWBOARDING

Alaska's main downhill ski area is **Alyeska Resort** (☎ 907-754-2111; www.alyeskaresort.com) in Girdwood. With an annual snowfall of 631in and 2500 vertical feet of terrain, Mt Alyeska can challenge the most die-hard downhillers and snowboarders with its season from November to April. This world-class resort has 68 runs, almost 40% black diamonds, which are serviced by nine lifts including a 60-passenger aerial tram.

The only way to achieve more exciting runs than what Alyeska has is to jump into a helicopter. **Chugach Powder Guides** (☎ 907-783-4354; www.chugachpowderguides.com) offers heli-skiing at Alyeska and in the Alaska Range. **Valdez Heli-Ski Guides** (☎ 907-835-4528; www.valdezheliskiguides.com) operates in the Chugach Mountains near Valdez, where the longest run through the deep powder is a descent of 6200 vertical feet.

ZIPLINING

That new-fangled thrill, ziplining, which involves riding a metal cable through the forest, isn't yet big in Alaska, but it has arrived. In Southeast Alaska it is bound to become more popular thanks in part to the rainforest that covers much of the region and the large number of cruise ships that pass through it. **Alaska Canopy Adventures** (☎ 877-947-7557; www.alaskacanopy.com) operates ziplines in Ketchikan (p90) and Juneau (p116).

Ziplining (p92), Ketchikan

⬊ DIRECTORY & TRANSPORTATION

DIRECTORY
ACCOMMODATIONS

Alaska offers typical US accommodations along with many atypical options such as a cabin in the mountains or a lodge in the middle of the wilderness. This guide includes recommendations for all types and budgets but it emphasizes midrange accommodations. In the regional chapters the accommodations are listed with budget first (under $100 a night) followed by midrange ($100 to $200) and top end ($200 and up).

Advance bookings are wise as the Alaskan tourist season is short, and in places such as Juneau, Skagway and Denali National Park rooms fill quickly. You will receive better accommodation rates during the shoulder seasons of April through May and September through October.

The rates listed in this book are all for high season: June through August. The listed rates do not include local taxes. In most towns you will be hit with a local sales tax *and* a bed tax, with the combination ranging from 5% up to 12% for cities such as Anchorage and Juneau.

As to be expected, Alaska is the land of wilderness lodges. Many of them are geared towards anglers and remote fishing opportunities, must be booked well in advance, and require floatplane transport to reach. Tribal companies and the cruise ship industry (for the land portions of their tours) are also responsible for a growing number of luxurious hotels popping up across the state.

B&BS

For travelers who want nothing to do with a tent, B&Bs can be an acceptable compromise between sleeping on the ground and sleeping in high-priced lodges. Some B&Bs are bargains, and most are cheaper than major hotels, but plan on spending $70 to $120 per night for a double room.

Many visitor centers have sections devoted to the B&Bs in their area, and courtesy booking phones. Details about specific B&Bs can be found in the regional chapters.

HOTELS & MOTELS

Hotels and motels are often the most expensive lodgings you can book. Although there are bargains, the average double room in a budget hotel costs $70 to $90, a midrange motel is $100 to $200 and a top-end hotel $200 and above a night.

RESORTS

Resorts – upscale hotels that have rooms, restaurants, pools and on-site activities – are not as common in Alaska as elsewhere in the USA but are increasing due to the patronage of large companies, such as Princess Tours. The finest is Girdwood's Alyeska Resort (p298), with a four-star hotel at the base of its ski runs. If you're near Fairbanks, head to Chena Hot Springs Rd to spend some time at the Chena Hot Springs Resort (p250) for good food, log cabins and a soak in an outdoor hot tub.

⬈ BOOK YOUR STAY ONLINE

For more accommodation reviews and recommendations by Lonely Planet authors, check out the online booking service at www.lonelyplanet.com. You'll find the true, insider lowdown on the best places to stay. Reviews are thorough and independent. Best of all, you can book online.

BUSINESS HOURS

Banks and post offices in Alaska are generally open from 9am to 5pm Monday to Friday and sometimes on Saturday mornings. Other business hours vary, but many stores are open 10am to 8pm Monday to Saturday with shorter hours on Sunday.

CLIMATE

From the north to the south, Alaska's climate changes drastically. The following climate charts extend from Barrow to Juneau and will provide a glimpse of temperatures and precipitation for whenever you plan to visit. See p44 for further information on choosing the best time of year for your visit to Alaska.

COURSES

Alaska is an outdoor classroom and outdoor leadership schools hold class there regularly. The **International Wilderness Leadership School** (☎ 800-985-4957; www. iwls.com) offers a half dozen courses including mountaineering, rock and ice climbing and sea kayaking. Courses last from 12 to 26 days and range in price from $2000 to $3500. The **National Outdoor Leadership School** (☎ 800-710-6657; www.nols.edu) has an equal number of programs that include sea kayaking, mountaineering and backpacking. Both schools can arrange for you to earn college credits while you're trekking through the wilderness.

Visitors who just want to try their hand at a new activity can turn to outfitters and guiding companies. Almost every kayak guiding company has a half-day, learn-to-paddle outing in which they teach basic kayaking skills in a calm setting and then lead you on a short trip. The cost is $50 to $70 per person and includes all equipment. The **Ascending Path** (☎ 907-783-0505;

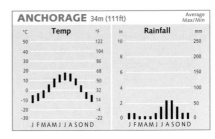
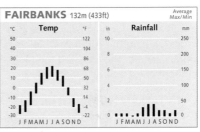
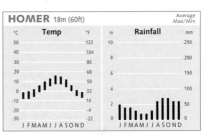
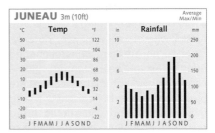

www.theascendingpath.com) of Girdwood has an excellent three-hour introduction to rock climbing for $129, while **Above & Beyond Alaska** (☎ 907-364-2333; www.beyondak.com) offers a seven-hour introduction to ice climbing on Juneau's Mendenhall Glacier for $189. For a list of outfitters, see p318.

ELDERHOSTEL

Nonprofit **Elderhostel** (☎ 800-454-5768; www.elderhostel.org) provides educational adventures and academic programs to older travelers, often senior citizens. Participants are 55 years or older, and take college-level courses taught by faculty members, but without homework, preparatory work or final exams. In short, you travel to the places that interest you, spend a few hours each day in the classroom learning the cultural or biological significance of the area and then join a number of extracurricular activities.

CUSTOMS REGULATIONS

For a complete list of US customs regulations, visit the official portal for **US Customs & Border Protection** (**www. cbp.gov**). Click on 'Travel' and then 'Know Before You Go' for the basics.

Travelers are allowed to bring all personal goods (including camping gear or hiking equipment) into the USA and Canada free of duty, along with food for two days and up to 100 cigars, 200 cigarettes and 1L of liquor or wine.

There are no forms to fill out if you are a foreign visitor bringing a vehicle into Alaska, whether it is a bicycle, motorcycle or car, nor are there forms for hunting rifles or fishing gear. Hunting rifles – handguns and automatic weapons are prohibited – must be registered in your own country, and you should bring proof of registration. There is no limit to the amount of money you can bring into Alaska, but anything over $10,000 must be registered with customs officials.

Keep in mind that endangered-species laws prohibit transporting products made of bone, skin, fur, ivory etc, through Canada without a permit. Importing and exporting such items into the USA is also prohibited. If you have any doubt about a gift or item you want to purchase, call the **US Fish & Wildlife Service** (**USFWS**; ☎ 271-6198) in Anchorage or check the USFWS website (www.fws.gov).

Hunters and anglers who want to ship home their salmon, halibut or rack of caribou can do so easily. Most outfitters and guides will make the arrangements for you, including properly packaging the game. In the case of fish, most towns have a storage company that will hold your salmon or halibut in a freezer until you are ready to leave Alaska. When frozen, seafood can usually make the trip to any city in the Lower 48 without thawing.

DANGERS & ANNOYANCES

Alaska is a relatively safe place with most of its dangers and annoyances occurring not in the cities but out in the woods. For how to deal with insects and paralytic shellfish poisoning (PSP), which affects some shellfish, see p307.

BEARS

Too often travelers decide to skip a wilderness trip because they hear too many bear stories. Your own equipment and outdoor experience should determine whether you take a trek into the woods, not the possibility of meeting a bear on the trail.

The **Alaska Department of Fish & Game** (ADF&G; www.adfg.state.ak.us) emphasizes that the probability of being injured by a bear is one-50th the chance of being injured in a car accident on any Alaskan highway. For an extensive review of bears and safety procedures go to the ADF&G website.

The best way to avoid bears is to follow a few commonsense rules. Bears charge only when they feel trapped, when a hiker comes between a sow and her cubs or when enticed by food. Sing or clap when traveling through thick bush, so you don't surprise a bear. Don't camp near bear food sources or in the middle of an obvious bear path. Stay away from thick berry patches, streams choked with salmon or beaches littered with bear droppings.

Leave your pet at home; a frightened dog only runs back to its owner, and most dogs are no match for a bear. Set up the spot where you will cook and eat at least 30 to 50 yards away from your tent. In coastal areas, many backpackers eat in the tidal zone, knowing that when the high tide comes in all evidence of food will be washed away.

At night try to place your food sacks 10ft or more off the ground by hanging them in a tree, placing them on top of a tall boulder or putting them on the edge of a rock cliff. In a treeless, flat area, cover up food sacks with rocks, or consider investing in a lightweight bear-resistant container. A bear usually finds a food bag using its great sense of smell. By packaging all food items in resealable plastic bags, you greatly reduce the animal's chances of getting a whiff of your next meal. Avoid odorous foods, such as bacon or sardines, in areas with high concentrations of bears. Avoid wearing scented cosmetics, including deodorant, as the smell attracts bears. Women who are menstruating should place used tampons/sanitary napkins in plastic bags and store them in bear-resistant containers up with the suspended food bag.

And please, don't take food into the tent at night. Don't even take toothpaste, hand lotion, suntan oils or anything with a smell. If a bear smells a human, it will leave; anything else might encourage it to investigate.

ENCOUNTERING A BEAR
If you do meet a bear on the trail, *do not* turn and run, it will outrun you. Stop, make no sudden moves and begin talking calmly to the animal. Speaking to a bear helps it understand that you are there. If it doesn't take off right away, back up slowly before turning around and leaving the area. A bear standing on its hind

PRACTICALITIES

- Alaska has more than 30 daily, weekly and trade newspapers with the *Anchorage Daily News* being the largest and the closest thing to a statewide newspaper.
- The largest cities have local TV stations while radio stations are found all over Alaska.
- Voltage in Alaska is 110V – the same as everywhere else in the USA.
- There is no national sales tax in the USA and no state sales tax in Alaska, but towns have a city sales tax plus a bed tax.
- Almost every town in Alaska has a Laundromat, the place to go to clean your clothes ($3 per load) or take a shower ($3 to $5).
- US distances are in feet, yards and miles. Dry weights are in ounces (oz), pounds (lb) and tons, and liquids are in pints, quarts and gallons (4 quarts). The US gallon is about 20% less than the imperial gallon. See the conversion chart on the inside front cover of this book.
- NTSC is the standard video system (not compatible with PAL or SECAM).

legs is not on the verge of charging; it's only trying to see you better. When a bear turns sideways or begins making a series of woofing sounds, it is only challenging you for space – just back away slowly and leave. If the animal follows you, *stop* and hold your ground.

Most bear charges are bluffs, with the animal veering off at the last minute. Experienced backpackers handle a charge in different ways. Some people throw their packs 3ft in front of them, which will often distract the bear long enough for the person to back away. Other backpackers fire a handheld signal flare over the bear's head (but never at it) in an attempt to use the noise and sudden light to scare the bear away. If an encounter is imminent, drop into a fetal position, place your hands behind your neck and play dead. If a bear continues biting you after you have assumed a defensive posture, then you must fight back vigorously.

Some people carry guns to fend off bear charges, but firearms should never be used as an alternative to common-sense approaches to bear encounters. Shooting a charging bear is a skilled operation if you are a good shot, a foolish one if you are not. You must drop the bear with one or two shots, as a wounded bear is extremely dangerous.

Other people are turning to defensive aerosol sprays that contain red pepper extract. These sprays cost $40 to $50 each and have been used with some success for protection against bears. They are effective at a range of 6 to 8 yards but must be discharged downwind. If not, you will just disable yourself.

DISCOUNTS

There are discounts to be mined in Alaska but you have to dig a little deeper than the rest of the country. Children do the best, often receiving discounted prices for transportation, entry fees, restaurants and even lodging.

Seniors citizens and, to a lesser extent, students can also find discounts. For example, most museums, parks and major attractions will offer reduced rates to seniors and students, but most accommodations, restaurants and small tour companies will not. The reason is simple economics: for most businesses the tourist season is too short and competition for rooms, tours or charters too high to be handing out discounts.

SENIOR CARDS

The best seniors card for US travelers to carry is the one issued by the **American Association of Retired Persons** (AARP; ☎ 888-687-2277; www.aarp.org), which can be obtained for $12.50 if you're over the age of 50 (you don't even need to be retired).

STUDENT & YOUTH CARDS

For student discounts your university identification is the best thing to have. The demise of Hostelling International in Alaska – there is now only one sanctioned hostel – makes its HI card of little use in the far north. It's worth purchasing an ISIC card before traveling to Alaska.

EMBASSIES & CONSULATES

International travelers needing to locate the US embassy in their home country should visit the **US Department of State website** (http://usembassy.state.gov), which has links to all of them.

There are no embassies in Alaska, but there are a handful of foreign consulates in Anchorage to assist overseas travelers with unusual problems:

Denmark (☎ 907-276-1221; Ste 610, 425 G St)
Germany (☎ 907-274-6537; Ste 650, 425 G St)
Japan (☎ 907-562-8424; Ste 1300, 3601 C St)
Norway (☎ 907-279-6942; Ste 105, 203 W 15th Ave)
UK (☎ 907-786-4848; Room 362, 2311 Providence Dr)

FESTIVALS & EVENTS

The vast majority of Alaskan festivals and special events, such as fishing derbies, take place during the summer and locals welcome visitors to their parties with open arms. For an extensive list of festivals in Alaska, see p46.

FOOD

Many travelers are surprised that food prices in a Fairbanks or Anchorage supermarket are not that much higher than what they're paying at home. Then they visit their first restaurant and a glance at the menu sends them into a two-day fast. Alaskan restaurants are more expensive than most other places in the country because of the short tourist season and the high labor costs for waiters and chefs.

In this book, restaurant prices usually refer to an average main dish at dinner and do not include drinks, appetizers, dessert or tips. Restaurants can be divided into budget, midrange and upscale. Dinner is an under-$10 affair in a budget cafe, $10 to $27 in a midrange restaurant and usually $27 and higher at an upscale place.

GAY & LESBIAN TRAVELERS

The gay community in Alaska is far smaller and much less open than in major US cities, and Alaskans in general are not as tolerant to diversity. In 1998 Alaska, along with Hawaii, passed a constitutional amendment banning same-sex marriages.

In Anchorage, the only city in Alaska of any real size, you have **Identity Inc** (☎ 907-929-4528; www.identityinc.org), which has a gay and lesbian helpline, and even some openly gay clubs and bars (see p69). The **Southeast Alaska Gay & Lesbian Alliance** (www.seagla.org) is based in Juneau and offers links and travel information to visitors. **Delta V** (http://dv-8.com) is also quite useful for travelers and offers, among other things, a list of gay, lesbian, bisexual and transgender organizations throughout Alaska. The list is short, however, because most towns do not have an openly active gay community. In rural Alaska, same-sex couples should exercise discretion.

HEALTH

There is a high level of hygiene found in Alaska, so most common infectious diseases will not be a significant concern for travelers. Superb medical care and rapid evacuation to major hospitals are both available.

BEFORE YOU GO
INSURANCE

The cost of health care in the USA is extremely high and Alaska is no exception. Health insurance is essential in the USA, where some hospitals will refuse care without evidence of insurance. It's essential to purchase travel health insurance if your regular policy doesn't cover you when you're abroad.

Be sure that the policy does not exclude wilderness trekking, mountaineering, kayaking, white-water rafting or any other activities you might be participating in while traveling in Alaska, or you may have a difficult time settling a claim. It is also prudent to be sure that the policy specifically covers helicopter evacuation, the most common way of reaching troubled backpackers in Alaska's wilderness areas.

DIRECTORY

FESTIVALS & EVENTS

If your medical insurance does not cover you for medical expenses abroad, consider getting supplemental insurance. Check the Lonely Planet website (www.lonelyplanet.com/bookings/insurance) for more information.

RECOMMENDED VACCINATIONS
No special vaccines are required or recommended for travel to Alaska or the USA.

MEDICAL CHECKLIST
Recommended items for a personal medical kit:
- acetaminophen (Tylenol) or aspirin
- anti-inflammatory drugs (eg ibuprofen)
- antihistamines (for hay fever and allergic reactions)
- antibacterial ointment (eg Bactroban) for cuts and abrasions
- steroid cream or cortisone (for poison ivy and other allergic rashes)
- bandages, gauze, gauze rolls
- adhesive or paper tape
- scissors, safety pins, tweezers
- thermometer
- pocket knife
- DEET-containing insect repellent for the skin
- permethrin-containing insect spray for clothing, tents and bed nets
- sunblock

IN ALASKA
AVAILABILITY & COST OF HEALTH CARE
In many small Alaskan villages health clinics serve as hospitals but may not have 24-hour emergency services, in which case call 911 for immediate assistance. If the problem isn't urgent, you can call a nearby hospital for a referral to a local physician or a walk-in clinic. Either one would be cheaper than a trip to the emergency room.

Pharmacies are common throughout Alaska, and in small villages they are usually part of the health clinic. You may find some medications that are available over the counter in your home country will require a prescription in the USA and, as always, if you don't have insurance to cover the cost of the medication, it can be surprisingly expensive.

INFECTIOUS DISEASES
In addition to more common ailments, there are several infectious diseases that are unknown or uncommon outside North America. Most are acquired by mosquito or tick bites.

GIARDIASIS
Giardiasis, which is commonly known as giardia and sometimes called 'beaver fever,' is caused by an intestinal parasite *(Giardia lamblia)* present in contaminated water.

ENVIRONMENTAL HAZARDS
HYPOTHERMIA
Perhaps the most dangerous health threat in Alaska's Arctic regions is hypothermia. Hypothermia occurs when the body loses heat faster than it can produce it and the core temperature of the body falls. It is surprisingly easy to progress from very cold to dangerously cold due to a combination of wind, wet clothing, fatigue and hunger, even if the air temperature is above freezing point.

Dress in layers for insulation – silk, wool and some of the new artificial fibers are all good insulating materials. A hat is important as a lot of heat is lost through the head. A strong, waterproof outer layer is essential, as keeping dry is vital. Carry basic supplies, including food containing simple sugars to generate heat quickly, and lots of fluid to drink.

INSECT BITES & STINGS

Alaska is notorious for its biting insects. In the cities and towns you will have few problems, but out in the woods you'll have to contend with a variety of insects, including mosquitoes, black flies, white sox, no-see-ums and deer flies. Coastal areas, with their cool summers, have smaller numbers of insects than the Interior. Generally, camping on a beach where there is some breeze is better than pitching a tent in the woods. In the end, just accept the fact that you will be bitten.

The most effective protection by far is a high-potency insect repellent; the best contain a high percentage of DEET (diethyltoluamide), the active ingredient. A little bottle of Musk Oil or Cutters can cost $6 or $7 (they contain 100% DEET), but it's one of the best investments you will make.

PARALYTIC SHELLFISH POISONING

In recent years, paralytic shellfish poisoning (PSP) has become a problem in Alaska. State officials urge people not to eat mussels, clams or snails gathered from unmonitored Alaskan beaches. PSP is possible anywhere in Alaska, and within 12 hours of consuming the infected shellfish victims experience symptoms of tingling or numbness in the lips and tongue (which can spread to the fingers or toes), loss of muscle coordination, dizziness, weakness and drowsiness. To get an update on the PSP situation, or to find out which beaches in the state are safe to clam, check the **Division of Environmental Health website** (www. dec.state.ak.us/eh/fss/seafood/psp/psp.htm).

HOLIDAYS

Public holidays for Alaskan residents, which may involve state and federal offices being closed, bus services curtailed, and shop and store hours reduced, include the following:

New Year's Day January 1
Martin Luther King Day Third Monday in January
Presidents' Day Third Monday in February
Seward's Day Last Monday in March
Easter Sunday Late March or early April
Memorial Day Last Monday in May
Independence Day (aka Fourth of July) July 4
Labor Day First Monday in September
Columbus Day Second Monday in October
Alaska Day October 18
Veterans' Day November 11
Thanksgiving Day Fourth Thursday in November
Christmas Day December 25

INSURANCE

A travel insurance policy to cover theft, loss and medical problems is a smart investment. Coverage depends on your insurance and type of ticket but should cover delays by striking employees or company actions, or a cancellation of a trip. Such coverage may seem expensive but it's nowhere near the price of a trip to Alaska or indeed, the potentially massive cost of being involved in a medical emergency in the USA.

Some policies offer lower and higher medical-expense options; the higher ones are chiefly for countries such as the USA, which have extremely high medical costs. There is a wide variety of medical and emergency repatriation policies and it's important that you talk to your health-care provider for recommendations. See Health on p305 for more information.

For insurance on car rentals see p317.

Worldwide travel insurance is available through the **Lonely Planet website** (www.lonelyplanet.com/bookings/insurance). You can buy, extend and claim online anytime – even if you're already on the road. The following companies also offer travel insurance:

Access America (☎ 800-284-8300; www.accessamerica.com)

Insuremytrip.com (800-487-4722; www.insuremytrip.com)

Travel Guard (☎ 800-826-4919; www.travelguard.com)

INTERNET ACCESS

It's easy to surf the net, make online reservations or retrieve email in Alaska. Most towns, even the smallest ones, have internet access at libraries, hotels and internet cafes. Access ranges from free at the library and from $5 to $10 an hour at internet cafes. If you are hauling around a laptop, wi-fi is common in Alaska at bookstores, motels, coffee shops, airport terminals and even bars. This guide uses the internet icon (▣) when accommodations offer either an internet terminal or wireless internet access. Ask exactly what is offered when reserving a room. If you're not from the US, remember you will need an AC adapter and a plug adapter for US sockets.

LEGAL MATTERS

Despite the history of marijuana in Alaska – it was once legal for personal use – possession of small amounts is now a misdemeanor punishable by up to 90 days in jail and a $1000 fine. The use of other drugs is also against the law, resulting in severe penalties, especially for cocaine, which is heavily abused in Alaska.

The minimum drinking age in Alaska is 21 and a government-issued photo ID (passport or driver's license) will be needed if a bartender questions your age. Alcohol abuse is also a problem in Alaska, and it is a serious offence if you are caught driving under the influence of alcohol (DUI). The blood alcohol limit in Alaska is 0.08% and the penalty for a DUI is a three-month driver's license revocation, and at least three days in jail. You'll also receive a $1500 fine.

If you are stopped by the police for any reason while driving, remember there is no system of paying on-the-spot fines and bribery is not something that works in Alaska. For traffic violations the officer will explain your options to you and violations, such as speeding, can often be handled through the mail with a credit card.

MAPS

Unlike many places in the world, you'll find Alaska has no shortage of accurate maps. There are detailed US Geological Survey (USGS) topographical maps to almost every corner of the state, even though most of it is still wilderness, while every visitor center has free city and road maps that are more than adequate to get from one town to the next. For free downloadable maps and driving directions there is **Google Maps** (www.maps.google.com).

In Anchorage the **USGS Earth Science Information Center** (☎ 907-786-7011; Grace Bldg, Alaska Pacific University; ☼ 8:30am-4:30pm Mon-Fri) has topo maps for the entire state. You can also order maps in advance directly from **USGS** (☎ 888-275-8747; www.usgs.gov) or you can view and order custom topo maps from cartography websites such as **Trails.com** (www.trails.com) or **Mytopo** (☎ 406-294-9411, 877-587-9004; www.mytopo.com).

MONEY

All prices quoted in this book are in US dollars unless otherwise stated. US coins come in denominations of 1¢(penny), 5¢ (nickel), 10¢ (dime), 25¢ (quarter) and the seldom seen 50¢ (half dollar). Quarters are the most commonly used coins in vending machines and parking meters, so it's handy to have a stash of them. Notes, commonly called bills, come in $1, $2, $5, $10, $20, $50 and $100 denominations. Keep in mind that the Canadian system is also dollars and cents but is a separate currency. For exchange rates, see the inside front cover.

ATMS

In Alaska ATMs are everywhere: banks, gas stations, supermarkets, airports and even some visitor centers. At most ATMs you can use a credit card (Visa, MasterCard etc), a debit card or an ATM card that is linked to the Plus or Cirrus ATM networks. There is generally a fee ($1 to $3) for withdrawing cash from an ATM, but the exchange rate on transactions is usually as good if not better than what you'll get from anywhere else.

CASH

Hard cash still works. It may not be the safest way to carry funds, but nobody will hassle you when you purchase something with US dollars. Most businesses along the Alcan in Canada will also take US dollars, though they might burn you on the exchange rate.

CREDIT CARDS

There are probably some isolated stores somewhere in Alaska that don't accept credit cards, but not many. Like in the rest of the USA, Alaskan merchants are ready and willing to accept just about all major credit cards. Visa and MasterCard are the most widely accepted cards, but American Express and Discovery are also widely used.

Places that accept Visa and MasterCard are also likely to accept debit cards. If you are an overseas visitor, check with your bank at home to confirm that your debit card will be accepted in the USA.

MONEYCHANGERS

Banks are the best place to exchange foreign currencies as the exchange counters at the airports typically have poorer rates. **Wells Fargo** (☎ 800-956-4442; www.wellsfargo. com), the nation's sixth largest bank, is the dominant player in Alaska with more than 400 branches, 13 in Anchorage alone. Wells Fargo can meet the needs of most visitors, including changing currency and offering 24-hour ATMs. You can usually count on banks being open 10am to 5pm Monday to Friday, with a few open on Saturday.

TIPPING

Tipping in Alaska, like in the rest of the USA, is expected. The going rate for restaurants, hotels and taxis is around 15%. It is also common for visitors to tip guides, whether it is a bus tour, a glacier trek or a white-water raft trip. If you forget, don't worry: they'll most likely remind you.

TRAVELER'S CHECKS

Although slowly becoming obsolete thanks to ATMs, the other way to carry your funds is the time-honored method of traveler's checks. The popular brands of US traveler's checks, such as American Express and Visa, are widely used around the state and will be readily cashed at any store, motel or bank in the major tourist areas of Alaska.

PHOTOGRAPHY

The most cherished items you can take home from your trip are photos of Alaska's powerful scenery. Much of the state is a photographer's dream, and your shutter finger will be set clicking by mountain and glacier panoramas, bustling waterfronts and the diverse wildlife encountered during paddling and hiking trips.

A compact, fixed-lens, point-and-shoot digital camera is OK for a summer of backpacking in the North Country, but if you want to get serious about photography, you need either a 35mm digital camera with interchangeable lenses, at least 6 megapixels and zoom capabilities. To photograph wildlife in its natural state, a 135mm or larger telephoto lens is required to make the animal the main object in the picture. Any lens larger than 135mm on a film camera will probably also require a tripod to eliminate camera shake, especially during low-light conditions. A wide-angle lens of 35mm, or better still 28mm, adds considerable dimension to scenic views, and a fast (f1.2 or f1.4) 50mm 'normal' lens will provide you with more opportunities for pictures during weak light.

If you want simplicity, check out the latest zoom lenses. They are much more compact than they have been in the past and provide a sharpness that's more than acceptable to most amateur photographers. A zoom for a digital camera from 18mm to 150mm is ideal and many camera companies, including Nikon and Canon, now offer vibration reduction (VR), which increases sharpness by reducing camera shake.

In the cities and major towns you can turn your digital photos into prints or have them burned onto a CD at self-serve photo counters in drugstores, large su-permarkets and chains such as Walmart and Fred Meyer.

For more on cameras and photography read Lonely Planet's *Travel Photography* book.

SHOPPING

Alaska is knee deep in gift shops, often selling terrifically tacky items. Moose nuggets will be seen from one end of the state to the other, but even if they are varnished, you have to wonder who is going to wear earrings or a necklace made of animal scat. Gold-nugget jewelry is another prevalent item, but more interesting and much more affordable is what is commonly called Arctic opal. This blue and greenish stone was uncovered in the Wrangell Mountains in the late 1980s, and is now set in silver in a variety of earrings, pins and other pieces.

Authentic Alaska Native–carved pieces, whether in ivory, jade or soapstone, are exquisite, highly prized and expensive. A 6-in carving of soapstone, a soft stone that indigenous people in western Alaska carve and polish, costs $150 to $300, depending on the carving and the detail. Jade and ivory will cost even more, up to $100 per inch in a carving. When shopping for such artwork, be especially conscious of who you are purchasing from. Non-Native art, sometimes carved in places as far away as Bali, is often passed off and priced as Alaska Native–produced. It is legal for Alaska Natives to produce and sell ivory work, which they obtain from the tusks of walruses that they hunt for food. Before purchasing such a piece make sure your country allows it through customs.

If you're considering investing in Native art look for the Silver Hand label, guaranteeing the item was made by an Alaska Native artist. For other art and items that are made by non-Alaska Natives, the state has created a Made In Alaska logo with a polar bear on it. For more on Native art see p291.

SOLO TRAVELERS

Maybe it's that Klondike spirit of adventure or the lack of large cities, but solo travelers are common in Alaska. Such travelers will find it easy to strike up conversations with locals in small towns, with waitstaff if they grab a stool at the counter and with bartenders if they're sitting alone at the bar. Women in particular will book nights at established B&Bs, knowing they will find friendly conversation, a sense of security and a lot of local knowledge and contacts.

The main concern of most solo travelers in Alaska is how safe is hiking, backpacking or paddling alone in the wilderness. This will depend on your skill level and where you're headed.

TELEPHONE
CELL PHONES

Cell phones work in Alaska and Alaskans (especially teenagers) love them as much as anywhere else in the USA. When calling home or locally in cities and towns reception is excellent but overall, in a state this large, cell phone coverage can be unpredictable and sporadic at times. Many injured climbers have been plucked off mountains in the middle of nowhere after calling for help on their cell phone. But drive north of Auke Bay in Juneau and it's hard to use your cell phone to make a dinner reservation downtown. The culprits in many cases are mountains.

Most travelers still find their cell phones to be more useful than not. Before you head north, however, check your cell phone provider's roaming agreements and black-out areas.

PHONE CODES

Telephone area codes are simple in Alaska: the entire state shares 907, except Hyder, which uses 250. In this guidebook, the area code is always 907, unless a different one is listed before the phone number. Phone numbers that begin with 800, 877 and 866 are toll-free numbers and there is no charge for using one to call a hotel or tour operator. If you're calling from abroad the country code for the USA is ☎ 1.

PHONECARDS

Every little town and village in Alaska has public pay phones that you can use to call home if you have a phonecard or a stack of quarters. The best way to make international calls is to first purchase a phonecard.

TIME

With the exception of several Aleutian Island communities and Hyder, a small community on the Alaskan/British Columbian border, the entire state shares the same time zone, Alaska Time, which is one hour earlier than Pacific Standard Time – the zone in which Seattle, Washington, falls. When it is noon in Anchorage, it is 4pm in New York, 9pm in London and 7am the following day in Melbourne, Australia. Although there is a movement to abolish it, Alaska still has Daylight Saving Time when, like most of the country, the state sets clocks back one hour in November and forward one hour in March.

TOURIST INFORMATION

The first place to contact when planning your adventure is the **Alaska Travel Industry Association** (ATIA; ☎ 907-929-2200; www.travelalaska.com), the state's tourism marketing arm. From the ATIA you

DIRECTORY

TOURS

can request a copy of the *Alaska Vacation Planner,* an annually updated magazine; a state highway map; and schedules for the Alaska Marine Highway Ferry service.

Travel information is easy to obtain once you are on the road, as almost every city, town and village has a tourist contact center, whether it is a visitor center, a chamber of commerce or a hut near the ferry dock. These places are good sources of free maps, information on local accommodations, and directions to the nearest campground or hiking trail.

Most trips to Alaska pass through one of the state's three largest cities. All have large visitors bureaus that will send out city guides in advance:

Anchorage Convention & Visitors Bureau (☎ 907-276-4118; www.anchorage.net)
Fairbanks Convention & Visitors Bureau (☎ 907-456-5774, 800-327-5774; www.explorefairbanks.com)
Juneau Convention & Visitors Bureau (☎ 907-586-1737, 800-587-2201; www.traveljuneau.com)

TOURS

Because of the size of the state and its distance from the rest of the country, Alaska is the land of cruise ships and packaged tours. For information on tours, including companies that handle specialized activities such as biking and wilderness trips, see p318.

TRAVELERS WITH DISABILITIES

Thanks to the American Disabilities Act, many state and federal parks have installed wheelchair-accessible sites and rest rooms in their campgrounds. You can call the **Alaska Public Lands Information Center** (☎ 907-271-2599) to receive a map and campground guide to such facilities. The Alaska Marine Highway ferries, the

Alaska Railroad, and many bus services and cruise ships are also equipped with wheelchair lifts and ramps to make their facilities easier to access. Chain motels and large hotels in cities and towns often have rooms set up for disabled guests, while some wilderness guiding companies such as Alaska Discovery (p318) are experienced in handling wheelchair-bound clients on rafting and kayaking expeditions.

The following organizations may be useful when planning your trip:
Access Alaska (☎ 907-248-4777; www.accessalaska.org) Includes statewide tourist information on accessible services and sites.
Access-Able Travel Source (www.access-able.com) A national organization with an excellent website featuring travel information and links.
Challenge Alaska (☎ 907-344-7399; www.challengealaska.org) A non-profit organization dedicated to providing recreation opportunities for those with disabilities.
Flying Wheels Travel (☎ 877-451-5006; www.flyingwheelstravel.com) A full-service travel agency specializing in disabled travel.
Society for Accessible Travel & Hospitality (☎ 212-447-7284; www.sath.org) Lobbies for better facilities and publishes *Open World* magazine.

VISAS

Since 9/11, the US has continually fine-tuned its national security guidelines and entry requirements. Double-check current visa and passport regulations before arriving in the USA and apply for visas early to avoid delays. Overseas travelers may need one visa, possibly two. For citizens of many countries a US visa is required, while if you're taking the Alcan or the Alaska Marine Highway Ferry from Prince Rupert in British Columbia, you may also need a Canadian visa. The Alcan begins in

Canada, requiring travelers to pass from the USA into Canada and back into the USA again.

Canadians entering the USA must have proof of Canadian citizenship, such as a passport; visitors from countries in the Visa Waiver Program may not need a visa. Visitors from all other countries need to have a US visa and a valid passport. On the website of the **US State Department** (www.travel.state.gov) there is a 'Temporary Visas to the US' page with tips on how and where to apply for a visa and what to do if you're denied.

Note that overseas travelers should be aware of the process to re-enter the USA. Sometimes visitors get stuck in Canada due to their single-entry visa into the USA, used up when passing through the Lower 48. Canadian immigration officers often caution people whom they feel might have difficulty returning to the USA. More information about visa and other requirements for entering Canada is available on the website of the **Canada Border Services Agency** (www.cbsa-asfc.gc.ca).

VISA APPLICATION

Apart from Canadians and those entering under the Visa Waiver Program, foreign visitors need to obtain a visa from a US consulate or embassy. Most applicants must now schedule a personal interview, to which you need to bring all your documentation and proof of fee payment. Wait times for interviews vary, but afterward, barring problems, visa issuance takes from a few days to a few weeks. If concerned about a delay, check the US State Department website, which provides a list of wait times calculated by country.

Your passport must be valid for at least six months longer than your intended stay

in the USA. You'll need a recent photo (2in by 2in) and you must pay a $100 processing fee, plus in a few cases an additional visa issuance fee (check the State Department website for details). In addition to the main non-immigration visa application form (DS-156), all men aged 16 to 45 must complete an additional form (DS-157) that details their travel plans.

Visa applicants are required to show documentation of financial stability, a round-trip or onward ticket and 'binding obligations' that will ensure their return home, such as family ties, a home or a job.

VISA WAIVER PROGRAM

The Visa Waiver Program (VWP) lets citizens of some countries go to the USA for tourism purposes for up to 90 days without having a US visa. Currently there are 27 participating countries in the VWP, including Austria, Australia, Belgium, Denmark, Finland, France, Germany, Iceland, Ireland, Italy, Japan, the Netherlands, New Zealand, Norway, Spain, Sweden, Switzerland and the UK.

Under the program you *must* have a round-trip or onward ticket that is nonrefundable in the USA, a machine-readable passport (with two lines of letters, numbers and <<< along the bottom of the passport information page) and be able to show evidence of financial solvency.

As of 2009, citizens of VWP countries must register online with the US Department of Homeland Security at https://esta.cbp.dhs.gov at least 72 hours before their visit; once travel authorization is approved, registration is valid for two years.

WOMEN TRAVELERS

While most violent crime rates are lower here than elsewhere in the USA, women should be careful at night in unfamiliar

DIRECTORY

WOMEN TRAVELERS

neighborhoods in cities like Anchorage and Fairbanks or when hitching alone.

The excellent **Alaska Women's Network** (www.alaskawomensnetwork.org) has listings of women-owned B&Bs and travel agencies across the state. **Arctic Ladies** (☎ 907-783-1954, 877-783-1954; www.arcticladies.com) arranges women-only trips. The **Anchorage Planned Parenthood Clinic** (☎ 907-563-2229; 4001 Lake Otis Pkwy) offers contraceptives, medical advice and services.

TRANSPORTATION
GETTING THERE & AWAY

For some travelers getting to Alaska can be half their trip. By sea it would take you almost a week on the Alaska Marine Highway Ferry to reach Whittier in Prince William Sound from the Lower 48. By land a motorist in the Midwest needs 10 days to drive straight to Fairbanks. Traveling to Alaska is like traveling to a foreign country.

If you're coming from the US mainland, the quickest, and least expensive, way to reach Alaska is to fly nonstop from a number of cities. If you're coming from Asia or Europe, it's almost impossible to fly directly to Alaska as few international airlines maintain a direct service to Anchorage. Today most international travelers come through the gateway cities of Seattle, Los Angeles, Minneapolis and Vancouver to Alaska.

ENTERING THE COUNTRY

Since the 9/11 terrorist attacks, air travel in the USA has changed and you can now expect vigilant baggage screening procedures and personal searches. In short, you're going to have to take your shoes off. Non-US citizens, especially residents from Middle Eastern and Asian countries, should be prepared for an exhaustive questioning process at immigration.

The process is not as time-consuming as it was in the years immediately following the attacks and once finished most visitors will be allowed into the country. Crossing the border into Alaska from Canada used to be a relaxed process – US citizens often passed across with just a driver's license. Now this process has also become more complicated, and all travelers can expect more substantial questioning and possible vehicle searches.

PASSPORT

If you are traveling to Alaska from overseas, you need a passport. Even Canadian citizens should carry one, as a driver's license alone may not be enough to satisfy customs officials. If you are a US resident passing through Canada you will need a passport to re-enter the USA. Make sure your passport does not expire during the trip, and if you are entering the USA through the Visa Waiver Program (VWP) you *must* have a machine-readable passport. For more on VWP or visas see p312. If you are traveling with children, it's best to bring a photocopy of their birth certificates.

AIR
AIRPORTS

The vast majority of visitors to Alaska, and almost all international flights, fly into **Ted Stevens Anchorage International Airport** (ANC; ☎ 266-2526; www.dot.state.ak.us/anc). International flights arrive at the north terminal; domestic flights arrive at the south terminal and a complimentary shuttle service runs between the two every 15 minutes. You'll find bus services, taxis and car-rental companies at both terminals. The airport has the usual services, including pay phones, ATMs, currency exchange and free wi-fi. For that 90lb halibut you want to take home there's **baggage and freezer storage** (☎ 248-0373; **per bag per day** $7) on the ground level of the south terminal.

LAND

What began as the Alaska-Canada Military Hwy is today the Alcan (the Alaska Hwy). This amazing 1390-mile road starts at Dawson Creek in British Columbia, ends at Delta Junction and in between winds through the vast wilderness of northwest Canada and Alaska. For those with the time, the Alcan is a unique journey north. The trip is an adventure in itself: the road is a legend among highways, and completing (or surviving) the drive is a feather in anyone's cap.

SEA

As an alternative to the Alcan, you can travel the Southeast's Inside Passage.

From that maze of a waterway, the **Alaska Marine Highway** (☎ 465-3941, 800-642-0066; www.ferryalaska.com) and cruise ships then cut across the Gulf of Alaska to towns in Prince William Sound. For more on cruising the Far North and selecting a ship see Cruising in Alaska (p267).

ORGANIZED TOURS

Package tours can often be the most affordable way to see a large chunk of Alaska, if your needs include the better hotels in each town and a full breakfast every morning. But they move quickly, leaving little time for an all-day hike or other activities.

GETTING AROUND

Traveling around Alaska is unlike traveling in any other US state. The overwhelming distances between regions and the fledgling public transportation system make getting around Alaska almost as hard as it is to get there in the first place. Come with a sense of adventure and be patient!

⮞ CLIMATE CHANGE & TRAVEL

Every form of transport that relies on carbon-based fuel generates CO_2, the main cause of human-induced climate change. Modern travel is dependent on aeroplanes and while they might use less fuel per kilometre per person than most cars, they travel much greater distances. It's not just CO_2 emissions from aircraft that are the problem. The altitude at which aircraft emit gases (including CO_2) and particles contributes significantly to their total climate change impact. The Intergovernmental Panel on Climate Change believes aviation is responsible for 4.9% of climate change – double the effect of its CO_2 emissions alone.

Lonely Planet regards travel as a global benefit. We encourage the use of more climate-friendly travel modes where possible and, together with other concerned partners across many industries, we support the carbon offset scheme run by ClimateCare. Websites such as climatecare.org use 'carbon calculators' that allow people to offset the greenhouse gases they are responsible for with contributions to portfolios of climate-friendly initiatives throughout the developing world. Lonely Planet offsets the carbon footprint of all staff and author travel.

AIR

As a general rule, if there are regularly scheduled flights to your destination, they will be far cheaper than charter flights on the small airplanes known in Alaska as 'bush planes.' This is especially true for **Alaska Airlines** (☎ 800-426-0333; www.alaskaair.com).

Other regional carriers include:

Era Aviation (☎ 800-866-8394; www.flyera.com) South-central Alaska and Kodiak.

Frontier Alaska (☎ 800-478-6779; www.frontierflying.com) Fairbanks and Arctic Alaska.

PenAir (☎ 800-448-4226; www.penair.com) Aleutian Islands, Alaska Peninsula and Bristol Bay.

BUSH PLANES

When you want to see more than the roadside attractions, go to a small airfield outside of town and climb into a bush plane. With 75% of the state inaccessible by road, these small, single-engine planes are the backbone of intrastate transport. They carry residents and supplies to desolate areas of the Bush, take anglers to some of the best fishing spots in the country and also drop off backpackers in the middle of untouched wilderness.

In the larger cities of Anchorage, Fairbanks, Juneau and Ketchikan, it pays to compare prices before chartering a plane. In most small towns and villages, you'll be lucky if there's a choice. In the regional chapters, bush flights are listed under the town or area where they operate.

Bush aircraft include floatplanes, which land and take off on water, and beach-landers with oversized tires that can use rough gravel shorelines as air strips. Fares vary with the type of plane, its size, the number of passengers and the amount of flying time.

Double-check all pickup times and places when flying to a wilderness area. Bush pilots fly over the pickup point and if you're not there, they usually return to base, call the authorities and still charge you for the flight. It's not uncommon to be 'socked in' by weather for a day or two until a plane can fly in. Don't panic: they know you're there.

BICYCLE

For those who want to bike it, Alaska offers a variety of cycling adventures on paved roads under the Arctic sun that allows you to pedal until midnight if you want. A bike can be carried on Alaska Marine Highway ferries for an additional fee and is a great way to explore small towns without renting a car.

Anchorage's **Arctic Bicycle Club** (☎ 566-0177; www.arcticbike.org) is Alaska's largest bicycle club and sponsors a wide variety of road-bike and mountain-bike tours during the summer.

If you arrive in Alaska without a bike, see the regional chapters for the towns with rentals and expect to pay $30 to $50 a day.

BOAT

Along with the Alaska Marine Highway (p268) the Southeast is served by the **Inter-Island Ferry Authority** (☎ 866-308-4848; www.interislandferry.com), which connects Ketchikan with Prince of Wales Island ($37) and Prince of Wales with Wrangell ($37); and **Haines-Skagway Fast Ferry** (☎ 766-2100, 888-766-2103; www.hainesskagwayfastferry.com) servicing Skagway and Haines ($31).

BUS

Regular bus service within Alaska is very limited, and companies come and go with alarming frequency.

TRANSPORTATION

GETTING AROUND

CAR & MOTORCYCLE

Not a lot of roads reach a lot of Alaska but what pavement there is leads to spectacular scenery. That's the best reason to tour the state in a car or motorcycle, whether you arrive with yours or rent one. With personal wheels you can stop and go at will and sneak away from the RVers and tour buses.

RENTAL

For two or more people, car rental is an affordable way to travel, far less expensive than taking a bus or a train. At most rental agencies, you'll need a valid driver's license, a major credit card and you'll also need to be at least 21 years old. It is almost always cheaper to rent in town rather than at the airport because of extra taxes levied on airport rentals. Also be conscious of the per-mile rate of a rental. Add up the mileage you aim to cover and then choose between the 100 free miles per day or the more expensive unlimited mileage plan. Affordable car rental places, such as the following, are always heavily booked during the summer. Try to reserve these vehicles at least a month in advance.

Alaska Car & Van Rentals (☎ 243-4444; www.alaskacarandvan.com; Anchorage)
Denali Car Rental (☎ 800-757-1230; Anchorage)
Rent-A-Wreck (☎ 800-478-1606; Fairbanks)
Valley Car Rental (☎ 775-2880; Wasilla)

MOTORHOME

RVers flock to the land of the midnight sun in astounding numbers. This is the reason why more than a dozen companies, almost all of them based in Anchorage, will rent you a motorhome. Renting a recreational vehicle is so popular you have to reserve them four to five months in advance.

ABC Motorhomes (☎ 800-421-7456; www.abcmotorhome.com)
Alaska Economy RVs (☎ 800-764-4625; www.goalaska.com)
Clippership Motorhome Rentals (☎ 800-421-3456; www.clippershiprv.com)
Great Alaskan Holidays (☎ 888-225-2752; www.greatalaskanholidays.com)

AUTOMOBILE ASSOCIATIONS

AAA (☎ 800-332-6119; www.aaa.com), the most widespread automobile association in the USA, has two offices in Alaska: **Anchorage South Service Center** (☎ 907-344-4310) and **Fairbanks Service Center** (☎ 907-479-4442). Both offer the usual service including maps, discounts and emergency road service.

FUEL & SPARE PARTS

Gas is widely available on all the main highways and tourist routes in Alaska. In Anchorage and Fairbanks the cost of gas will only be 10¢ to 15¢ per gallon higher than in the rest of the country. Along the Alcan, in Bush communities such as Nome, and at that single gas station on a remote road, they will be shockingly high.

Along heavily traveled roads, most towns will have a car mechanic, though you might have to wait a day for a part to come up from Anchorage. In some small towns, you might be out of luck. For anybody driving to and around Alaska, a full-size spare tire and replacement belts are a must.

INSURANCE

Liability insurance, which covers damage you may cause to another vehicle, is required when driving in Alaska but not always offered by rental agencies because most Americans are already covered by their regular car insurance. Agencies offer Collision Damage Waiver (CDW) to cover damage to the rental car in case of an accident. This can up the rental fee by $10 to $15 a day and many have deductibles as high as $1000. It's better, and far cheaper, to arrive with rental car insurance obtained through your insurance company, as a member of AAA or as a perk of many credit cards including American Express.

ROAD CONDITIONS & HAZARDS

For road conditions, closures and other travel advisories for the Alaska highway system, even while you're driving, contact the state's **Alaska511** (in Alaska ☎ 511, outside Alaska ☎ 866-282-7577; http://511.alaska.gov).

ACTIVITY TOURS

Whether you want to climb Mt McKinley, kayak Glacier Bay or pedal from Anchorage to Fairbanks, there's a guide company willing to put an itinerary together, supply the equipment and lead the way. Guide companies are also listed in regional chapters.

ABEC's Alaska Adventures (☎ 877-424-8907; www.abecalaska.com) Rafting and backpacking the Arctic National Wildlife Refuge and Gates of the Arctic National Park.

Alaska Discovery/Mt Sobek (☎ 888-687-6235; www.mtsobek.com) Kayaking Glacier Bay, bear viewing at Pack Creek and raft trips on the spectacular Tatshenshini River.

Alaska Mountain Guides (☎ 800-766-3396; www.alaskamountainguides.com) Week-long kayaking trips in Glacier Bay and mountaineering schools in Haines.

Alaskabike.com (☎ 245-2175; www.alaskabike.com) Fully supported cycle tours along the George Parks, Richardson and Glenn Hwys.

Arctic Treks (☎ 455-6502; www.arctictreksadventures.com) Treks and rafting in

the Gates of the Arctic National Park and the Arctic National Wildlife Refuge.

Arctic Wild (☎ 888-577-8203; www.arcticwild.com) Floats and treks in the Brooks Range and Arctic National Wildlife Refuge.

CampAlaska (☎ 800-376-9438; www.campalaska.com) Camping tours with hiking, rafting and other activities.

St Elias Alpine Guides (☎ 888-933-5427; www.steliasguides.com) Mountaineering, rafting, trekking and glacier-skiing at Wrangell-St Elias National Park.

Tongass Kayak Adventures (☎ 907-772-4600; www.tongasskayak.com) Kayaking LeConte Glacier & Tebenkof Bay Wilderness in Southeast.

TRAIN

ALASKA RAILROAD

It took eight years to build it (see p72), but today the Alaska Railroad stretches 470 miles from Seward to Fairbanks, through spectacular scenery. You'll save more money traveling by bus down the George Parks Hwy, but few travelers regret booking the Alaska Railroad and viewing pristine wilderness from its comfortable cars.

SERVICES

The Alaska Railroad operates a year-round service between Fairbanks and Anchorage, as well as summer services (from late May to mid-September) from Anchorage to Whittier and from Anchorage to Seward.

The most popular run is the 336-mile trip from Anchorage to Fairbanks, stopping at Denali National Park. Northbound, at Mile 279 the train passes 46 miles of Mt McKinley, a stunning sight from the viewing domes on a clear day. It then slows down to cross the 918ft bridge over Hurricane Gulch.

ALASKA RAILROAD

TRANSPORTATION

GETTING AROUND

The ride between Anchorage and Seward may be one of the most spectacular train trips in the world. From Anchorage, the 114-mile trip begins by skirting the 60-mile-long Turnagain Arm on Cook Inlet and then swings south, climbs over mountain passes, spans deep river gorges and comes within half a mile of three glaciers.

The Anchorage–Whittier service, which includes a stop in Girdwood and passes through two long tunnels, turns Whittier into a fun day trip. So does riding Alaska Railroad's *Hurricane Turn*, one of America's last flag-stop trains, which departs from Talkeetna (p226).

RESERVATIONS

You can reserve a seat and purchase tickets, even online, through Alaska Railroad (☎ 800-544-0552; www.akrr.com); highly recommended for the Anchorage–Denali service in July and early August. See regional chapters for prices and departures.

↘ GLOSSARY

Alcan or **Alaska Hwy** – the main overland route into Alaska. Although the highway is almost entirely paved now, completing a journey along this legendary road is still a special accomplishment; the Alcan begins at the Mile 0 milepost in Dawson Creek (northeastern British Columbia, Canada), heads northwest through Whitehorse, the capital of the Yukon Territory, and officially ends at Delta Junction (Mile 1390), 101 miles southeast of Fairbanks

AMS – acute mountain sickness; occurs at high altitudes and can be fatal

ANWR – Arctic National Wildlife Refuge; the 1.5-million-acre wilderness area that oil-company officials and Alaskans have been pushing hard to open up for oil and gas drilling

ATV – all-terrain vehicle

aurora borealis or **northern lights** – the mystical snakes of light that weave across the sky from the northern horizon. It's a spectacular show on clear nights and can occur at almost any time of the year. The lights are the result of gas particles colliding with solar electrons and are best viewed from the Interior, away from city lights, between late summer and winter

bidarka – a skin-covered sea kayak used by the Aleuts

blanket toss – a traditional activity of the Iñupiat, in which a large animal skin is used to toss a person into the air

BLM – Bureau of Land Management; the federal agency that maintains much of the wilderness around and north of Fairbanks, including cabins and campgrounds

blue cloud – what Southeasterners call a break in the clouds

breakup – when the ice on rivers suddenly begins to melt, breaks up and flows downstream; many residents use this term to describe spring in Alaska, when the rain begins, the snow melts and everything turns to mud and slush

bunny boots – large, oversized and usually white plastic boots used extensively in subzero weather to prevent the feet from freezing; much to the horror of many Alaskans, the company that manufactured the boot announced in 1995 it would discontinue the style

Bush, the – any area in the state that is not connected by road to Anchorage or is not part of the Alaska Marine Highway

cabin fever – a winter condition in which Alaskans go stir-crazy in their one-room cabins because of too little sunlight and too much time spent indoors

cache – a small hut or storage room built high off the ground to keep supplies and spare food away from roaming bears and wolves; the term, however, has found its way onto the neon signs of everything from liquor stores to pizza parlors in the cities

calve – (of an ice mass) to separate or break so that a part of the ice becomes detached

capital move – the political issue that raged in the early 1980s, concerning moving the state capital from Juneau closer to Anchorage; although residents rejected funding the move north in a 1982 state election, the issue continues to divide Alaska

cheechako – tenderfoot, greenhorn or somebody trying to survive their first year in Alaska

chum – not your mate or good buddy, but a nickname for dog salmon

clear-cut – a hated sight for environmentalists: an area where loggers have cut every tree, large and small, leaving nothing standing; the first view of a clear-cut in Alaska, often from a ferry, is usually quite a shocking sight for the traveler

d-2 – the lands issue of the late 1970s, which pitted environmentalists against developers, over the federal government's preservation of 156,250 sq miles of Alaskan wilderness as wildlife reserves, forests and national parks

dividend days – the period in October when residents receive their Permanent Fund checks and Alaska goes on a spending spree

Eskimo ice cream – an Iñupiat food made of whipped animal fat, berries, seal oil and sometimes shredded caribou meat

fish wheel – a wooden trap powered by a river's current that scoops salmon or other large fish out of a river into a holding tank

freeze-up – the point in November or December when most rivers and lakes in Alaska ice over, signaling to residents that their long winter has started in earnest

glacier fishing – picking up flopping salmon along the Copper River in Cordova after a large calving from the Childs Glacier strands the fish during the August spawning run; practiced by both bears and people

humpie – the Alaskan nickname for the humpback or pink salmon, which is the mainstay of the fishing industry in the Southeast

ice worm – a small, thin black worm that thrives in glacial ice and was made famous by a Robert Service poem

Iditarod – the 1049-mile sled-dog race run every March from Anchorage to Nome. The winner usually completes the course in fewer than 14 days and takes home $50,000

Lower 48 – an Alaskan term for continental USA

moose nuggets – hard, smooth droppings; some enterprising resident in Homer has capitalized on them by baking, varnishing and trimming them with evergreen leaves to sell during Christmas as Moostletoe

mukluks – lightweight boots of sealskin trimmed with fur, made by the Iñupiat

muktuk – whale skin and blubber; also known as *maktak*, it is a delicacy among Iñupiat and is eaten in a variety of ways, including raw, pickled and boiled

muskeg – the bogs in Alaska, where layers of matted plant life float on top of stagnant water; these are bad areas in which to hike

North Slope – the gentle plain that extends from the Brooks Range north to the Arctic Ocean

no-see-um – nickname for the tiny gnats found throughout much of the Alaskan wilderness, especially in the Interior and parts of the Brooks Range

NPS – National Park Service; administers 82,656 sq miles in Alaska and its 15 national parks include such popular areas as Denali, Glacier Bay, Kenai Fjords and Klondike Gold Rush National Historical Park

Outside – to residents, any place that isn't Alaska
Outsider – to residents, anyone who isn't an Alaskan

permafrost – permanently frozen subsoil that covers two-thirds of the state but is disappearing due to global warming
petroglyphs – ancient rock carvings
portage – an area of land between waterways over which paddlers carry their boats
potlatch – a traditional gathering of indigenous people held to commemorate any memorable occasion

qiviut – the wool of the musk ox, often woven into garments

RV – recreational vehicles (motor homes)
RVers – those folks who opt to travel in an RV

scat – animal droppings; however, the term is usually used to describe bear droppings. If the scat is dark brown or bluish and somewhat square in shape, a bear has passed by; if it is steaming, the bear is eating blueberries around the next bend
scrimshaw – hand-carved ivory from walrus tusks
sourdough – any old-timer in the state who, it is said, is 'sour on the country but without enough dough to get out'; newer residents believe the term applies to anybody who has survived an Alaskan winter; the term also applies to

a 'yeasty' mixture used to make bread or pancakes
Southeast sneakers – the tall, reddish-brown rubber boots that Southeast residents wear when it rains, and often when it doesn't; also known as 'Ketchikan tennis shoes,' 'Sitka slippers' and 'Petersburg pumps' among other names
squaw candy – salmon that has been dried or smoked into jerky
stinkhead – an Iñupiat 'treat' made by burying a salmon head in the sand; the head is left to ferment for up to 10 days then dug up. The sand is washed off and the treat is enjoyed

taku wind – Juneau's sudden gusts of wind, which may exceed 100mph in the spring and fall; often the winds cause horizontal rain, which, as the name indicates, comes straight at you instead of falling on you; in Anchorage and throughout the Interior, these sudden rushes of air over or through mountain gaps are called 'williwaws'
tundra – vast, treeless plains

UA – University of Alaska
ulu – a fan-shaped knife that Alaska Natives traditionally used to chop and scrape meat; now used by gift shops to lure tourists
umiaks – leather boats made by the Iñupiat people
USFS – US Forest Service; oversees the Tongass and Chugach National Forests, and the 190 cabins, hiking trails, kayak routes and campgrounds within them
USFWS – US Fish & Wildlife Service; administers 16 federal wildlife refuges in Alaska, more than 120,312 sq miles
USGS – US Geological Society; makes topographic maps, including those covering almost every corner of Alaska

↘ BEHIND THE SCENES

THE AUTHORS
CATHERINE BODRY

Coordinating author, This Is Alaska, Alaska's Top 25 Experiences, Alaska's Top Itineraries, Planning Your Trip, Anchorage & Around, Prince William Sound, Kenai Peninsula, Katmai & Kodiak Island, Alaska in Focus

Catherine has spent most of her adult life rebelling against her suburban upbringing. As soon as she finished university in Washington State, she headed north to wilder lands. After a few stints of summer work in Anchorage, she decided to brave a winter. It turned out she liked it just fine, and after she completed a Master's degree in English she moved to tiny Seward where she feels right at home in hiking boots. When she's not daydreaming about traveling, she's usually out on the trails. Besides Alaska, Catherine has also contributed to Lonely Planet's *Thailand, Pacific Northwest Trips,* and *Canada.*

Author thanks First, thanks to Cat Craddock for commissioning me for this fun title, and for answering all my questions along the way (Sasha Baskett gets a shout-out for that, too). Jim DuFresne paved the way long ago; his Lonely Planet *Alaska* guided my first trip up here. He and Greg Benchwick left me awesome text to work with. Finally, Kari, Micheley and Nathaniel get special thanks for providing me with roofs over my head during write-up – thank you, thank you, thank you.

GREG BENCHWICK   Denali & the Interior, Fairbanks & the Bush

Greg has rumbled in the jungles of South America, walked across Spain and challenged the peaks of Alaska. He specializes in adventure and sustainable travel, and has written more than a dozen guidebooks. Greg first came to Alaska in 1996, when he dirt-bagged it at the Dragnet parking lot in Kenai and worked in a remote cannery on the Bristol Bay. He has since hitchhiked from Girdwood to Haines, picked fights in Ketchikan (and lost) and, for this research trip, traveled through Alaska's Bush and Interior. When he's not on the road, Greg develops his new-media company www.monjomedia.com.

LONELY PLANET AUTHORS

Why is our travel information the best in the world? It's simple: our authors are passionate, dedicated travelers. They don't take freebies in exchange for positive coverage so you can be sure the advice you're given is impartial. They travel widely to all the popular spots, and off the beaten track. They don't research using just the internet or phone. They discover new places not included in any other guidebook. They personally visit thousands of hotels, restaurants, palaces, trails, galleries, temples and more. They speak with dozens of locals every day to make sure you get the kind of insider knowledge only a local could tell you. They take pride in getting all the details right, and in telling it how it is. Think you can do it? Find out how at lonelyplanet.com.

JIM DUFRESNE Juneau & Southeast Alaska, Kenai Peninsula, Katmai & Kodiak Island, Directory & Transportation

Jim has lived, worked and wandered across Alaska and even cashed a Permanent Fund Dividend check. As the sports and outdoors editor of the *Juneau Empire*, he was the first Alaskan sportswriter to win a national award from Associated Press. As a guide for Alaska Discovery he has witnessed Hubbard Glacier shed icebergs the size of pick-up trucks off its 8-mile-wide face. Jim now lives in Michigan but is constantly returning to the Far North to write books on Alaska including Lonely Planet's *Hiking in Alaska*.

THIS BOOK

This 1st edition of *Discover Alaska* was coordinated by Catherine Bodry, and researched and written by her, Greg Benchwick and Jim DuFresne. This guidebook was commissioned in Lonely Planet's Oakland office, and produced by the following:

Commissioning Editors Catherine Craddock-Carrillo, Heather Dickson
Coordinating Editors Nigel Chin, Katie O'Connell, Martine Power
Coordinating Cartographers Andy Rojas, Brendan Streager
Coordinating Layout Designer Adrian Blackburn
Managing Editors Sasha Baskett, Liz Heynes, Annelies Mertens
Managing Cartographer Alison Lyall
Managing Layout Designers Indra Kilfolyle, Celia Wood
Assisting Editor Carly Hall
Cover Research Naomi Parker
Internal Image Research Nicholas Colicchia

Thanks to Glenn Beanland, Michelle Glynn, Brice Gosnell, Darren O'Connell, Raphael Richards, Alison Ridgway, Rebecca Skinner

SEND US YOUR FEEDBACK

We love to hear from travelers – your comments keep us on our toes and help make our books better. Our well-traveled team reads every word on what you loved or loathed about this book. Although we cannot reply individually to postal submissions, we always guarantee that your feedback goes straight to the appropriate authors, in time for the next edition. Each person who sends us information is thanked in the next edition and the most useful submissions are rewarded with a free book.

To send us your updates – and find out about Lonely Planet events, newsletters and travel news – visit our award-winning website: lonelyplanet.com/contact.

Note: we may edit, reproduce and incorporate your comments in Lonely Planet products such as guidebooks, websites and digital products, so let us know if you don't want your comments reproduced or your name acknowledged. For a copy of our privacy policy visit lonelyplanet.com/privacy.

Internal photographs
p4 Cruise ship in Sitka Sound, Sitka, Ernest Manewal; pp10-11 Brown bears trying to catch salmon, Brooks River, Katmai National Park, Imagebroker/Bernd Zoller; pp12-13 Bald eagles on beach, Katmai National Park, David Tipling; p31 Mt Sanford, Wrangell-St Elias National Park, Mark Newman; p39 Ice climbing, Chugach Mountains, Chugach National Forest, Mark Newman; p3, pp50-1 Aerial view of downtown Anchorage reflected in Cook Inlet, Mark Stadsklev/AlaskaStock.com; p3, p79 Arrowhead Mountain from summit of Mt Vestovia, Sitka, Brent Winebrenner; p3, p137 Valdez harbour and Chugach Mountains, Valdez, Sune Wendelboe; p3, p159 Hikers, Harding Ice Fields, Kenai Fjords National Park, Brent Winebrenner; p3, p201 Air-taxi plane, Ruth Ampitheatre, Denali National Park, Mark Newman; p3, p233 Aurora borealis, Thomas Sbampato; pp260-1 Moose crossing road, Denali National Park, Mark Newman; p299 *Lively Lady* fishing boat, Petersburg, Emily Riddell

↘ INDEX

INDEX

E-H

000 Map pages
000 Photograph pages

INDEX

H

INDEX

H-K

INDEX

K-M

INDEX

P-S

INDEX

S-T

000 Map pages
000 Photograph pages